This book was purchased to commemorate the life
of our dear Bedlington Terrier, Simon Barnsley,
a great friend and very faithful companion.

13th December 1984 to 17th February, 1995
(Joined us on 8th October 1985)

Brian T. Fountain   Catarina B. Fountain

Other Bedlington Terriers

Theodore Henry   3-08-69 —   24-02-86
(Dorey)

Jiminy Mungo 10-69-70 —   11-06-86
(Jiminy)

Rondo   Mid 83-82 — 07-04-95   (transferred Sept 86)
(Rondi)
                                        (transferred to Leslie Philpot 11-08-05)
Tinker   3-10-94   — 18-09-08   (transferred to us 11-03-95)

Leah   9-01-90   — 23-04-04   (transferred to us 23-04-95)

THE BEDLINGTON TERRIER

RAY'S KENNELS

Bedlingtons of Quality and Temperament since 1966.

Ray and Sandy Herman

811 Sharon Circle
West Chester, PA.
19382   U.S.A.
215-4312530

THE
BEDLINGTON
TERRIER

Ken Bounden

DICKSON  PRICE

Dickson Price Publishers Ltd.
Hawthorn House
Bowdell Lane
Brookland
Romney Marsh
Kent TN29 9RW

First published 1990
© Ken Bounden

British Library Cataloguing in Publication Data

Bounden, Ken
   The Bedlington terrier.
   1.   Bedlington terriers
   I.   Title
   636.755

ISBN 0–85380–137–1

Set by R. H. Services, Welwyn, Hertfordshire
Printed and bound by Biddles Ltd, Guildford and King's Lynn.

Contents

Normally a work is dedicated to an individual but I am mindful that the Bedlington has introduced me to some wonderful people and so I would like to dedicate this book to:

My father who introduced me to the Bedlington and taught me dogs and my mother who tolerated the pair of us. Among the true lovers and workers for the breed met along the way have been Camilla Best (Pitt), Phil Cooper, Sidney Lay, Jessie and Virden Wilson, Elizabeth Brewer, Betty Davids and Ann Heron. All gave more to the breed than they received in wins or glory.

Introduction

It is 55 years since we had a work on the breed and much prompting from well meaning lovers of the Bedlington eventually resulted in my agreeing to shoulder the responsibility. If it is true, as so often claimed, that I regard the preservation of the true Bedlington as something worthy of dedication, then the challenge had to be accepted, the task undertaken. It is with humility I present this work in the hope that it will be of some use to those good people interested in the Bedlington Terrier.

Although one may regret that competitive breeding can mean change in animals it is up to the individual to decide whether the breed or personal success is the more important. If the former, as we hope, then a degree of singlemindedness is required, plus stubborn perseverence. Although it would be an exaggeration to assert that devotees of the true type must always row against the tide of fashion, it is nonetheless true to say that constant awareness of the dangers of trends must be present. Study of the breed and discussion among breeders are our best weapons. Time spent educating ourselves and others is never time wasted. Opinions on any given subject vary and we must be prepared to listen to many points of view and be ever ready to learn. At no time do we stop learning and must be prepared to revise our ideas when genuinely persuaded.

In the Bedlington Terrier we have a distinctive breed, both in physique and character, and it is my sincere hope that it will be appreciated for itself alone by sufficient people to preserve in purity this prince of tykes.

Ken Bounden, Exeter, 1989

— 1 —
Buying and Caring for a Puppy

WHY THE BEDLINGTON?

When faced with the choice of a breed to own, whether as a pet or a breeding proposition, the newcomer hopes to find out the virtues and failings of the alternatives before making a decision. To those of us who appreciate the Bedlington we often fall into the trap of thinking it obvious to the world at large that there is nothing to surpass our breed. When asked to substantiate such a claim, in simple language, we are forced to stop and think. What is second nature to us has to be explained to the uninitiated.

Extreme loyalty to the Bedlington must have some weight in the argument. It is not a popular breed by any means but the owner is repeatedly confronted by complete strangers who stop to admire the dogs and tell stories of past Bedlingtons, in the family or among acquaintances, and what wonderful animals they were. It is often said that the Bedlington can introduce us to more people than anything else we possess. We submit there must be something of significance here!

Where do we start, though, and which virtue do we select as number one for this dog?

To begin with, he has a noble character, loyal, affectionate and possessed of depths which are fascinating to discover. He is versatile, being ideal as a pal, worker or show animal. As a pal he can walk us off our feet, adapt to our every mood, being serious or clownish and can alternate between boisterous bouts and lying perfectly still and quiet when master needs peace. As a worker he has no betters. Be it fox or rat, he will have a go and as a poacher (sorry – hunter) no rabbit is safe from him. Training is required to make a first class worker but even the house pet will surprise its owner if given half a chance. The show world has learnt to respect the Bedlington as a worthy opponent in all-breed competition and the most

1

humble beginner can rise to the heights with application and work. We do not have professional handlers in the breed and it is certainly one for the amateur with limited means.

Physically, it is big enough to be really active yet small enough to be carried in comfort when need be. The coat never sheds so the most house-proud of folk can relax in the knowledge that the furnishings will never be spoiled by dog hairs. Also, this coat is non-odorous and easily kept tidy. To trim, the pet owner needs but scissors and the ability to follow instructions. There is no need for expensive trips to the dog beauty parlour (more often than not they can't do a proper trim anyway), for an owner can soon learn a do-it-yourself-trim and if grooming is carried out every day it need only take five minutes a session.

Clean in its habits, the Bedlington is sometimes fastidious in his toilet and it is a known fact that he preens himself after a trim.

When it comes to breeding there are no snags to worry about. The narrow head and supple joints make for easy whelping and the bitches make excellent mothers.

For those who like to train a dog for obedience work the Bedlington has proven ability in this field, although it must be said he does show a certain pitying tolerance and indulges the wretched master in pointless repetition.

Having so easily listed the virtues we should keep faith by telling the faults of the breed. Never a bully or troublemaker he will tolerate offence more than most but when he does become riled he will fight to the death. For this reason an owner should not be careless and allow a Bedlington to suffer indignity or abuse from other dogs for retaliation there will finally be for always remember he is a terrier. But who can say that self-respect in our terrier is a failing? Therefore, one could say that on the debit side the Bedlington has no faults!

CHOOSING A PUPPY AS A PET

If the dog is wanted as a pet the selection is made easier, the only requirements being good health and temperament.

A healthy puppy is firmly bodied with good bone, clear eye, sweet breath, scurf free skin, a bloom on the coat and plenty of energy. A pup that comes out of his kennel to investigate friends and strangers alike is usually sound in temperament and the poor little wretch that runs away to hide should be discarded at once.

CHOOSING A PUPPY FOR SHOW

To select the best of a litter in terms of show quality is much more difficult and cannot be done with certainty unless the remainder are hopeless specimens. All one can do is pick what appears to be the best and live in hope. Puppies change a lot as they develop and what, at one stage, appears to be a very ordinary member of the family suddenly shoots into being the star of the troupe. Not only as small puppies do dogs change. The

Bedlington is a late maturing breed and, as such, is not really at its best until at least two years old. Examples of this changing comes to mind among our own dogs (citing other people's may offend, for the modern fancier is inclined to be supersensitive).

Juno of Pitt (whelped in 1938) was so gawky that war came along before she was fit to be seen in the showring. She had no feathering, the legs being dark blue and she invariably looked in need of a good feed. After a litter on her second season she blossomed out, developed glamour, and commenced winning and went on winning until she was nine years old, when it was thought she should give way to the youngsters. At eight she won Best in Show all breeds at an Open show.

Quite the reverse was the career of Tol-pedn Smuggler, her grandson. If ever there was a pup to rave about this was it. At six months he won Best of Breed at an Open show (beating a good champion) and at seven months landed a Challenge Certificate. Then came a collection of Reserve Best of Sex awards and he never did achieve the title. He 'went off' and became a very ordinary looking animal, although he still measured up to the Standard when taken point for point. In his late years he turned the clock back, but operations for persistant canker precluded a return to the show ring.

From the above it must be agreed that there is no such thing as a certainty and we can only gamble on our judgement.

Experience of a distinct type makes a great difference and family characteristics can be noticed and taken into account. Knowing the stock behind puppies makes things easier and anyone with ambitions to produce good specimens should make a point of learning as much as possible about the forebearers before buying.

The breeder is not likely to tell you all the dam's faults so have a look at her yourself if possible, but remember she won't look capable of winning Best of Breeds at the time.

Let us assume you have 'genned up' on the parents and grandparents of the puppies which interest you, have checked to what extent they are line or in-bred, in which case you will have an idea what to expect in the whelps, and have come to the great moment of decision.

Never pick a puppy that crawls away when you approach. He is unlikely to be a showman and will be handicapped before entering the ring. Look for the imp that is fearless and full of its own importance. Watch the litter playing in the run. If this pup stands foursquare, head carried high, nose arrogantly down and neck crested he is the chap that will have presence in the ring. Beware of the big bully. Usually he grows up no bigger than the rest and, as often as not, completely without personality.

Bedlington action is very distinctive but don't expect it to be ready made in the youngster. As an adult the movement should be mincing in the slower paces and a steady roll when the dog is in full stride. If there is a hint of this in the pup, well and good — but be more concerned with action as viewed from in front and behind. Faults to be avoided are cow-hocks, stilted hind movement and plaiting or crossing of the front legs.

3

Remember though, there is a very fine line between excessive rolling and plaiting.

The ideal adult head is long with deep, rounded skull and well filled up under the eye. In the pup, look for the 'brick' shape with plenty in front of the eye not only in length but strength as well. Avoid the snipy muzzle which never grows to any real length of power. The skull must be smooth without any hint of bumpy cheek bones. A well developed occiput is a breed feature often overlooked by reason of the top-knot.

The neck has to be long, set into well sloped shoulders. In a scruffy pup this is not obvious, but the short neck gives it a cloddy, thick-set, servile look whereas the correct appearance should be 'snaky' and wicked.

Teeth should be scissors in bite but sometimes an undershot or overshot jaw corrects itself during the growing months. Play safe and start with a scissors bite rather than pray for miracles.

The eyes should be fairly small, triangular and sleepy when in repose, but when roused they flash. Bold, round, headlamps are out. However, puppies' eyes change very much in colour as they grow older and the beginner lacks that all important thing, experience, which is needed at this point. Compare the eyes in direct light and deduct from the pup that has eyes much lighter than his companions.

Ears should be low set and carried close to the cheek. Some claim that teething puppies do strange things with the carriage of their ears and it is not possible to assess them. True but only in a matter of degree and I feel that good ears are always good ears. Avoid thick, spongey ears like the plague. Not only are they incorrect but seem more prone to canker and the like, being immobile curtains over the well of the ear and certainly difficult to breed out.

The front legs have to be straight, viewed from the front, but one foot slightly turned out is not listed as a fault and at one time appeared as a feature in the Standard. The pastern should be sloped, not vertical as in most terriers, and the feet hare-shaped with thick pads and close, arched toes. The puppy will not have such obviously correct feet which can be needing strength at this age. The experienced breeder will trim any puppy before considering it seriously and the novice would be wise to ask that the feet are cleaned off for examination. The toes may not be as tight as in an adult but on no account accept splayed or flat feet. The hind legs should be springy with nicely bent stifles. Watch the puppy strolling around and if he has a jaunty, bouncey stride and does not appear to be knockkneed at the back or hinting at the Chippendale at the front then he may be a good mover later.

In the pup the slight roach should be evident as, also, the brisket. The arching is at the loin and is gentle and supple and no regard can be given to the youngster having a high point somewhere behind the withers from which the topline falls away in an almost straight line to the tail. That is a camel-back in the making. If the ribs are round with no hint of flat sides the pup will not develop any real depth. The back should be medium length and the short one avoided as untypical of the breed.

The tail in the young Bedlington is inclined to be very gay but usually settles down as time goes on. However, the root should be low set and a tail curled firmly over the back is not likely to improve sufficiently.

The Bedlington coat is not at all easy to assess in the youngster because at birth it is black or dark brown and ends up blue, liver or sandy. At two months the close baby jacket has given way to a floppy lot of hair like neither baby nor adult coat. Look for a twisty, springy coat of great density. Mixed colour of hairs is a good sign as is plenty of twist in the area of the knees. A straight, open coat in a puppy usually means a poor one in an adult. A silky texture is to be avoided. A 'dirty' looking coat of mixed colour density usually develops into a better jacket than the shiny, even hued blue.

If you find the puppy that conforms to all the above points – look again. Accept the fact that there has never been a faultless dog, and never will be, and go for the balanced whelp with no glaring faults and plenty of personality.

SOME BASIC TRAINING

House breaking should start as soon as possible. If they have been well trained to go to the toilet on newspaper puppies usually have a good idea what is required of them so that taking them outside to relieve themselves presents no problems. The main advice is **always** to take the puppy out not just put it out. Use the same word at all times to encourage the puppy to perform and be very lavish with your praise as soon as the deed is accomplished; it does not matter if the neighbours think you have flipped! Do not punish for any mistakes made indoors until you are really sure the puppy understands what is required of it, for after all, some of the mistakes can be your fault for leaving the puppy too long, or for not reading his signals that he wants to relieve himself. Night training takes a little longer but one tip is to see that his bed is really warm and comfortable, then he will usually be reluctant to leave it during the night and if you are up early enough you should be able to catch him to take him out as soon as he wakes.

Lead training

This should start as soon as possible. Try to get the puppy to follow you about the garden at first, then put on a very light collar and lead and try to encourage him to continue to follow you but, if necessary, be prepared to follow him; make it all seem like fun and he will want to join in. Once he has got the idea, you can then start to direct him to walk beside you and go where you want to go, all the time talking in an interesting voice to him and giving lavish praise when he does well. When you go out on the road, see that he learns to wait at kerbs and not rush ahead and into the road, likewise if you stop to talk to anyone he should learn to wait quietly and not to bowl people over or keep pulling to get on with the walk. Never make the mistake of always picking him up when another dog comes along, particularly if it is a large dog as this is a sure way to give him a complex about other dogs. Adult dogs will seldom harm a puppy and if you do have doubts about the other dog's intentions, just bring your puppy in close and bring your leg forward to hold off the other dog.

Coming back

Teach him to come to you before you ever let him off the lead in the countryside or parks. Tone of voice will do a lot here as it should always appear interesting to the puppy to come back to you, a dull or snappish tone will only send him in the other direction! Never, ever be tempted to lose your temper and shout or smack him if he does not come straight away, have patience and lighten your tone even further and turn as if to walk away from him, patting your own leg as you do so. If all this fails, then you can go to him, pick him up without a word (at least any that he can hear) and put him in his bed and ignore him for an hour, then try again as if the incident had never happened and usually you will get a rewarding result. When you do let him off in the countryside do not put him back on the lead only when it is time for home as he will cotton on to this very quickly. At various times during the walk call him to you, pat him and maybe even give him a titbit, then let him run off again, at times you can put the lead back on for a moment and then let him off again, this way you will keep him guessing and he will always come when called.

Sit, lie and stay

You can further teach the puppy to sit, lie down and stay fairly easily though there is a distinct advantage in joining a local training club (addresses will be supplied by the Kennel Club) in this part of the dog's training as the pup will learn to obey **you** despite the distraction of other people and dogs around him.

First teach the puppy to sit by gently pushing down his hindquarters, at the same time giving the command 'sit', and remember be lavish with your praise and keep the training sessions short. When he has mastered this it is time to train him to lie. The procedure is equally straightforward but as your dog might find this exercise a bit more tedious be extra careful not to overdo it as this will make future training sessions more difficult. First get the puppy into the sit position and then giving the command 'lie' push his forequarters down. Given 10 or so minute sessions twice a day your puppy will soon sit and lie to your verbal command only.

Teaching a dog to stay is not quite so easy and you should be prepared to be very patient. No matter how frustrating it might seem never show the puppy this by shouting at him as this will only make your job even harder. First get the dog to sit or lie and then, facing it, start to walk slowly away repeating the command 'stay'. It will probably do no such thing but come running towards you tail wagging, just stay calm pick it up and carry it back to the same spot and start the exercise again.

After a few training sessions your puppy will get the idea that something is required of him and after a few more will understand that it is to stay where he has been put. It is difficult for the puppy to overcome his quite natural desire not to be left behind when his beloved owner walks away and for some time he will continue to creep forward, but just persevere returning him to the spot where the command was first given until he stays perfectly. Remember to give him plenty of praise, never get cross with him and have a play time at the end of each training session.

The show ring

Training for the show ring can best be accomplished by attending ringcraft classes and here again, the dogs learn to show themselves off whilst not being distracted by others and the novice handler can learn the correct method of showing and presenting his dog to best advantage.

HOUSING

A puppy must be housed to maintain its good health, safety and to its owner's convenience.

From the health angle the sleeping quarters must be dry and free from draughts, the bedding has to be clean, the dog must be able to retire to its own lair at will and a supply of clean fresh water should always be accessible.

If the dog is to live indoors one should resist the temptation to buy a wicker dog basket. There is always the danger of injury to the eye from a projecting end, a hazard greatly increased in a well chewed basket. An ideal arrangement is a tea chest on its side, raised on blocks out of the draught with a gate fixed to the open end. Tastefully painted externally the box can be an unobtrusive piece of kitchen furniture. Care must be exercised on choice of paint as some dogs will chew and swallow paintwork. Train the puppy to sleep in the box at night with the gate shut and to accept 'locking-up' for spells during the day when the owner wishes. In this way the dog is out of the way when the housework is being done and can be left at home at night or during the owner's absence without fear of his doing any damage. If the dog is to be kennelled outside the same needs of a dry, draught-free bed apply, and ample room for the animal to move about is necessary.

Whether indoors or out a dog should be left to rest when it chooses and not disturbed to supply amusement for humans young or old.

Cleanliness in the sleeping quarters is essential. Blankets should be washed weekly, straw, shredded paper, shavings or sawdust should be changed daily and woodwork washed down with hot water and soap weekly. Some sawdusts are from treated timber and can cause weeping of the eyes or more deadly illness and care should be taken in its use. Sawdust and wood shavings are not ideal for Bedlington bedding as they do get into the coat. They are better used as absorbent covering for an indoor run.

EXERCISE

A fast disappearing habit of the human being, but the dog still needs exercise to develop and maintain a healthy mind and body, strong muscles and soundness of wind and limb.

A healthy glow cannot be applied from a bottle and no amount of medicines or coat dressings can substitute good food and correct exercise. It should be noted that the term is correct exercise rather than plenty of exercise. Never overtire a youngster. A puppy up to four months gets all the exercise it needs in play, given plenty of space to scamper. At that age a half mile walk on the lead on hard ground teaches deportment and develops the muscles brought into use when moving in the show ring. Distance can be increased until the adult dog enjoys three or four miles a day on a hard surface, which wears down the nails and strengthens legs and feet. Free galloping over open country and 'working' hedge and rock all benefit the dog. It often does wonders for the owner as well! The Bedlington is a tough little terrier possessing stamina. We have walked 20 miles over moorland with dogs dashing here and there and surely covering four times our distance. Returning home the same animals were keen to join the evening walk after feeding.

Growing youngsters kept in runs and standing for hours on two legs scrabbling at chain link fencing will develop some muscle but certainly not in the right places or adequate amount. It must be borne in mind that a dog spreads the feet on ground that 'gives', a factor in deciding floor material for kennel runs.

WORMS

Round worms occur in puppies and adults and all youngsters should be treated on the assumption that they are infected. There are many proprietary treatments on the market these days and if the manufacturers' directions are followed no real difficulty should be encountered.

Although it eats well a badly infected puppy will waste and even die if some cure is not quickly obtained. The stomach becomes abnormally large whilst the rest of the animal wastes to grotesque thinness. Rickets, enteritis and even death can result from neglect. At any time during its life a dog can become infected with round or tape worms and worming should be a routine annual precaution. Also any symptoms, such as bad breath, dragging of the bottom, loss of weight, staring, rough coat, biting the hindquarters, or evidence in the motions should be acted on immediately.

Certain dogs have a habit of picking up the droppings of other animals and this should be prevented especially on sheep land. The flea can be a source of infestation which is another reason for keeping the dog free from this parasite.

FEEDING

It is commonsense for the purchaser of a puppy to find out the diet it has had previously and, if that has been satisfactory, to stick to it. A change of home and or diet can mean a tummy upset and the new owner should not rush back to the breeder claiming that the puppy is unhealthy. But as such an upset can be potentially very serious for a young puppy it makes sense to minimise the chances of its occurring so keep to the same diet if possible.

From seven weeks onwards a puppy should be fed three times a day. It is not desirable to give any milk to replace the dam's milk as Bedlingtons so often get tummy upsets from being on cow's milk and get very little benefit from it as they cannot digest it properly. The modern foods produced for dogs are so complete and balanced they do not require the multitude of supplements that were once commonly given to try and make sure the dogs got all the requirements for good growth and healthy maintenance; in fact you can undo the goodness by adding and thus upsetting the balance.

Puppies usually give up the midday meal at about 12 to 16 weeks old and can be kept on just the two feeds for up to one year, according to their requirements, as they vary so much in growth patterns according to their type and breeding this is an area where the owner's own judgement has to be used. If in serious doubt your vet should be consulted.

Puppies can go to their new homes from seven weeks onwards but if they are required for the show ring it is wisest to run them on till they have had their inoculations as this extra time will help to show up the differences in make, shape and temperament.

INOCULATION

Do not take the puppy out of your house or garden until it has been inoculated. Telephone your vet in advance to check his procedure but normally the inoculation against distemper, hepatitis, leptospirosis and parvovirus is done in two parts with the first injection when the puppy is 12 weeks old and the second three weeks later. Thereafter the dog should have an annual booster to ensure its immunity to these fatal diseases is maintained.

CONCLUSION

No matter how well-bred your puppy is you will only get out of him what you are prepared to put into him; this not only means good feeding but general care and training and also involving him in what you do as much as possible. Bedlingtons are very intelligent but also rather sensitive and are inclined to read your moods and you must learn to understand this. He will then not only become your pet but also your friend and a more faithful one is not to be had.

— 2 —
Caring for the Adult

It is not my intention to go into great detail, but a few general hints may be useful to the person owning his first dog. If in doubt on any point concerning your dog's health you should always consult your vet.

ACNE

Believe it or not, dogs also can be afflicted with this form of pimples. After squeezing out the pustules wash with boracic lotion. Sulphur, magnesia and boiled nettles given internally all help.

ANAL GLANDS

In the anal passage there are two glands containing a lubricating fluid to assist the expulsion of hard objects in the motions. These are essential to the wild dog which eats bone, hair, etc. However, the domestic animal does not have the same needs with the result that these glands sometimes become a source of discomfort to the dog and require emptying. It can be done by a veterinary surgeon or by the owner once he has been shown how to perform the operation.

    The dog indicates that he is uncomfortable sometimes by dragging its bottom along the ground (worms will also promote this attempt at relief) or by trying to bite the quarters. On occasions the glands will burst and there is no mistaking the dreadful stench.

BATHING

A simple enough operation but it must be remembered that a dog cannot suffer the temperatures a human would want to soak in. A tepid bath of about 60°F, 15.5°C is ideal. The floor of the bath must not be slippery, making the dog fearful of not keeping his feet, and the ears must **always** be plugged with cotton wool to keep out any water.

Some soaps and shampoos remove the natural oils in the coat which then becomes more likely to pick up dirt. Also such agents as vinegar to remove soap particles softens the coat further. Dogs only need to be bathed when prepared for a show or when really dirty. Good brushing with a shampoo powder or pine sawdust should normally be sufficient.

Among the soaps to be recommended are Fairy Green and Lux and of the shampoos Loxene serves well, as does Vosene, but when using the latter care must be taken to protect the eyes. There are, of course, many preparations on the market for dogs but often they are more expensive and one must always watch out for the advertising blurb claiming that 'X' will make the coat 'lovely and silky'. Most preparations made for dogs seem to be for silky coats. Shop assistants are there to sell the goods displayed and must never be relied upon to advise on doggy matters. Pushing something as that 'used by the breeders' is often so much twaddle and to be treated with contempt.

BITES

Do not ignore the wounds inflicted by one dog on another. Cleanse with antiseptic and consult the vet. There is always a risk of surface healing and the formation of a nasty abcess which professional attention could avert. Experience will teach one to judge and deal with dog bites but the beginner must not take chances.

CONJUNCTIVITIS

The eyelids become red and the eye waters, sometimes a pus causes the eyelids to stick together. Simple cases can be treated by bathing the eye but anything persistent should be passed to the veterinary surgeon for treatment. An old fashioned eye bath consists of cold tea but this, if used on a Bedlington, will stain the coat in the area around the eye.

CONSTIPATION

Mainly a problem of diet. Either the food content or lack of water. Check to see if the diet is really balanced making sure there is plenty of liquid content and green vegetables. A small sulphur block permanently in the drinking bowl is a cheap benefit to the dog and a little oil or Milk of Magnesia can do the trick when trouble starts.

CYSTS BETWEEN THE TOES

Sometimes called Interdigital Cysts. We are assured the correct medical term is Interdigital Abcesses. Some Bedlingtons are really prone to this and suffer badly. Whether one takes umbrage at the suggestion, the fact remains that the condition is often caused by dirt working into the skin between the toes. Usually after much swelling, the abcess bursts but causes a lot of pain to the animal whilst developing and, unless the wound is thoroughly cleansed, can re-form in an adjacent or the same spot. In its early stages iodine applied above and below the web may help. If the swelling continues poulticing will help soften it and it can be lanced. The meat content of the diet should be cut out for a while and a blood tonic given. Stinging nettle tea is an excellent blood medicine.

A dog that seems prone should have its feet examined and washed regularly and thought given to where the dog walks that could possibly encourage trouble. Standing the feet in T.C.P. is helpful as a preventative, and this is also an excellent treatment for dermatitis in the feet brought about by the chemicals man throws around. Lumps of dirt, mud, etc. should never be allowed to gather between the toes. Excessive hair between the toes collects dirt and should be trimmed out.

DIARRHOEA

In puppies and adults it can occur for many reasons and there are some very good curative preparations on the market. However, care must be taken to study the dog and decide whether the reason is simple and obvious (Diet, etc.) or whether the condition of the animal otherwise suggests that the diarrhoea is one symptom of something much more serious. The veterinary profession cannot perform miracles when a case is left too long without expert treatment. Whilst it is appreciated that some vets are not worth calling in, the profession as a whole must be expected to know more than the layman and this should be recognised.

DOSING

Attempts to dose an unreceptive dog with medicine can be comic or hazardous. To begin with the animal should be sitting on the ground with the owner's feet on either side and the legs firmly trapping the dog behind the shoulders. If a pill is to be given the dog's head is held back, the jaw opened, the pill placed on the back of the tongue, mouth closed and held shut tight. To encourage swallowing, the throat should be stroked. If the victim is stubborn and decides to show who's boss, then a hand over the nostrils usually makes him gulp air through the lips and swallow. When liquid is prescribed it should be poured in the loose corner of the mouth at the flew. Do not release the lips until the dog has swallowed, otherwise the medicine will run out again and down the jaw and neck. Although firmness must be the order, care has to be taken that the animal does not panic, and reward, either in fuss or food, should always follow.

A novel way of giving liquid was shown to me recently. Take a pair of table spoons, cut one across halfway along the bowl, weld the lower portion to the whole spoon with a hole cut at the points. To this hole is welded a tube two inches long and about one eighth of an inch in diameter. The whole is chromium plated and provides a very sophisticated instrument. The dose is poured into the spoon, the tube inserted between the lips and teeth, the handle of the spoon tilted, and down goes the dose.

EARS

Wax forms in the ear and there are many other problems from parasites and infection. Excessive probing and pulling can do more harm than good and common sense is called for. Removal of hair is best achieved by using warmed artery forceps, pulling a few hairs at a time rather than clumsy fingers pulling on thick wads. Wax can be broken up by use of Otodex drops then wiped free. One per cent Cetavlon solution is also a good cleansing agent but, whatever method adopted, the ears should always be left dry.

Ear tips must be kept clean and scurfiness avoided at all costs. If it does occur, wash weekly with three per cent mercurial soap and treat twice daily with a dressing of Resorcin, Cyllin and Almond oil. Consult your vet for mixture.

If problems persist, one should always consult the vet rather than experiment and, possibly, make matters worse.

EXERCISE

A dog needs regular and correct exercise to maintain a healthy body and alert mind. An adult dog will benefit from three to four miles a day of good walking on a hard surface to keep its legs and feet strong and its nails short. The chance to gallop over open country and to 'work' hedges and rocks will do wonders for the dog's general level of fitness and will help maintain an alert and keen mental state.

FEEDING

There are as many theories on feeding as there are makes of food, from the extremist who insists that a carniverous animal **must** have vast quantities of meat 'as it did in the wild', to the equally adamant who advocates a meat-free diet. The ancestor of the modern dog was, undoubtedly, a meat eater foremost, but its daily routine was so different that it is illogical to assume that the modern animal has the same food requirements. Not only do breeds differ (terriers burn up far more nervous energy than the more placid breeds) but individuals vary in the same way as do we humans. It has to be a trial and error affair with a fair amount of common sense.

As in our diet it is wise to concentrate on wholesome food and avoid 'processes', dyes and synthetic flavourings as much as possible.

The minced meat or offal in frozen blocks is a convenient food but one cannot condemn too strongly the folly of giving it to dogs with ice particles still formed. Sledge dogs may chew chunks of frozen meat quite happily with no ill effects but we are not concerned here with feeding sledge dogs conditioned to the practice. Young stock, particularly, can die from enteritis, brought about by, either sitting around on cold concrete or eating frozen food. The former lesson has been learned by bitter experience.

13

The variations worth considering are fresh, frozen or dried meat, thick vegetable and marrow soups, sheep's head broths, fish, paunch, liver (too much scours), ox heart, etc. Mixed with soaked wholemeal biscuit meal such a diet should satisfy. There is a theory about that says that meat should not be fed at the same time as biscuit but that, surely, is a case for study by the individual. Never should soaked biscuit meal be mushy nor the liquid be at a boiling temperature to destroy any of its values.

We now have a number of all-in-one dry feeds on the market and more and more tinned foods have become available as well as the frozen fish and meat. All are labour saving and most are excellent food but one needs to be selective, watching for dyes, etc. and if possible fresh food should still form the bulk of the diet. Beware of caponised flesh preparations due to possible adverse affects on the fertility of breeding stock.

Dogs themselves often decide what food should be on the menu but a lot can depend on the owner's approach to the feeding ritual. Like children, dogs can play on the sentiments of normally intelligent adults and firmness at the outset can save a lot of fuss later. Never leave food containers on the floor for more than 10 minutes and the dog will learn to eat when invited, otherwise he goes without. Not only is it a nuisance to have food lying about but it is a health hazard to the dog and humans. Also, a normal feeder that suddenly refuses food gives warning to the owner that something is amiss with the dog.

Quantity varies, also, according to the dog's ability to convert intake into bone, flesh and energy but a guide would be to see the animal after a feed. The tummy should be firm and the dog lively. If it is bloated and listless it could be overfed or wormy.

We now have preparations guaranteed to give our dogs every mineral, vitamin and what-have-you ever discovered. A correctly fed and properly exercised animal in good health should not need such supplements and recently people have had serious doubts about the harmful effects of forcing more than is required into a dog's system.

FLEAS AND LICE

Bathing in some pretty noxious mixtures used to be the only cure for lice, but today we have effective powders, provided frequent use is made of them until a cure is brought about. In Bedlingtons it is simple to cut all the coat off thus affording little cover for parasite and its eggs. Bedding, brushes, collars, etc. should be treated and when the dog seems clear it is as well to destroy or thoroughly clean this gear as it is possibly harbouring further outbreaks. When treating parasites, skin disorders, in fact anything affecting the dog's well being half measures are out and persistent thoroughness pays dividends.

Fleas are less serious, but more easily come by and whenever grooming a weather eye has to be on the lookout. Not only the flea but its dirt and eggs must be tracked down in the bedding and all treated by catching and killing, washing and powdering. It is of little use being fastidious or stuck up about destroying fleas – hunt them down with gusto, even to the odd 'tally ho'.

GRASS SEEDS

The feet and legs should be examined after the dog has been in rye grass or similar plant life where the seed is designed in nature to propel itself by an arrangement of stiff 'hairs' in one direction only. If the seed punctures the dog's skin it can travel in an alarming manner under the surface. The result can be serious, causing much pain to the dog. Withdrawal of the seed can be effected without professional aid in the early stages but care must be taken to remove every particle and to cleanse the wound.

GROOMING

Daily grooming is an ideal which should be attempted. Most of us are busy or lazy (or both) and find it difficult to achieve such efficiency but it is beneficial to both dog and owner.

The coat should be combed in the 'normal' way first and then in 'reverse', or back combed, so that it stands off instead of lying flat. Then a stiff brush in the 'reverse' direction takes out the loose dirt and dead hair and massages the skin. Thorough combing is necessary and one must not skip over the hidden or difficult spots. Tangles often occur behind the ears, in the 'armpits', on the pastern and between the toes when a casual job is done. A dog will gib at the more sensitive parts of his body being combed but the owner has to be quietly firm, at the same time taking care to be gentle and not cause pain. Attacking a dog with grooming tools deserves resentment, but on the other hand man must have authority over animal and nothing is more degrading to both than the statement that the dog will not *allow* the owner to groom him.

Whilst grooming one looks out for signs of fleas, skin disorders, cuts, objects stuck between the toes and pads or any condition which calls for remedial action.

HAIR SPRAYS

Never use aerosol hair sprays in the room if a dog is there. Inhaling the fine lacquer can be very dangerous to pets.

HOUSING

Whether the dog lives indoors or out the sleeping quarters must be dry and free from draughts. The bedding must be clean, fresh water should always be accessible and the dog able to retire to its own lair at will.

Avoid wicker dog baskets as a projecting end can cause serious eye injury and instead use the plastic variety which are safe, can not be damaged by teeth and are easy to keep clean, or an old tea chest. Blankets should be washed weekly; straw and shredded paper changed daily; woodwork washed down weekly with hot soapy water.

15

HYSTERIA

Puppies will sometimes have attacks of hysteria when teething and both pups and adults are liable, when they can find no relief from a blazing sun or when the stomach is filthy. Immediate action consists of keeping the animal in a cool, quiet, dark place. Quiet includes the owner who should keep a still tongue. As soon as possible, bromide should be given and when practicable the root cause treated.

INOCULATION

All dogs should be given a booster injection by a vet once a year to protect them against distemper, hepatitis, leptospirosis and parvovirus.

NAILS

The long foot of the Bedlington allows of a longer nail which the dog needs for digging. However, it is a disadvantage to the animal not working regularly and so wearing down the nail, and treatment has to be given to prevent overlong growth.

Care must be taken not to cut through the quick and cause pain. If the dog has a white nail the extent of the quick can be readily seen, but when the pigment is good and dark then the position is not so obvious. The blunt end formed by the cut should be filed to a wedge shape. Filing with a coarse rasp is a more efficient method of keeping nails short than cutting as the nail can be narrowed and shaped into a downward sweeping curve. From this shape the nail will continue to grow downwards and be subject to wear. However, if the nail is trimmed to encourage horizontal growth the result will be faster growth with less chance of the animal wearing the nail down himself.

Hind nails should not be cut at the same time as clipper work on the head or cleaning of the ears. If there is any irritation and the dog decides to scratch the likelihood of skin damage is greater from sharp edged nails.

Opinion differs on the wisdom of dew claw removal. Their removal does give a neater leg line and makes for regular growth of hair. In some countries the Kennel Club demand that dew claws be removed, going so far as to make the presence of dew claws a point for disqualification. One can only wonder why such strong measures for a relatively unimportant state of affairs.

SKIN

Dogs are subject both to eczema and mange and it again pays to get an expert diagnosis. It is unfortunate that so many people will take dogs to shows whilst suffering from some form of skin complaint. Not all judges bother to comment on it and thoughtless and selfish people spread trouble willy nilly. Luckily Bedlington exhibitors are not culprits here but a dog meets other than Bedlingtons at shows and the skin should be examined regularly for an early indication of trouble.

STAINING

To remove those ugly stains some find the following powder most effective: Four parts zinc oxide powder, four parts boracic powder and one part iodoform powder.

SUNSTROKE

In extreme heat dogs can suffer from sunstroke. Prevention is always better than cure and a dog should never be in a position where it is impossible for him to retreat to the shade either in its run or when out with its owner. Beach parties are a human delight, and if humans decide to soak up the sun on the sands they have no right to expect the dog to suffer for them. On these occasions the dog should be left at home (maybe with his favourite tele program!). Neither should an animal be taken for long walks under a blazing sun. In hot weather exercise has to be given during the cooler hours of the day.

When sunstroke occurs the dog collapses to the ground, the breathing is laboured, the pulse races and the mouth turns blue. Sometimes it vomits. An ice bag should be applied to the head, the rest of the animal immersed in water at about 100°F, 38°C and expert help sent for.

TAR AND ANTI-FREEZE

In the summer melted tar can become stuck to the feet and its removal is achieved by patience and a supply of lard.

During the winter months of very low temperatures the highway engineers put a chemical on the surface to alleviate the danger of icy roads. This chemical unfortunately attacks the skin and the dog's pads can become sore and even bleed. So keep a dog off the main roads, hills and anywhere the chemical may be used.

TEETH

The teeth should be large, strong and clean. To maintain healthy gums and teeth a dog needs to use its powers of tearing and gnawing. Even so, some of the muck present in our food produces deposits on the teeth and care should be taken to clean this off. A rough linen wrapped around the finger is useful and practice makes one quite adept with a tooth scaler in the more heavily coated cases. There are various cleaning preparations and a favourite with many is lemon juice on the cloth. Abrasives have to be studied and care should be taken not to damage the enamel on the tooth. When scaling, work from the root and towards the point of the tooth. This brings the tartar off in large pieces leaving the tooth quite clean. Scratching away horizontally part way down the tooth can produce but half a job and damage the enamel.

TEMPERATURE

The normal temperature of a dog is 101.5°F, 36.6°C but perhaps because he really is a superior being, the Bedlington has to be different. Very often it will be found that a Bedlington's norm is slightly below this but it cannot be taken as a strict rule.

VOMITING IN AN EMERGENCY

If a dog swallows something which calls for immediate expulsion to save its life then a piece of washing soda, the size of a pea, can be popped down the throat at once to induce vomiting.

WORMS

At any time during its life a dog can become infested with round or tape worm and 'worming' should be a routine annual precaution. Worming treatments can be obtained from your vet or pet shop.

Watch out for such symptoms as bad breath, bottom dragging, loss of weight, rough coat, biting of hindquarters or evidence in the faeces.

— 3 —
The Standard

The breed Standard is of the greatest importance. It is the basis of all work and study and it is therefore necessary to devote space at length here to discuss its detail and implications. The reader is reminded that much that follows is a personal view but it cannot be otherwise for we are dealing more with an art than a science. Wiser heads may disagree with some detail but the author's words are offered humbly as a reference for study.

At one time, each breed club had its own Standard, or description, of the ideal. These often differed, either in minor detail or major essential, and, finally, the Kennel Club realised the advantages of one Standard for each breed. The ruling body adopted the Standard of the Bedlington Terrier Association, which dated from 1924, with amendments proposed by that club in the ensuing years. This served for many years until 1981 when the Kennel Club decided to attempt a common format for all Standards. It was hoped that this would lead to internationally agreed Standards. Some breeds had the briefest of Standards whilst others were marathons of words. Fortunately, the Bedlington Standard conformed to some extent to the proposed format which meant few actual changes.

The Bedlington Terrier Association and National Bedlington Terrier Club seized on the opportunity to improve the Standard and co-operated in joint advice to the Kennel Club. In this way any naive shortcomings of bureaucrats at the Kennel Club were, it was hoped, avoided. Not all the suggestions were accepted, but many were, and the current Standard is a definite improvement.

Sometimes people will refer to a club Standard as if it were a different thing from that of the Kennel Club. This is incorrect – there is only one Standard for each breed in this country. However, all Standards of the past should be studied to stimulate thought and give added insight into the breed's type, characteristics and nature.

A Standard is merely a framework on which we build. There are those who would have it that, armed with a copy of the Standard, a veterinary surgeon's telephone number and a supply of cash, the way would be there to produce good specimens of a given breed. This is not so and the sooner it is realised the quicker progress will be achieved. A Standard is limited in its scope and it would be impossible to deal perfectly with all the points in such a brief description of an ideal. Some Standards are too scant and some have been so wordy as to destroy clarity, thus defeating the purpose. That Standards have, in the past and still do, fall short of their aims, is quite true but such should not handicap the person blessed with commonsense. Neither should they be the hunting ground of the habitual critic. To criticise is all too easy.

If we study natural history, without becoming too engrossed, read all we can about dogs, observe dogs in general and Bedlingtons in particular, discuss dogs (and not people) until the jaws ache, then we can begin to understand. We begin and never finish learning. A hard fate that can befall the beginner is to have early success in the ring followed by a number of defeats. Lack of experience makes it difficult for the novice to comprehend and, unfortunately, such a person is often lost to the breed because of bewildering disappointment.

The Standard could be quoted in whole and parts taken for discussion but it is hoped that the reader will accept the following method of studying it a part at a time.

THE KENNEL CLUB STANDARD

GENERAL APPEARANCE
A graceful, lithe, muscular dog, with no signs of either weakness or coarseness. Whole head pear or wedge-shaped and expression in repose mild and gentle.

The first sentence above is of paramount importance and should not be read hastily without absorbing its full import. The Bedlington is a working terrier, strong enough to kill a tough opponent, yet supple and fast enough to accomplish this in differing circumstances, conditions and against various foes. To do its job this terrier has to be light enough for speed in deploying its resources, yet possessing the strength, substance and stamina to withstand the rigours of combat at length. This demands strong, flat bone, strong muscle and sinew and great courage. There can be no hint of softness or shelliness. The old National Bedlington Terrier Club Standard used the term 'lathy' and when one considers the wooden lathe used for so long in the building trade the aptness is apparent – hard yet flexible. Another parallel could be that of the lighter weight boxer compared to the powerhouse of the heavyweight.

The description of the head shape is very general but suggests an attempt to describe a head different to that of all other terriers. Some pears have the required shape but, no doubt, those who first thought of this description were aware that, if used alone, some wag would surely ask which type of pear. So the words **wedge-shaped** were added and these, plus a little commonsense, should give an idea of what is required. A head without exageration, well filled up under the eye and with greater depth through the skull than the jaw. Viewed from above, the cheeks should be clearly defined and not too narrow, as seen in the modern Fox Terrier. Coarseness is not wanted, but neither is ultra refinement. The expression can be said to be mild, gentle, diffident, bored, in fact there are many ways to describe the Bedlington's expression in repose – and people do so – but never should the 'sleepy' look be used as an excuse for stupidity, sloth or lack of mettle.

CHARACTERISTICS
Spirited and game, full of confidence. An intelligent companion with strong sporting instincts.

This is a new clause in the Standard and part of the Kennel Club's changed format. It is very much to the point and one can only stress that it be taken seriously. Few of the modern Bedlingtons are called upon to work but the breed was created for that purpose and must be preserved as such. Like humans, the truly game ones with spirit are not the noisy ones but have a quiet confidence in themselves. Only when the demand is there will the dog become a fury that will give no quarter. The yapper, throwing his weight about, when mated to a shy one, will often produce neurotics which seems to prove that this characteristic needs to be watched in the planning of matings. The carriage of the head is indicative of the Bedlington's character. The head is carried high with crested neck and nose well below the eye. Reminiscent of the poised cobra – controlled power ready to strike.

Fools are found in all breeds as in humans but, by and large, the Bedlington has an intelligence that, at times, surprises the most experienced owner. Faced with a situation, a Bedlington does not dash into action but considers for a second and then makes his move. As a companion the dog has no betters. Absolutely loyal, protective, a handy size, accepting as much or as little exercise as possible, free of doggy odours, compatible with some asthma sufferers and others allergic to pet hair and very affectionate.

The fact that the sporting nature of the breed is well developed is confirmed by the repeated use of Bedlingtons crossed with sighthounds to produce lurchers. Go to any game fair where there is a goodly turnout of lurchers and their owners will approach anyone with a Bedlington and recount stories of the value of our terrier in putting 'guts' into their workers.

TEMPERAMENT
Good tempered, having an affectionate nature, dignified, not shy or nervous. Mild in repose but full of courage when roused.

The Bedlington is good natured if the world treats him properly and adoringly affectionate to his owners. Humans he likes, but his dignified manner in dealing with other than his dearest seems to indicate a condescending pity for the rest of us. It must be said that he is sensitive, stubborn and jealous. The sensitivity is shown dramatically when admonished by someone to whom it gives limitless loyalty. A mild rebuke will produce a look of suffering and shame. This is a handicap in training the breed, for the soft-hearted owner will feel guilt at causing such reaction and there is the risk of avoiding confrontation and allowing the stubborn streak to get the upper hand.

The jealous side of the breed's nature can also show in the suffering look when the owner indicates affection for another. The jealousy is a serious problem when it occurs with other dogs, particularly of the same sex. At one time breeders never kennelled two of the same sex together. The Brambledene line changed that, for Eileen Marsh insisted on animals that were easy to cope with and that stock is behind nearly all the breed today. However, owners should study their dogs, watch for the signs of tension and take appropriate steps, separating them until moods relax. The mild manner and sleepy expression should not be confused with shyness or lack of spirit. He does not look for trouble and, sometimes, will even walk away from a challenge but, when the patience is exhausted, the Bedlington is a fury that will kill.

HEAD AND SKULL
Skull narrow but deep and rounded; covered with profuse, silky top-knot which should be nearly white. Jaw long and tapering. There must be no 'stop', the line from occiput to nose end straight and unbroken. Well filled up beneath eye. Close fitting lips, without flew. Nostrils large and well defined.

To describe a skull as narrow is to use a relative term and one must study examples of the correct, narrow skull to know what is required. The skull has to carry a jaw of length and depth and an ultra fine one would be too weak for the job. The cheeks should not be bumpy, because of the bone structure beneath the skin, and the dome should be smooth, well rounded and the occiput must be well pronounced to the touch. This latter feature of the Bedlington is only seen when the coat is wet or, for some reason lying flat. The skull is deeper than it is wide. Note that the top-knot is described as nearly white for it is not a fault to have coloured hairs among the white or for the whole to be an offwhite.

The straight line from occiput to nose is of course literally impossible and we need only use the old grey matter to see what our predecessors were trying to attain. Early terriers had small forefaces with pronounced stops – many were 'apple-headed' and the sporting lads set out to produce heads with really punishing jaws. We have a deep skull and, if we conjure up a picture of this depth being continued forward with a slight taper, but no appreciable stop, and with bone and muscle forward of the eye, large teeth and large nostrils we can visualise a powerful piece of machinery. There may be two reasons why the lips should be tight fitting, without pronounced flews. A pendulous flew would be vulnerable in combat but, also, its prescence could indicate some line of descent not to be retraced without loss of desired type. There appears to be a definite hint of the hound (Otterhound?) in the breed (large nose, domed skull, pronounced occiput, ringing voice, etc.) and reversal to a hound type would not be impossible. The large nose, with well defined nostrils, usually goes with large, strong teeth and deep jaws. The pretty 'button' nose, too often, goes with small teeth and weak muzzles.

In 1877, Mr A. N. Dodds was involved in correspondence on the breed and published his own version of a Standard. It is interesting to read his words on the head and to note what little difference there is between the concept of a hundred years ago and today. *Skull narrow, parallel and well rounded; entirely free from flatness and not receding, but extra high at occiput and covered with a nice silky tuft. Jaw long, tapering and sharp, as little dent as possible between the eyes, no dish, so as to form a line, if possible, from the nose end along the joint of the skull to the occiput. The lips close fitting and no flew.* In close on a hundred years this has been the desired head, with the various breed clubs having Standards expressing the same demands with very little change in the wording.

EYES
Small, bright and deep set. Ideal eye has appearance of being triangular. Blues have a dark eye; blue and tans have lighter eye with amber lights, liver and sandies a light hazel eye.

In other breeds of terriers animals have been produced with allegedly small, dark and well sunk eyes, which would have been better described as tiny, beady, almost black and so deeply sunk as to give an unnatural, piercing expression. None of these exaggerations are required in the Bedlington and it is as well to remember the relationship of the Dandie Dinmont and the Bedlington when appreciating these terms. Comparing the two, the Bedlington is a racier dog with finer lines and a smaller, less prominent eye. The eye is relatively small, it should not be round, neither should it be elongated, hence the use of the word 'triangular'. In the terrier breeds where the exaggerated has become the norm, many otherwise good specimens have been discarded because the eye did not resemble a currant. However, the Bedlington has been luckier in this respect and, whilst some top animals have lost out in eye shape or colour, very few breeders or judges have had a misguided fetish about beady eyes.

At one time there was a theory that breeding to livers or blue and tans produced light eyes in blues. This could account for so many bicolours being exported before the last war. History has shown the lack of genetic knowledge to have been wasteful for some excellent specimens were lost to English breeders. In the fifties, Ch Goldstrike Of Foxington, a very pale coated liver dog, had an exceptionally dark eye which he passed on to his progeny of whatever colour.

Sometimes the eyerim will be more apparent because it is properly pigmented and, if the coat around the eye is dark then the uninitiated will think that the eye is 'bold'. The impression is certainly of a larger mass.

This state of excellent pigment must not be confused with an oversized eye.

Black or sepia eyes are definitely not required and we have to guard against criticising the hazel eye in a liver as too light. A sparkling, healthy, expressive eye is much more desirable than one of exaggerated colour not called for in the Standard.

In passing, it is interesting to note that the eye changes colour with different moods. When a Bedlington is busy fighting, his eyes can become frightening for the gentler owner. The livers' eyes become red coals of fire and the blues' take on an ice green. When this happens it is as well to take the situation seriously and drop the mild words of persuasion. Old Dunmail of Pitt did enjoy a scrap, believing himself to be the only stud dog in the world. When the green lights flashed it was wise to remove every other male in striking distance – at the double.

EARS
Moderate sized, filbert shaped, set on low and hanging flat to the cheek. Thin and velvety in texture; covered with short, fine hair with fringe of whiteish, silky hair at the tip.

Describing the ear as triangular with rounded tip has a weakness in that no idea of proportion, width to length, is indicated and the 'rounded' could be well rounded or just a blunted point. The men who first coined these Standards were nearer to nature than the urban people of today and often used comparisons with natural forms to express themselves. Study of the filbert nut and the filbert water colour brush, using a modicum of commonsense, should give an idea of what is required in shape. Size ? To say that the tip should reach the corner of the mouth is a dangerous guide for set-on can influence such measurements. However, it is a rough guide and the student needs to observe examples in the company of an experienced person. Too small an ear is usually set too high on the head and gives an over alert expression foreign to the breed. Although the ear should not be small, large, thick, soft or folded ears are all faulty and give a dog a foreign expression also. Some of the old stagers used to say that the ear should be thin enough so that, when held up, one could see daylight through it. Not scientific but the point was made.

The ideal ear should be thin, hard, and not at all fleshy, with thin cartilage, set on low, carried close to the cheek on its inner edge with an outward turn at the lower end.

The amount of coat on an untrimmed ear reveals the changes that have taken place since the early days of the breed and there is an overabundance of hair both outside and inside the ear. The better the quality of the coat generally, the shorter the hair will be on the ear. Another valid reason for breeding good coats. To perpetrate soft, dense hair growing into the well of the ear to cause discomfort to the dog is nothing less than cruelty and no apology is made for stressing the fact. Trimming the ear for the show ring has become a must. A small tassle, shaped to a natural appearance is harmonious. Unfortunately, some favour a crude, pom-pom like lump of fluff which looks ridiculous on a sporting terrier and destroys much of the animal's true beauty. Better no fringe at all than such clownish confections.

MOUTH
Teeth large and strong. Scissor bite.

The Kennel Club ignored the suggestion that the excellent American Standard description be used. A pity, for the above does little to educate the person clueless as far as anatomy is concerned. The reader is urged to study the American Standard at the end of this section. 'Level' bite has been removed from the English Standard and 'scissors' is now the recognised term. The term 'level' has never been satisfactory because different people have different interpretations of its meaning. The old Standard said 'Level or pincer' and many thought that 'level' meant 'scissors'. The 'pincer' bite is not in the dog's best interest for, with age, the teeth become worn down and loosen more readily. It is a condition when the incisors meet edge to edge. In the 'scissors' bite the incisors touch but the inner face of the upper teeth touch the outer face of the lower ones at the **edge**.

An 'overshot' mouth occurs when the upper teeth are far enough forward to leave a gap between the two rows. An extreme case is referred to as 'pig jawed'. The 'undershot' jaw is the opposite – where the lower row of teeth are in front of the upper. As the lower jaw usually grows more slowly than the upper an 'overshot' mouth in a small puppy is more likely to right itself than an 'undershot'. Another fault found in long headed breeds is the misplaced canine. Caused sometimes by slow shedding of the milk teeth or by a narrow or crowded jaw the lower canines will sometimes grow in line with, and not infront of, the upper ones and take position inside of the mouth. Although there have been champions with this fault it remains a serious defect. In a working terrier a perfect mouth is a must and, although it may seem unnecessary to state the obvious, the importance of the correct mouth is too often overlooked.

NECK
Long and tapering, deep base with no tendency to throatiness. Springs well up from the shoulders and head carried rather high.

Length to give reach and depth at the base to give our little worker the muscular power to use that length. At the time of writing, there is a regrettable tendency to overlong, slim necks which, although elegant and stylish, are not suitable where strength is required. The high head carriage on a slightly arched (crested) neck let into sloping shoulders make for more strength and agility than the weak 'ewe' neck sometimes found in dogs. One anatomical defect is often coupled with another in some other, balancing, part of the animal. Usually, the ugly 'ewe' neck is found with steep shoulders and 'goose' rump with the accompanying weak hindquarters. With ewes and geese fixed into doggy jargon it is obvious that the old timers used as few words as possible to convey their thoughts. Such a contrast to the modern ways of talking a lot and saying nothing. However, back to the job in hand – the high head carriage has already been shown as indicative of the animal's temperament and mood.

The fact that throatiness, or loose hanging of the skin of the throat, is a fault is because such would be vulnerable in fighting and, possibly, it could indicate a throwback to an ancestry not wanted in that form.

FOREQUARTERS
Forelegs straight, wider apart at chest than at feet. Pasterns long and slightly sloping without weakness. Shoulders flat and sloping.

The description of the forequarters would seem clear enough, but the beginner is bound to hear of the 'horseshoe front' at some stage so it would be as well to mention it here. This is another of those pithy expressions from more colourful times and men. Again, one cannot take it to be literally meant, but to give a guide, a hint, an illustration of the fact that the space between the front legs at the top is greater than between the feet. Also, the untrimmed coat of the earlier days would lend itself to the effect. To delve into the different designs of horseshoes and make parallels between metal and bone would be petty and defeat the purpose of a witty expression. Surely it was quicker to say 'horseshoe front' than 'wider at the chest than at the feet front'.

A too common failing and one often condoned, or even encouraged, by ignorant judges is the gun barrel front as seen in the Fox Terrier, where the legs, viewed from the front, are perfectly vertical and the chest relatively narrow. This is foreign to the breed and not to be tolerated.

The forelegs are straight when viewed from the front but logic dictates that this cannot be literally true. If the leg, because of the difference in chest width and spacing at foot level, slopes inwardly and the foot is placed evenly on the ground then it follows that there must be a turn at the wrist. Very slight but definite. Otherwise the dog must walk and stand with a bias to the outer edge of the foot.

The sloping pastern is capable of sustaining shock and producing spring, more readily than a rigid, vertical one and is the logical extension of a long foot. There must be no confusion between the normal slope of the pastern and weakness. A strong pastern gives a spring to the step whilst a weak one produces a plodding action. A weak one is also incapable of great speed and tires too readily.

The slope of the shoulder is of prime importance to permit a free, ground-devouring stride but the steep, upright shoulder placement is becoming too common and overlooked because many are seduced by overdeep briskets which, in themselves, are faults. Much has been written over recent years about the angle of the shoulder being 45 degrees with the horizontal. This has been argued as the ideal for most breeds. However, it has been learnt from more careful observation that the angle is more than 45 degrees, something like 50. Otherwise the legs would be too far under the animal. Whilst the upper arm must bring the legs under the dog, the smaller angle inhibits full reach of stride. The flatness required in shoulder is that which produces the adequate but not overabundance of shoulder muscle. Too much muscle (loaded shoulder) produces an ungainly, although powerful, animal which would be handicapped in both speed and manoeuvrability.

BODY

Muscular and markedly flexible. Chest deep and fairly broad. Flat ribbed, deep through brisket which reaches to the elbow. Back has natural arch over loin creating a definite tuck-up of underline. Body slighter greater in length than height.

'Muscular and flexible'. These words should always be in mind when viewing the Bedlington. The ribs must be flat to allow the legs maximum stride but a narrow, slab sided creature of exaggerated depth would be awkward, lacking stamina and impeded when trying to crawl underground. The ribs spring away from the spine and, when turning downwards, flatten out somewhat allowing movement of the forelegs in galloping and in confined spaces. The rib cage has to be shaped so as to permit supple movement but giving sufficient space to allow ample lung development. For, without a good supply of oxygen, a worker cannot work.

Few breed standards mention the sternum or the fact that it should be well forward in the chest. When this is not so, the dog is 'hollow chested' with poor leverage for the chest and arm muscles. This failing is often accompanied by upright shoulders and poor front action.

The arching of the loin gives the Bedlington a speed and agility advantage over the other terriers. For some years the word 'roach' was used in connection with the curve of the topline but, thankfully, the Kennel Club agreed to accept recommendation to change the description. D. H. Smythe was not only a famous veterinarian and writer of dog books in the first half of the century but he also had experience with the Bedlington and corresponded with the author on a number of subjects relative to the breed. He had observed that some animals had 'fixed' roaches with the high point in the middle of the back and the dog could not flatten the back even if it wanted to. Further study of the spine revealed the condition to be a deformity of the components that make up the spine. The end result meant that the animal would have great difficulty in confined spaces and would be useless underground. This condition has been referred to in the past by breeders as the 'wheel back' and considered a fault. Another faulty conformation is the so called 'camel back' wherein there is a high point just behind the withers from where the backline falls to the rear in a straight line. This restricts supple movement and reduces the galloping ability. Although the terms to describe wheel and camel backs are old, the conditions are still with us today.

As with all galloping dogs a short back is out of keeping and the Bedlington should be longer than it is high. Too frequently, ignorant all-round judges will praise a Bedlington for shortness of back but such people should be noted for lacking knowledge. It is sometimes said that power in the vertibrate is based in the back and our terrier is no exception, the Bedlington back must be well muscled, particularly between the last rib and the pelvis.

HINDQUARTERS
Muscular and moderate length. Hind legs, arched loin with curved topline immediately above loins. Hind legs have appearance of being longer than forelegs. Hocks strong and well let down, turning neither in nor out.

The new Standard has omitted a phrase: 'muscular quarters which are also fine and graceful'. A pity this for it was put there for a very good reason. The Bedlington hind leg, when viewed from the side, is not very wide but this is compensated by a thickness laterally which results in great propulsive power as well as the ability to change direction at speed. Needless to say, the second thigh, in any working breed, should be well developed. Failure here is partly responsible for the inability of some dogs to flex the hocks properly when moving. The term 'well let down' means that the hind leg from hock to ground should be relatively short. How short can only be learnt from observation. The correct length at hock is essential to propulsion and to see a properly constructed animal moving as it should is the only way to study action and the correct proportion and juxtaposition of the components of what is surely a beautiful machine. The so-called art of trimming has given us the fake bend at stifle and the mini-hock, and even experienced breeders can be brainwashed into accepting these phoney shapes. The result is that fewer people are bothered about the real stifle and hock. We have reached the sorry stage where the hind leg, to some, is merely an accommodating frame on which to shape an 'elegant angulation'. The Bedlington is not a breed with accentuated angulation and many of the elegantly thighed specimens are too long from stifle to hock. Too great a length here is a weakness every bit as undesirable as too straight a leg at the stifle. This construction is often indicated by a swinging hind action described by some as 'going like an Afghan'.

Viewed from behind, hocks turning inwards (cow hocks) are very weak, and hocks turning outwards are equally weak and undesirable. It should be noted that there are occasions when a dog will stand for a judge with hocks in but as soon as it moves the true alignment is taken up without any hint of the cow hock. This is caused by apprehension and not a fault of construction. The dog may not like being handled by strangers or is ill at ease standing on a table.

FEET
Long hare feet with thick and well closed up pads.

Because of incorrect trimming of the legs where too much coat is left at the lower end, and so many all-rounders coming from the ranks of other terrier breeds, there is always the risk of round feet being passed without comment. The Bedlington foot is quite different from most other terriers and its influence on the complete picture of the dog, making or marring type, is considerable. For, with the true foot comes the true pastern, gently sloping but strong and elastic; together influencing stance, style and action. The foot is longer than it is wide with arched toes and relatively long nails which accentuate the length of the foot. The toes are held closely together and, on the underside, the pads are deep and pliable. Not smooth so as to be easily pierced but definitely not rough. The sloping pasterns and deep pads are very necessary shock absorbers.

Many Bedlingtons turn out one forefoot and, if not excessive, this is acceptable in a digging dog. This is little referred to today but at one time it was a requirement. On no account should the feet turn inwards for this would surely occur with outward turned and weak elbows. In common with the Irish Terrier and the Dandie Dinmont Terrier the Bedlington can be afflicted with varying conditions of the pads referred to as 'corny feet', or 'cracked feet'. This is a symptom of vitamin deficiency (H) which is of a hereditary nature and therefore the symptom apparent to us is hereditary. There are two conditions, the more serious being known as cracked pads. In this state the pads are dry, hard, fibrous and split in deep fissures. The pads grow sideways, with hard, insensitive corns that can be cut through without the dog feeling a thing. However, the fissures cause the dog great discomfort, indeed pain, and anyone using an afflicted animal for breeding purposes would not only be doing the breed a disservice (for it can be dormant for generations) but is guilty of downright cruelty. A milder form of bad foot, but equally undesirable is the giant, spongey, coarse textured, although soft, pad. The foot as a whole is over large, clumsy and smells. In neither condition can the animal operate over rough ground and in its worst form the dog is a pathetically wretched creature. There is an old saying among sporting men, 'No foot – no dog.' and one has to agree that therein lies much good sense.

TAIL
Moderate length, thick at root, tapering to a point and gracefully curved. Set on low and never carried over the back.

The whippet tail is not thick at the root and the thin tailed Bedlington is often whippety in type. We were told quite firmly that in the early days the Bedlington used its tail in fighting and it had to be 'strong, not too short and not too long'. Sometimes it was referred to as the 'whip', a term in keeping with a lithe, muscular, yet flexible animal.

The tail carriage should, ideally, be a continuation of the curve of the spine – but in reverse. In a sporting dog, when the spirit is roused, or in a stud dog, it can be expected that the carriage will be way above the horizontal but at no time should the tail be over the back. Unfortunately, there are those who are horrified to see a tail above the horizontal at all, yet will quite happily accept the whip hanging like a lamb's tail or tucked between the legs. Rarely does one hear comment on this state although it is usually indicative of a lethargic disposition. It is more than likely that there exists confusion between 'over the back' and above the backline. A Bedlington can carry its tail almost vertically and still conform to the Standard. One cannot emphasise too often that the Bedlington is a **sporting terrier** and what price the terrier that does not show the flag at times? Occasionally one cannot help but favour the theory that it is easier for some eyes to see a tail but be incapable of assessing the merit of anything less simple.

GAIT/MOVEMENT
Capable of galloping at high speed and have the appearance of being able to do so. Action very distinctive, rather mincing, light and springy in the slower paces and slight roll when in full stride.

The Kennel Club has made Movement a separate section of the written description but has kept most of the previous wording. The omission was the phrase 'when galloping must use the whole body'.

The Bedlington is so built that its ability to gallop at speed should be apparent. When stationary, it has the appearance of being poised on the surface of the ground rather than planted in a static manner. On moving over short distances without obvious objective, one might say sauntering, the spring in the step is indicative of preparedness for sudden action at speed. This mincing comes from flexing strong wrists and hocks and must not be confused with the hackney action resulting from a short upper arm and steep shoulder placement. Over angulation at the rear will prohibit anything approaching a mincing step. The preparedness for sudden action is a mental state that dictates stance and movement just as much as does conformation. When the dog is moving steadily towards a definite objective at a walking pace, it lengthens its stride, drops the head a little, does not spring off the ground so much and is inclined to roll because of the width of chest, difference in height, front and back, suppleness of loin and desire to place the feet down in an almost continuous line in front. The roll is sometimes confused with plaiting which is a fault. At no time should the feet cross. Some dogs will cross the feet, one in front of the other, and place them down; others will cross, only to bring the foot back again before touching the ground. Neither is correct.

When the old Standard called for the galloping dog to 'use the whole body' it reminded us that the spring in the supple back was brought into action. The hind legs push against the ground and the forequarters reach forward to cover the maximum amount of territory. The forefeet having been planted, not by bending at the limb joints alone but also by bending the loin in a jackknife action and thus gaining the most forward travel of the hind feet. The animal of ideal conformation, when galloping, is seen to be running close to the ground with very little rise and fall but all effort going into forward projection in fluid rhythm.

COAT
Very distinctive, thick and linty, standing well out from the skin, but not wiry, a distinct tendency to twist, particularly on head and face.

It is sometimes claimed that pedigree dogs have improved with the passing of years, a sweeping statement with which one must take issue on certain points.

In the Bedlington there is no doubt that the coat, as in many breeds, has deteriorated sadly but it must be recognised as a failing by indifference and lack of appreciation rather than disagreement with the laid down ideal. One handicap has been the use of the word 'linty', for many people have put an interpretation on the term to suit the animal in front of them at the time. The true coat is made up of an admixture of soft and hard twisty hairs of great density giving a jacket springing away from the body. The texture, as a whole, is harsh to the touch but not as hard as in the correctly coated Wire Fox Terrier. Soft coats, be they silky or woolly, are incorrect. The twist is more pronounced on the face and head but nowhere should the coat be curled. The curl is more common now than before and there are some inexperienced exhibitors who, mistakenly, favour it. It has an appeal of cuteness quite foreign and nothing to do with the Bedlington.

Why coat texture has declined in many terrier breeds has brought forth a number of theories but one with which experienced hands often agree argues that the craze for heavy leg furnishings is the culprit. When one considers that wild animals have most coat on the body to protect vital organs we must appear a little silly wanting to reverse the natural order of things. Be that as it may, history has shown that the cult of furnishings has gone together with the deterioration in quality of coat generally.

The conditions under which a dog lives does affect the coat and central heating or any other form of artificial heat is bound to spoil any jacket. The best coats are found on animals living in kennels and bedded in ample straw.

COLOUR
Blue, liver or sandy with or without tan. Darker pigment to be encouraged, blues and blue and tans have black noses, livers and sandies must have brown noses.

This is a new format and, with the Kennel Club's intent to improve things, it may be uncharitable to ask what colour the noses of the liver and tans and sandy and tans should be. It should be obvious that brown is the desired colour. What is pleasing is that for the first time in many years due recognition is given to liver and tan for this colour, ancient though it is, was omitted for many years as the prejudice of one person resisted this rare colouring.

For many years the Standard referred to dark blue as one hue but, sadly, this was dropped in favour of blue. Some years before the present changes, pressure was brought upon the Kennel Club by the Bedlington Terrier Association to include the sentence 'Darker pigment to be encouraged'. Early writings refer to a blue black dog, with or without grizzle legs, from which it is obvious that very definite pigment is required. This precludes acceptance of pale grey, silver or white.

Liver and sandy have become very confused and there is a tendency to label any pale brown as sandy. This is too easy and quite wrong. Liver is a purple brown and when seen on a Bedlington in really strong tint it is usually found with a coat of correct density and texture. Sandy belongs to the yellow range of colours and the word must not be used to excuse a washed-out liver. The mustard in cousin Dandie Dinmont is the companion of the sandy in the Bedlington. One can find pale livers and pale sandies but there must be no confusion between them.

If we are to be objective we have to consider another colour. According to genetisist Haagedorn, dilute black (blue) to liver over a long period of many generations will produce apricot. Is it not possible then, that without intending to do so, this is what breeders have produced in the Bedlington? In passing it is interesting to note that when Miniature Poodles were becoming money spinners in the fifties, a very clever breeder used a Bedlington with good effect. This accounts for the fact, no doubt, why nowadays we find so many miniatures with flat sides and roached toplines and silvers with white leg hair. It should be stressed that the crossing was for the 'benefit' of the Poodle – not the Bedlington.

When studying colour inheritance one learns that breeders of Dutch rabbits mate blues (dilute blacks) after a few generations to blacks in order to maintain good blue colour. We do not have blacks but there have been many blue/blacks through the years which could have been of great value to the breed in preserving good colour but, sadly, we have ignored long term policies for short term gains.

To throw a bone of possible contention into the arena one recalls the fact that in the distant past reference was made to the 'red'. What was the red like and what happened to it? Likely, we will never know.

Blues, livers and sandies are to be found with tan markings on face, chest, vent, tail, legs and feet. The colouring has become rare but there are some around although the tan pales so that it has become difficult to recognise one. In 1985 we saw Champion Dalip Venus in Blue Genes become the first blue and tan title holder in over a quarter of a century.

Like the puzzle, as to why coat texture has deteriorated, the loss of pigment has been a source of debate and the same argument holds. Too much emphasis on the amount of leg hair regardless of the colour of the animal as a whole. The top-knot should be 'nearly white' be it noted and nowhere has there been a written call for leg hair differing in colour from that of the body. However, the vogue for many years has been to have animals with white top-knots and white legs. The legs can be trimmed to a very smart appearance and faults 'aided' in line with the other rough coated terrier breeds requiring ring preparation. Not many would be willing to put the clock back and there are very few advocates of the untrimmed dog. However, there is no reason why Bedlingtons with coloured, even dark, legs should not be acceptable and just as smart. On no account should a judge penalise a dog for having coloured legs. The judge who suggests that a Bedlington will be better when its colour 'clears' is ignorant of the finer points of the breed and is to be educated into better ways.

The novice breeder may have a shock on breeding his or her first litter to find that the whelps are either black or dark brown with, or without, white patches. This is perfectly normal and the pups should not be destroyed as mongrels for the colour changes as the youngsters grow and after six weeks this change becomes obvious. As an adult the colour changes through stages when it is sometimes pale and sometimes darker. When there is any injury to the skin and coat is lost, the new growth will always be the colour of the newborn, slowly paling so as to merge finally with the surrounding coat. Colour change can and does occur. It has already been stated that the tan on blue and tans does pale in modern times but there have been occasions when a blue has developed tan markings after reaching adulthood and we had a champion in the fifties which did not become so until three years of age. The moral is that we should have open minds on the question of colour and not be fearful when seemingly strange things happen.

SIZE
Height about 16 inches at withers. This allows for slight variation below in the case of a bitch and above in the case of a dog. Weight between 18 and 23 pounds.

The country accepted a government's decree that we should go metric to fit in with our European neighbours with some reluctance but metric is the official form of measurement. It is therefore all the more surprising that the Kennel Club, with its avowed aim of internationalism of Standards should rebel against the official measurement and stick to the extinct Imperial. On a purely selfish note the author is delighted for a decrepit mind finds the old ways so much easier to comprehend.

No part of the Standard has given rise to more heated argument than the question of height, although usually expressed as size. It is the most easily appreciated from the ringside provided the norm is in the majority. However, as already hinted at, it is often confused with size generally and many a dog has gained a reputation in this sector not borne out by the measuring stick. Two dogs of identical height but differing in build, one light and racey and one heavier and more compact, are rarely recognised as being the same height. A perfectly balanced dog always looks smaller than one not so well proportioned.

What variation above and below the Standard height should be regarded as acceptable is another debating point and there are opinions that, outside certain limits animals should be liable to disqualification. There are too few Bedlingtons to discard breeding stock in this way and there could be a danger of an otherwise superb specimen being cast aside in favour of the inferior. A sense of proportion must be sustained and dogs judged as a whole within the general climate of breed merit. An animal of outrageous over or under height always fails in type somewhere and soon loses our interest.

For some inexplicable reason weight is rarely mentioned when discussing the qualities of an animal, yet in the modern show Bedlington the Standard height dog is too light in weight according to the same

Standard. The reason is twofold. The modern dog is often shorter in back and lacks the bone and muscle of the earlier specimens; however, condition comes into play here also. Given more spartan lives our modern tykes would be heavier, and less money spent on veterinary and cosmetic products and more on walking-shoe leather would benefit the health of both dog and owner and produce an animal nearer to the Standard in substance. In recent times a Wetop Bedlington left home for three months living rough and fending for itself. When it was finally captured it was found to be exactly Standard weight and, being a bitch of Standard height, could be regarded as proof that perhaps the modern Bedlington is not too far adrift as regards size.

Size has always varied in the breed so one should not be misled into thinking it is a problem of our times. If ever a judge signed a Challenge Certificate with responsibility it was the late Leo Wilson. Yet he gave the top award to both Ch Spring Dancer and Ch Joyventure. They were poles apart in size but he judged them as a whole with no prejudice against any one feature. However, although the actual position is given rather as a fact of life, it must not be thought that great variance in size is condoned or encouraged here. The Standard is, and should be, the aim but no one point can be given exaggerated importance in relation to other points of the breed.

FAULTS
Any departure from the foregoing points should be considered a fault and the seriousness with which the fault should be regarded should be in exact proportion to its degree.

This is a new clause introduced by the Kennel Club. It is general and logical in its form but one would wish for more guidance for the learner. The Bedlington Terrier Association (whose Standard the Kennel Club had adopted before the latest format) did not include a faults section but those other breeds which did do so made a point of accentuating those items that fell short of the already stated ideals. Those things which they considered either more important or more vulnerable were referred to in a faults clause. The Kennel Club has not done so here but it is the author's personal view that such is necessary. Some emphasis needs to be shown wherein there may lie danger. The following faults do occur if we are not vigilant:
Soft, woolly or silky coats lacking colour. Thick ears with thick cartilage, carried flying away from the cheek. 'Camel' or 'wheel' back. Cracked or corny pads. Weeping eyes. Short back. Hackney movement. Pinched nostrils. Gunbarrel front. Any weakness of character.

In applying assessment of a dog we take into consideration values as well as conformation to the Standard of a particular breed, one of which is quality. What do we mean by quality?

Quality

This must be a personal interpretation of the word so the author can give only his own. When the larger masses of any composition are in due proportion to one another we can say that there is balance. When the details are in like due proportion then we can say that we have achieved quality. There are those, no doubt, that will not agree with this definition but it has served well over a long period and will be retained until a more convincing one is presented.

At one time Standards ended with a scale of points for each part of the dog with the total adding to the ideal 100. Using such a measure for judging was a hopeless tactic for many a specimen could score high in the individual parts but the picture as a whole was far from a thing of beauty. Balance and quality were missing.

Beauty

Long ago someone was credited with the wise (sic) saying that beauty lies in the eye of the beholder. There is no intention of arguing with that here, but the reader is asked to consider beauty and glamour as applied to our Bedlington and the show world where he is judged for better or for worse. Glamour is that which captures the attention immediately but does not retain our appreciation whereas beauty has a subtle merit that calls us back again and again. With so much thought put to presentation in the hope of winning the top prize in the show ring there has developed a confusion between beauty and glamour and the reader is urged to ponder in this field for a while. One lasts and the other, not only of brief life, can actually be destructive of quality.

In common with all other breed Standards the Bedlington Standard ends with a sentence inserted by order of the Kennel Club some years ago:

Note:

Male animals should have two apparently normal testicles fully descended into the scrotum.

It should be obvious that the reproductive organs must be absolutely healthy and anything other than the normal is not to be tolerated. When the problem of monorchidism (one testics descended) was first discussed among show people there were those that insisted that there was no harm in breeding from afflicted dogs. The error was brought to light when the results of such policies produced cryptorchids (no testes descended) and they in turn finally proved to be incapable of siring puppies.

EARLY STANDARDS

There follow descriptions and Standards of the breed which will, hopefully, give further information and stimulus to the student. The first quotation is from *Dogs of the British Islands* (1867) by Horace Cox. Style and forthright manner make it an enjoyable piece in itself. It has to be realised that early writers and breeders had varying ideas on what constituted the ideal and one should not be tempted to select an item from early writings that suits one's own purposes and declare it to be the 'original Standard'.

STANDARD OF 1867

Before proceeding to give a description of the Bedlington as he is, I will put on record descriptions of these two famous progenitors of the modern dog. Anderson's Piper was a slender built dog, 15 inches high and weighing only 15 pounds; he was liver colour, the coat being of a hard, linty texture; ears large, hanging close to the cheek and slightly feathered at the tips. Phoebe was black, with brindled legs and a tuft of light coloured hair on the top of her head; she was 13 inches high and weighed 14 pounds. This shows that more than 50 years ago some of the features peculiar to the Bedlington of today characterised their ancestors.

In general appearance the Bedlington terrier has little to recommend him; to strangers he must be known to be appreciated. He looks lean and leggy, his flat sides, cut-up flank and light thighs give him a starved appearance; in fact, as a rule, he is an indifferent feeder and never carries much flesh; he has, too, in quiescence, a soft look, although when roused he is all fire; he is a remarkably courageous dog – deadly to vermin of every kind, from the rat to the otter and badger; rather too fond of a free fight, but not the vicious brute he has been described. I may mention that the two dogs, Nailor and Rosebud, were in my keeping for two days whilst Mr Baker sketched them and, although I had never seen them, except a few times on the show bench, I let them run loose in the street and fields, and found them most tractable, under perfect command and instantly obedient to voice or whistle.

1. **Head:** This is long and narrow, and wedge shaped; the skull, however, is not long, it is the jaw that gives the length, and in thickness it is a medium between the tapering muzzle of the English Terrier and the broader muzzle of the Dandie Dinmont; the skull is high, narrow and peaked at the occiput.

2. **Ears:** These are filbert shaped, lying close to the cheek and set on low, leaving the outline of the head clear. They should be slightly feathered at the tip.

3. **Eyes:** In blue and blue and tans the eyes have a dark amber shade; in liver and sandy specimens they are lighter, commonly called 'hazel eyes'. They should be small, well sunk in the head and placed close together.

4. **Jaws and teeth:** As already said, the jaw is long, lean and powerful. In most specimens the upper jaw is slightly longer, making the dog overshot. The level mouthed dogs are termed 'pincer jawed'. The teeth should be large, regular and white.

5. **Nose:** The nose should be large, standing out rather prominently. The blue and blue and tans have black noses; the livers and linties have them red or flesh coloured.

6. **Neck and shoulders:** The neck long and muscular, rising gradually from the shoulder to the head; the shoulder is flat and light, set much like the Greyhound's.

7. **Body:** Moderately long, with rather flat ribs, low at the shoulder, especially in the bitches; arched, light and muscular loins, slightly tucked up flank, deep chest.

8. **Legs and feet:** Forelegs perfectly straight and rather long; feet large, furnished with long, strong claws.

Note the word 'linties' under section 5. This reminds one of a reference once to 'linty' being likened to dressed flax. Was the word first used to indicate colour or texture?

STANDARD OF 1877

In 1877 two Bedlington enthusiasts took up their pens and we are fortunate in having these first hand accounts from famous names. The first is taken from the *Book of the Dog* (1880) and the second from *The New Book of the Dog* (1907). The fact that these two pieces were allegedly written in the same year may give rise to cynicism on coincidence. However, another reference says that Thomas Pickett wrote to *The Livestock Journal* as late as 1875 and we feel that both can be taken on face value.

In August 1877, Mr A. N. Dodds, of North Shields, who had been for some time taking a considerable part in a correspondence which had been going on, published the following table of points and description of the breed, which was certainly the most elaborate published up to that time. Mr Dodds writes as follows:

From the following it will be seen that I have divided the points into three – head, body, colour and tail. I contend that a good body is just as essential as a good head and just as difficult to breed. I contend also that, under present circumstances, hard blue or liver hair is just as difficult to breed good as either. I am also well aware that as soon as they can be bred true to colour and hardness (then and not till then) the scale of points can be modified. It will also be seen that I have thrown in 'the tail', thus giving preference to head and body properties. Some of the 'head' properties are seldom, if ever, seen in such perfection as I give them, but I am laying down general rules, which I hope will be easily understood.

Skull: Narrow, parallel and well rounded; entirely free from flatness, and not receding, but extra high at occiput and covered with a nice, silky tuft.

Jaw: Long, tapering and sharp; as little dent as possible between the eyes, no 'dish', so as to form a line, if possible, from the nose end along the joint of the skull to the occiput. The lips close fitting and no flew.

Nose: Large, broad and well angled, the more acute, the better. Blues have black noses, livers, linties, sandies, have flesh coloured.

Teeth: Pincher or over a little.

Ears: Large, well forward, flat to the cheek, and pointed, thinly covered and well tipped with fine silk.

Legs: Tall, not wide apart, straight, stout, square set, very high behind, good sized feet.

Tail: Short, thick at root, tapering and scimitar shaped, feathered on the lower side.

Neck and shoulders: Neck long, deep at the base; shoulders flat.

Body: Short coupled, flat ribs and deep, not wide in chest, well arched back, and well 'clicked-up' loins, light quarters.

Hair: Hard and wiry, standing up, but not curled, each individual hair having its own twist, as if it had been slightly singed, and about an inch long.

Colour: Deep Blue, deep brown, usually called 'liver', linty, resembling loose flax, silkies of both blue and liver shade, and the commoner colours of blue and tan and liver and tan.

Value of Properties

Head:		Body:			
Skull	7	Neck & shoulders	5	Tail	5
Jaw	7	Chest	8	Colour	8
Nose	6	Short couples	8	Hair	20
Teeth	6	Arched loins	8		
Ears	7	Legs	5		
	33		31		33

From the opening words, it would seem that there had been a fair amount of correspondence on the Bedlington and, maybe, controversy. Much, we accept today in words but not always in practice. There are some words, though, that beg comment. Would anyone in any breed, nowadays, take a flesh coloured nose as normal? The use of the word 'pincher' with reference to the mouth is unlikely to be a misprint for 'pincer' for I heard the expression used often as a youngster. When describing the legs we have to remind ourselves again that all terms were relative and have to be understood in the context of conditions at the time. These words were written at a time when the Bedlington and Dandie had more in common and nowadays we may be wise to think that the author wanted to convey that the former was taller and straighter and narrower in front than the latter. It is in coat and colour that Mr Dodds really conveys his views with emphasis. He allocates 28 per cent of the points for coat. He stresses the need for weather resisting coats but mentions 'silkies'. He makes the point that the coat should not curl and his likening the twist to singed hair is a gem of description. On colour he stresses the desirability of strong pigment and uses the term 'linty' to describe a colour and uses the word 'flax'.

Now for Mr Pickett's words from the *Book of the Dog*.

Mr Thomas J. Pickett, of Newcastle-on-Tyne, was perhaps the earliest supporter of the breed on a large scale, and his Tyndedale and Tyneside have left their names in the history of the Bedlington. Referring to the origin of this terrier, Mr Pickett wrote in *The Livestock Journal* in 1877.

Whilst a schoolboy I recollect one day wandering in the woods of the Brandling Estate of Gosforth, in Northumberland, gathering primroses, when I met a woodman named David Edgar, who was accompanied by a Northern Counties Fox Terrier, and who gave me a whelp by his celebrated dog Pepper, this whelp was the first of the breed I ever possessed. Being an ardent admirer of this description of dog, I followed up the breed, and have seen as many of them as most people. . . . . I have in my possession a copy of Tyneside's pedigree, dated 1839, signed by the late Joseph Aynsley, who was one of the first breeders of this class of dog, and who acted as a judge at the first Bedlington show, and I quote the following as a description of what a Northern Counties Fox Terrier should be:

Colour: Liver, sandy, blue black, or tan.

Shape: The jaw rather long and small, but muscular; the head high and narrow with a silky tuft at the top; the hair rather wiry on the back; the eyes small and rather sunk; the ears long and hanging close to the cheek, and slightly feathered at the tip; the neck long and muscular, rising well from the shoulder; the chest deep but narrow; the body well proportioned, and the ribs flat; the legs must be long in proportion to the body, the thinner the hips are the better, the tail small and tapering, and slightly feathered. Altogether they are a lathy-made dog.

A shorter description which is a pity but Mr Pickett or Mr Ainsley? was very much to the point. Again the coat description indicates one that is weather resisting and a narrower animal than the Dandie.

STANDARD OF 1903

The book, *British Dogs* was published in the 1880s and 1903 and the extracts given here are from the later edition. Among other things, it makes it clear that clubs sprang up and faded away a number of times in the breed's history. Indeed, there has been a Yorkshire club, a Scottish club and even a West of England one. The National Bedlington Terrier Club has had its periods of inactivity but is nearly a hundred years old now and, fortunately, as healthy as can be.

The following description was formulated by the old Bedlington Terrier Club, which ceased to exist some years ago. It must, however, be said that the comparison of the Bedlington's head to that of a ferret is neither a correct nor a happy one.

Head: The head rather resembles that of a ferret, and though wedged shaped, like most terriers, should be shorter in the skull and longer in the jaw, and narrow or lean muzzled; it should have a narrow, high skull, coned or peaked at the occiput and tapering away sharply to the nose.

Ears: They should be filbert shaped, lie close to the cheek, and set on low like a Dandie, thus leaving the head clear and flat, and they should be feathered at the tips.

Eyes: In blue, or blue and tan, the eyes have an amber shade; in livers, etc. it is much lighter, and is commonly called the 'hazel eye'. It should be small, well sunk into the head, and placed very close together; very piercing when roused.

Jaws and teeth: The jaw should be long, lean and powerful. Most of these dogs are a little 'shot' at the upper jaw, and are often termed 'pig jawed'. Many prefer what is called 'pincer jawed' – that is, the teeth should meet evenly together – but it is not very often they are found so. The teeth should be large, regular and white.

Nose: The nose, or nostrils, should be large, and stand out prominently from the jaw. Blues or blue and tans have black noses; livers and sandies red or flesh coloured noses.

Neck and shoulders: The neck is long and muscular, rising gradually from the shoulders to the head. The shoulder is flat and light, and set much like the Greyhound's. The height at the shoulder is less than at the haunch. More or less this is the case with all dogs, but it is very pronounced in this breed, especially in bitches.

Body, ribs, back, loins, quarters, and chest: A moderately long body, rather flat ribs, short, straight back, slightly arched, tight, and muscular loins, just a little 'tucked-up' in the flank, fully developed quarters, widish and deep chest, the whole showing a fine, muscular development.

Legs and feet: Legs perfectly straight and moderately long; the feet should be rather large – that is a distinguishing mark of the breed; long claws are also admired.

Coat: This is the principal point on which fanciers differ; some prefer a hard, wiry coat, but the proper hair of these dogs is linty or woolly, with a very slight sprinkling of wire hairs, and this is still the fancy of the majority of North Country breeders.

Colour: The original colours of this breed of dog were blue and tan, liver and sandy, and these are still the favourite colours of the old breeders. The tan of these dogs is of a pale colour, and differs greatly from the tan of the black and tan English Terriers; and the blues should be a proper blue linty, not nearly black, which is sometimes seen now. In all colours the crown of the head should be linty or nearly white, otherwise white is objectionable.

Tail: The tail should be of moderate length (eight to 10 inches), either straight or slightly curved, carried low and feathered underneath. The tail should by no means be curled or carried high on to the back.

Weight: The weight of these dogs varies greatly, but the average is from 18 to 23 pounds, or at the outside 25 pounds.

THE BEDLINGTON TERRIER CLUB STANDARD

The present Bedlington Terrier Club (1903) has issued an altered descriptive Standard, as given below, but it cannot be regarded as a model of lucidity. A descriptive Standard of excellence adopted and published by a club should largely aim at instructing the ignorant, as well as furnishing a criterion by which to test the merits of the dog described; but that many fall far short of this is very well known.

Skull: Narrow but deep and rounded; high at occiput, and covered with a nice silky tuft or top-knot.

Jaw: Long, tapering, sharp, and muscular; as little stop as possible between the eyes, so as to form nearly a line from the nose end along the joint of the skull to the occiput. The lips close fitting, and no flew.

Eyes: Should be small and well sunk into the head. The blues should have a dark eye; blue and tan, ditto with an amber shade; livers, sandies, etc., a light brown eye.

Nose: Large and well angled. Blues and blue and tans should have black noses; livers and sandies flesh coloured noses.

Teeth: Level or pincer jawed.

Ears: Moderately large, carried well forward, flat to the cheek, thinly covered and tipped with fine silky hair; they should be filbert shaped.

Legs: Of moderate length, not wide apart, straight and square set and with good sized feet, which are rather long.

Tail: Thick at root, tapering to a point, slightly feathered on lower side, nine inches to 11 inches long and scimitar shaped.

Neck and shoulders: Neck long, deep at base, rising well from the shoulders, which should be flat.

Body: Long and well proportioned, flat ribbed and deep; not wide in chest; back slightly arched, well ribbed up, with light quarters.

Coat: Hard with close bottom, and not lying flat to the sides.

Colour: Dark blue, blue and tan, liver, liver and tan.

Height: About 15 inches to 16 inches.

General appearance: A lightly made-up, lathy dog, but not shelly.

Weight: Dogs about 24 pounds; bitches, about 22 pounds.

Reading between the lines one has the impression that ideas on what constituted the correct type of Bedlington differed and much argument took place. When studying type in any breed one should not make the mistake of accepting a defect which is of frequent occurrence as 'typical', as if desirable.

The hard coat of the majority of terrier breeds is not true for the Bedlington but neither is the soft and the dog, as a working animal, has to have a weather resisting jacket. It is a pity we have not treated this as seriously as the flesh coloured nose. This is the first time we read of the teeth as 'level or pincer' and this description has stayed with us until the recent change of the Kennel Club Standards. The earlier Standard above refers to the pig-jaw as common and one wonders if this was accompanied by irregular placement of the teeth. Otherwise, why the use of the word 'level'? Note the change of the width of chest! Who was the strong minded committee member who forced the changes, one wonders?

STANDARD OF 1910

About 1910, Harold Warnes wrote on the breed in *The New Book of the Dog* and he gives a Standard used by two clubs but, most interesting, differing in scale of points. Apparently, there must have been strong feeling on this issue at some period. The practice of having a scale of points at the end of a Standard was common at one time but has, thankfully, ceased. It could have been valuable once but the level of quality has evened out and today it would be possible to have a dog scoring heavily in points but presenting a sorry sight when the picture is viewed as a whole.

This Standard was still used by the National Bedlington Terrier Club in 1935 (and possibly later) with two differences. The second paragraph is headed **Jaw** instead of **Muzzle** and the word **Jaws** appears instead of **Joint** in the first sentence.

The Standard of points as adopted by the National Bedlington Terrier and The Yorkshire Bedlington Terrier Clubs is as follows:

1. **Skull:** Narrow, but deep and rounded; high at the occiput, and covered with a nice silky tuft or top-knot.

2. **Muzzle:** Long, tapering, sharp and muscular, as little stop as possible between the eyes, so as to form nearly a line from the nose end along the joint of skull to the occiput. The lips close fitting and without flew.

3. **Eyes:** Should be small and well sunk in the head. The blues have a dark eye, the blues and tans ditto, with amber shades; livers and sandies a light brown eye.

4. **Nose:** Large and well angled; blues and blue and tans should have black noses, livers and sandies flesh coloured.

5. **Teeth:** Level or pincer jawed.

6. **Ears:** Moderately large, well formed, flat to the cheek, thinly covered and tipped with fine, silky hair. They should be filbert shaped.

7. **Legs:** Of moderate length, not wide apart, straight and square set, and with good sized feet, which are rather long.

8. **Tail:** Thick at the root, tapering to a point, slightly feathered on lower side, nine inches to 11 inches long and scimitar shaped.

9. **Neck and shoulders:** Neck long, deep at the base, rising well from the shoulder which should be flat.

10. **Body:** Long and well proportioned, flat ribbed, and deep, not wide in chest, slightly arched back, well ribbed up, with light quarters.

11. **Coat:** Hard, with close bottom, and not lying flat to sides.

12. **Colour:** Dark blue, blue and tan, liver, liver and tan, sandy, or sandy and tan.

13. **Height:** About 15 inches to 16 inches.

14. **Weight:** Dogs about 24 pounds; bitches about 22 pounds.

15. **General appearance:** He is a light made, lathy dog, but not shelly.

Value of points adopted by the National Bedlington Terrier Club

Head	15
Size	10
Teeth	10
Colour	5
Legs and Feet	10
Ears	5
Eyes	5
Nose	5
Body	15
Coat	10
Tail	5
Total	100

The Yorkshire Bedlington Terrier Club Scale of Points

Skull	15
Jaw	5
Eyes	5
Nose	5
Teeth	5
Ears	5
Legs	10
Tail	5
Neck and shoulders	5
Body	15
Coat	10
Colour	5
Height	5
Weight	5
Total	100

THE F.C.I. STANDARD

Most countries abroad use the Standard of the Federation Cynologique Internationale (usually referred to as the F.C.I.) which was the English Kennel Club Standard before the recent change. It is hoped that again the international body will adopt the English Standard.

General appearance: A graceful, lithe, muscular dog, with no sign of weakness or coarseness. The whole head should be pear or wedge shaped, and expression in repose mild and gentle, though not shy or nervous. When roused, the eyes should sparkle and the dog look full of temper and courage. Bedlingtons are capable of galloping at great speed and should have the appearance of being able to do so. This action is very distinctive. Rather mincing, light and springy in the slower paces, could have a slight roll when in full stride. When galloping must use the whole body.

Head and skull: Skull, narrow but deep and rounded; covered with profuse silky top-knot which should be nearly white. Jaw long and tapering. There must be no 'stop', the line from occiput to nose end being straight and unbroken. Well filled up beneath the eye. Close fitting lips without flew. The nostrils must be large and well defined. Blues and blue and tans must have black noses; livers and sandies, must have brown noses.

Eyes: Small, bright and well sunk. The ideal eye has the appearance of being triangular. Blues should have a dark eye; blue and tans have lighter eyes with amber lights; and livers and sandies have a light hazel eye.

Ears: Moderate sized, filbert shaped, set on low, and hanging flat to the cheek. They should be covered with short, fine hair with a fringe of whiteish silky hair at the tip.

Mouth: Teeth level or pincer jawed. The teeth should be large and strong.

Neck: Long, tapering neck, deep at the base; there should be no tendency to throatiness. The neck should spring well up from the shoulders and the head should be carried rather high.

Forequarters: The forelegs should be straight, but wider apart at the chest than at the feet. Pasterns long and slightly sloping without weakness. Shoulders flat and sloping.

Body: Muscular, yet markedly flexible; flat-ribbed and deep through the brisket well ribbed up. The chest should be deep and fairly broad. The back should be roached and the loin markedly arched. Muscular, galloping quarters which are also fine and graceful.

Hindquarters: Muscular and of moderate length. The hind legs, by reason of the roach back and arched loin, have the appearance of being longer than the forelegs. The hocks should be strong and well let down.

Feet: Long, hare feet with thick and well closed up pads.

Tail: Of moderate length, thick at the root, tapering to a point and gracefully curved. Should be set on low and must never be carried over the back.

Coat: Very distinctive. Thick and linty, standing well out from the skin but not wiry. There should be a distinct tendency to twist, particularly on the head and face.

Colour: Blue, blue and tan, liver, or sandy. Darker pigment to be encouraged.

Weight and size: Height should be about 16 inches at the shoulder. This allows of a slight variation below in the case of bitches and above in the case of a dog. Weight should be between 18 and 23 pounds.

THE AMERICAN STANDARD

The breed has been well established in the States for many years and the Bedlington Terrier Club of America has had its own Standard. After a great deal of thought it was changed in 1967 and there is no doubt, whatever, of the endeavour to produce the most useful Standard humanly possible. In many instances it is superior to the original but there are a number of points of difference with the English Standard which illustrates the dangers of different Standards producing different breeds in time.

The American Standard describes the eye as almond shaped, which suggests a longer, narrower shape than we visualise as true of the breed. On a flippant note it is interesting to observe that a geometric shape (triangular) has been replaced by a nut (almond) here whilst, when describing the ear 'triangular' has ousted the 'filbert', a nut used to illustrate shape for a hundred years. The subtlety of the filbert as a shape is more accurate than the round tipped triangle and the almond is truer of the poodle eye than the Bedlington. Also, we must regret that the 'twist', for some reason has given way to 'curl' in the coat which, frankly, is just not right. We have many coats that curl rather than twist but we do not change the standard to fit certain dogs.

On the credit side there are certain items that are welcomed as invaluable. Ear carriage, colour, teeth, body length, coat texture and gait are all dealt with superbly. The American Standard did influence some of the changes made in the new Kennel Club Standard but our ruling body ignored the clubs' request that the American section on the mouth be taken in its entirety. A pity.

Although the following is the Standard for the American breeder and judge, it should be made use of to stimulate thought everywhere. In the same way as one would hope that people using that Standard would study ours and all of us study the Standards compiled over the last century or so.

General appearance: A graceful, lithe, well balanced dog with no sign of coarseness, weakness or shelliness. In repose the expression is mild and gentle, not shy or nervous. Aroused, the dog is particularly alert and full of immense energy and courage. Noteworthy for endurance, Bedlingtons also gallop at great speed, as their body outline clearly shows.

Head: Narrow but deep and rounded. Shorter in skull and longer in jaw. Covered with a profuse topknot which is lighter than the color of the body, highest at the crown, and tapering gradually to just back of the nose. There must be no stop and the unbroken line from crown to nose end reveals a slender head without cheekiness or snipeyness. Lips are black in the blue and tans and brown in all other solid and bi-colors.

Eyes: Almond shaped, small, bright, and well sunk with no tendency to tear or water. Set is oblique and fairly high on the head. Blues have dark eyes; blues and tans less dark with amber lights; sandies, sandies and tans – light hazel; liver, livers and tans slightly darker. Eye rims are black in the blue and blue and tans and brown in all other solid and bi-colors.

Ears: Triangular with rounded tips. Set on low and hanging flat to the cheek in front with a slight projection at the base. Point of greatest width approximately three inches. Ear tips reach the corners of the mouth. Thin and velvety in texture, covered with fine hair forming a small silky tassel at the tip.

Nose: Nostrils large and well defined. Blues and blues and tans have black noses. Livers, livers and tans, sandies, sandies and tans have brown noses.

Jaws: Long and tapering. Strong muzzle well filled up with bone beneath the eye. Close fitting lips, no flews.

Teeth: Large, strong and white. Level or scissors bite. Lower canines clasp the outer surface of the upper gum just in front of the upper canines. Upper premolars and molars lie outside those of the lower jaw.

Neck and shoulders: Long tapering neck with no throatiness, deep at the base and rising well up from the shoulders which are flat and sloping with no excessive musculature. The head is carried high.

Body: Muscular and markedly flexible. Chest deep. Flat ribbed and deep through the brisket, which reaches to the elbows. Back has a good natural arch over the loin creating a definite tuck-up of the underline. Body slightly greater in length than height. Well muscled quarters are also fine and graceful.

Legs and feet: Lithe and muscular. The hind legs are longer than the forelegs, which are straight and wider apart at the chest than at the feet. Slight bend to pasterns which are long and sloping without weakness. Stifles well angulated. Hocks strong and well let down, turning neither in nor out. Long hare feet with thick, well closed up, smooth pads. Dewclaws should be removed.

Coat: A very distinctive mixture of hard and soft hair standing well out from the skin. Crisp to the touch but not wiry, having a tendency to curl, especially on the head and face. When in show trim must not exceed one inch on body; hair on legs is slightly longer.

Tail: Set low, scimitar shaped, thick at the root and tapering to a point which reaches the hock. Not carried over the back nor tight to the underbody.

Color: Blue, sandy, liver, blue and tan, sandy and tan, liver and tan. In bi-colors the tan markings are found on the legs, chest, under the tail, inside the hindquarters and over each eye. The top-knots of all adults should be lighter than the body color. Patches of darker hair from an injury are not objectionable as it is only temporary. Darker body pigmentation of all colors to be encouraged.

Height: The preferred Bedlington Terrier dog measures 16½ inches at the withers, the bitch 15½ inches. Under 16 inches or over 17½ inches for dogs and under 15 inches or over 16½ inches for bitches are serious faults. Only where comparative superiority of a specimen outside these ranges clearly justifies it, should greater latitude be taken.

Weight: To be proportionate to height within the range of 17 to 23 pounds.

Gait: Unique lightness of movement. Springy in the slower paces, not stilted or hackneyed. Must not cross, weave or paddle.

We see from the foregoing that Standards have and do vary and we may ask ourselves whether at some future date further changes need to be made. There are still some the author would like to see but the two clubs making recommendations to the Kennel Club in 1981 accepted so much that was offered by him and perhaps too much medicine from one source is not always palatable in group therapy. Cowardly maybe, but the peaceful progress of the breed always seems more worthwhile than personal assertion.

47

Only the romantic would think that the history and type in our Bedlington is clear for there is so much that conflicts. Mention of crossing with the Bulldog for courage and the hound connection both argue against the idea of 13 inch and 15 pound animals. The coat, like that of litter mate Dandie, is different to all other terriers – yet 'grizzle' has been recorded and that has been a terrier colouring. Also, as has been said before, so much is relative and one must try to imagine the context in which descriptions were evolved. The book has to be left open and we have to go on trying to understand and see.

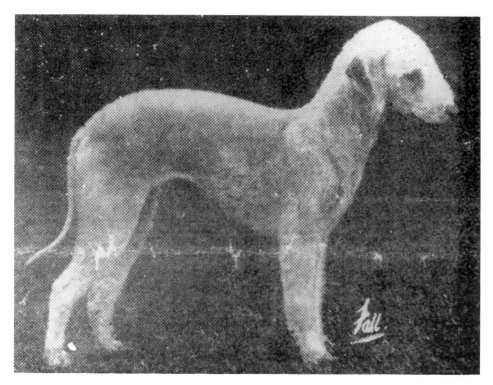

Gay Miss of Simonside
(Ch Deckham Oprecious – Ch Miss Gaysum)

This photo of a bitch whelped in 1934 has been selected to illustrate breed type. The correct height to length, crested neck, gentle arching over the loin, not too much depth through the chest and not too much cut-up at the loin. The photograph does show that many of the present day Bedlingtons are too short in back or too long in the leg, are camel or wheel backed, have exaggerated keels which handicap a dog underground, have small waists which limit development of internal organs or carry the head in a fawning and submissive manner. One or more of these faults are found in the modern dogs. There never has been, and never will be, a perfect dog and Gay Miss had her faults but her photograph serves a purpose in the belief that a picture is worth a thousand words.

PROPORTIONS IN THE BEDLINGTON
(Some exaggeration has been indulged to make a point)

From the 'smooth' specimen it can be seen that the lines and proportions are that of a terrier and NOT of a Whippet.

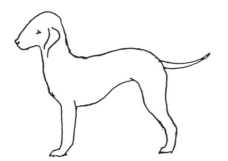

Bedlington outline

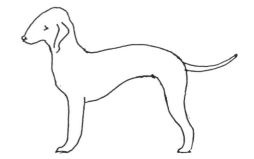

Long back

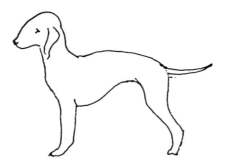

'Camel' back

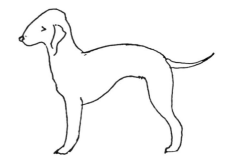

'Wheel' back

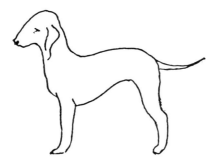

Long hock

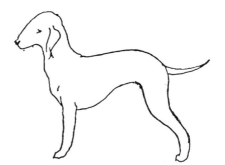

Too long stifle to hock

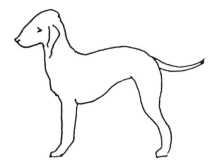

Short back

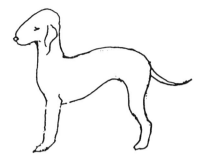

'Ewe' neck and 'Goose' rump

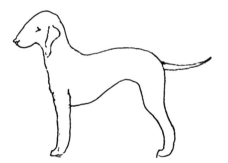

Foreleg not under dog

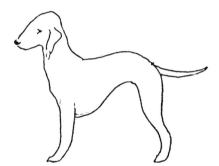

Too deep in body

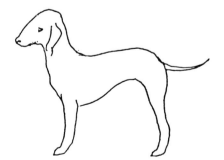

'Sickle' hock

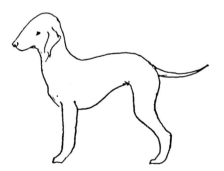

Overangulated hind leg

Correct front

Correct rear

Fox Terrier front

'Cow-hocked'

'Out at elbow'

'Out at hock'

— 4 —
Trimming

In the last 50 years the terrier breeds have been subjected to more and more skilful trimming and have now reached a stage where an untrimmed, or badly trimmed, exhibit is severely handicapped in the show ring. This does not mean that a really good specimen, badly presented, could never win; indeed under a specialist judge or an all-rounder familiar with, and interested in the breed, the dog would, in breed classes, be examined, placed and the owner tactfully told to study trimming. However, generally speaking, an untrimmed or poorly trimmed dog would rarely reach the prize lists in variety classes.

In the early days of shows trimming consisted merely of a little tidying up process with finger and thumb plucking out the odd, untidy dead hair. The scissors later came into play in the preparation of the Bedlington and the exhibits were 'improved' to such an extent that in 1882 Mr A. N. Dodd sarcastically registered a dog as 'Hairdresser'. Finally, Mr Dodd, who was quite an authority, gave up showing his dogs as he was so disgusted with the 'faking'. I am afraid that if the gentleman saw our present day efforts he would resort to physical expression of his feelings.

Mr Harding Cox, in his work *Dogs of Today* follows in the Dodd tradition, referring to the contemporary dogs as 'grotesque fakements' and seeing the head trimming as 'deplorably ugly'. Seemingly he attributes such sinful behaviour to the ladies. Discretion being recognised, we flatly refuse to pursue the subject.

Although these gentlemen may have been somewhat extremist in their views they are not alone in thinking that we tend to ridicule a sporting terrier. Such writers must obviously influence some people hesitant in choosing a breed as a pet.

We now have to guard against any further advance on a style which, if approached with good sense, can be both beautiful and practical. It would be so easy to destroy the flowing lines of the Bedlington by allowing the dog to grow large 'cowboy chaps' or outsize tassles on the ears resembling pom poms, etc. Any such caricature of the breed can only interest the cute pooch type of people without regard to quality, soundness or essential breed type. The rapid rise to popularity of the poodle and its pathetic consequences should be a warning to us. One recent tendency that does call for comment is the practice of cutting down to the skin in areas and not graduating length of coat from one part of the dog to another. If the coat is too short it is virtually impossible to assess the texture, although a really good jacket is never in doubt. Exaggerated trimming does destroy breed type and character.

The reason, then, for trimming is to present the dog in a smart, business-like manner, minimising the faults and accentuating the virtues. The judge, if he knows his job, will find the faults anyway and not be deceived but no dog is perfect and a well turned out exhibit is bound to create a good impression.

Dr Muriel Binns, of the Pynello prefix, once said that a well trimmed Bedlington should look as if its coat were naturally so. To add to this would be superfluous.

To become adept at trimming requires a knowledge of the points of the breed, practice and constant observation of the work of the experts. To the beginner, attendance at dog shows is suggested when opportunity permits so as to study the finished products of the old hands. Some examples of superb trimming come to mind as these notes are written. Miss Marsh's Brambledenes, Fred Gent's Foggyfurze and Ida Sills' Vistablu. The latter breeder is one for the novice to copy. It may be quite some time before you attain anything like that standard; however, keep trying and do not be afraid to ask for assistance. If you live somewhere near an expert in the art of trimming it would be invaluable if you could watch that person at work. Should you be fortunate in this respect do not make the mistake of plagueing your tutor or taking him or her for granted. It has happened, so may we offer a mild warning?

EQUIPMENT

If we made a survey of all the equipment used by different breeders the list, in all probability, would be a very long one. As time goes by, individuals improvise and produce all sorts of gadgets of their own and quite ingenious some of them are! However, here we will take only the basic tools required to trim a Bedlington for the show ring.

The scissors should be light, preferably the hairdresser's type, with the screw set so that the instrument is easily manipulated with no hint of stiffness. There is always the risk of the dog suddenly moving when being trimmed, so the ends of the blades must be nicely rounded. A second pair of scissors of a different design can be found useful, especially when trimming the legs. Sometimes referred to as marking scissors (cattle drovers cut brands in the ears of cows with the heavier type) the blades are parallel but set in a different plane to the grips, there being a double bend between them. With this instrument it is possible to hold the scissors flat against the leg hair without the fingers brushing the coat askew. See Fig. 1.

Use a steel comb with teeth as round pins set into a back. For half the length the teeth should be ⅛th of an inch apart and the remainder ¹⁄₁₆th.

Not all hand or electric clippers are suitable for the Bedlington coat and some clog with hair too easily. The better the texture of coat the less likely this will happen but, as the modern coats are generally bad, this is a problem. Also, unless one is careful, a dog with a sensitive skin can suffer from clumsy work with an overheated electric clip held too close. This was learnt the hard way with livers who seem to have more sensitive skins.

A small pair of hand clippers is sufficient for cheeks, ears, throat, etc. and the Hauptner No. 2 or Diamond Edge are quite the best obtainable. Areas where clippers have been used should be dusted with talc, witch hazel or after-shave. If a dog scratches violently where it has been clipped, sore patches can develop and these can take a long time to heal properly on account of the dog's attentions.

When trimming, the scissors should not be opened wide but a method of snipping, as opposed to cutting, should be adopted, using the ends of the blades rather than the whole. This avoids scissor marks showing on the coat and sometimes encourages the twist in the coat. Do not cut too deeply at first as, although it is quite easy to go over the dog a second or third time, it is recognised as somewhat difficult to replace coat once it has been removed.

Different people, different methods, and in time you will no doubt develop your own style. I was fortunate indeed in being given instruction at an early age by a number of breeders who were only too willing to encourage a kid with the benefit of their experience, (absolute confidentiality, be it noted!). By comparing the different methods, and reasons, I was able to develop a style of my own which is humbly offered here as a basis for the novice to work on.

METHOD

When trimming a Bedlington, wander about the dog and do not complete any one part before carrying on with the next. The reason for this is that each dog is an individual and must be trimmed as such. It would not do to trim to a fixed pattern, working systematically from one end of the animal, completing each part before going on to the next. **Each mass is contributary to the whole** and as the subject is to be viewed as a whole at completion, it must be viewed as a whole at commencement and throughout the whole process of trimming. However, it will be easier to explain, and also to follow, how the various parts are trimmed if they are taken as quite separate items.

First, bath the dog in tepid water, making sure to plug the ears with cotton wool so that no water penetrates the well of the ear. If you use a soap, rinse the dog thoroughly afterwards. Some people put a few drops of vinegar in the rinse to clear the suds but this only serves to soften the coat. Normal rinsing is sufficient if you are not too heavy handed with the soap but for preference a shampoo is recommended. There are many on the market but those sold in the pet shops and at dog shows with flea ridding additives, etc. seem to be on the sellers' market and the cheaper supermarket product for humans does just as well at half the price. Some of the preparations contain colouring and texturing properties and, praise be, the Kennel Club is now outlawing any such faking. I have seen black sulphur emerging from a Mason Pearson as a vet, of all people, brushed his dog at a show, and billiard cue chalk on the bench of a famous lady exhibitor. The modern human hair dyes are not easily detected, unless it is the same tone as used by the handler. Do not be tempted to faking. You may get away with it for a time but other exhibitors will not make cheats welcome and the new attitude of the ruling body could mean banishment. One hopes so. Of the soaps, there is nothing quite like Lux flakes but rinsing is important here.

Having washed the dog, dry briskly. Hair dryers save time but not all dogs tolerate them. When the dog is still damp, powder the head, tassles, forelegs and hind legs below the hock with magnesium powder. This powder is extremely light and should not be applied in a high wind otherwise a minor snowstorm is likely to develop and very little will find its way where wanted. Powdering completed, carry on with the rubbing down until the dog is thoroughly dry. When you are satisfied that it is so, comb the dog all over, making sure to remove every tangle and knot. Be it noted that, under new Kennel Club ruling, no trace of chalk or powder should be present in the show ring. In grooming this breed, the coat is combed finally in the reverse direction, i.e. from tail to head and from foot to top of leg.

This done, ward off the risk of the dog becoming chilled by taking him for a short, brisk walk – weather permitting. Keep him on the lead because, if free, he is certain to roll on the ground. If it is raining this is out of the question so bring him in front of the fire for a few minutes. Stand him on a newspaper otherwise the furniture is likely to get a dusting if he shakes himself. Close work with the clippers should be done before bathing as the soaping and rinsing will help ease any irritation set up by the clippers.

Ears
All hair is removed from the inside of the ear, taking care around the well. On the outside the flap is cleaned off except for a tassle left at the end. The size of the tassle is a matter of choice but it should never resemble a pom pom. It is shaped with a point at the end which harmonises with the flowing lines of the breed (Figures 2 and 3). A straight, horizontal line is crude, ugly and foreign to the breed. The ears should look 'natural'. If the ears are on the small side in proportion to the rest of the dog, commence the tassle near the extreme tip and have the hair fairly long. On the other hand, if the ear is on the large side, commence a little higher than the norm and finish almost in line with the tip. This will not deceive the judge in respect of the quality of the ears themselves on close examination, but if they are obviously incorrect at a casual glance the whole picture is marred and can handicap a little unjustly a dog of otherwise excellent quality. Scissors are used for removing the long hair, but for finish,

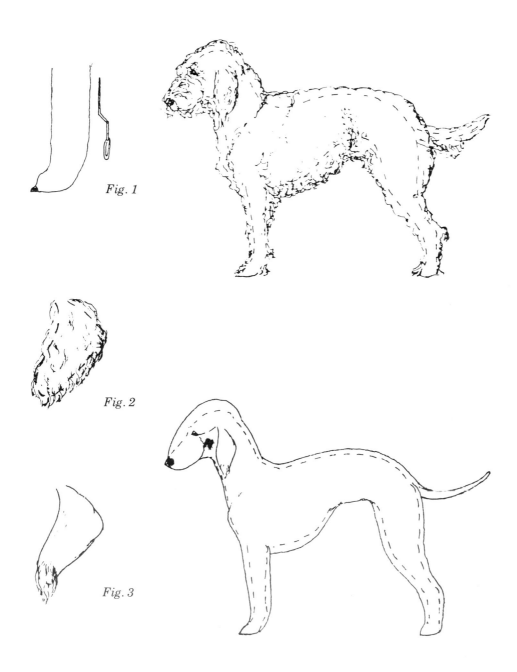

Fig. 1

Fig. 2

Fig. 3

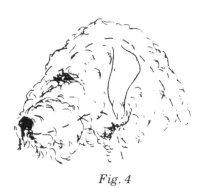

Fig. 4   *Fig. 5*

Fig. 6   *Fig. 7*   *Fig. 8*

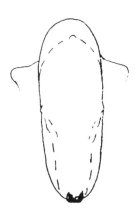

Fig. 9   *Fig. 10*

clippers are quicker, easier and kinder on the dog for there is less chance of nipping the skin. All clipper work should be done three or four days before the show to allow the ends of the hairs to heal and produce a natural sheen. Indeed, it is preferable if the whole trim is completed a week before a show and just the legs and head washed the night before the event. The odd hair can be removed in a more relaxed atmosphere when time is not the master. After finishing the ears they should be wiped with a damp cloth and dusted with talc or other powder to avoid irritation.

Head

Taking a line from the corner of the eye to the top of the ear, remove the hair from the cheek, continuing down the throat and under the jaw (Figures 4 and 5). Here again it is advisable to make use of clippers to get a good finish.

Standing in front of the dog, place the scissors flat against the cheek and cut vertically into the top-knot, so continuing the line of the cheek (Figures 6, 7 and 8). Comb the top-knot carefully and shape it as shown in the diagram, viz. a dome with the hairs at the peak being the longest and graded down in length until very short at the eye-ear line. Now, looking down on the head, similarly trim the sides of the muzzle to make a continuous, almost straight, line from the nose to the cheek (Figures 9 and 10). We now have to consider the head in profile. The desired shape is that of a thick wedge formed by the natural jawline underneath and a graceful, parabolic curve on the top (Figures 11 and 12). Do not hurry this part of the job as it is the most exacting and, done well, the most pleasing. A good finish is important when trimming the head as it can make a world of difference to the impact your dog has on the eye of the judge when seen on first entering the ring. After the head has been shaped as described above, proceed slowly and with even more caution than before, continually combing the hair off the face and skull so that each is imagined as extended to its full length. If you look at the head in profile you will observe that on the 'horizon' you will have a haze, as it were, formed as shown in the diagram by hairs of different lengths (Figure 13). From now on do not cut into the top-knot proper, but snip carefully at this haze, bringing the hairs to a uniform length. The reason for this work is that the outline so produced will have a more definite line and solid shape to arrest the eye. The back of the top-knot is rounded in profile and runs gradually into the shorter neck hairs in the form of a 'V' when viewed from the rear (Figures 14 and 15).

Neck

The neck hair varies in length, being graduated from the close cutting of the clippers on the throat to about a quarter of an inch at the side of the neck to half an inch on the back. These lengths are not to be taken as definite but are mentioned so that an idea may be formed of the graduation in length on different parts of the neck. When trimming the shoulders, hold the scissors at an angle of approximately 45 degrees or roughly at the angle of the shoulder blade. Any scissors mark will give the

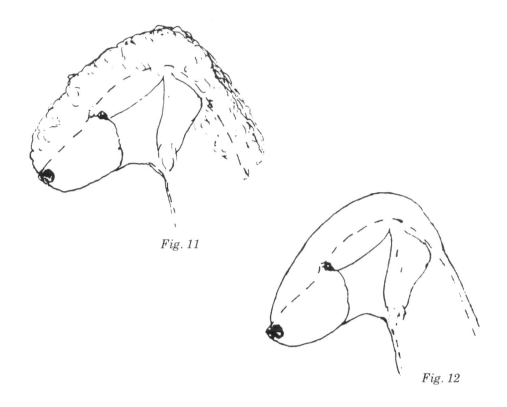

Fig. 11

Fig. 12

Fig. 13

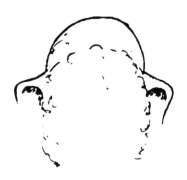

Fig. 14

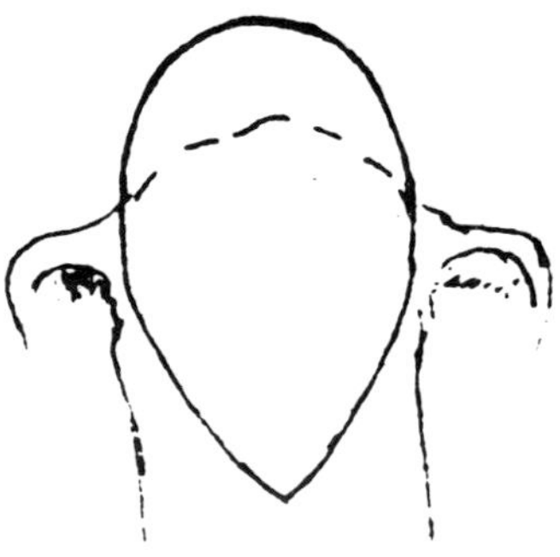

Fig. 15

immediate impression of a neck flowing into correctly placed shoulders. This is not meant to deceive the judge when the shoulders are incorrect but the undesirability of giving the wrong impression when the shoulders are in fact correct by vertical cut lines is fairly obvious. Just an optical illusion, one might say, but one worth taking into consideration. The dog that looks right to the practised eye before detailed examination makes a lasting impression.

Body

Remove all hair from the belly of the dog commencing immediately behind the brisket and continuing a little way down the inside of the hind legs. Not too far, otherwise the effect viewed from behind is that of a bandy legged clown. The skin should be absolutely clean with little hint of coat. You will find an apron of skin running from the ribs to the hind legs. In itself it would not seem to be an important part of the dog's anatomy but in any trimmed breed it assumes some importance as it lends itself to the creation of impressions which can either enhance or mar a dog's appearance. The Standard requires that the loin of the Bedlington be arched and the backline over be curved. If this length of skin is trimmed off along its edge, giving a clean line it will accentuate the arch and curve and give the desired impression of a lathy, springy dog capable of galloping at speed. Great care must be observed when trimming the loin, however, as, although an asset when done properly, it can be a real howler sometimes, making the animal look pinched in the waist and barrel in rib. It is the edge that is cut close and not the whole apron. The novice will be well advised to practice carefully and be critical of the result.

The outline of the Bedlington is that of a flat-sided animal with gracefully arched back and deep, capacious chest. Trim accordingly, going a little closer to the sides than on the back and closer on the withers than on the middle of the back. This must not be exaggerated in the same way as the actual depth and flatness must not be exaggerated. The body is not that of a Whippet but a terrier.

Legs and feet

Trim off all the hair between the pads and toes. Clean off the coat from the toes as far as the knuckle and from the sides and back of the foot with a clean outline against the floor (Figure 16). Avoid making the foot look round and the pastern vertical as the Standard calls for a hare foot and sloping pasterns, neither of which can be apparent in a Fox Terrier trim (Figures 17 and 18). Neither should the whole foot be trimmed clean to produce a Poodle effect (Figure 19). The front legs are trimmed with the same technique as the head; slow, careful snipping of the hazy outline to give a bold, definite line and shape. Viewed from the front, the legs should be perfectly straight, though wider at the chest than at the feet (Figures 20 and 21). If too much coat is left on the elbows it is inclined to flop outwards as the dog moves and may give the idea that the dog throws its elbows out. Standing in front of the dog, lift each foot in turn and trim off the offending elbow hair as the leg bends into the position it takes up on

Fig. 16

Fig. 17

Fig. 18

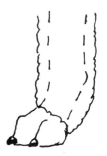

Fig. 19

Fig. 20

Fig. 21

the move. Trim the hind leg, continuing the flowing line of the arched back and accentuate, only very slightly, the natural bend at the stifle joint. On no account exaggerate the bend as the Bedlington is not a breed with great angulation. From hocks to feet trim as in the front legs making sure to achieve a clear outline. Care is necessary in trimming the hocks. Stand behind the dog, placing the hand between the legs, lift gently an inch off the ground and then let him drop. This is not always possible with a young or playful dog which may look around to investigate. However, if the dog does not take kindly to the affront to his dignity, have someone hold his head. By this procedure, the hind legs will take up their natural position according to the dog's conformation. The hocks will also take up their true position and can be trimmed with the angle at the back and (less so) at the front with the outer and inner rising as straight lines from the foot to the upper leg.

Tail

First remove all the coat from the underside from tip to root. Standing behind and holding the tail horizontally, trim the sides from tip almost to the root. Finally, trim the upper side from tip to within three inches from the root where it should be graduated from nil length to body length at the root (Figure 22). There must be no bump or sudden change of coat length but a continuing, flowing line. Care is necessary here for any sudden change will give a jarring note and too much removed could give the impression of a high set-on of tail. We have come to accept the close trim on the tail but how much better the picture would be were we to leave a little hair on for the whole length and shaped to follow the line of the tail! Some dogs will sit down when working on its stern. One counter is to place the hand under the belly and along to the tail end and another is to stand a small box between the legs so that the scamp cannot sit.

The Bedlington does not shed his coat as other terriers do and when out of coat has to have the dead hair removed. Little is gained by cutting the dead hair and leaving part still attached to the dog and hoping that a new coat will burst through. The old must be stripped out with finger and thumb or stripping comb and the remainder cut back very close. When the new coat is through a good method of keeping it thick and healthy is an occasional session with a singeing taper or lamp. Not to be attempted outdoors otherwise the slightest breeze may result in the dog suffering a nasty burn.

In Holland, France and Germany trimming styles are much the same as in Britain but elsewhere the glamour dogs often seen would have Mr Dodd revolving in his resting place at great speed. Some lose the true lines altogether, giving the dogs ugly pantaloons for legs, crude manes producing thick necks, giant tassles on the ears and Fox Terrier front legs. These efforts surely tell that the perpetrators do not know breed type at all.

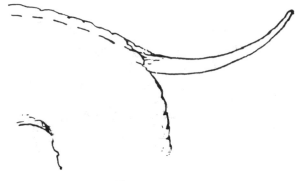

Fig. 22

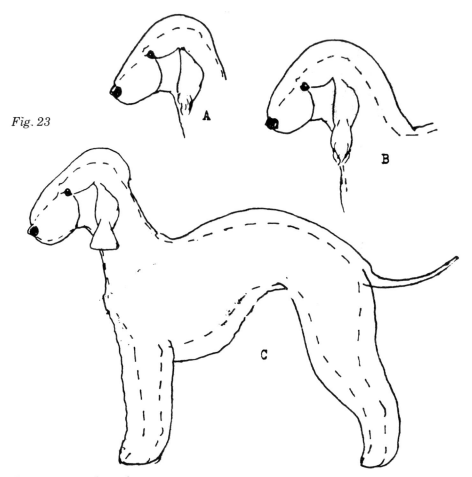

Fig. 23

Incorrect trimming

(A) *Too flat on foreface giving weak appearance.*

(B) *Extension of top-knot to form a mane. Coarse and false.*

(C) *Lacking in the flowing line and with clumsy ear tassle. Does not conform to Standard description of a 'graceful, lithe dog apparently capable of galloping at great speed'. Note 'camel' back and cloddiness.*

— 5 —
Showing

Dog shows began because a few sporting people decided to get together to compare their dogs. The first was held at Newcastle upon Tyne in 1859 for gundogs. The accent in the early days being very much on shooting and hunting breeds. Since those days the picture has changed somewhat. The first all-breed show was held in Birmingham and the Birmingham Dog Show Society is still with us. The first Bedlington specialist show was held in 1870. Shady characters in the early days meant that rules and control were needed and so the Kennel Club was set up. At times the social side seemed to take precedence over the doggy needs but things have improved in recent years, especially since women were allowed to be members. The problems are different in modern times in that the sheer size of the dog world is such that bureaucracy has become a danger and people without the necessary interest in dogs have too much power.

All recognised dog shows are licensed by the Kennel Club and anyone found exhibiting at, or organising, 'unofficial' events is liable to a lifetime ban from participation in the orthodox dog world. By registering an animal at the Kennel Club, which one must do before it can be exhibited or bred from, the owner does not become a member of that body. It is a private club, with membership by invitation only, but it is surprising how often one finds people unaware of the fact.

However, there is an Associate Membership, although application for same does not necessarily mean acceptance. This associateship entitles one to a copy of the Kennel Gazette each month, the Kennel Club Stud Book and Year Book, admission to Crufts and the privilege of nominating two dogs for entry into the Stud Book. These dogs, although not winning places therein, must be either parents or progeny of dogs already entitled to entry.

1889. Mrs P. R. Smith (Breakwater) nearest the judge, Mr Harding Cox.

There are five categories of shows:

SANCTION SHOW

Confined to members of the organising society at which no class higher than Post Graduate is offered. Therefore, it is limited to dogs which have not won more than five first prizes, each of the value of £1 or more, in Post Graduate, Minor Limit, Mid Limit, Limit and Open classes, whether restricted or not. The restriction could refer to colour, sex, owner-bred, etc.

LIMITED SHOW

Again an event for members of the organising society but the competition is drawn from a wider field and only bars dogs which have won a Challenge Certificate or obtained any points which count towards the title of Champion. It is not necessary to be a member of a society running a Limited or Sanction show prior to the event. The subscription is forwarded with the entry fees and no formal letter of application is required.

OPEN SHOW

As the name implies, this show is open to all dogs registered at the Kennel Club, including Champions. It is not necessary to be a member of the society, but sometimes reduced entry fees are offered to members. The membership of dog clubs covers a period of 12 months so the members' concession at Open shows can be an advantage.

CHAMPIONSHIP SHOW

An Open show with a difference that gives it great importance in the dog world. The Kennel Club issues, at its discretion, a number of Challenge Certificates which entitle a dog, winning three such, under three different judges, and one after the age of 12 months, to the title of Champion. The word 'Champion' prefaces the dog's name for all time thereafter. Shows at which these certificates (or C.C.s) are on offer are called Championship shows but not all breeds classified at such events necessarily have C.C.s available. Where C.C.s are competed for, the best of each sex in the breed is awarded a Certificate but, although the word 'Challenge' is printed on the coveted piece of card, it must not be supposed that all unbeaten animals have a right to compete, or challenge, for the award. The judge may call for as many unbeaten animals as he chooses and, although he usually has all in the ring, can make a decision based on assessments made during the class judging. As with all awards, however, the winner must be in the ring at the time the award is made. Normally, the judge will have the second in the Open class paraded as well, or standing in the corner of the ring, to compete for the Reserve Best of Sex award. The Kennel Club requires that a reserve best of sex be declared in the event that the Certificate winner is disqualified. The reserve dog is then awarded the Certificate. The Reserve Best of Sex card is often referred to as the Reserve C.C. but this is not strictly correct.

EXEMPTION SHOW

The Kennel Club will grant exemption from its normal rules to anyone wishing to organise a small show in aid of charity. A registered dog society cannot organise such an event but individual officers may take part. The only stipulations the Kennel Club make are that there are a maximum of four pedigree classes and that prize cards are black print on white card. This should indicate the inferiority of the event as show competition but, unfortunately, greedy people will exhibit top specimens at these shows. More regrettable is the fact that people set some value by such wins. Also, we find the Exemption show run in aid of football clubs, political parties, etc., which cannot be truthfully regarded as charities. On reflection, though, perhaps politicians, by their deeds or lack of, need all the charity we can muster. At one time the Exemption shows were informal affairs taken lightly by the exhibitors with 'money for a good cause' as the theme, but this no longer applies and the sooner the Kennel Club discards them the better.

DOG MATCH

A variation on the accepted dog show is the match in which two clubs sometimes compete on a team basis. No prize money is on offer and there is a limit to the number of animals in each team. The system by which points are awarded is left open to the organisers.

A very young Fred Gent with his first Champion, Foggyfurze Ace High 1935.

Bath 1950. Mary Taunt with Ch Ragea-tail, judge Herbert Winder and the author with his first Champion, Ch Tol-pedn Merry Maid.

BENCHED SHOWS

Some shows are 'benched', that is pens are provided for the dogs and a charge is made for this with the entry fees. Use of the bench is not optional and the Kennel Club demand that all dogs must be on their benches except when being shown or exercised. The dogs must be securely chained to the benches and, for their comfort, a blanket should be included with the show gear.

The reader may have bought a Bedlington without any intention of showing it but, if it is a good specimen, the breed will be done a service by bringing it before the public eye. There are far too few specimens of this fine breed about and every opportunity should be taken to advertise it.

These notes are written to assist such owners and also the beginner with decided ambitions in the show world.

DOCUMENTS

To be shown a dog must be registered at the Kennel Club. The system is about to be changed again and any detailed information we may give here would certainly be out of date by the time it is read. A golden rule, before buying, is to contact the Kennel Club at 1, Clarges Street, Piccadilly, London, for regulations on registration and then demand the appropriate documents from the breeder. Should the breeder be unable to furnish the necessary certificates because he is awaiting issue of same by the Kennel Club, then the purchaser must obtain a statement to this effect, in writing. The Kennel Club is taking a stricter stand on authenticity of particulars and an intending exhibitor may find himself with an animal unacceptable to the ruling body because the seller was ignorant or an old fashioned villain. Buyers are advised of the desirability of buying from a breeder rather than from a middleman. The genuine breeder will be interested in the future of his stock and will be glad to help and guide. Be it remembered, though, that the breeder is not accountable for the puppy beyond any reasonable expectation. The fascination of breeding is that one applies theory and planning but experience teaches that there is a lot of hoping and luck attached to the pastime.

HOW TO ENTER FOR A SHOW

Dog shows are advertised in the canine press, and you will find a subscription to one of the weekly dog papers *Dog World* or *Our Dogs*, is a must if you are to keep au fait with what happens in the world of dogs. A postcard to the secretary will bring you a schedule of the classes, and an entry form, almost by return. After a show or two you will find yourself on the mailing lists and schedules will arrive from the most unlikely places. Read the schedule carefully and make sure you understand the classes for which the dog is eligible. Secretaries do not check the entry forms but send them directly to the printers and an incorrect entry can mean disqualification and, sometimes, a fine by the Kennel club. Check the forms before posting. Mistakes often cause a lot of unnecessary work for the secretary, who is normally working in an honorary capacity.

SHOWING YOUR DOG

Before attempting to exhibit a dog yourself go along to a few dog shows and

Leeds 1952. Tom Barker and Ch Karswell Cassadora, of the superb liver coat, and Herbert Winder with Ch Gayboy of Foxington.

Manchester 1954. Mrs C. G. Worrall with Ch Golden Sun of Manaton, judge Vernon Hirst and Norman Stead with Ch Amanda Mirabeau of Nonington. (C. M. Cooke).

sit at the ringside watching carefully the work of the exhibitors. Take note of the different temperaments of the various dogs and how one owner differs in his handling of two different animals. Watch and listen. If anything puzzles you do not hesitate to ask help of one of the exhibitors, but have a little consideration and do not approach when he is obviously

Glasgow 1956. Fred Gent with the first Bedlington to win best in show all breeds at a British Championship show, Eng. Am. & Can. Champion Foggyfurze Sugar Baby. (C. M. Cooke).

Birmingham 1956. Ken Bounden with Ch Tol-pedn Fairmaid, judge Miss Enid Nichols and Norman Stead with Ch Gents Cut. Fairmaid was the first to win Best in Show at an English Championship Show – L. K. A. 1957 (C. M. Cooke).

busy. By your third show you should be looking at things with something of a critical eye and watching for points good and bad. When you think you can do no worse than some of the less skilful, have a try at it yourself. The performance seen in the ring, however, is the result of much work done at home and training your dog to stand still when told and to walk in a straight line on a slack lead is time well spent. Many general canine societies run weekly ringcraft classes and the beginner can benefit a great deal by attending these sessions. The procedure is to act out the judging of a class of dogs in a makeshift ring. The novice owner is trained how to show a dog under fairly typical conditions and meets people who will be able to help and advise. Excellent ground work for novice dog and novice owner.

Let us run through the general procedure used by most judges although the reader must be prepared for individual judging styles. For this reason one should always watch a few classes beforehand to see the technique used.

The diagram shows a fairly average ring, although they do differ slightly, some secretaries taking great pride in providing the last word in amenity to both judge and exhibitor alike.

Normally there are at least two stewards – one to marshall the exhibits and the other to hand out the ring numbers and prize cards. Find out, from the catalogue, **before** entering the ring, the number of your dog as it will waste a lot of precious time if the steward has to sort out the dogs as well as issue the cards. Also neither you nor the dog is as relaxed as could have been after taking part in a scrimmage. Having received your card, glance at the judge. If he is not ready to commence, or not looking your way, run the comb through your dog, especially if you have had to elbow your way through a crowded ringside and the dog's coat has been brushed askew. From now on you are only concerned with your own charge and forget the others. This does not mean you should be impolite but **your** dog is on show and all your attention must be focussed on him. Do not admire the other exhibits, do not apologise for being among the old hands but, trying to hide your nervousness, concentrate on the job in hand. A good judge will sense the novice and not do anything to make the debut more difficult. Some go out of their way to reassure and encourage.

Have one eye on the dog and one on the judge so that every time he glances in your direction, whether directly at your dog or not, your exhibit must be showing itself off. There are times when the judge cannot catch you off guard and then you can relax a little and give the dog a rest. Usually, when all the exhibits are reported by the steward as being present, the judge will stand in the middle of the ring and ask everyone to parade around him, keeping as near the perimeter as possible. Have your dog on the inside, between yourself and the judge, and walk him at a steady pace without pulling, dropping the head or dragging behind. This is where the home practice shows results. After halting the parade, the judge will examine each dog in turn and have the exhibitor 'move him'. When asked to move your dog take him in a straight line away from the judge to the far end of the ring, turn slowly, and come straight back again. Some judges will ask you to move 'in a triangle' which enables him to see

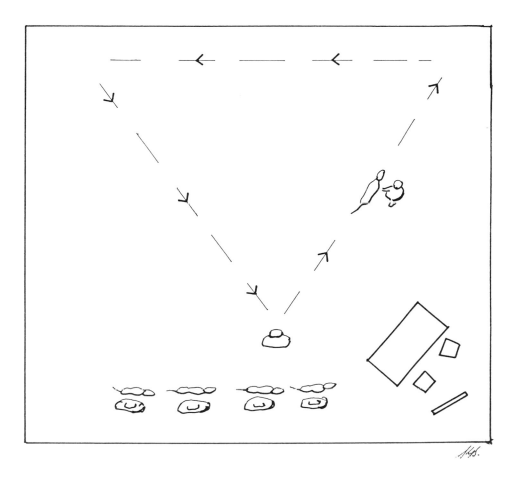

Fig. 1. Plan of an average ring, with one dog moving in a triangle and the others lined up waiting examination. The judge's table, chair and blackboard are in the corner.

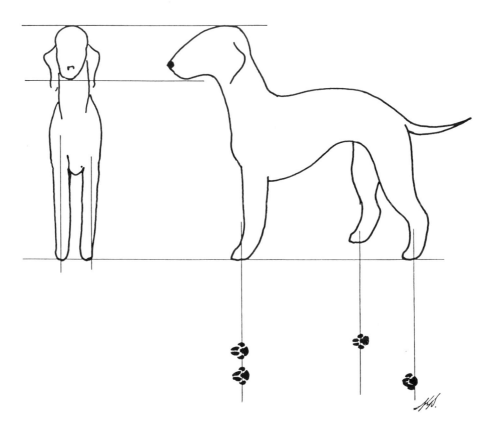

Fig. 2. Stance from the front and from side nearest judge.

the action from behind, in profile and in front when the animal approaches him. The judge may want you to move again so be prepared for a further command, which is sometimes nothing more than a vague wave of the hand. The judge will carry on to the next dog and you will return to your place in the line. If the dog's coat has been ruffled, then a quick run through with the comb is required; then let the dog relax but keep an eye on the judge in case he should look back at your exhibit.

When he is examining the last dog, rouse your animal's interest and place him with his feet as shown in the second diagram. The dog must be comfortably balanced on his feet and not over extended.

The judge will now sort out those of his choice and place them in order, usually in the centre of the ring. Have your wits about you to obey the judge's commands as soon as issued. Dithering sometimes allows a Smart Alec to nip into line ahead of you. If you are the meak type he is likely to get away with a higher placing than was intended. Remember – do not relax until the judging book has been marked.

When standing, if your charge refuses to hold his head up it must be held up for him as the judge is not likely to place an animal with nose to

Leeds 1958. Ch Foggyfurze Sugar Puss winning her qualifying Challenge Certificate from Spring Cut. Left to right: – Norman Stead (Cut), J. W. Dawson (Cloverway), R. R. Seaton (Northcote) and O. Gowing (Wederbi). A change in style from page 66.

ground. Do not break the outline as seen by the man in the middle by enveloping the muzzle in four fingers and a thumb. Hold the near jaw bone between the index finger and the thumb tips. If he is the type of scamp that fidgets, place the other hand under the tummy and very gently stroke the last rib making sure again that the outline of the dog, as seen by the judge, is not broken by a large area of human hand. This rib tickling exercise need not be continuous, in fact is not always necessary, but is offered as a little tip to make your dog conscious of the fact that you are on parade and in charge. If you find it makes him want to play more than ever – hold still.

Be sure to have plenty of elbow room for yourself and see to it that you do not crowd your neighbour. On the walk around, keep your dog under control and prevent him from upsetting the others. Exhibitors, understandably, become annoyed if their charges, maybe good dogs, showing well, prepared superbly, have their chances of winning impaired because someone else's pup wants to play.

Some youngsters take to showing without any bother but others are shy and uncertain of themselves. A nervous dog can never give of its best so, from an early age, let your pup become accustomed to loud noises, traffic, people and other animals. Take him shopping, into stations, indeed many swear by the good old fashioned pub crawl as most beneficial to dog and owner. Get him used to being handled as by the judge. Prevail on your friends to run their hands over him frequently so that he becomes

Manchester 1960. Mrs O. Stones with Ch Stanolly Sapphire, judge W. Burrow and Ted Smith with Ch Shenstone Master Mack. (C. M. Cooke).

accustomed to being handled and takes it as a matter of course. Include in this the examination of the teeth. By the way, when the judge asks to see the dog's teeth or mouth, do not open it wide but just turn the lips back so that he can see the arrangement of the teeth.

Get to know, by practice, the best pace at which to move your dog, neither too fast nor too slow, but at a smart speed at which he impresses as a fit and active dog. Have him on a slack lead well away from you so that he is never partially hidden by flapping clothes.

The ordinary collar and lead are not suitable for showing, something thinner and less obvious is required. Our favourite show lead is the fine nylon slipover which not only serves the purpose admirably but costs little. A half inch band of leather creates the impression of a shorter neck than does a piece of fine cord or nylon.

The exhibitor's dress is also worth considering as it must not detract from the dog and it is as well to choose something plain and contrasting in colour to the dog. A small point, maybe, but in competition it all helps.

All show dogs become bored at some time or other (some are rumoured to make blase remarks to kennelmates) and an essential part of your equipment should be a few lumps of boiled liver or other titbit to arouse interest in the ring. On no account throw the liver about the ring or have Uncle George make noises from outside the ring. Very bad form that will land you in trouble sooner or later.

Do not enter in too many classes at your first shows. You may have a large purse, but, rich or poor, nothing can be more disheartening to the self-conscious beginner than to return to the ring again and again only to be thrown out with the discards. Be prepared for much disappointment, develop stamina, sense of proportion and humour and – good luck.

The beginner should not postpone exhibiting until a show comes along that schedules classes for the breed. The Bedlington is not often classified at smaller shows and, whilst this is a pity in one way, there is a distinct advantage in that a well trimmed Bedlington is an eyecatcher in variety competition. Seasoned exhibitors exploit this advantage and some even bemoan the fact that the win of the coveted C.C. prevents the dog 'having fun at the locals'.

A dog should be only shown when it is looking the part and sufficient work has been done to ensure that this is so. It is an impertinence to grumble and refer to leading exhibitors as 'professionals' or 'in the clique' if their dogs are put down to the minute, properly trained and carefully handled whilst one's own exhibit looks tatty and no effort is made to show it properly. The poor novice does not have to stay so but application and effort are required if anything is to be achieved.

JUDGES

A judge places in order of merit the animals brought before him. He may approve of all and enjoy the task immensely, on the other hand he may dislike all intensely but his job is to place them in order. He is empowered to withhold prizes for want of merit but still the placings have to be made. It is always possible to fault the leading animal and sad reflection on the critic who does so as a comment on the judge's ability. We have yet to see the dog not possessing at least three faults but the degree and relativity of the faults must be the criteria.

Ringside judging is an inefficient pastime, at the best, particularly in a trimmed breed and, despite the cynics who sneer at 'the laying on of the hands', thorough examination is necessary for assessment of merit. Trimming can aid or spoil a dog and, although skill with the scissors will not change an animal, to say that trimming should make no difference in the awards is naive over-simplification. If an animal is presented in long

77

National Terrier 1963. Fred Gent with Ch Foggyfurze Statacco, judge Dave Fenby and Ida Sills with Ch Shenstone Blue Bliss of Vistablu. (C. M. Cooke).

Crufts 1963. Fred Gent with Ch Foggyfurze Honey Chile, B.O.B., and Walter Clark with Ch Amerdale Delight.

body coat and legs so trimmed as to resemble baggy trousers then it cannot have the appearance of being able to gallop at great speed — neither can it look lithe. Although close examination may lead one to believe that the dog could look the part differently presented, it is not in order to judge on probabilities. In a similar way an immature youngster should not be adjudged on what it promises to be but as it is on the day.

It is unintelligent and bad manners to assume the reasons for the judge's placings based on any other than the relative merits of the entry. When a preponderance of one colour features among the prizewinners the claim that the judge has a bias towards that colour is pitiable and embarrassing to hear.

This colour 'rivalry' may have been planted in people's minds by writers whose efforts at reporting reveal them incapable of more than counting the numbers of each sex and colour with the odd reference to the weather.

Judges come in various packages. Good, bad and indifferent, honest, dishonest and fools. However, exhibitors also fall into these categories, as do critics and the easiest task of all is that of the critic. It is most interesting to take note of the performance, as a judge, of the person who has spent many years carping on the efforts of others. There is some sort of justice in seeing biter bit, so to speak. The more vindictive the critic the more painfully embarrassing is his debut in the centre spot.

It is sometimes said that the all-rounder puts up soundly constructed animals whereas the specialist will sacrifice soundness for quality, type or mere fad. History does not prove this to be any truer than the idea that fat people are always cheerful. A specialist can fall into the trap of not seeing the wood for the trees but if he gives prizes to unsound dogs it can be for two other reasons – that he has nothing better to put over them or, sadly, that he does not understand soundness. There are all-rounders who appreciate the whole animal without placing exaggerated value on any one department and give soundness its due recognition. However, there are also all-rounders, uncertain of the points of a breed, who base their placings on action alone and justify this by declarations on the subject of soundness.

Carnival time in Bedlington.

— 6 —
Breeding

For the dog fancier there can be few greater pleasures than breeding and rearing a litter of puppies from a favourite bitch. In the case of the Bedlington terrier, a litter is of the very greatest interest as well, not least of all because of the almost metamorphosis-like changes the whelps go through from black (or, in the case of livers, brown) splashed with white. They look like cross-bred labradors, turning into dead ringers for lurcher pups at about 12 weeks, only to emerge at six months old (and usually when the breeder has almost given up hope) as the most beautiful and graceful of all breeds. The impish charm of the Bedlington puppy is an added bonus that the strictest disciplinarian will find hard not to be melted by.

From a practical point of view, and having already decided that he can afford to breed a litter and is certain of having really good homes lined up for the pups, the novice need have few fears, as Bedlington bitches have few problems in whelping, seldom needing any help at all during parturition and only plenty of good food and clean, dry surroundings to make a superb job of rearing her litter.

CHOICE OF THE STUD DOG

The best advice for a novice about to breed his first litter is to approach the breeder of his bitch and ask him to recommend a stud dog of a line that he knows will stand a good chance of tying in with the bitch's pedigree and type, he might even be able to supply a suitable dog from his own kennel as most of the larger breeders keep more than one stud dog and the progeny from one will often compliment the other. Taking your bitch to a kennel with more than one dog can also ensure a better chance of a mating as your choice of stud may not be that of your bitch, a reluctant maiden bitch can be most difficult, even impossible, to mate. Offered the chance of a different dog, the most ferocious and chaste miss will often become a wanton madame.

The dog should not only compliment the pedigree of your bitch but also her faults and virtues. Do not be lulled into the very mistaken idea that two opposites will produce a happy medium as you will be sadly disappointed when the litter arives. So do avoid exaggeration at all costs, e.g. if your bitch is very long in back and has thick, large ears, mating her to a dog that is very short in back with small, thin, fly-away ears will usually produce puppies with all or some of these faults. Better to mate such a bitch to a dog with correct length of back and correct ears. Whilst you will still get some pups with the faults of the bitch you also stand a chance of getting one or two that have the correct points of the dog.

Do give some regard to temperament. A really vicious bitch should never be mated, no matter what her other qualities, as it is she who will have the greatest influence on the puppies and no matter how superb a dog may be it is nothing if it is impossible to live with.

WHEN TO BREED

The usual time to consider mating a bitch is at her second season which usually falls between 15 and 18 months of age. If the bitch is being shown you may wish to delay mating her and this is perfectly all right up to three years or so, a mating after that age can still be safe and fruitful but the chances of trouble are increased as time goes by and I do not feel that a mating of a maiden bitch should be attempted once she is over five years of age.

THE STUD SERVICE

When the bitch comes into season, inform the owner of the dog at once to make sure the stud is available on the day(s) you will require him. If the bitch is not to be boarded at the kennels you will have to estimate the right day for the service. This is usually on about the twelfth day but it can vary by a week or more, so be on your guard. If stroked down her back and over the hindquarters, the bitch usually indicates her readiness to mate by switching her tail tightly to one side and elevating the vulva. The amount of colour of her discharge is a poor guide and should be ignored.

Many bitches are best mated without their owners present, though I usually call the owners in to witness the tie once it has been effected. The tie, when the dog will turn back to back with the bitch and remain connected to her, usually lasts from about 10 to 20 minutes and 45 minutes is not rare. But matings without a tie can be fruitful though I prefer to give a second service a day or two later in this event. Once your bitch has been mated, guard her carefully as she will be more than willing to mate again and a second mating to the village Romeo could result in a mixed litter in which you could not be sure of the parentage. Never attempt to mate a bitch who is not in the very best of health and sleek, hard condition.

CARE OF THE PREGNANT BITCH

The gestation period is 63 days but this can vary by five days either way without any effect on the bitch or her puppies. Whelps born more than five days premature are difficult to rear and not really a job for the novice. If the bitch goes more than five days overdue the advice of your vet should be sought though the outcome is not necessarily bleak. I have had a bitch go nine days overdue and proceed to selfwhelp a fine, healthy litter.

The diet and routine of the bitch should not be changed in any way at all for the first five weeks. It is a mistake to start feeding up a bitch too soon as she will only lay fat on herself and this can cause problems when she whelps. Usually, an examination by palpation of the abdomen on the twenty eighth day after the service will reveal whether the bitch is pregnant, though do not give up hope if whelps cannot be felt as they can often be carried high up in the ribcage where they remain hidden almost to the end. You may suspect this if the bitch starts to look barrel ribbed and the teats become pronounced and rather pink at the base. Often, a marked change of personality will also reveal her secret.

From five weeks on the diet should slowly increase, feeding at least twice a day and allowing plenty of protein and vitamin rich foods rather than filling up with pills as these can even be dangerous if overdone. Avoid milk as experience has shown that Bedlingtons are often allergic to this and it will cause them to scour. Dogs digest cow's milk very poorly, anyway, and are best provided with calcium and protein in other forms. If in doubt, the best way to ensure that she is being correctly nourished is to feed her 50/50 on fresh, raw or cooked, meat mixed with a complete food such as Chappie. Bedlingtons do not require huge bones so go easy on the bone meal or calcium tablets, an excess of either puts a strain on the kidneys which is not a good thing as they will already be working overtime during her pregnancy.

Milk fever, or eclampsia, is not necessarily caused by a lack of calcium in the diet but, most often, by a bitch being unable to fully absorb it fast enough into her system at a time of high demand. Hence it most often occurs at the actual time of whelping or when the pups are three or four weeks old.

Signs to look for are: sudden change in the behaviour of the bitch, such as lying away from, and even snapping at, the pups. Trying to crawl under furniture or hide in a corner; shivering and having a frightened or wild-eyed look; unable to stand. Any or all of these signs may present themselves and will rapidly lead to total collapse and the death of the bitch. A vet **must** be called immediately as there is no way that this condition can be home treated. An injection will bring about a recovery very quickly, often in only a matter of minutes. The vet may advise further injections but sometimes even this is not required. If the pups are near to weaning anyway, it would make sense to wean them off straight away and thus remove the drain on the bitch.

If you wish to breed from the bitch again, the vet will probably advise that she is given precautionary doses by injection of calcium glutanate even though it does not always follow that a further litter may bring about the same condition.

Right up to the moment of parturition the bitch should be exercising daily, cutting down on the more boisterous gambols during the last week. An overdue bitch can often be stimulated into labour by several brisk walks, letting her lay about all the time will only make her sluggish and going into labour with slack muscles is far from being a good thing.

One week before the expected date I like to bath the bitch, trim her very short, particularly around the mouth, tail and hindquarters, as it is easier to keep her clean during the nesting period and by the time the pups are six weeks or so her coat will be looking a nice length and she will be attractive to show off to prospective buyers rather than looking bedraggled and moth eaten.

THE WHELPING BOX

If it is intended to breed more than one litter then investing in a properly constructed whelping box with front and top opening will be a very worthwhile thing, or the handyman may even be able to construct one at a reasonable cost. Failing this, the next most suitable box is probably a large cardboard packing carton, if several are kept the dirty ones can be burnt as necessary and they have the great advantage of being free.

Most kennels have either a room in the house or a specially designed puppy house outside, a spare bedroom with the carpet rolled up is equally suitable. To be avoided is the placing of the whelping box in a busy room with a lot of light and noise and, worst of all, with other dogs around. Quiet surroundings and dim light for the first two weeks will help to create the correct atmosphere for a relaxed mother and thriving puppies. Warmth is essential. In a properly constructed and insulated box this can best be supplied by the bitch, in other circumstances heat in the form of a plate or pad that the pups can lie on and which is kept at the exact, correct body temperature are to be preferred to a lamp which keeps the family in a constant light, can cause burns if the height is not judged correctly and, a point to be well considered, costs more per hour to run than a pad does in 24 hours. Do not allow too much heat, whatever the method, as this will cause the bitch to lay away from the puppies in an effort to get cool and hence fail to suckle them.

Bedding is best made up of very thick layers of newspapers, I have tried all types from wonder blankets to straw but have yet to find anything that betters newspapers and, again, they come free!

SIGNS OF LABOUR

There are many signs that labour has started, from the bitch pacing about, tearing up the newspapers, refusing food, vomitting, shivering or simply turning her back on the world and lying curled up in a tight ball. Just to be perverse, some bitches show no signs at all that labour has started, will gobble down their meal, chase the cat round the garden, belt into the house and deposit a puppy at your feet! The one sure way to know whether the bitch is about to whelp is to take her temperature regularly over the last week. It will vary just a little from a.m. to p.m. but will be around 101.1. As soon as labour starts, the temperature will take a decided drop and will settle down at about 98 degrees. Use a rectal thermometer and dip it in a little vaseline, insert it for a couple of inches and hold it slightly to one side so that it is against the bowel wall, then count sixty saying 'one and two and three' etc. Remember to shake it down to below 98 degrees after use.

THE BIRTH

The first puppy should appear shortly after the first visible signs of straining occur. Should the bitch strain for two hours and not produce a puppy you must get her to the vet as soon as possible. Should the straining start to fizzle out after an hour or so, again, get help as this is uterine inertia, thankfully very rare indeed in the Bedlington.

The first puppy is usually preceded by the water bag which will break and soak the papers, so be ready to remove these down to the dry layers. A swelling between the anus and vulva that gets larger with each push will tell you that number one is about to arrive. Some bitches deliver standing, others lying on their sides and some even sitting up in an impossible (from the pup's point of view) position, do not interfere but just watch quietly the wonder of nature about to unfold before your eyes. The bitch will usually start to tear at the bag that contains the puppy as soon as it arrives. As soon as it is released the pup will squeak and gasp and the dam will lick and ruffle it about in quite a rough way, eating the placenta and severing the cord at the same time. Should she be a bit bemused, as a maiden bitch can sometimes be, you may find that you will have to break the first bag yourself. I do mean break. Never put scissors near, even if you have to go so far as to separate the cord; do this by grasping it between both thumbs and forefingers, a couple of inches from the puppy, and tearing it apart. This way, you will not have any bleeding from the puppy afterwards and there should be no need to tie the cord off. Always do the minimum and encourage the bitch to take over as soon as possible.

The interval between puppies can vary from a few minutes up to an hour or more but a good average is 20 minutes. Once number two has arrived, I remove the first pup and take off the dew claws, using fairly blunt scissors and pressing well into the leg. Just snipping off the claw will rsult in certain regrowth. If you feel you just cannot do this yourself the vet will do it at three days old, but I prefer it done at birth as there is no bleeding and no pain and it does not seem to upset the bitch as her attention is diverted anyway.

When you are sure the last whelp has arrived, take the bitch out to relieve herself, clean up the bed while she is out, then quickly clean her up if necessary with the minimum of fuss, place her back in the nest with her babies against her and let her have a well earned rest. A drink can be offered but no food at this stage.

Malpresentations can occur but are rare and not for the novice to deal with and the vet should be called in, except for a breach birth which does not usually cause trouble anyway. Malformation of a puppy can also occur but, again, it is rare. Should this happen, it is best to remove the puppy straight away and take it to the vet who will inject it to destroy it at very little cost and without pain; drowning in a bucket is both slow, cruel and distressing.

AFTER CARE

Just light meals should be offered for the first 24 hours and the bitch disturbed as little as possible. For the first three weeks there is little to do except to keep the bed clean, the bitch well fed and to check that each pup is thriving and the bitch's teats not sore or red and swollen; do not fail to get help if they are as this is mastitis and can result in great pain to the bitch and the death of her puppies.

The nails of the pups should be kept short as they are very sharp and can badly scratch the teats of the bitch. Also check that the anal area of the puppies is kept clean, most bitches are very observant about this but should she neglect this duty you will have to wash the puppies with cotton wool and warm water, dry them and rub a little olive oil in the area.

WEANING

The usual age to commence weaning is four weeks but one must use one's own judgement on this as it may be advisable to start up to a week earlier if it is a large litter or the dam does not make a plentiful supply of milk. Likewise, you can delay for up to a week if the litter is one of only one or two puppies as there is no finer food than the mother's milk and better to feed her up and let her feed them than to wean early.

Start with a little finely minced fresh, raw beef offered at about 11 a.m., having taken the dam away at least one hour previous to this. If the pups do not go to the dish themselves place their heads and front legs into the dish and if this fails to get their interest, roll a very small portion of beef up and push it into the mouth of each puppy. Usually puppies take to solid feeding very quickly. Straight after feeding, place the puppies out on a newspaper and they will relieve themselves, thus you have made a start on house training as well.

After the first feed is being taken well for at least a couple of days you may give a second feed of the same at about 3 p.m. and, of course, remove the dam as before. By five weeks or so you may start to add a little cereal based food to the meat; I prefer tinned Chappie but there are so many makes on the market of complete foods, dry pelleted, moist morsels, tinned, flaked, etc. You can even forego meat altogether and feed these on their own but I have found that this method of feeding makes the puppies produce large amounts of soft faeces which makes the job of keeping them clean very hard work whilst meat fed, they usually have only one firm motion per day, this makes final house training a lot easier too. Whatever

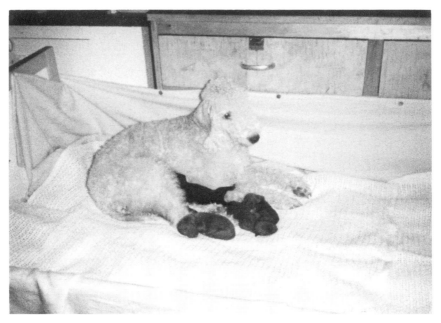

Champion Highquest Holly Girl and puppies.

method you wish to use to feed your puppies, if it suits them and also your pocket and time, do stick to it, chopping and changing is the very worst thing both for pups and adults alike. Dogs do not look for constant changes in their diet unless trained to this by the methods of feeding used by their owners, kennel dogs are used to a plain and constant diet and are the better for it.

At seven weeks or so the puppies should be taking all they can eat in 10 minutes (never leave food down) three times a day and can then be considered weaned.

BREEDING STOCK

The serious breeder with hopes of producing dogs that can win in the show ring has to consider what constitutes a suitable brood bitch and suitable stud dog. A number of essentials are common to both – perfect health at the time of mating, correct conformation, adequate substance, good width in pelvis, strong hindquarters, good musculature, sound action and good temperament. Where do they differ? The dog must be masculine in appearance and the bitch feminine to an extent that both have the look of being able to 'give' to their offspring as the old stockmen would say. The male should look like a stallion and the bitch have that fruitful, matronly appearance.

The question is often asked as to which is the more important, the dog or the bitch, and experience over the years teaches one that most people believe the bitch has more influence. Not very scientific but there are many who claim that there is more mystery and art than science in the breeding of livestock. The top winning show bitch does not necessarily make the best brood and sometimes this is explained by the fact that she is eye-catching but lacks femininity, sometimes even being doggy. A less glamorous litter sister with the right credentials could outshine the winner as a brood bitch. Whilst this argument is often true one should never think that the runt of the litter 'will do as a brood', that way lies disappointment.

A bitch should never be mated if she has cracked and corny feet, is neurotic or is unwilling to mate naturally. Artificial aids to fertility and injections to cancel a mismating can be harmful and are to be shunned. The latter can upset a bitch's cycle and even make her barren. If a bitch is too small to receive a stud, artificial insemination is wicked for a cesarian delivery will follow and such a state of affairs indicates that nature is saying, 'Enough – end of line'. Tales of the dogs knowing more than the humans have often been told by experienced breeders. On one such occasion a keen stud dog sniffed at a bitch full in season and proceeded to lift his leg on her. It was revealed later that the bitch had been bowled over by a car some months before and the vet found her to be twisted inside. Another time a bitch that had had a litter on her second season refused to mate thereafter. Five years later she was force mated and had a healthy litter of three pups, then 10 days later she dropped dead.

A keen Romeo and a shameless hussy that are healthy animals are the ideal pair for producing lusty pups. When choosing a stud dog, the wise person selects one that has already proved itself as a successful sire of quality stock. A proven sire is a better bet than a young (or old) hopeful.

LINE AND INBREEDING

Linebreeding is the mating of distantly related animals and inbreeding the pairing of close relatives. In a linebred pedigree one may find a common ancestor appearing half a dozen times or more in an extended pedigree of four or five generations. Examples of inbreeding are father to daughter, mother to son, half brother to half sister and full brother to sister. Father to daughter and half brother to half sister are usually reckoned to be the most successful and the full brother to sister not worth the bother. In layman's terms such close breeding 'doubles up' on the genes. It fixes certain characteristics already in the stock and is very useful for that reason. However, what must be borne in mind is that undesirable as well as desirable traits can be fixed so one should only start with sound, quality stock and be absolutely ruthless in discarding the inferior, even starting all over again. There is no credit in close breeding animals of correct shape and type that are also very faulty in other ways.

Inbreeding itself is not harmful but the material must be good to start with and the results culled whenever necessary. When outcrossing is demanded it must be done but one must then be prepared to wait for another generation or two to achieve one's objective.

In the last 40 years we have had three distinct lines developed from line and inbreeding. The post war Foggyfurze were based on Brambledene (which were not inbred) and after the infusion of Mahidap and Wederbi blood were closely bred until crossed with Stanolly in the last decade. The Wetop line came from Foxington and Brambledene and the close breeding in the former strain has been continued ever since. The Stanolly taproot was the product of unrelated animals but a policy of line and inbreeding has been followed with one outcross to Amerdale which, in itself, was all outcross breeding. The result is that we have three distinct types. Each has its virtues and faults but lucky and patient people have combined them with some success.

There are those who view inbreeding as something distasteful and unnatural. However, it does happen in the wild and a dominant male street mongrel will mate its own daughters and grand daughters whilst he is the king of the heap. Were he not superior to his rivals he would not command the breeding programme. Also, in the domestic world, geographic restrictions such as small islands have often meant close breeding. Channel Island cattle are a case in point.

COLOUR DOMINANCE

The theory that a dog inherits one gene from each parent on any given feature does not always work in such a simple way in practice and a specialist study of genetics can be fascinating as well as hard work. Here we will only go into the subject of colour inheritance in the Bedlington. Blue is referred to as **dominant** and liver **recessive**. This means that if a blue of 100% blue breeding is mated to a liver that has no blue ancestory then the whole litter will be blue. However, if two blues are mated and both have some liver breeding in the background then some of the pups can be liver. If, though, two livers are mated, no matter how much blue lies behind them, every pup will be liver.

Blue is dominant but no study has been made to prove whether liver is

Three strong healthy puppies.

dominant to sandy. Blue and tans and liver and tans have cropped up when least expected in blue matings so the bi-colouring must be recessive.

THE STUD FEE

The fee paid to the owner of the stud dog is for the mating, not for puppies, and should a bitch fail to have a litter her owner has no right to demand a return of monies. There are many reasons why the bitch fails to produce, it can be the fault of either animal, and the fact that a fee is accepted does not constitute an agreement that puppies will result. However, most stud dog owners, if informed on the day that the bitch should whelp that nothing has happened, will offer a free service in the future. There is no obligation to do so, though, it being a matter of honourable conduct.

Sometimes a stud dog owner will accept a puppy in lieu of a fee and this can be to the advantage of the owner of the bitch at times. It is, however, unwise to agree to the owner of the dog having the pick of the litter, as the breeder may want a bitch and if there is only one in the litter under such an agreement it may be lost. Second choice is reasonable and can be to the advantage of the novice breeder if a successful breeder takes a puppy and campaigns it with success. A repeat of the mating will then find a ready market with other exhibitors. The policy should be to accept with gratitude the help of the experienced but stay in control of one's own destiny.

For years there has been a recurring debate on whether a repeat mating produces a litter as good as a first that turned out to be of top quality. There have been those who could give instances proving one argument was correct and then others who would come up with records that said the opposite. It is my opinion that a repeat mating can give stock of as good a quality but not necessarily. Also, a second litter may give a pup or pups better than any of the first mating.

CULLING

Culling, or the destruction of inferior stock, is rarely practised these days but at one time breeders often made a practice of inspecting each puppy as it was born and, if it was weak or deformed, consigned it immediately to the waiting bucket of water. Nowadays while we would not put a puppy down in this way there is much to commend the principle. The vet should be asked to put to sleep anything that could not survive without assistance and should not be encouraged to 'save' a throwout which could, possibly, be bred from later and perpetrate its defects. If a bitch pushes a puppy away and refuses to suckle it, it is certain that there is something wrong with it and it should not survive. Let the bitch say what should be done for it is not our place to play God.

— 7 —
The Bedlington Overseas

It had been the intention to give a full history of the breed abroad but sufficient information to do justice to all countries has not been forthcoming and rather than give unbalanced emphasis brevity will have to be the order of the day.

Just how long the breed has been in other European countries it would be nigh impossible to say but it has certainly been established for many years. It is appreciated in Holland, Belgium, France, Germany, Italy, Poland, Finland, Norway and Sweden and has reached the top places at shows in these countries. Thirty years or so ago the Bedlington reached as far east as the Soviet Union and has won the supreme award of best in show at the big show in Moscow where there are about 50 of the breed.

The Bedlington has been in North America for over a hundred years, it being uncertain whether it turned up first in Canada or the United States. Imports, Young Topsy, Chief and Fancy were exhibited at St Louis in 1880 and may have been the first of the breed in the States. Two litters were bred in Canada in 1883 from Vixen to Pioneer and Tyneside 11 to Elswick Lad. Tyneside 11 was bred in England in 1881 and could have been a granddaughter of the illustrious Ch Tyneside. The breed was first given its own classes in the States at Chicago in 1883 and in Canada at Toronto in 1884.

Susana Saevich spent some time in North America and when she returned to her home in Argentina she took with her stock of Rockridge breeding and, with Vistablu blood from England, she and brother Carlos set to put the breed on the map in South America.

In 1961 Dorothy Aitkenhead bred Ch Foggyfurze Dandy which Fred Gent later exported to Australia and the breed soon found favour so that it is well established although not great in numbers.

More recently the Bedlington has been successful in the ring in Singapore where it thrives despite the climate although the owners have to take it into consideration in the daily routine.

Spread over the globe as it is there is bound to be the risk of type changes and gradual drifts without the realisation of the breeders. Some, and only some, American dogs have become too round and heavy whilst a proportion of European animals have become light and shelly. However, there is enough common ground at the moment to say that type is not in danger of drastic change in one quarter. However, it is only by study of and adherence to the Standard that true type can be retained.

Show trimming can have much influence here and exaggeration of any sort must be avoided at all costs. The Bedlington is a sporting dog with flowing lines and an appearance of controlled power and speed. Never should it look static. Over-abundance of coat anywhere and concealing the feet in leghair can never illustrate the true picture. One must harp on the statement that beauty should never be confused with cheap glamour.

The following photographs are merely a few representatives of their countries and again we see that photographs do not always do justice to the subject.

The Bedlington is now found in all corners of the world but the amount of information available varies and the following should be taken as a guide rather than the final word as to the position in various countries.

NORTH AMERICA

The breed reached North America over a hundred years ago but we do not know whether the first appearance was in the United States or Canada. The National American Kennel Club was formed just two years after the English one but not all dogs that competed in the showring were registered at one or either. Mr W Blythe of Iowa showed his imports Young Topsy, Chief and Fancy at St Louis in October 1880 and they were placed in that order in a mixed terrier class. In September of the same year Mr W Dempster's Wasp and Sting won in Toronto in a similar mixed class. In 1883 the Bedlington was given its first breed classes in Chicago and in 1884 the first North American Champion was made in Blucher, unregistered and owned by Mr J F Scholes of Toronto and bred in England by Mr J A Baty. The breed certainly had followers from the early days and was soon established.

English expatriates Anthony and Anna Neary settled in the United States and, as managers of the Rockridge kennels that started in 1929, had great influence on the breed for many years. In 1932 a group of enthusiasts met to form the Bedlington Terrier Club of America and this well organised body has nurtured the breed ever since.

From those days the Bedlington has been a force to be reckoned with on the American dog scene and today we have a nucleus of breeders who have been loyal to the breed over many many years. Elizabeth Funkhauser, Connie Willemson, Gene McGuire, Martha McVay and Aquina Meyer are a few of those who have served the breed so well and still hold it dear although not all are quite as active as in former years.

Being scattered over such a large land mass, type has varied at times and there is a danger that the often exaggerated trimming styles will give

American Champion Alquinas Sportsman. Owned by Mary and Gene McGuire. Aquina Meyer has produced many winners for herself and others, as well as her stud dogs having had an influence on the breed throughout the States.

American Champion Persimmon of Rowanoaks.

American Champion Barma's Rudi of Riegal Road. Owned by Frank Majocha.

American Champion Sunburst of Tamarack. Winning Best of Breed at the Bedlington Terrier Club of America Speciality show under the author in 1971. Sally de Kold's Tamarack Bedlingtons have been successful in the showring and obedience, winning top honours in both fields.

Am. Champion Willow Wind Centurian owned by D. Ramsay, A. Sheimo and M. Silkworth. Bred by D. Ramsay. The top winning Bedlington of all time in the United States.

Canadian and American Champion Siwash Desert Daisy, owned and bred by Shirley Martin was top Bedlington in Canada 1975 and 1976.
Shirley Martin's Siwash Bedlingtons have been the leading kennels in Canada in recent years and have had great success crossing over into the United States.

newcomers a false impression of what true type should be. Exaggerations are never good for education. Nevertheless one's hands tell the truth when applied to the dog and there are some excellent specimens around.

The breed is not so numerous in Canada but the standard is as high and breeders regularly cross the border to make American champions.

SOUTH AMERICA

Susana Saevich spent some years in the United States and when she returned home to Argentina in the 1960s, took with her some Rockridge stock. With brother Carlos she set about establishing the breed, Vistablu dogs were imported from England (Champion Freddie the Gent of Vistablu, Champion Womens Lib of Vistablu and Champion Blue Happening of Vistablu), and very quickly the Bedlington became a force in South America with Buenos Aires being the centre of activity. The breed became successful in group and Best in Show wins and held the stage for some years but in the last 10 there has been a decline in the number of enthusiasts. It is hoped that this situation will change for the better in the near future.

Argentine Champion Wildwind Clown of Blue Happening. Owned and bred by Carlos Saevich.

AUSTRALIA

An early book on dogs published in Australia made brief mention of two Bedlington terriers being shown at the Victoria Poultry and Kennel Club Show of 1896, Mr H Beckford showed Jack (imported). No other record is known until 1933 when two were shown at Adelaide rings, these were Mrs S Bailey's imported Tambi and Miss H Crabb's Jazz Dancer of Tambi. There then seems to have been another gap in the history and it is not known if the breed dropped out of existence or merely failed to get a mention for the next 30 years until 1963 when Mrs Olive Smalley of

Australian Champion Lynstar Foggy Spring. Mrs Joan Tucker's winner bred from two English imports in the early days of the breed in Australia in the fifties.

Victoria imported English Champion Foggyfurze Dandy, bred by Dorothy Aitkenhead, and Foggyfurze Tango Twist, bred by Fred Gent. About the same time Miss O'Brien (Victoria) brought in Lucy Locket of Wetop from Wally Topham. Also in 1963 Mr G Blamey and Mr Elliott imported Nadworna Aussie and Nadworna Sundance and English Champion Nadworna Statesman also went to the southern hemisphere.

The Bedlington Terrier Club of New South Wales was formed in 1967 and the first breed show took place the following year. The breed has not become very popular and is scattered over a large area. Bill and Helen Carney of the Myander affix, active in the breed for some years, produced a useful news sheet at one time which helped to keep people scattered over this vast country informed. The breed seems to be on a sure footing but judging from photos, again one cannot enthuse over some of the trimming.

EUROPE

Language makes it difficult to trace the history of the breed in other countries but some facts are known. In Europe, although the Bedlington seems to have arrived much earlier the general advance only took place in the twenties and thirties.

Germany
The first Bedlingtons recorded in Germany were bred by Englishwoman

95

Mrs W. S. Magee of Dresden, with the affix Langebruck. A Mrs W. S. Magee held the Bluehouse prefix in England at the same time. It has not been possible to discover if it was the same lady and a misprint with the initials. It is more than likely that there was a relationship for the former imported Bluehouse Precious Penelope of Langebruck. In 1930 Gyp of Langebruck was registered, the dam Cramling Peggy being imported in whelp to English Champion Night Express. Later registrations were Peggy of Langebruck and Bluehouse Precious Penelope, bred in England by Champion Deckham Oprecious ex Rytonian Golden Dawn.

Continental International Champion Foggyfurze Ferrari. An import that was campaigned with great success. The author made him Best of Breed at the 1973 Winners show in Amsterdam and considers him to be one of the best ever.
Ingeborg de Rijke has been a keen supporter of the breed and produced some fine dogs at home and abroad in her Vom Klovensteen Kennels.

When the Langebruck kennels ceased almost at once in 1931 the stud dogs were taken over by Frau Schnorr of the Karlsfeld affix. This lady imported many English dogs, mainly from Freda Sturt of the Knowlton kennels. In 1932 the first breed club was formed and amongst its members was Helma Cloppenburg of Berlin, who was to become the most successful breeder the world has known with her Helmburg affix being carried by over a hundred champions. She started with imports Knowlton Peterson and Woodland Jenny and from them produced the first of a long line of winners. There followed many other English imports, including Sunshine Susie and Sunshine Princess bred by Jack Flint, and Woodrow Bluebird and Woodrow Hunters Moon from Valerie Cross of the Woodrows. Susie had already proved a good brood for Miss Cross and it is more than likely that it was this Woodrow blood that accounted for the perfect coats found in Holland in later years when Ms Cloppenburg moved there after the war. In 1941 Frau Hemmen based her Wetterstein kennel on Gilde van Helmburg. Come 1948 these ladies, with Frau Wendemuth of the Anster affix, started a new club in Hamburg and nowadays over a hundred Bedlingtons are registered each year.

East Germany became somewhat isolated after the war, there being an embargo on imported dogs. However, the breed did prosper and the Bannwald line of the Franke family was not only successful at home but exports to the United States proved themselves by winning there and producing winners of top class. It is a pity that we do not have good photos of Bannwalds to illustrate their undoubted true type and quality. Some of the blood also travelled eastward to help the breed there.

Holland

The Bedlington was known in Holland at the beginning of the century but great strides were not made until the 1920s and there is no doubt that it really caught on when Queen Wilhelmena fell for and owned the breed. Cago van der Meulen trimmed the royal dogs and certainly made the most of the fact to publicise the breed. Cago was a great ambassadress, helped novices to get started, encouraged the international approach and was proud of the fact that she attended over 50 Crufts.

After the war the Helmburg kennels settled in Holland and it was here that it had its busiest and most successful years, reigning supreme on the continent. However, many other breeders competed against this powerful kennels making their champions and in the sixties the country could muster an entry of dogs that could compete anywhere in the world with their perfect coats. Unfortunately forsaking old lines for new English imports some features of the breed were improved but the coats lost. The Helmburgs moved to Switzerland a decade ago and were replaced in the limelight by Harry van der Loo's Weiendaal kennel. Started with Dutch stock the line has been crossed with many imports from the Foggyfurze kennel.

The breed has dropped in numbers in recent years and it is hoped that there will be a revival and a return to the days when a Clubmatch in Holland saw a show of Bedlingtons to delight the eye of the enthusiast.

Switzerland

The Bedlington was first mentioned in Swiss records with Medo Straightforward and Whittingham Vic but not until the 1930s did the breed take off. In 1932 Dr W Scheitlin, President of the Swiss Kennel Club, registered Mottisfont Jim and Twilight Shiela, the former certainly bred in England. At the same time Fraulein H Rey of Zurich registered Greenroyd Jo,

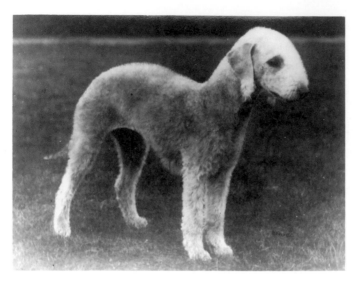

Continental International Champion Adna Van De Helmburg 1935. An ideal stamp. Beginners should look at this photo again and again.
Helma Cloppenburg must go down in the history of the Bedlington as the most successful breeder of all time. In over 50 years she has produced more than 100 Champions. A record that it is unlikely will ever be beaten.
  It is a tragedy that the woman has not judged for her objectivity and love of the breed would have been safeguards against the whims of fashion. The reader would do well to study the photographs of the Helmburg dogs. They are true Bedlington Terriers with no hint of the shelly or overrefined.

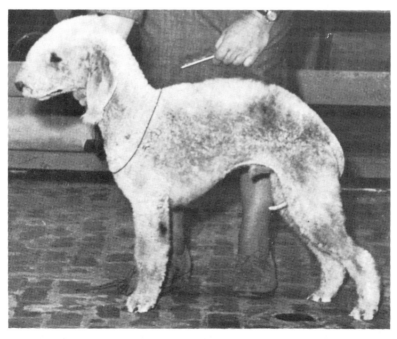

Continental International Champion Solln Van De Helmburg.

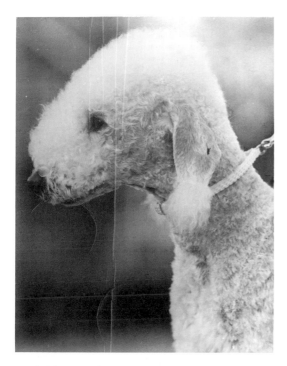

German Champion Cyrrius vom Bannwald.
Heinze Frank's Bannwald dogs were not only successful in Germany but were of international importance. His Champions Orpheus and Joker vom Bannwald had an influence for the good in the American bloodlines.

Dutch and Continental International Champion Sugar Push van de Weiendaal.
For two decades Harry van de Loo, of Holland, produced a series of top winners, importing liberally from the Foggyfurze line. The author recalls seeing the lovely Colette van de Weiendaal as one of the best bitches ever.

and a year later living in East Prussia (now Poland) registered a litter by Bluehouse Patrick (imported) out of Haga Phoebe. Dr Scheitlin's daughter Margotta also registered a litter and the breed became established. However, numbers were not big until 1949 when 22 dogs were registered, many from Germany. Frau Baltzer started her Bustello kennels in 1954 with a bitch Tula van Helmburg; and was active for 20 years. Helma Cloppenburg went to live in Watenwil a decade ago and the Helmburgs continued their successful way until recent times when numbers were drastically cut.

Soviet Union

In the late 1960s four Bedlingtons were imported into the Soviet Union. Happy Day Diamond (owned by Mr Artobolevsky), Happy Day Densy (Ms Matynova), Nimbus von Merkhenland (Ms Rabukhina), and Happy Day Escapade (Ms Rabukhina). These were from Eastern Europe and were the nucleus of the breeding stock. Later, Mr Petricenko brought Sancho in from Poland and in 1974 two more arrived from the German Democratic Republic in Bassam von Haus Shamburg (Ms Sil'eva) and Bellgis von Haus Shaunburg (Mr Dvorin).

The breed has made steady progress since then and is well established, especially in Moscow where a Bedlington has gone Best in Show. Recently two English bred pups went there and should be valuable additions to the gene pool. The dogs are notable for substance and excellent feet but teeth formation seems to be a problem. A weekly dog magazine would be a great help to the enthusiastic Soviet breeders.

Aribica Elsi. Owned by Anna Kriveleva, Moscow. A typical bitch and granddam of the first Bedlington to win Best in Show at the big Moscow show. Obviously not in show trim when the photograph was taken.

Italy

Nothing is known to the author of the breed's history in Italy and approaches to the Italian Kennel Club and terrier club there have been fruitless but in the early 1960s Dr Dionosi imported Shenstone dogs and showed with success.

France

It was only in the 1930s that the Bedlington made a modest appearance at French shows, until then it was rare and considered the pet of the snobs. In 1935 a Russian emigre, living on the Côte d'Azur, imported dogs from the Gardners kennel of Ted Metcalfe in Bedlington. However, the man thought the breed unsuited to the Mediterranean and passed them on to the Count and Countess Stenbock-Fermor who lived near Paris. These Skye breeders fell for the breed and, with the guidance of Mrs R J Martin, produced many winners and the breed became a force to reckon with at the shows.

No breeding took place during the war years but in 1946 shows were organised and people again took an interest in the Bedlington. The breed never became popular but attracted some real enthusiasts. Madame L Vivies and her daughter Madame A Pfohl made their Clos de l'Ill kennels well known and with the infusion of Wetop blood, were in the forefront.

Today there are few breeders but those that there are are almost fanatics and produce top quality animals. There are 50 members of the terrier club and the breed is in a firm position. At the moment there is a worry that breeding working dogs may not maintain quality, but dogs doing the jobs for which the breed was originally produced can only do good though producing animals for guard work can only result in oversize and the wrong temperament.

French Champion Igor du Clos de L'Ill.
This French kennel was formed in the thirties by the late Mme L. Vivies and its successes have been continued by her daughter Mme Antoinette Pfohl. This strain has always scored in type and quality.

Denmark

The Bedlington was introduced into Denmark to deal with the rat infestation which was bad enough to warrant rat catching competitions, thus encouraging people to have working terriers. The first was bred in 1906 by Mr John Ollier of Merthyr, South Wales. Mr Borreson, the Managing Director of the Copenhagen Electricity Works, brought in Merthyr Nell in whelp to Royal Rover and among her pups was Roston Rover, considered to be the king of the ratters. Although Mr Borreson bred many litters he was not interested in showing and did not register all his dogs. In 1923 a teacher imported six English Bedlingtons and these, also, were bred only for work.

It was not until Mr Thomsen, a horticulturist, started his Premiere kennel, in 1924, that the breed was established as dual purpose. Three years later Mr Herold Moller, founder of the Danish Terrier Club, took up the breed with the Westend affix. He was followed in 1931 by Consul Aage Dujardin, chairman of the Danish Kennel Club, whose Vestkysten kennel heralded real advance. With such obviously influential men the breed made steady progress until 619 were registered in the sixties. In 1950 Mrs Elsi Dykoy started her Jalna kennel which supplied the first Bedlingtons in Finland. Since those times there has, unfortunately, been a decline and nowadays there are only Jalna and Eiler Hack's Zardoz kennels, which have been active for any length of time, and in 1989 only four Bedlingtons were registered.

Finland

A foreign restaurateur came to Finland in 1907 and brought with him the first Bedlingtons. Unfortunately this stock faded into history as did further imports in 1925 and 1930.

The breed was really launched when Mrs Margot Nystedt imported a Danish dog in 1956, Julnus Furstinnan Bae Bae. A year later Mrs Rea Hannula, of the Peggan kennels, brought in another Danish dog in Blue Light and later Jalnus Sabina, Jalnus Blue Bonnie and Jalnus Afrodite. All these dogs won their titles and the breed was established. In the 1960s Mrs Hannula imported Leasowes stock from Mary Taunt, and more English stock was brought in by Mrs Tienius, of the Eho affix. By now Foggyfurze, Tol-pedn, Rathsrigg and Stanolly blood could be found in the pedigrees.

The breed has made steady progress since and its leading position in the ring was proved when Ilpo Malmioja's Scandinavian International Champion Jessica was the first Bedlington to be Terrier of the Year in 1974. The same owner's Scand. Int. Ch Marilena Marketeer, bred in England by Charles and Mary Metcalfe, was runner-up for the award. The top winning dog has been Ritva Kohijoki's Scan. Int. Ch Kisapirtin Perro and the Bedlington is now a force to be reckoned with at the shows.

The Finnish Bedlington Terrier Club was formed in 1988 and the breeders have made great progress in tackling the problem of Copper

Continental and Nordic Champion Kisapirtin Fenman. Owned and bred by Ritva Kohijoki, Finland.

Toxicosis. Puppies whelped after 1985 have shown 70% healthy livers and this must be the best record in the world to date.

Sweden

The Bedlington first arrived in Sweden at the same time as in Denmark, 1906, with a dog, Clyde Boy, by Bobrikoff out of Tweedside Girl bred by R. C. Irving. This information is interesting as there was an English Champion of the same name whelped in 1894.

The breed was popular with the officer class families around Stockholm and has had a following ever since. Miss Gudrun Bratgard started her Jycken kennel some 50 years ago and among her imports was Pynello Princess, bred by Dr Muriel Binns. In the late forties, Mrs Dorothy Mattsson brought in Foggyfurze blood. In the fifties, Mrs Dorothy Dovertie started the Flamengo line and it is said that this breeder has done more than anyone to foster the interests of the Bedlington. Through her and, later, Mr Adenby (Ingheden) all the English strains are to be found in Sweden. In recent years the Bla Skuggans kennel of Mr and Mrs Rolf Lyberg have come to the fore. Most Swedish breeders use only biopsied stock for breeding and they are to be congratulated on this commonsense and responsible attitude.

Other countries

Other countries where our tyke has made an appearance are Poland, Belgium, Spain, South Africa (Helmburgs were found here), the Republic of Singapore and Japan, and it is fair to say it has travelled the world over.

Nordic Champion Velvety Perfect Angel. Owned by Lise-Lotte Nilsson, Sweden.

— 8 —
The Working Bedlington

The Bedlington originated to do a job of work for man as well as to provide companionship. Physical features sometimes indicated abilities and characteristics that were desirable to do the job in hand and it was by mating animals with these outward indicators the breed type evolved. Along came the days of dog showing and Bedlingtons were kept by people who were not interested in working their dogs or who, as much as they wished otherwise, were unable to take part in working in the field. Some fortunate folk were able to do both show and work.

In recent years we have found a group of people who decry the world of the show Bedlington and claim that the dog of today is not a true Bedlington and that their goal is to reproduce the real Bedlington as of yore. At first one could be excused for thinking this a praiseworthy and noble venture but second thoughts reveal it all as something akin to romantic self-delusion. That the breed has changed, as all have, sometimes for the better and sometimes for the worse is obvious to anyone who has been involved for many years. However, there are points of argument that must be made before anyone can dare claim a monopoly of the truth and knowledge. The show bred dogs are not all useless in the field, some having proved themselves time and again, with or without training or encouragement from the owner. Some have shown themselves to be useless for work but, unpalatable as it may be to the so-called working Bedlington fraternity, so also have some of the working bred (sic) animals. Dogs purchased from the self styled experts on working dogs for the purpose of sport have shown themselves 'not interested'. So as far as the breed's character is concerned the show world has not betrayed the trust.

On physical features the show world is not on such secure ground. A working dog does need a coat that protects it in adverse weather conditions. There are too few coats of the correct texture in the ring today but the claim by the 'working men' that the breed should have a hard coat is a nonsense. Criticisms can be levelled at other features. There are many dogs too big – but there are also as many of the correct size. There are many that are exaggerated in depth of brisket and too flat in sides – but there are more whch have correct bodies. There are many shelly ones, lacking substance and muscle – but there are many (but not enough) who satisfy here.

On make and shape of the animal the show people can be criticised but their efforts certainly not dismissed as totally wrong.

One fallacy that does persist in some quarters is that the so called working strains go back to the early days without pollution by the show-bred 'degenerates'. Study of pedigrees proves that to be silly. The early Rillingtons came from Ann Heron's Tynefield dogs and the Gutch Commons came from the Pitt and Foxington lines. So these 'working' lines are 30 to 40 years old and the Bedlington has been recorded for 200.

Ideally, Bedlingtons that are worked regularly and of proven ability should be bred into the show families but there are influences that act against this. First, the Kennel Club decided some years ago to accept for registration only dogs from registered parents. This was a betrayal of their own boast to be acting in the interests of dogs, for many people who work their dogs do not show and therefore have no desire to pay the high price of registration. So these dogs are denied us in any breeding programme. Secondly, the men who criticise the show world so scathingly make no attempt to influence matters by mixing with the show folk and arguing their case. Sadly they prefer to isolate themselves and pontificate through their own specialised press. It could be said that the show people do not become involved in the working side and so express themselves in debate, but they live in ignorance of the working activities whereas the show world is well publicised. Working classes are put on at club shows but these are sneered at by those whose involvement is sought.

We think we have some idea what the early Bedlingtons looked like but we can have no certainty and to claim any is a conceit. The ideal situation is rare in life and we are denied ours in that showing and working do not exist in close alliance so it is essential for breeders at all times to keep uppermost in mind that the Bedlington **is** a working terrier and that we must breed animals that we hope fulfil that role. We can be excused mistakes out of ignorance but **never** can we be forgiven for pursuing the falsity of glamour at the expense of the attributes of the true working dog.

Those becoming interested in the breed for the first time may ask what sort of work we are talking about. As ratters they are fast and lethal, having the sense to adopt immediate team practices. Fox holds no problems as far as temperament is concerned but here the oversized animal finds it impossible to follow its quarry underground. Before the introduction of the present legislation protecting the badger it was the boast of partisans of the breed that the Bedlington was the only terrier that could deal with a badger single-handed. A prejudiced view and, some would say, foolhardy in practice but the Bedlington would have tackled Brock with a will. Calling for little courage but other attributes the Bedlington has long been a provider of food in the form of rabbit and, even, hare. Those who scoff at the suggestion that the breed could cope with the

Anyone at home? Granitor dogs at work.

speed of the hare would do well to see a photo in the author's possession of a show bred pet with owner and bag of hare. Unfortunately, the print is too faint to reproduce here.

Mr J Piggin is a rodent officer in the North of England who swears by his team of Bedlingtons who work **daily** in the task of exterminating vermin. From abroad we hear tales of the breed killing off large vermin not found in its land of origin so there is not unreasonable faith that the Bedlington can still do a job of work calling for courage, tenacity, power and speed. The Bedlington is also extensively used in the production of lurchers and it must be said that show bred ones are often found in the pedigrees.

In summary, the show world must never forget that the Bedlington is a working terrier and features to make it capable of that job must be retained. At the same time, those fortunate to be able to put theory into practice must not divorce themselves from the show world but register their stock with the Kennel Club and so make it available to all and, at the same time, use the show press to educate and hammer home the arguments. Preaching to the converted has never produced anything other than the warm glow of self-satisfaction.

— 9 —
History and Redmarshall's Stud Book

In 1932 a book was published under the title *A List of Leading Bedlingtons* and was so successful that a second edition came out in 1935, but now entitled *The Bedlington Terrier, History and Origin, a Stud Book*. The authors were Redmarshall and Others. It has since become known as *Redmarshall's Stud Book*. Who the Others were we are unlikely to discover at this late date but Redmarshall was T. ff. Carlisle Esq., a founder member and one-time President of the Bedlington Terrier Association. He gave the work to the Association whose present day committee has kindly given permission for it to be included in this work, it being understood that it will not be abridged in any way. No one in possession of his faculties would wish to do so. Some photographs of early dogs, breeders and a map of Northumberland, the land of the Bedlington, have been omitted.

Redmarshall gives us a clear picture of a nucleus of pure, closely bred stock, only occasionally outcrossed to obtain fresh blood but does not dwell much on these crosses other than bull for courage. What he does do is stress that two likely crosses did not occur, yet commonsense dictates that, if we are to be objective, they must be considered seriously.

The breed has long had a tendency to increase in size quite dramatically if breeders are not careful and one must surely ask the question why a breed supposedly founded on Anderson's Piper (15 inches) and Coates' Phoebe (13 inches) will shoot up to 19 inches or more if given the chance. The Bedlington has many houndlike features and the possibility of hound blood being introduced, intentionally or otherwise, has to be given a fair hearing. Many early breeders were associated with hound packs and we remember the cry of the notorious Piper Allan, 'When my Hitchen gives mouth I durst always sell the otter's skin.' The opportunities for crossing, planned or not, were there but more informative evidence is surely to be found, physically, in the dog itself. As well as the tendency to increase in size, there is the gaunt structure to be found in the really big ones, the low set, sometimes heavy, fleshy ear, sometimes the pendulous flew, the tendency to heavy dewlap or throatiness, the domed skull, pronounced occiput, the gentle disposition when not working and the constant reminder that the Bedlington is different to the other terriers – that peculiar, ringing bark.

One should not consider the modern 24 to 27 inch Otterhound in this debate. A hundred years ago the Bloodhound was introduced into the Otterhound packs to increase height from the then 20 inches so that the animal could stand in deep water and not tire itself in swimming. Why Redmarshall was so adamant that there was never an introduction of Otterhound blood is mystifying unless one subscribes to the theory that the giants produced in the last 50 years came from a line not fashionable but existing in his time. Amma Blue (1937) was credited with being 19 inches at the shoulder and, although his descendants are legion, he was not the first of the big ones and cannot be blamed, alone, for size variation.

The other cross spurned by Redmarshall is the Whippet. It has been a common error of ambitious authors producing large tomes on all breeds, yet knowing little on any, to declare flatly that the Bedlington is the result of a Whippet/Dandie Dinmont cross. Any book of that calibre is best put aside as suspect in its entirety. It is recognised that the Bedlington and Dandie spring from the same tap root, the former being bred for more length of leg and the latter for less. However, Redmarshall is very definite in not accepting the possibility of a cross. On that we have to deduce that the lighter boned, leggier animal came about by selective breeding. That is more than likely, for many people confuse quality with over refinement and exaggerated raciness. To achieve elegance, some will pay the price of changed type and feel no guilt. At the same time we must not overlook other attributes that crept in at some stage: weak forefaces, the staring eye, the high set, sometimes small ear, the thin tail, the flighty temperament – all to be found at times and suggestive of the Whippet.

Many are the times we are puffed with pride to hear that a first cross Bedlington/Whippet is a superb worker (certain in our faith that the Bedlington contributed most of the good qualities), and the lurcher community regard the Bedlington crosses, be they to Deerhound, Saluki, Greyhound or Whippet, as excellent workers. Being genetically dominant very often the question must be posed whether it is not likely that a crossbred specimen, looking much a Bedlington, was not, in all innocence, mated to a pure Bedlington and the progeny thought to be pure. Until recent years the Kennel Club accepted for registration dogs without papers who were declared by leading judges as typical of a certain breed and it is from such sources the 'impure' blood could have come.

Lurcher breeding has been with us for many years and flourishes today. At a game fair a while back the owner of a three-quarter bred Bedlington saw my Champion Red Eagle and asked if the dog could be used on the bitch. The joke was on me when I suggested a nominal fee of £10 for such an alliance only to be told the figure was cheap and the gentleman's other common looking mutt commanded a £50 price. It is on these occasions we wonder if we do sound patronising.

The hound crosses are very much open questions but signs do seem to indicate the possibilities. The same cannot be said of the rumoured Poodle cross.

Because the Bedlington is a trimmed breed its coat has been neglected for too long but some breeders have recognised the folly, a few have made great efforts to redress things and one went so far as to experiment with the Poodle. The experiment was carried out in the proper manner, the stock registered with the Kennel Club as Interbreds, kept separate from the normal show animals and disposed of when it was learned that nothing was being gained for the breed. In another quarter, a pet owner first had a Bedlington/Poodle cross, fell for its character and decided to go out and get a pure bred Bedlington. The lady bred a few litters but never from the cross. It cannot be stressed too strongly that in neither case was Poodle blood introduced into the breed. Dark remarks made at the time, and later, seem to stem from people disappointed with their lot in life and ever ready to see fault in others. Sadly, the 'knowing' ones usually ignored the state of coats in the breed, particularly those on their own dogs.

Having said that the Poodle was not introduced into the Bedlington it is true that the reverse did certainly happen. That the Bedlington was used to help out the Miniature Poodle in its rocketing popularity in the forties is a fact. In the thirties there was a dog by the name of Barnacle Ben which was shown and bred to produce some good stock. There was another Barnacle Ben, though, that was not shown and owned by a Poodle breeder churning out puppies in a sellers' market. Many of the silvers from this kennel had strong muzzles, flat sides, roached backs, low set tails and white or pale coat on the head and legs. Apricots were becoming much prized and this made the Bedlington very useful. According to Haagedorn, blue and liver over many generations produces apricot. Incidentally, this could explain some of the indefinite colours passing for liver in the pure Bedlington. The Poodle expert, Margaret Fife-ffailes hammered away on occasions against this use of the Bedlington which she blamed for introducing the 'rat' eye into her breed. We never did think that very flattering to our tykes.

This may be argued as of little interest to the Bedlington enthusiast but it has been laboured to stress the point that the traffic was the other way and rumour should not be allowed to become history. It is the author's firm conviction that we do not have Poodle blood in the Bedlington.

Redmarshall's history took us up to the time of dog shows starting in earnest and it is a great pity he did not gather information on that most important era of dog breeding, the first quarter of this century. Records were being kept, competition was keen and the art of the photographer was well advanced in dogdom. Had he taken us to his own day we could have picked up the threads from there and observed the progress or otherwise from then until today.

The author will only take up the story during his own time with the breed for the number of false 'legends' experienced in that time has made one wary of the second-hand story.

WAR YEARS

During the war years there was little breeding, travel was difficult and many show societies and breed clubs suspended operations. However, the dedicated persevered with a will. What shows that took place had larger entries than we have seen since and everyone broke the law by habit to feed the precious stock. In Bedlingtons we had a dynamic person in Camilla Brewer whose passion for the breed savoured of a crusade. At Harrogate show, the day before war broke out, she won the Challenge Certificate, his second, with Dunmail of Pitt who must have been one of the best ever not to have carried the title of Champion. However, 'D', as we knew him, has his place in Bedlington history as a great sire. Miss Brewer became in turn an ambulance driver and lorry driver as her war effort and always had a dog in the cab. It was almost a case of 'Have dog – will travel'. With her talent for obtaining illegal petrol she took her stud dogs to virtually stranded bitches, visited litters to advise the owners, sold puppies for novices and generally acted as the breed's go-between. She married, became Mrs Best and it was by this name that some remember her today. Sadly, after making Champions of Ruler of Pitt, Bracknel Rowland of Pitt and Brightstone Sunflower of Pitt her health failed and Camilla spent the last years of her life in hospitals. Her contribution to the breed can never be measured. There cannot be a Bedlington in England and, possibly, the world that does not trace back to Dunmail.

In 1939, Dr Muriel Binns bred Pynello Jacques, born at the wrong time for a show career before or after the war. He did win the C.C. at the 1949 Bedlington Terrier Association show under Mrs Ben Holgate, before a watery eyed ringside, but his greater triumph was as a sire. Muriel Binns served the breed well in different offices within the association and started the B.T.A. Bulletin, paid for out of her own pocket. Jacques' most famous get was Ch Lindum Lightning. Bred by Mrs Florrie Franks this ordinary, but expertly presented, dog launched Herbert Winder to the forefront and from this dog stemmed the Foxington kennel. Fortunately the kennel also housed a superb bitch in Ch Moorsraike Moonlight, a Dunmail daughter of true type and the strain owed more to her than Lightning. Close breeding produced an excellent type of Bedlington but the price had to be paid, for on occasions temperaments fell to the neurotic and coats were either excellent or dreadful. However, a Foxington with good coat and temperament was a Bedlington par excellance. The ultimate was reached in Blue Blazes of Foxington whose quality was so intense as to qualify for the doggy term of being 'overdone'. Used wisely, the dog had much to offer and one can see the superb head qualities of his family in the present day Wetops.

A year after Lightning Miss Eileen Marsh bred Ch Brambledene Baron and the dogs were as great rivals as undoubtedly were the owners. Despite the fact that Baron's sire, David of Harnish, had nothing but character to commend him, being heavy, plain and poor coated, Baron and the Brambledenes have had more influence on the modern Bedlington than any other strain emerging from the post war recovery. The Brambledenes were the first to hit the high spots at Crufts for, in 1939 the author watched wide-eyed as the immaculate Ch Brambledene Buccaneer was in the last six for the supreme award. A beautiful dog, he was little used at stud but perhaps this was as well as he had the infamous Khaki, of the cracked feet, as granddam. David and Buccaneer don't sound much like pillars of the breed and we have to ignore them in the evolving story. After her first pet Bedlington, David, introduced her to the breed, Miss Marsh bought a top class bitch, Welhead Whisper, from Mrs Ben Holgate. Whisper was as good as David was poor and, mated to Amma Blue, produced Brambledene Brione. At the same time Miss Marsh had from the author Brambledene Ballerina and the two bitches were campaigned at the wartime London shows. Ballerina was the flyer in the ring but Brione was the winner-producer. To David she threw Ch Baron and to Wansbeck Nobleman she gave Ch Brambledene Brendan. A Brendan daughter, Norman Stead's Ch Spring Dancer, mated to a Baron son, Mrs Jessie Fenby's Ch Westfen Panther, gave us Fred Gent's English and American Champion Foggyfurze Classic Cut. A Classic Cut daughter mated to Spring Dancer's litter brother, Ch Curly Cut gave the breed the great Ch Foggyfurze Classic. Classic Cut went to Lewis Terpenning in the United States where he played his part as a stud force and Classic became the cornerstone of the modern Foggyfurze strain. Modern, because the Foggyfurze kennel was established in the thirties from a different line.

Fred Gent started the Foggyfurze kennel with a working bitch but soon decided where he was going and produced Ch Foggyfurze Ace High to hit the high spots. The last Bedlington to win a Challenge Certificate before the war was Foggyfurze Starlight and the first post war Champion was Ch Foggyfurze Glamorous, a big but glorious bitch of superb type. Glamorous does not have much of a breeding record which is sad for had she passed on her obvious qualities the breed would surely have stood a better chance of retaining real Bedlington coats. Among the many bitches he served, Classic mated Drewcote Marie Belle, owned by Andrew Tait, and Fred Gent bought in the litter. Two sensational bitches were the result. Between them Foggyfurze Baby Mine and Foggyfurze Sugar Baby won all the bitch classes at the B.T.A. show of 1956, their first show and whilst still puppies. Baby Mine won the C.C. on the day but was retired to become a winner-producer whilst Sugar was the showgirl, became a Champion and went Best in Show at the Scottish Kennel Club show, the first Bedlington to do so at an all breed Championship show in Britain. After a short career in this country, Sugar joined Virden and Jessie Wilson in Texas and she gained her American title. From Baby Mine came a line of Champions for the kennel which has sent stock all over the world in the ensuing years. The strain has produced many first class animals but the author's favourite was Continental Champion Foggyfurze Ferrari, owned by Mrs de Ryke. The great feature of the line has been correct conformation. This has been of inestimable value in combating the straight stifles and upright shoulders which come down from Lightning and, further back, Ch Robin of Simonside. Faults that persist for generations.

Another kennel to bridge the war years was Mr and Mrs C G Worrall's Manaton strain. Charlie Worrall insisted that a Bedlington was a working dog and always offered this as the reason for the unruly behaviour of his dogs at the shows. True in type, with ideal proportion, height to length, and superb heads, this small kennel was of the highest standard and, with a limited amount of stud work, Ch Golden Sun of Manaton did much for the breed.

Mrs M E O'Brien made up her first Champion in the early thirties and from Ch Bubble of Harnish and Ch Miss Gaysum came the Nonington family which was to produce Champions for the next quarter of a century.

In 1938 Mrs R J Martin made up Ch Folly to her title. After the war, the Cullercoats suffix was taken out and later transferred to her daughter, Peggy Lay, to carry on the family tradition of producing Champions.

It was in that year that the author was to have his first bitch in his own name, Blue Bliss. The first that owned him was his father's Maid of Harnish, whelped in 1926 and by Ch Shothanger Rector out of Lady in Waiting. Blue Bliss was out of Juno of Pitt, a half sister of the great Dunmail, and was first mated to Ch Brambledene Buccaneer to produce Brambledene Ballerina. Her second litter, to Brambledene Beacon produced Tol-pedn Piper who, in turn sired Tol-pedn Crinoline, the dam, to Ch Rag a tail, of Leasowes Humpty Dumpty and Leasowes Simple Simon who featured in Bill Smith's Shenstone line. The third litter was to Rover of Pitt, a son of Dunmail, and this produced Ch Tol-pedn Merry Maid, the first Champion to carry the prefix. Her daughter by Ch Goldstrike of Foxington, Ch Tol-pedn Mermaid, went to Rip Gowing to start the Wederbi line, and a granddaughter, Ch Tol-pedn Fairmaid, went best in show at the 1957 L.K.A. and followed on by producing Champions in every litter.

With Florrie Franks (Lindum), Norman Stead (Cut) and Tom Barker (Mahidap), the above shared the honours of the decade after hostilities ceased.

FIFTIES

In the fifties Mrs Wardman started showing a dog, Ch Moscar Red Ensign, bred by Mr and Mrs Barnes, later the bitch Ch Burleydene Mischief (bred by Mrs Elwick, the owner of Ch Brambledene Brendan) and from her came the Daleview dogs. Husband Laurie began to take an interest in this breed Mrs Wardman had become involved with and so commenced an era when the man worked for and supported the Bedlington wherever and whenever he could.

In 1948, a Mr E J Furze mated his Newlyn Fashion to Lightning and produced a dog which finally ended in the ownership of Mary Taunt, a real dog lover who helped so many animals and owners during her time with us. This dog became Ch Rag-a-Tail and the founder of the Leasowes kennels, a line known for coats and correct size.

At the end of the fifties along came a group of new people who are still with us. In 1958 Annie Clark and son Walter arrived upon the scene with a superb bitch which was later to become Ch Knotts Bluebelle and so started the Amerdale kennels. The most illustrious member of the family, of course, was Ch Amerdale Amanda who broke all records and was even honoured by the town of Bedlington. We lost a great character when 'Our Annie' passed away.

In the same year Mrs Franks started to win with Ch Lindum High Octane of Vistablu, bred by Ida Sills and the following year the breeder made up her first champion in Ch Little Willie of Vistablu. Vistablu have won consistently ever since and, with American Rockridge stock, have established the breed in South America. Racey lines with reachy foreheads and good coats have been the hallmarks of this kennel.

In 1984, Mrs Sills bred a dog called Ch Vistablu Nelson Touch which has had a great show career, winning an all time record number of Challenge Certificates, group wins and Best in Show at the National Terrier Championship Show. His record is unlikely ever to be equalled, let alone beaten.

The 1958 Bedlington Terrier Association championship show saw Olive Stones win both puppy classes with litter brother and sister by Moyvallee Minstrel out of Shenstone Miss Tesha, a sister of Ch Shenstone Master Mack. The bitch became Ch Stanolly Sapphire, the first of a long line of Champions to come from the Tean stable. The most famous dog was Ch Stanolly Scooby Doo, a phenomenal winner and popular sire. The strain has been strongly line bred with only one outcross in Ch Stanolly Starbow (1970) a bitch bred by the Clarks from Ch Amerdale Astralita (by Ch Chartlands Fair Dinkum ex Ch Amerdale Delicious). The ideal size of Sapphire has been retained but her beautiful colour has been lost.

Mrs Stones had been familiar with the breed before Sapphire but a real novice was Wally Topham who turned out with two good daughters of Ch Brambledene Baron which had top-knots and leghair but little else. The unkind critics were to learn that these bitches and their owner would carve their place in the breed history. Fortunately, Bert Winder set about teaching the newcomer with the result that in 1959 Ch Cinderella became the first Wetop Champion. One of the best of the line was Tweedle-dee of Wetop, a dog that died young without getting his third C.C. and foolishly ignored as a stud force. This, again, has been a strongly line and inbred strain to fix an easily recognised type of perfect heads, true Bedlington width of chests, correct proportion, length to height and true type. In this line also, sadly, coat colour is not now as good as it was with animals like Ch Cinderella, Ch Gun Metal, and the perfect liver of The Count.

Someone whose interest in the breed goes back much earlier but whose first C.C. was won in 1959 was Dorothy Aitkenhead whose Craglough Champions have always been lathy, hardbitten terriers who looked as if they could work. English and Australian Champion Foggyfurze Dandy was bred here and featured very much in the early days of the breed on the other side of the world. Although not a champion, the author has always regarded Craglough Denarius as one of the best.

Mr and Mrs Dick Ratcliffe became regular showgoers but great success did not come until the eighties when Ch Moorside Quite Quaint started a trail of wins that were just reward for someone who had supported the breed with mixed fortunes for many years.

SIXTIES

Roy Highfield joined the ranks and in 1960 bred Ch Maydew Moonraker, the dog with the perfect balance and outline, which was followed by other homebred champions.

The sixties saw Fiona Craig winning with her Highquests, not always presented to advantage but true to type, the star being Ann Heron's Ch Highquest Holly Girl.

In 1965 Ian Phillips came to the fore with Ch Rathsrigg Little Ceasar winning his title from the puppy classes. His wife, Margaret, had been breeding Bedlingtons in her own right and the partnership has established a line of first class dogs adorned with real coats to withstand the elements.

A successful breeder starting in the sixties was Barbara Clifton whose Ch Vardene Blue Grenadier was a big winner, including the Terrier Group at Crufts. There followed the Anderson family (Birkonbrae), Marie and Mervin Sugden (Lieberlamb), John Holden (Granitor), Audrey Norgate (Petacrest) and Ernie Hill (Tynccourt). All have produced a string of Champions and top winners, possessing good colour coats, and it is a pity that others have not made more use of their stock for breeding.

SEVENTIES AND EIGHTIES

One must ask the question now as to what has been the results of these years of breeding and showing.

We have three distinct strains – Foggyfurze, Stanolly and Wetop, each with its virtues and faults. The oldest is Foggyfurze, based on Brambledene but Stanolly was introduced 10 years ago with Ch Avilas Lucky Lad of Foggyfurze. It is difficult to see any of his forebearers in this dog but there is more influence of Northcote than anything else and Northcote went back to pure Foggyfurze. Mated to Foggyfurze bred bitches he has, mostly, produced the same racey stamp but it will be interesting to see the results when the blood has become diffused in the next two or three generations crossed to other stock. The Foggyfurze strain scores, undoubtedly, over the others in conformation, soundness, and colour, although sometimes they have lacked power before the eyes and can be narrow in front.

The Stanollys have this strength of foreface coupled with the correct Bedlington width of front and are, generally, standard in size. Faults inherited from a mixed background have, by selective breeding, been eradicated but it can only be regretted that the perfect coat of the first Champion has been lost.

Wetop dogs are recognised on sight with their superlative heads of power and delicate chiselling, typical fronts and correct proportion, length to height. Again, coats have deteriorated since the early dogs.

To list further the faults and virtues of these families would create more heat than debate so the matter will be left with a plea to the reader to study with hand and eye objectively, always keeping in mind the dictum that there has never been a dog that cannot be criticised in at least three departments. Maybe not so much defect as needing improvement but, however one plays with words, assessment must be based on degree of fault and relative detriment to the breed at a given time. A defect can be penalised more lightly when it is rare than when it is commonplace and threatening to become the norm.

As the breed stands in the eighties one must regret the poor coats on our terriers. Although there has been some improvement in recent years, the really good coats are in the minority. The culprits are indifference and the cosmetic 'show preparations' which make possible a neat, orderly trim. Silky or woolly and white jackets with or without curls are not true for the breed. Insufficient regard has been given to the Standard on this feature.

Also, one has to admit to the loss of substance in so many animals. Confusion on the meaning of 'quality' is partly to blame in so many breeds as well as our own but one must accept that the use of effeminate looking stud dogs sometimes, over the years, has been detrimental and cannot be expected to produce substantial terriers. Action has been poor for many years and the rears of some animals are appalling. It is acceptable that a judge may consider the movement of two exhibits and still put up the inferior mover because it had enough in hand on other points. However, one cannot accept a critique which says that a dog moved well behind when one witnessed a cow hocked animal staggering across the ring.

On the credit side we can congratulate ourselves that corny feet have become rare. It can skip generations and appear, to surprise the breeder who, without knowledge of the past, will be at a loss to know where it came from. The main source of the gene was Ch Cribden Chutney from whom it went to Khaki, the dam of Ch Woodrow Wizard, a much used stud dog. Also, it appeared in the Gardners line. As almost all liver lines of today go back to Wizard there is ever the chance that it could occur. The golden rule is **never** breed from an animal afflicted with cracked or corny feet. It is downright cruel and inexcusable to perpetrate the defect.

Size has been a problem from the early days and there has always been variety in any great line-up of Bedlingtons. There is, however, more conformity these days.

The thing that makes any breed distinctive is type and we have to address ourselves to the question whether we have retained it or moved on to some other stamp of dog. Excessive amounts of coat left on the legs with big top-knots and chunky tassles on the ears destroy the visual effect one wants but it would be dangerous to ignore this as mere fashion and having no influence on breed progress. This caricature trimming makes it difficult for the novice to learn type and is no way to educate the learner all-round judge. The Standard says that the breed should look capable of galloping at great speed but this does not mean it should be built on the lines of the Whippet with hocks standing six inches behind the tail root. The Bedlington should appear poised on the ground, ready to move quickly at a second's notice. This is achieved by high head carriage, crested neck and hind legs longer than the front. Pondering on this many years ago I found it reminded me of the wretched cobras I had seen being abused by the snake charmers in India. So the idea that the Bedlington should look like a cobra ready to strike became a conversation piece and it is satisfying to know that it has found favour with the purists. A matter of type, this outline is still with us but we have too many that stand in a servile manner with the head poked forward.

In common with a number of breeds where flat sides are called for there have been exaggerations resulting in narrow chests, sometimes referred to in our breed as 'Fox Terrier fronts'. This did seem to be taking hold in the breed but the situation has improved in recent times.

The other type feature which has given cause for alarm has been the length of back which, in some instances has been too short. This may please the all-rounder looking for the short coupled terrier but it is not true of the Bedlington and is to be resisted.

To answer the question we asked on the results of the last 50 years breeding we can say that substance, coats and action have suffered whilst size, feet and fronts have improved.

The future of the breed lies with smaller breeders and it is hoped that they will realise that they are being entrusted with a responsibility that supercedes the vainglory of show wins. The Bedlington, because of its trimming, is vulnerable and it cannot be stressed too strongly that it was created as a working breed and must remain so. Trimming can help present a dog to advantage but **never** should points be awarded for presentation.

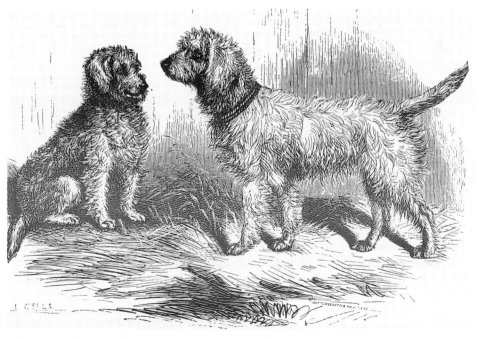

The first published picture of Bedlington Terriers.

Redmarshall's Stud Book

PART I
EARLY HISTORY
OF THE
BEDLINGTON
TERRIER

In the latter part of the Eighteenth Century, a breed or strain of terriers existed in Northumberland in and around Rothbury Forest and in Coquetdale which was held in high esteem in the neighbourhood for its excellent qualities and especially for its gameness. I will make some surmises later as to the origins of this breed; for the present, I merely ask the reader to accept the fact that there were at that time, and possibly for long before, some very staunch and sporting terriers in this district, and, which is equally important, certain people who were interested in procuring the best and gamest of them, and of mating them together suitably so that they should produce their like. When I speak of a breed of terriers existing at this time, I do not mean to imply that these dogs were all alike as two pins, in the manner of a recognised breed that we see at dog shows nowadays. Their matings were probably arranged in the first place entirely with a view to perpetuate their qualities rather than their mere outward appearance; to get dogs with strength, courage, endurance, nose and the like. Of course physical qualities would be of importance too; if a dog was wanted mostly for going to ground after badger or fox he would need to be not too big; if he was also wanted to hunt above ground for rabbits and such, and to catch them, he must not be too short in the leg. Whatever he was wanted to do in the animal killing line – which either for business or sport was no doubt his principal vocation – he would want a powerful, punishing jaw and good teeth. The men who used these dogs no doubt bred from those that they knew from their experience of them had these qualities. Then it would, after a time, strike them that certain dogs who were, say, of a certain colour, or had a certain shaped ear, or a certain arrangement of hair, were better at their work than the others. No doubt this was so – a good, hard-bitten, working sire who has a tuft of hair on his head, or a long pendulous ear, is as likely to transmit those properties to his offspring as he is to transmit his courage, his endurance or his powers of scent. So those outward marks would come to be accepted as signs that

Northumberland 'Land of the Bedlington Terrier'.

the dog possessing them was more likely to have the necessary working qualities than a dog without them. And so gradually people who wanted to breed the best working dog would reject those who did not possess the outward marks which they had learnt to believe were always possessed by the most useful dogs. And then, to perpetuate the marks and the qualities which they indicated, they would breed together dogs possessing them in a notable degree, even if they were closely related – brother and sister, father and daughter, etc. And so the outward marks would become fixed in that particular strain.

In this way breeds of dogs arose in the days before Dog Shows, and before people thought it worth their while to breed dogs for their appearance only, as we do now.

It is probable therefore that these working terriers round about Rothbury of which I am speaking – in days long before such a thing as a Dog Show had ever been thought of – had a general, rough similarity of appearance, although what they were prized for was their gameness and prowess in the field.

At Flotterton, which is some four miles west of Rothbury, there lived in the early part of the Nineteenth Century, a certain Mr Edward Donkin, who hunted a pack of foxhounds in the district. I do not know how long he or his family had been at Flotterton. It is said that he was familiarly known as 'Hunting Ned,' which suggests that he was a devotee of the sport. He had in his kennels some of these local terriers, and among them two who became very celebrated in the district – Peachem, generally known as 'Old Peachem,' and Pincher. It is this Old Peachem whom we must regard as the great patriarch of the Bedlington tribe.

I am now going to adopt the practice which I have followed in my 'Stud Book' list of Bedlingtons, and add certain numbers preceded by the letter R to the names of dogs when there is any possibility of their being confused with other dogs similarly named. This precaution is very necessary, for the early breeders rang the changes over a limited number of names, and the effort to keep the various holders thereof distinct in one's mind becomes very severe. I refer to this Donkin's Pincher, then, as Pincher R7. Peachem can remain in this narrative as Old Peachem, although I enter him in my list as Peachem R1.

It is probable that Pincher R7 was the son of Old Peachem. Two of my authorities (about whom more anon) do not give the name of Pincher's father, and two (including that which I consider the most reliable) state that it was Old Peachem. As will be seen, there was another Pincher (R5) who was certainly Old Peachem's son. It is just possible that both Pinchers were really the same dog, or that some confusion has arisen between the two. In any event Old Peachem will appear twice after this in the pedigree, and any uncertainty as to whether he really was the sire of Pincher R7 does not much diminish the light in which I regard him as the veritable ancestor of the breed.

I do not know who the dam of Pincher R7 was (unless indeed he was identical with Pincher R5), but in due course he was mated to a bitch (whose name has not been recorded) belonging to William Wardle, of

Framlington, a village about four miles as the crow flies to the east of Rothbury. One of our authorities precises it as Long Framlington as distinct from Low Framlington, which is near by. Among their offspring was a dog which was acquired by a certain Sherwood (I have seen the name also given as Sheawick) of Longhorsley, which is some seven miles south-east of Rothbury. This dog was given the name of Matchem (R9), and was mated to a bitch called Phoebe (we will call her Phoebe R8) belonging to John Dodd, also of Longhorsley.

Henry, 3rd Duke of Buccleuch, painted by Thomas Gainsborough c. 1770. The family did have connections with the Trevelyans and there is a possibility that the dog was a Bedlington. The present duke is interested in the theory but cannot confirm. We have to keep an open mind on this one.

This Phoebe R8 was of the same strain as her mate Matchem. She was by his grandsire Old Peachem out of a bitch named Vixen (R6) belonging to Andrew Evans of Holystone, which is some three miles west of Flotterton on the Coquet. Vixen R6 had been got by the miller's dog at Felton (eight miles on the other side of Rothbury, namely nearly due east of it) out of a bitch belonging to a Mr Carr of Felton Hall. Her known pedigree ends there.

We thus have Sherwood's Matchem and Dodd's Phoebe R8 mated together at Longhorsley, both, as I believe, descended from Old Peachem. They had, among others, a bitch pup who came into the possession of Christopher Dixon of the same place, and was also called Phoebe (R12). She thus had Old Peachem's blood on both sides. She in turn was mated to another Peachem (R13) which had been purchased by one Joseph Ainsley from a certain Cowen, either William of Rothbury or Robert of Rocklaw. This Peachem R13 (generally known as Cowen's) was by a dog called

Burdett, also belonging to Cowen, out of a bitch of David Moffat's of Horwick. I can find nothing about their ancestry. Howick is on the coast a little north-east of Alnwick. From his name I should be inclined to suspect that Peachem R13 came from the same strain as Donkin's Old Peachem.

From the union of Cowen's or Ainsley's Peachem R13 with Dixon's Phoebe R12 there was born Piper (R15) or Old Piper, of whom more anon. He came into the possession of one James Anderson (whose habitat is described as Rothbury Forest) and is therefore often known as Anderson's Old Piper.

We are now getting near to the rise of the dogs known as Bedlington Terriers, but before proceeding further must turn back a little.

Donkin's Old Peachem was also mated at some time to a bitch named Venom (R4) belonging to William Turnbull of Holystone, which as we know was near Donkin's kennels at Flotterton. Venom was out of her owner's Fan (whose parents we do not know), and sired by a dog called Matchem (R2) belonging to Mills or Myles of Netherwitton, a village about seven-and-a-half miles south of Rothbury. Matchem R2 was the son of Old Flint, a dog belonging to Mr Trevelyan, the squire of the village. We do not know who Matchem's dam was, but an interesting point is that Old Flint is said to have been born in the year 1782. Another authority, however, gives it as 1792. Whichever is right this is the earliest date that can be given in the History of Bedlingtons, and, by comparison with most other breeds of terriers, gives a ripe antiquity to the race. Old Peachem and Venom R4 had among their progeny a dog pup which was kept by Turnbull, and received the name of Pincher (R5). It will be remembered that Donkin's Pincher R7 was also by Old Peachem and out of an unnamed dam, and in one pedigree I have seen this dam is said to have been Turnbull's Venom R4. In that case there would seem a probability that the two Pinchers were identical, but I doubt whether it was so. I imagine that the designation of Venom R4 as the dam of Donkin's Pincher R7 was due to a confusion between the two Pinchers. It is however rather curious that both Pinchers seem to have been mated to an unnamed bitch of William Wardle's, and it is possible that they really were the same and merely changed owners.

(At the risk of causing further confusion I am bound to point out also that there is another version of the ancestry of Turnbull's Pincher R5. This omits Venom, and makes Fan his dam instead of his granddam, and makes Fan the daughter of Old Flint, instead of the 'daughter-in-law'. I think that this has clearly originated from an error in transcribing a pedigree, a generation having been skipped by mistake, and I much prefer the version first given, which has three out of four of my authorities in its support.)

At all events, Turnbull's Pincher R5 was a son of Donkin's Old Peachem, and was descended on his mother's side from Squire Trevelyan's Old Flint of 1782. Pincher R5 in turn was mated to an unnamed bitch of William Wardle's, but whether or not it was the same bitch that Donkin's Pincher R7 was mated to, I cannot say. The result of this mating was a dog pup, known afterwards as the Rennington dog (presumably from having gone to live at Rennington, which is 3½ miles north of Alnwick) and a bitch called Wasp (R10) which was acquired by Andrew Riddell of Framlington, the village where Wardell lived. Riddell mated Wasp R10 to her brother the Rennington dog, and Wasp gave birth to a bitch called Phoebe (R14), generally known as Coates's Phoebe. Her parents being brother and sister, it will be seen that she was descended on both sides from Donkin's Old Peachem.

Pedigree of James Anderson's Old Piper R15.

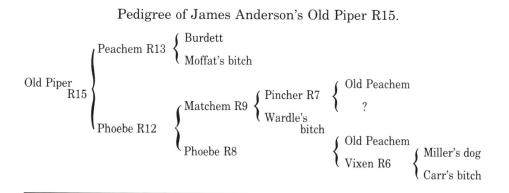

We now come to another date in our history, for in the year 1820 a Mr J. Howe of Alnwick came down to Bedlington to visit a friend, and brought with him this bitch Phoebe R14 belonging to Riddell. He left her in the keeping of Mr Edward Coates at the vicarage, from which circumstance she has gone down to history as Coates's Phoebe, but Riddell subsequently gave her to Joseph Ainsley, whose name we have already heard as the purchaser of Peachem R13.

It was from that visit of Mr Howe to Bedlington that the chain of circumstances arose which led to the mining village giving its name to the breed. But for that, the strain, if it had been perpetuated, might have been known now as Rothbury or Framlington or Longhorsley terriers. All those places were really nearer to the centre of its origin than was Bedlington.

It must be said however that but for this visit the breed might not have been perpetuated at all, as its continuance in purity seems to have been largely due to Joseph Ainsley himself who lived at Bedlington.

Ainsley, having been given Coates's Phoebe R14, decided to mate her to Anderson's Old Piper R15, which, as we have seen, was the offspring of Ainsley's Peachem R13 and Dixon's Phoebe R12.

Let us see if we can what manner of dogs these were. They were both, we know, descended from Donkin's Old Peachem – Piper twice on his dam's side, and Phoebe on the side of both sire and dam, as she was bred from brother and sister. Piper R15 is described as 'a dog of slender build, about 15 inches high, and 15 lb. weight; he was of a liver colour, the hair being a sort of hard woolly lint; his ear was large, hung close to the cheek and was slightly feathered at the tip'. As to Phoebe R14, 'her colour was a black or black-blue, and she had the invariable light-coloured silky tuft of hair on her head. She was about 13 inches high and weighed 14 lb.' Elsewhere it has been said that she had 'a sort of branded legs' which suggests that she may have been what we should call a dark blue and tan. Evidently these dogs were smaller and lighter built than the prize-winners of today.

Pedigree of Coate's Phoebe R14.

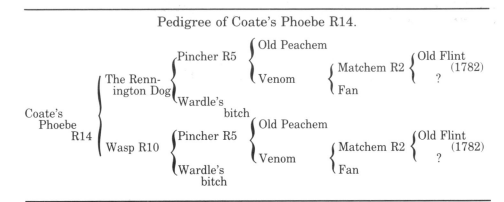

Ainsley then in the year 1825 mated these two terriers together, and among the first results of the union in that same year there was born Piper or Young Piper, generally known as Ainsley's Piper, and said on good authority to have been the first dog to be called a 'Bedlington Terrier'. Joseph Ainsley having so named the strain which he had founded. I number him Piper R16.

So far, it will be seen, the breed had been a purely local one, confined to the district of Rothbury Forest and its immediate neighbourhood. With the possible exception of the unnamed bitch of David Moffat's of Howick, all the terriers named up to this point seem to have been born at a distance of not more than 8 miles from Rothbury. But with the establishment of the breed at Bedlington (some 18 miles, as the crow flies, south-east of Rothbury) they acquired a wider range, and gradually spread from there all over Northumberland.

In a letter in the *Field* in 1869 signed 'A' (to which I shall presently allude again), the writer states that at the same time that Mr Edward Donkin kept his kennel at Flotterton, viz., the first quarter of the 19th century, 'a colony of sporting nailers then flourished at Bedlington, who were noted for their plucky breed of terriers'. A writer in the *Newcastle Chronicle* in 1872, quoted in Dalziel's book on dogs, is also of opinion that 'it is not all unlikely that the Staffordshire nailmakers who some eighty or ninety years ago were brought from the south and employed at Bedlington crossed the pure-bred native terrier with some of the stock they brought with them, having, probably, fighting purposes in view'. If any such crossing did take place, it must have been after the mating of Old Piper and Coates's Phoebe, and the birth of Ainsley's Piper, for up to that time, as we have seen, there is no sign in the pedigrees of any dogs from the Bedlington district having been bred with the original Rothbury stock. I do not know what sort of dogs these nailmakers' terriers were, but surmise that they probably had a good deal of bull in them, and it is quite possible that some of the descendants of Ainsley's Piper were crossed with them.

Joseph Ainsley c. 1830.

W. Clark 1830.

We know that a good deal of crossing did take place, and I will refer to it again a little later. It is quite possible too that the nailers had themselves also got some of the Rothbury dogs to Bedlington, and crossed them with their own stock before Ainsley's Piper was born, so that their dogs had already much of the same blood. But what does not seem likely is that there was any of the nailmakers' blood in Ainsley's Piper, or that there can have been much, if any, of it in his direct descendants whom we are going to trace down to Clark's Scamp.

It has been said that in their early period, before their association with Bedlington, these dogs were actually known as Rothbury or Rodbury terriers, but allusions to this are very vague, and I cannot find any statement as to when or by whom they were so known. Any contemporary reference to Rothbury terriers that could be found would be most interesting.

A point which must now be dealt with is as to what connection, if any, there was in the early days between Bedlingtons and Dandie Dinmonts. It is a truism which one hears at nearly every Dog Show that 'Dandies and Bedlingtons are first cousins'. The silky top-knots, the long pendulous ears, the high-domed skull, the grave demeanour, and the twin colours of blue and liver or pepper and mustard, all seem to point to some relationship, despite the great dissimilarity in body and legs and eye between the two breeds. I have always felt that the dogs must have a common origin somewhere back in the past. I do not profess to be a deep student of Dandie Dinmont history – which appears to be beset by much controversy – but I have read a little to see what bearing it had on the present subject, and I may almost say that I was startled to find that Piper Allan, the legendary founder of the race of Dandies, is said to have lived near Rothbury at Holystone, the very centre of the ancestors of the Bedlington.

To give honour where honour is due, let me here say that the data concerning the history of Dandie Dinmonts which I give here have been obtained from the magnificent book *Dogs: Their History and Development*, by Mr Edward C. Ash, published by Ernest Benn Ltd. in 1927. It is unfortunately rather an expensive work, but a perfect mine of information

Unconfirmed but thought to be Tynesider.

and illustration, and a joy to any dog-lover. I do not entirely agree with all Mr Ash's conclusions on the subject of Bedlington history, but that is by the way.

Mr Ash quotes the writer Mr Francis Somner, who 'without any attempt to suggest a clue as to their origin, stated that, in his opinion, the terriers (Dandies) were at one time confined to the Coquet Water district, the property of the tinkers and muggers who worked that area. From his letter we glean that amongst these tinkers and muggers were the Allans, Anguses, Andersons and Faas, who treasured their sporting, four-footed companions. Piper Allan was a tinker-sportsman who lived near Rothbury at Holystone, spending much of his time hunting otters and playing on his bagpipes. He owned a pack of terriers, among which were the three favourites "Hitchem," "Charlie" and "Phoebe". It was Hitchem, often printed as "Peachem," of which Piper Allan would say "When my Hitchem gives mouth, I durst always sell the otter's skin." Piper Allan died in 1779 at the age of 75.' His son and grandson carried on the breed of his terriers after him.

A Mr Davison also has given a contribution to the history of the Dandies which is reproduced both by Mr Ash and by 'Stonehenge' in his book *The Dog* (1879 edition). He also attributes their origin to the Border muggers, and names the Andersons, Faas, and Camells among them. He describes how they used to meet once or twice a year at Longhorsley, Alwinton, or other Border villages and indulge in badger-drawing, dog-fighting and kindred diversions, with apparently some hard drinking. It was, this writer says, after such a meeting at Alwinton (which is in Coquetdale, a very few miles above Holystone) where Willy and Adam Bell (noted terrier breeders) were present, that after a badger-drawing and a subsequent heavy carouse a red bitch belonging to Jack Anderson, and a wire-haired dog belonging to Geordy Faa, were mated, and afterwards produced the first pepper and mustard Dandies, which were presented by Faa to the Mr Davidson who was the original of 'Dandy Dinmont' in Walter Scott's *Guy Mannering*, which popularised these dogs and gave them their name. *Guy Mannering* was published in 1814.

This Mr Davison (who was writing in 1878, and said that he was more than 60 years old) also recorded that 'the last pair I saw of what I consider perfect Dandies were Robert Donkin's at Ingram near Alnwick, just before I left the north in 1838. I have been at shows, but could never identify any Dandies shown as at all like the original breed belonging to the Telfords of Blind Burn, the Elliots of Cottonshope, the Donkins of Ingram and other Border farmers'.

In his 1859 edition 'Stonehenge' wrote that the Dandie Dinmont was originally bred by a farmer named James Davidson at Hindale in Roxburghshire 'who is generally believed to have got his dogs from the head of Coquet Water'. He also said that at the time he wrote 'occasionally in a litter there may be some with the short folding ear of a bull-terrier, and also with some greater length of the legs; these are not approved of by fanciers, but nevertheless are pure, showing a tendency to cast back'. In his 1867 edition 'Stonehenge' says that 'between the Skye and the Dandie

Dinmont there is a very close affinity, the two breeds running into one another so nearly that it often happens that there is a difficulty in deciding to which an individual belongs. Our own belief is that in all probability the two came from the same stock by selection, the longer-haired ones being Skyes, and the shorter Dandie Dinmonts, but the different carriage of the tail is somewhat against this hypothesis'.

There seems a general agreement that Dandies have altered considerably from the original type, and Mr Ash says that 'the original Dandie Dinmont, though long-bodied, had longer legs than the modern dog'.

In Mr Rawdon B. Lee's *Modern Dogs* (1894) he says that the resemblance between Bedlingtons and Dandies seem to have been 'much greater fifty years ago than it is now'. And he mentions that 'some eight or so years ago, at one of the South Country Shows, the Earl of Antrim exhibited two terriers from the same litter, one of which won in the Dandie Dinmont class, the other receiving an honorary award in the division for Bedlington terriers'.

I may also mention that 'about 1872 two hawkers, brothers, Robert and Paul Scott, of Jedburgh, were noted for their terriers (Dandies), one of these, "Peachem," winning at the Crystal Palace Show that year'.

What conclusion is to be drawn from all this? To me, it is plain and unmistakable. The early ancestors of Bedlingtons and Dandies were the same dogs.

Mr Edward Ash says, 'I am constantly forced to the opinion that the early history of the Bedlington is somewhat confused with that of the Dandie Dinmont'. I do not think there is any confusion, for it seems to me clear that the history was the same. We do not really know what Piper Allan's terriers looked like, but I would wager that they frequently or generally had long, pendulous ears, silky tufts on the crowns of their heads, and in short the characteristics which are distinctively common to the two breeds. I do not suppose Piper Allan created them himself, but that he originally got together likely local terriers and bred them judiciously. I should say that Donkin's Old Peachem was almost certainly of the same strain as Allan's dogs (even if Allan did pronounce the name Hitchem), Donkin at Flotterton being only three or four miles from Allan's reputed headquarters at Holystone. Holystone was actually the home of Evans's Vixen and of Turnbull's Venom, to both of whom Old Peachem was mated. To me it seems evident that these ancestors of the Bedlingtons which inhabited the Coquetdale and Rothbury neighbourhood were the same race as Piper Allan's dogs, which are traditionaly reputed to be the ancestors of the Dandie Dinmonts.

I would like to point out that the first Bedlington which I have found with the name Piper is James Anderson's Old Piper, which I call Piper R15. I do not know who this James Anderson was, but it seems possible that he was a connection of or descended from the Andersons who are mentioned by both Mr Somner and Mr Davison as one of the families of Border muggers who were keen dog fanciers, and that he named his dog after old Piper Allan, whose memory among local terrier fanciers was no doubt still green. Old Piper's sire, it will be remembered, was called Peachem. Anderson has been described as 'of Rothbury Forest,' which is a rather vague address, and suggests that his vocation may not have tied him down to one particular spot.

At the same time it is interesting to note the recurrence of the name Phoebe in these early records, when we remember that a bitch named Phoebe is said to have been one of the three favourites of Piper Allan at Holystone.

As to how the Dandies developed their separate existence and distinctive shape, we need not, I think, take literally Mr Davison's story that they sprang ready-made, so to speak, from the union of the terriers of two intoxicated tinkers at Alwinton. I have no doubt in my own mind that the longer body and shorter legs came from an admixture of the blood of a long-bodied, short-legged terrier, which certainly seems to have existed in Scotland in early times, and which was the ancestor of the breeds now known as the Skye, the Scottish Terrier or Aberdeen, the West Highland White and the Cairn. I suggest that this crossing possibly commenced first among these same Border tinkers, who wandered over both sides of the Border with their dogs, and sometimes mated their dogs of the Rothbury strain to bitches of the locality where they happened to be, but I expect that probably the Rothbury dogs' fame spread across the Border, and that specimens of the breed were brought over for the express purpose of crossing them with the local terriers. This must be pure conjecture, but I feel satisfied in my own mind that Bedlingtons and Dandies were both descended from the terriers of Rothbury, and that Dandies were afterwards crossed with the long, low-to-the-ground terriers of Scotland. The facts and legends which I have recited above all seem to point to this conclusion.

I suggest also that the longer-legged Dandies which Stonehenge in 1859 said occasionally appeared in litters may have been a throw-back to the original Rothbury type, though I confess that I am at a loss to suggest where 'the short folding ear of a Bull Terrier' came from, unless it was a throw-back in the other direction, i.e. to some ancestor of the Scottish Terriers. Skye Terriers' ears were described by Stonehenge in 1859 as 'large and slightly raised, but turning over,' and Dalziel describes the old Scotch Terrier of about 1840 as having 'ears small . . . semi-erect, falling over at the tip'.

As for the Earl of Antrim's mixed litter, it would be interesting to know whether the parents were supposed to be Bedlingtons or Dandies. If the latter (as I expect, for I do not remember hearing of the Earl as a breeder of Bedlingtons) the terrier which received an award as a Bedlington may also have been a throw-back to the original strain, always supposing that, firstly, there had been no recent Bedlington cross, and, secondly, that the judges knew their business.

I have now finished with the Dandie relationship, but would like to refer to the fact that Piper Allan seems to have used his dogs regularly for otter-hunting, and it has been suggested that the Bedlington has been produced by a cross with the Otter Hound. I can find no evidence of that, and it seems to be very unlikely. The writer 'A' to whom I refer below said that the crossing of the Bedlington with the Otter Hound had been indulged in, but the result was disappointing. I cannot believe that the Otter Hound took any part in the production of the Bedlington. I may mention, however, that Bedlingtons used to hunt with the Carlisle Otter Hounds some sixty years or more ago. That is stated by Mr Taprell Holland in the article to be mentioned shortly. He also mentions that at the time he wrote (probably 1872) 'the Reedwater Foxhounds (Northumberland) are attended by some four or five of the breed, descended from Donkin's strain, as good as are to be procured'.

Before proceeding with the narrative I will take this occasion to refer to the authorities upon which I rely mainly for the history of the pedigree and breeding of the early Bedlingtons and their ancestors. These authorities are four in number. First and most important is a letter signed 'A', which appeared in the *Field* on March 27th, 1869. Bedlingtons then were just emerging into publicity, questions had been asked as to what this breed was, different answers had been given, and 'A' wrote in reply as one who really knew. His letter is quoted in full by Mr S. Taprell Holland, himself at the time a well-known and enthusiastic breeder of Bedlingtons, in his article on the breed in a book entitled *Dogs; their Points, Whims, Instincts and Peculiarities*, edited by Henry Webb, the second edition of which was published in 1876. In his letter 'A' states that he had made the acquaintance of the breed in its native district, and in his account of its origin was 'supported by the high authority' of Joseph Ainsley himself, 'the first owner and breeder of the Bedlington Terrier proper'. He also states that he has been given the benefit of the experience of Mr Thomas Sanderson, 'a breeder of forty years' experience,' and knows others who have bred and owned these dogs for twenty and thirty years. I consider that his letter, therefore, is the best account we have of the early days of these terriers. He gives the pedigree of Ainsley's Piper, which I have mainly followed in the above account – though with one important exception.

Champion Tyneside 1869. Owned by T. J. Pickett and bred by Sir Thomas de Wheatley.

131

Mr Ash in his book which I have already mentioned seems to have overlooked Mr Webb's book on dogs, and Mr Holland's article on Bedlingtons therein, as he states that the first mention of a Bedlington (he must mean in a book, for he refers at length to the *Field* correspondence ten years earlier) is in Dalziel's first edition, published in 1879. I believe that the first edition of Webb's book appeared in 1872; the second edition is certainly 1876, and in his article on Bedlingtons Mr Holland refers to the 'National Dog Club at the Show last year (1871)' which seems to date his article sufficiently. Mr Ash also does not mention that there is a notice of the Bedlington in Stonehenge's third edition, which was published in 1879, with a portrait of Mr Pickett's 'Tyneside'.

This important letter of 'A' published in the *Field* of 1869 was apparently afterwards reproduced by Mr W. J. Donkin, who as Secretary of the Bedlington Terrier Club wrote a letter or article in almost the very same words which is reproduced in Dalziel's book. The Bedlington Terrier Club was not founded till 1875. It is possible that Mr Donkin was the real writer of the 'A' letter of 1869, who now shed his anonymity, or it is possible that he merely copied 'A's' letter, as giving the best account available of the start of the breed. At all events Mr Ash must be wrong in stating that the letter of 'A', to which he is clearly referring on page 243, 'substantiates the account . . . given earlier by Mr Donkin'. 'A's' letter of 1869 is the earliest authoritative account of Bedlington history that we have in print, and Donkin, when writing as Secretary of the B.T.C. must have done so years after it had appeared.

The second of my four authorities is the pedigree of Lieutenant-Colonel John A. Cowan's 'Ask 'im II' who was born in 1874, and whose descent is traced back to Old Peachem, Old Flint, etc., on the lines that I have given. It differs in certain small details from 'A's' pedigree, the most notable being that Pincher R5 is given as the son of Venom, not of Fan, and that Phoebe R8 is said to have been by Donkin's Old Pincher (no doubt merely a slip of the pen for Old Peachem) out of Andrew Evans's Venom, whereas all the other authorities call Evans's bitch Vixen. The other differences are slight, but sufficient to indicate that the pedigree has not been slavishly copied from that given by 'A'. The date of Old Flint's birth is given in this pedigree as 1782.

My third authority is a printed card, which purports to set out the 'pedigree from 1792 to 1885 of Mr D. Ross's liver-coloured Bedlington Terrier dog Strathblane'. This follows the 'Ask 'im' document with regard to the dam of Pincher R5, but differs from it in one important particular regarding the grandparents of Meg, who was mated to Ainsley's Piper, a point we have not yet reached in our narrative. It gives the date of Old Flint's birth at 1792 instead of 1782.

The fourth authority is a manuscript in tabular form, written on a portion of the back of an 'Advertising Sheet,' which is dated at North Shields in 1877. This was among some papers which the late Mr W. E. Alcock (himself a great breeder of Bedlingtons in the eighties and nineties of the last century and later) gave to the Bedlington Terrier Association not long before his death. I do not know who wrote it. It was not Mr Alcock, for it is not his handwriting. It mainly follows 'A', but there is one notable exception. It originally made Pincher R5 the son of Fan, as 'A' does, but this has been carefully corrected, and he is made the son of Venom, as the 'Ask 'im' and Strathblane pedigrees have it, and as I feel is probably correct. A minor difference is that whereas 'A' speaks of 'William Wardle's bitch of Framlington,' this writer defines the place as Longframlington – a slight variation, but sufficient, I think, to suggest that he did not merely copy 'A'.

I may add that a pedigree of Scamp which seems to be practically the same as that given in the Strathblane document, appears in a letter to the *Shooting Times* of July 14th, 1888, signed 'Homeros'.

Having now given an account of all the documents, so far as I know, on which we have to rely, I will continue my narrative which has been in suspense since the birth of Ainsley's Piper R16, and the foundation of the breed of dogs known by the name of Bedlington Terriers.

Joseph Ainsley was a mason by trade, and seems to have been very keen on his dogs. Mr Holland, in the article already mentioned, says that Ainsley kept a written record of the breed, but closed it when his Piper died in 1840, although 'he still preserved it'. Mr Holland must have written this about 1872 when, I think, the first edition of *'Dogs, etc.'* appeared, and when Ainsley must have been a very old man. I wonder what has become of that record. It would be a very valuable document for students of the history of the breed now.

Ainsley's Piper seems to have been an extremely game dog, as was to be expected, having been bred from parents who were no doubt chosen mainly for their sporting prowess. There is a tradition (not mentioned by 'A') that he was entered to badger when only eight months old, and that at the age of thirteen years, when he had scarcely a tooth left in his head, he drew a badger when other dogs had failed. Truly a notable achievement if he weighed no more than his parents! He is also said to have earned much fame by having in his old age once saved his mistress's baby from the attack of a savage sow.

During his life Piper had a numerous progeny. I have however, only succeeded in tracing the descendants of one of his daughters. The blood of many others among his progeny must appear in the dogs of today, but pedigrees showing the connection are missing. The same may be said with regard to the other pups that were born to Anderson's Piper R15 and Phoebe R14. They are said to have produced many dogs well known in their time, and their progeny no doubt formed the nucleus of the breed. One of them however, Jean or Jin R17, does appear in our pedigrees. She, being a sister of Ainsley's Piper R16, was mated to a dog named Tug belonging to Robert Bell of Wingate, a village a little to the west of Longhorsley. According to 'A', Tug was by Dusty belonging to Robert Dixon of Longhorsley, 'out of a bitch of the Makepiece breed, presented to J. Ainsley by John Thompson'. From other sources we learn that the bitch's name was Music. How Dusty and Music were bred we do not know, but I have heard that the Makepieces, especially one Old Nicholas, were celebrated rat-catchers, who lived near Howick and made their living by going from one gentleman's house to another to kill vermin. They always had first-rate terriers, mostly of the small wiry sort, who were splendid ratters. (I must say here that the Strathblane pedigree makes Music the name of the sire and Dusty that of the dam. This is evidently an error. It is this difference between the Strathblane and Ask 'im pedigrees that I have referred to above.)

Jean, the sister of Piper R16, being mated to this Tug, which evidently came of a good working strain, gave birth to a Meg (R19) which belonged to J. Anderson. Meg was then mated to her uncle, Ainsley's Piper R16, the old strain being thus again doubled. From this there was born a bitch pup, Nimble R20, who came into the possession of one Bagalee. Nimble R20 was chosen as a mate for a certain Tip. They had a daughter, another Nimble, R28, who belonged to Thomas Thompson, and was mated to the same owner's Old Tip. Now I have not found any pedigree given for either of these Tips, but I feel pretty confident that they were really the same dog, and that Nimble R28 was mated to her own father. I also have reason to believe that this Tip was the dog also known as the Bow (or Boa) Alley Dog, and a brother of Ainsley's Piper. Thompson certainly had a dog called Boa Alley Tip. And in the letter of 'A' already quoted he mentions as amongst the best-known specimens of the offspring of Piper R15 and Phoebe R14, the 'Bow Alley Dog'. Mr Holland in the article already mentioned refers to 'the celebrated Bow Alley Dog and Tom Thompson his owner'. So I think that the probabilities are that Tip was the brother of Piper R16 and Jean R17, and that therefore when he was mated to Nimble R20 the original strain from Old Peachem was again doubled, and that this happened yet again when, if I am right, he was mated to his own daughter Nimble R28.

Thompson's Old Tip and his Nimble R28 being then mated together produced a dog which was acquired by Bagalee, and was named Viper (R21).

Bagalee mated this dog Viper R21 to a bitch of his named Daisy (R30), who was by a certain 'Viper, the Moor House Dog' out of an unnamed dam. Now the question arises were these two Vipers identical, and was it another case of a dog being mated to his own daughter? In this instance, I do not think it was, one reason being that in the pedigrees we have the one dog is called Bagalee's and the other the Moor House dog in such a manner as to lead me to infer that the compilers wish to show the distinction between the two. But what really clinches the matter is that, in a letter to the *Fanciers' Gazette* on April 24th, 1877, the then Secretary of the Bedlington Terrier Club, who no doubt was or had been in touch with people who had actually known these old dogs, discussing the question of colour and coat, said that among the 'linty-coated' had been the Moor House dog (blue and tan) and Bagalee's dog (sandy), which I have little doubt refers to these two Vipers and clearly differentiates them. It may be of interest to record what was the official view of the Fancy on the points alluded to fifty-five years ago, so I quote what the writer, speaking for the Club, said on the matter: 'We prefer a linty or woolly coat, which we maintain to be the proper and original coat, and all the best dogs have been that way if anyone goes back for any number of years. I may mention two or three of the old dogs, viz.: the Moor House dog (blue and tan), Bagalee's dog (sandy), A. Armstrong (sen.'s) Rush (sandy), D. Patterson's (blue and tan), which were linty-coated dogs, and many others we could mention, which were all good and hard dogs. In the second place, as to colour, we maintain that the blue and tan or livers were the two original colours, and what blues there were in former years were a proper blue linty, not nearly black as they are often seen nowadays. Lastly, as to weight we do not fancy a dog over about 23 lbs., and think the average should be from 18 lbs. to 23 lbs., or at outside 25 lbs. weight.'

In the list of best-known specimens of Old Piper's offspring given in 'A's' letter already referred to occur the names of 'Rinside Moor House Dog' and 'Angerton Moor House Dog'. It seems likely that Viper, the Moor House dog, was one of these, or the offspring of one of them, and I have little doubt but that he brought into the line another reinforcement of the old strain.

The idea has also occurred to me that it is possible that these two Vipers were really Pipers, and that the old name was altered by an accident in copying or in hearing. At all events Bagalee had at one time a Piper, whose name I have seen mentioned as among the ancestors of an afterwards famous bitch Tyneside. But the point is not of much importance.

Pedigree of Clark's Wasp R22.

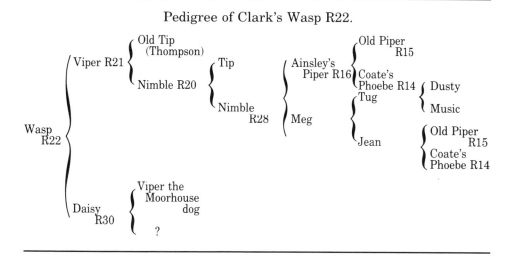

Bagalee's Viper R21 and his Daisy R30 being mated together produced a bitch named Wasp R22. And here we come to the name of another man who built up the breed – Wlliam Clark of Bedlington, into whose hands Wasp came. In another letter signed 'Homeros' in the *Shooting Times* of April 7th, 1888, the writer quotes a fellow fancier as describing Clark to have been an intelligent man, a retired farmer, who was a true lover of the breed, and who was seldom seen without a gun and two or three Bedlingtons at his heels, he being attired in a velvet shooting coat and breeches, and a low-crowned hat. At all events at some time after Ainsley's Piper died and Ainsley, as we have mentioned, had closed his written record of the race, although still maintaining great interest in it, and after also the death of the Messrs Coates (who had been early supporters of the breed, and whose name is always associated with Phoebe R14), the pure strain seems to have been in some danger of being submerged in a flood of out-crosses, and it was mainly due to the persistence of a few individuals that it was kept pure and saved from extinction. Mr Taprell Holland says in the book which I have already mentioned, which was written about 1872, that the last thirty years had been the most unfavourable period of the breed, which had fallen largely into the hands of poachers, pitmen and 'other sporting characters' who seldom committed pedigrees to paper. Many of the men also were of migratory class, and difficult to get hold of. He says that 'there however existed between them a rivalry, which partly was the cause of the race being saved from extinction, it having been preserved with some of them by a system of in-breeding, foreign blood being sparely introduced, and when absolutely required, procured from an acquaintance who was known to possess it pure'. But with others the case was different, and 'many were the crosses indulged in, varying according to the taste of the owners or the purpose to which the dog was to be applied – fighting, badger-baiting, or rabbit-coursing, the special sports of the pitmen. The descendants of these mongrels often trading under the name of the Bedlington Terrier, are now plentiful in Northumberland, and frequently bought as pure specimens, to the great subsequent discomfiture of the purchaser and prejudice to the breed.' But he adds that luckily we are not 'entirely indebted to the most trustworthy of the men mentioned for the present existence of this terrier. There are several instances in which individuals of a different standing have the breed, procured by themselves or their relatives in the first instance direct from Ainsley or one of the early breeders, and conscientiously preserved in its former purity. Several families might be mentioned in which it has existed from twenty to forty years.'

Of these people we in the present day are certainly most indebted to William Clark, as it is through his Scamp that we are able to trace our dogs step by step back to Old Peachem.

With reference to the out-cross indulged in during this period, 'A's' letter of 1869 is also instructive. He says that 'the old and true breed is now scarce, and there are few indeed, even in Northumberland, able to furnish a reliable pedigree of the original doughty specimen ... The Bull strain has been introduced, it is supposed, for fighting purposes; and for rabbit-coursing the leggy beast has been bred; but one and all diverge from the original, either in size, shape, or some other important particular. The model Bedlington should be rather long and small in the jaw, but withal muscular; the head high and narrow, and crowned with the tuft of silky hair of lighter colour than the body; the eyes must be small, round and rather sunk, and dull until excited, and then they are piercers; the ears of filbert shape, long, and hang close to the cheek, free of long hair, but slightly feathered at the tips; the neck is long, slender, but muscular, and the body well proportioned, slender, and deep chested; the toes must be well-arched, legs straight, and rather long in proportion to the height, but not to any marked extent; the tail varies from eight inches to twelve inches in length, is small and tapering, and free of feather. The best, and indeed only true, colours are: first, liver or sandy, and in either case the nose must be of a dark-brown flesh colour; or, secondly, a black-blue, when the nose is black. The Bedlington Terrier is fast, and whether on land or in water is equally at home. In appetite these dogs are dainty, and they seldom fatten; but experience has shown them to be wiry, enduring, and in courage equal to the Bulldog.'

At this point I may mention that in a letter in the *Field* in April 1869 (quoted in Mr Ash's *Dogs*) a correspondent reports that 'several years before' when bargaining with a pitman over the purchase of a red-coloured terrier, the man had claimed that it was 'one of the Peachem strain – the real Bedlington,' which seems to bear out Mr Holland's contention that the pure blood was prized, even among the 'sporting characters'.

I have just mentioned Tyneside. She was a very famous bitch in her day, belonging to Mr T. J. Pickett, whelped in 1869. I have not been able to connect her with any of the present-day dogs. She was entered in Vol. I of the K.C.S.B. as No. 3433, bred by Sir Thomas de Wheatley and coloured blue. She was by Spoor's Rock out of Breeder's Nimble, and became a champion. A writer in the *Newcastle Chronicle* of July 24th, 1872, quoted in Dalziel's *British Dogs*, says that she was descended from Thomas Thompson's strain 'and in-bred to a most curious extent, the name of Hutchinson's Tip occurring no less than five times in the course of her pedigree, while on the part of both sire and dam she is descended from such grand dogs as Bagille's (Bagalee's) Piper, Thompson's Jean, Burn's Twig, Thompson's Boa Alley Tip, and Bagille's Nimble, etc.' Tyneside was 14¾ inches high and weighed 20 lbs. There is a picture of her (very rough and untrimmed, but an unmistakable Bedlington) on page 120 of Stonehenge's book (third edition, 1879). But a newspaper cutting in my possession (I think from the *Fanciers' Gazette* of 1876) gives a letter from an exhibitor of that period, Mr John Parker of Newcastle, which throws a somewhat dubious light on Tyneside's pedigree. He was evidently annoyed at the time at unkind criticisms which had been made on the breeding of some of his own dogs, and what he called the 'endeavour to puff up Tyneside'. He is comparatively kind about the sire of Tyneside, Rock, who he merely states was by the Tynemouth dog, whose pedigree was unknown, and out of a bitch of Hutchinson's breed. But Tyneside's dam, Nimble, was by 'the Brewer's dog, which latter is grandson to Jimmy Forster's pure-bred Bulldog Fuddler' and out of Luke Herring's bitch, which 'was bred by Joseph Young from a dog and bitch, brother and sister, which were got by Lance Crozier's dog out of Old Nancy – terrier-looking but pig-jawed – pedigree unknown'; Lance Crozier's dog was by Tommy Thompson's Tip (probably the Old Tip or Boa Alley Tip with whom we have already had acquaintance), out of Andrew Hogg's bitch. The latter was by Ainsley's Piper out of 'Tom Pattison, the horse-breaker's, blue-and-white bitch,' and Pattison's bitch was got by the Jingling Gate dog, a pie-bald Bulldog, out of a bitch at Hotchpudding. The Jingling Gate dog's father was Carrick's Billy, a pure-white Bulldog. If this scathing commentary on Tyneside's lineage is correct there does not seem much room in it for the close in-breeding of which the writer in the *Newcastle Chronicle* speaks, except in the case of Rock's dam, who was of Hutchinson's breed. Possibly also the Brewer's dog had only the one regrettable interlude of Fuddler in his family tree. I do not know what, if any, reply was made to this scandal, nor how much Mr Parker's criticism was actuated by a feeling of dislike to Tyneside, but on the face of things it certainly looks as if the latter's dam had two Bull crosses in her.

I have introduced this reference to Tyneside because I do not want it to be thought that I am trying to make out that the Bedlingtons in the early days were all entirely bred from the original pure strain. The general practice seems to have been to breed them in very closely for a couple of generations, and then to have an outcross – and the outcross no doubt was sometimes Bull, to give added courage and stamina. It must be remembered that what was called a Bulldog in those days was very different to the grotesque and often deformed-looking animal of to-day. Unless there had been some mixture of outside blood sometimes the breed, if continually in-bred from the descendants of Ainsley's Piper alone, would have perished after a few generations, or, at all events, would have suffered from diminished vitality. But William Clark does seem to have kept the main current of the original strain flowing.

While on the subject of crosses I would refer also to the question of the Whippet strain, which is often said to have been introduced to give Bedlingtons the great speed which they possess. There may at times have been some breeding with dogs possessing Whippet blood, but I do not think that Whippets can have taken any appreciable part in the evolution of the modern Bedlington, or our dogs would show the results of such crossing in other ways. What I think is much more likely (and indeed believe to be a fact) is that Bedlington blood has been sometimes introduced into the breeding of Racing Whippets to give them more stamina and courage.

To resume the thread of our narrative, Clark obtained Wasp R22, the offspring of Bagalee's Viper R21 and his Daisy R30, which, if I have been correct in my deductions hitherto, was very full indeed of the blood of Anderson's Old Piper and Phoebe R14. He mated her to a dog called Billy (R29) belonging to W. Cowney. This Billy was by J. Maugham's Bustle out of a bitch of William Weatherburn's. No record of their parentage exists, and this may have been an outcross, but a Weatherburn's Phoebe appears among the names quoted by 'A' as 'best-known specimens' of the original Bedlington family, and I have not much doubt in my own mind that this bitch of Weatherburn's was either that Phoebe or one of her descendants.

From this union of Billy R29 and Wasp R22 there was born Clark's Billy R23. And now the in-breeding began again, for he was mated to his own mother, Wasp R22, and the result was Clark's Meg R24.

Meg R24 was mated to a dog called Scamp belonging to one J. Curley, about whose antecedents I can find nothing. IIe must be carefully distinguished from his grandson, Clark's Scamp, to whom we shall come shortly. Meg R24 (whose mother and grandmother, as we have seen, was Clark's Wasp R22) and Curley's Scamp, had a daughter, Clark's Daisy R25.

Clark then mated Daisy R25 to a dog called Joicee's Piper (R26). This dog was by R. Hoy's Rock (R32) out of the Meg R24 who was Daisy's dam. Rock R32 (also known at the time as Rocky III) was by Dodd's Pincher out of an unrecorded bitch. Referring once more to 'A's' names of best-known specimens of the original stock, we find a 'Hoy's Rocky,' so I think we may make a pretty safe guess that Hoy's Rocky III was also descended from the old strain.

Piper R26 and Daisy R25, being half-brother and half-sister, had a very famous son, Clark's Scamp (R27). He is another of the pillars of the breed, and the chief connection between the modern dogs and the ancient ones that we are able to trace.

Pedigree of Clark's Scamp R27.

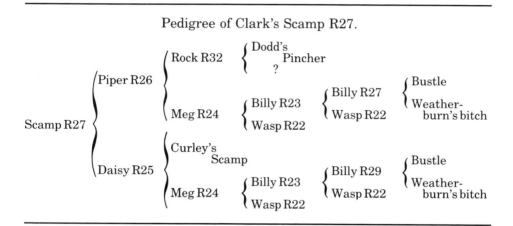

Scamp R27 was in due course mated to his mother, Daisy R25, and produced the champions, Tearem (dog) and Tyne (bitch), belonging to Mr T. J. Pickett, whom I have already mentioned as the owner of Tyneside. They were born in the year 1868. Mr Pickett, who lived in Newcastle-on-Tyne, had been breeding Bedlingtons, we are told, since 1844. He was very keen on the breed and did much to popularize them; in fact he was so much interested in them that he was often known to his friends as the 'Duke of Bedlington'. The days of Dog Shows had now arrived, the Kennel Club was founded in 1873, and in the first volume of the Kennel Club Stud Book, that of 1874 for the year 1873, Tearem and Tyne both appeared as Nos. 3429 and 3430 respectively. They in due course, although brother and sister and already closely in-bred, were mated together and produced, among others, Soulsby's Weardale. It is said that when Weardale was shown at Bedlington, William Clark, who was present, 'fairly gloated over' him 'as a rare good specimen of the old breed'. The pedigree of Weardale is an interesting study of close breeding to Clark's strain.

Scamp R27 was also mated to a bitch named Wassy (R5702) belonging to Joicee, which was by Piper R26 (Scamp's sire) out of another Daisy of Clark's (which I must call R25A). This Daisy was by Clark's Billy R23 out of another Meg of Clark's (R24A). (Really if these old breeders had known the terrible confusion and trouble they were going to cause in the future by their apparently simple method of nomenclature, I think they would not have done it.) Of this Meg R24A all we know is that she was by a certain Captain Potts' dog. Scamp R27 and Joicee's Wassy being mated had a daughter called Gyp (R5701) which belonged to John Ainsley (I do not know if he was any relation of Joseph). Gyp was mated to her father Scamp, and had a son Piper R50 which Ainsley kept. He was mated to a bitch called Topsy who was by Pickett's Tearem (Scamp's son), and they had batty's Mat, K.C.S.B. 5580, a very famous dog in its day. Gyp was also the mother of Ask 'im and grandmother of Ask 'im II belonging to Mr John Cowan, whose pedigree given in Dalziel's book is one of the authorities I have referred to.

Pedigree of Weardale (G. J. Soulsby).

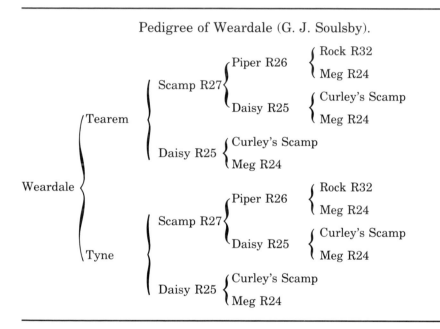

It is not absolutely true to say, if I have done so, that Scamp R27 is the only connecting link which I have been able to trace between the dogs of the present day and those of the pre-Show past. There was a brother of Clark's Meg R24 who has also left a line whose perpetuation is on record. This dog, which does not seem to have had a name, is known as 'Gibbs's liver-coloured dog'. He was of course by Clark's Billy R23 out of his Wasp R22, whose pedigree we have dealt with. J. Gibbs who acquired him founded a strain which was well known in its time, and lasted for several generations. He mated the liver-coloured dog to a bitch, about which nothing – not even her name – is known, and they had a son Rattler (R34) which Gibbs kept. Rattler had a son and two daughters, who come into our pedigrees, but the question of who were their respective mothers is

Mr J. Cornforth's Newcastle Lad (K.C.S.B., 6668). Sire, Mr Liddell's Tip; Dam, Mr Morris's Sut.

Champion Humbledon Blue Boy 1887. Owned by W. E. Alcock. Never beaten.

somewhat involved, and I leave it to be dealt with under their names in the list which follows. The most famous of the three was Gibbs's well-known dog Dante (R46), eight of whose offspring appear in the list. The bitches were Betty R47 and Daisy R44.

141

As regards early pictures of Bedlingtons, the first I know of is one of which a reproduction appears in Mr Ash's book, Plate 119, where it is described as 'the first Bedlington illustrated,' and is said to be from the *Field* of 1853, which is an error. It is really (as appears in the text) from the

Rosebud and Nailor 1878.

Champion Clyde Boy 1894.

Field of 1869, and it represents Mr Taprell Holland's Peachem and Fan. They are very shaggy-looking and quite untrimmed, but unmistakable Bedlingtons, especially the one standing up. Then there is the portrait of Tyneside which I have already mentioned as appearing in the 1879 edition of Stonehenge, and an interesting one of Mr Pickett's Tartar (by Tearem out of Tyneside) accompanying Mr Holland's article in Webb's *Dogs*. Dalziel's 1879 edition shows a picture of Newcastle Lad, and Mr Ash also gives small reproductions of A. Armstrong's Nailer (1878), and of Clyde Boy who was whelped in 1894. There are no doubt other early portraits in existence, but I have not been so fortunate as to come across them.

One word as to the reliability of the early pedigrees. It has been rather the fashion to refer in sceptical tones as to the authenticity of pedigrees going so far back. Stonehenge does so, and Mr Ash is inclined to follow his example – at least he says that he thinks the Ask 'im pedigree is 'very doubtful'. Well, I expect I have studied these pedigrees as carefully as anybody in the present day, and I can see no reason whatever to doubt their genuineness or that they are, broadly speaking, correct. I do not dispute that errors and omissions may have crept in at times in certain places; I have pointed out certain discrepancies and certain doubtful details, but I think that the pedigrees on the whole bear the impress of truth. I believe that William Clark and Joseph Ainsley, who between them covered nearly fifty years of Bedlington history, carefully recorded the pedigrees of the dogs they bred from, and did not seek to ascribe ancestors to dogs whose breeding was in fact uncertain. I do not see any evidence or suggestion of pedigree faking in the particulars given. And I feel no doubt, after weighing all the probabilities, that Clark's Scamp was in fact descended from Ainsley's Piper in the manner here shown, and that Ainsley's Piper in turn was descended from Donkin's Old Peachem and Trevelyan's Old Flint. In the absence of Kennel Club and Stud Book records one cannot have official documentary proof of these old genealogies; one must rely on a certain amount of pains having been taken to keep records at the times, and on a certain amount of good faith in the transmission of them. There seems reason to suppose that these were present, and I am satisfied that, making due allowance for the human propensity to err by inadvertence, the old pedigrees which I have here described do in fact represent the truth in their main lines.

I have now brought the record down to the time of Dog Shows and K.C.S.B. numbers, and will leave it there. The Stud Book list which follows gives the parentage of all the well-known dogs of the last ten years, and the parents of their parents, when I have been able to identify them, and so on, so that their descent can be traced backwards until either one comes up against the letter N.T. signifying that I have been unable to discover the parents, or else one arrives at the very beginning of things, and gets back to the days of Old Peachem and Old Flint.

Redmarshall's Stud Book

PART II
STUD BOOK

The great difficulty in compiling a list of this kind is that only a proportion of the dogs and bitches concerned have ever been registered at the Kennel Club. A record of their parentage therefore only exists in written pedigrees in private ownership, and these, when frequently transcribed, are liable, either through poor handwriting or mistakes in copying, to contain many errors. I have been only able in this list to give a small proportion of the pedigrees of unregistered Bedlingtons. I have checked these as well as I could, and have drawn attention to any doubtful cases. I have not included anything that is manifestly wrong.

I must point out that this list is only intended for pedigree or Stud Book use. Therefore a dog of, say, twenty years ago, however distinguished its show career may have been, does not appear in it unless some descendant is among the leading winners of the present day.

I have compiled it on the following basis. I have taken all the Bedlingtons who have won places in the Kennel Club Stud Book from 1925 to the present year, and have traced their ancestors back as far as I can, and have thus made a list of over 1,100 Bedlingtons. It is brought down to about the end of March, 1935.

I have no doubt that errors and discrepancies will be found in the list. I can only hope that critics will be lenient and will believe that I have done my best to be careful. It has taken a long time and much work to compile. I have consulted all the Kennel Club Stud Books from 1875 to 1914 (besides of course the recent volumes), and all the *Kennel Gazettes* from 1892 to date, besides a number of MS. pedigrees, notes, letters and printed articles. And I have amassed memoranda giving particulars of some thousands of dogs, all arranged alphabetically, from which I have selected those given in this list.

I feel that I am weakest in my record of unregistered Bedlingtons of recent times; so many people still breed from unregistered 'Pipers' or 'Nells,' of which it is difficult to get any reliable information.

It is evident that some method is necessary in a work of this kind for distinguishing between dogs which bear the same name. I have therefore given a number preceded by the letter R (for Redmarshall, to show it is not an official number) in all cases where one dog might be confused with another of similar name whether in this list or not. But where the dog in question has a K.C.S.B. number which I know, I have given that number in preference. I have given K.C.S.B. numbers wherever I know them — that is, in the great majority of cases, and, I think, for all the modern dogs. To save space and labour I have not put the letters K.C.S.B. before these numbers.

I wish to emphasize the fact that the R number is a purely private matter invented by me for convenience sake.

When I have been unable to discover the parentage of a dog I have put the letters NT (i.e. 'not traced') in brackets after its name. Readers will therefore be saved the trouble of looking up the dog in question in the list.

After the dog's name I put the name of its owner in brackets when I happen to know it. These, I fear, will sometimes turn out to be mis-spelt: I have to depend upon my authorities. It must be remembered also that some dogs change hands frequently. I have not attempted to trace changes of ownership, but have simply put the name of any owner of whom I have found a record.

The date which follows the name of the dog is the date of its birth. It is seldom that this can be supplied if the dog was not registered.

I have also, when possible, added a note of the dog's colour and any other points of interest.

In the previous edition dogs who had won a K.C.S.B. number in 1924 were included in the list. To economize space I have now eliminated these and their ancestors in all cases where none of their descendants appear in the list. The names so removed from the list are Ch. Blue Betty, Blue Hawk, Bluey R6100, Brownhylda, Bulawayo, Chaucer Lady, Chloe, Cribden Captain, Ferry Lassie, Funny Face, Ginger Son, Goxhill Diana, Gripwell, Hermit, Highland Queen, Jenny R5200, Jyp R5197, Lady Highstep, Lady Peggy, Lintz Jess, Massey's Wendy, Midmoor Peggy, Peel Duchess, Peter Pan, Prinnie R5198, Redcloud O'Phipson, Rose and Crown Premier, Ryehill Blue Rascal, St. Cuthbert, Silverlocks of Massey's, Somme Miss, Veralda, Vixen R5939, Wannyscrag, Wass II R5196, Whitbarn Silver Bill. I shall be happy to supply particulars of the breeding of any of these dogs to anyone who may be interested.

At the same time may I appeal to anyone who can supply information to fill up any of the gaps in the list where dogs are marked as NT (not traced) to forward it to me? I shall be very grateful for any help which may be given in this direction, will return promptly any pedigrees which may be lent me, and will embody the information in any future edition of the book. There must be many fanciers who are in possession of old pedigrees which would assist in identifying some of these untraced dogs.

To conclude, I would say that this list is not nearly so complete as I would like, or as I had hoped to make it, but, such as it is, I hope it may be of some use or interest. I think you may be confident, supposing that your dog is of any of the leading strains, that you will, if you have the patience, be able to trace his pedigree by its means through at least one line back to the very beginning of the Bedlington era.

HEATHER MOUNT,
    CAMBERLEY.   REDMARSHALL.
       April, 1935.

STUD BOOK

(I am indebted to the Kennel Club for their courtesy in permitting me to quote their K.C.S.B. numbers.)

NOTES FOR THE READER.

(NT) means that I have not traced the parents of the dog in question, and that it is no use looking them up further in this list.

Numbers *preceded by* the letter R are merely Redmarshall numbers and are not official. I have only used them to distinguish between dogs of the same or similar names. Numbers *followed by* a letter or letters (including R), or without letters, are official K.C.S.B. numbers.

Dates, unless otherwise stated, are dates of a dog's birth.

Names in brackets after a dog's name refer to owners.

K.C. means Kennel Club.

K.C.S.B. means Kennel Club Stud Book.

A.

Abbeydale Wonder 1806PP (Alderson) 1931 by Pitswood General out of Thread of Gold. Bred by owner. Blue.

Abus Vic. See Vic R5217.

Active Lad (R. Walker) 1922 by Handyman out of Christmas Daisy. Bred by Mrs M. Thompson.

Afton Actress by Shemer (NT) out of Beauty (NT).

Afton Daisy by Death or Glory out of Blue Adeline.

Afton Gem 1913 by Craghead Piper out of Moss House Beauty. Bred by White.

Afton Ida 1910 by Askme out of Nellie R5682. Bred by Taylor.

Afton Jessie 1286G Champion (J. Blench) 1899 by Blyth Bob out of Sweet Afton. Bred by Hunter and Bell. Blue.

Afton Topic 1620J (J. Bell) 1899 by Blyth Bob out of Sweet Afton. Bred by Hunter and Bell. Blue.

Afton Wallace (Hunter and Bell) 1899 by Blyth Bob out of Sweet Afton. Bred by owners.

Afton Water 1289G (J. Blench) 1901 by Afton Wallace out of Miss Afton (NT). Bred by J. Bell. Blue.

Alexander of Cromdale 199W 1915 by Sperkeforde Jackanapes out of Cranley Peggy. Bred by W. W. Savage.

Alnwick Cadger (Edminson) 1892 by Clyde Peach out of Nellie (NT). Bred by Millburn.

Alston Peggy 327FF (H. Hartley) 1922 by Eccleshill Trumpeter out of Comicator. Bred by M. Fish. Liver.

Ambrose 523JJ (W.W. Young) 1926 by Pugnacity out of Masquerade. Bred by G. W. Kent. Blue.

Angustura 501QQ (Mrs E. M. Bartlett) 1933 by Gardeners Supremacy out of Esperanza. Bred by owner. Blue.

Apple Tree Blossom (M. Lewis) by Charlie R5266 out of Queen (NT). Bred by W. J. Gingell.

Arrah-go-on (Misses Maunsell and Hamilton) 1926 by Hop-a-long out of Don't be Talkin'. Bred by R. G. Moir. Originally registered as Dragon Fly.

Askme 445P (Mrs Bell) 1908 by Cranley Sentinel out of Nellie R5682. Bred by owner. Blue.

Awauni 502QQ (Mrs N. Bullivant) 1933 by Cribden Centaur out of Blue Tinsell. Bred by owner. Blue.

Azure Cast 1217JJ (S. Mercer) 1927 by Cribden Chutney out of Tamar Implacable. Bred by A. T. Sutton. Blue.

Azure Model 1297LL (D. Morgan) 1930 by Azure Cast out of Tam's Wares. Bred by G. Nicholson. Blue.

B.

Badger by Beaconsfield Tavy out of Tibbie (NT).

Bagatelle 14412 (Watson) 1879 by Twig 10907 out of Wasp (NT). Bred by Hall. Liver.

Bagpipes 297U 1913 by Doneraile Boy out of Doneraile Gem.

Banzai 505PP (J. Flint) 1931 by Cribden Chutney out of Toppin. Bred by Major P. Groves. Blue grey.

Barber (J. Barnes) by Hairdresser out of Berwick Lass.

Barley of Bransways (Miss E. S. M. Branfoot) 1929 by Bluehouse Barnabas out of Philwood Tess. Bred by Mrs H. C. Branfoot.

Barnaby Rudge (J. Flint) by Triumph out of Machen Pride. A bitch in spite of her masculine name.

Barney Boy by Barney Camwal out of Vectis.

Barney Camwal (G. Coulter) 1906 by Barmoor Squire (NT) (J. Steele) out of Madam Camwal. Bred by owner.

Barny (Miss K. West) 1922 by Sperkeforde Jackanapes out of Gypeena. Bred by Mrs Martin.

Battery Girl (H. Seddon) 1927 by Sporting Chance out of Biddy R5711. Bred by C. Webster.

Beaconsfield Tartaress 1319A (J. Cook) 1894 by Piper R360 out of Phoebe R361. Bred by Armstrong. Blue.

Beaconsfield Tavy 652L (J. Cook) 1904 by Deansfield Piper out of Pride of Dudley. Bred by Robson. Blue.

Beaconsfield Teaser (J. Cook) 1895 by Beaconsfield Triumph out of Nettle (NT). Bred by Patterson.

Beaconsfield Technical 483N Cham-pion (J. Cook) 1906 by Baker (NT) (Peacock) out of Nell (NT). Bred by J. Hore. Blue.

Beaconsfield Tamianka 377Q (J. Cook) 1909 by Benwell Prince out of Beaconsfield Teneriffe. Bred by Dodds. Blue. Formerly known as Strickland Daisy.

Beaconsfield Temporize, Champion registered by K.C. in 1901 as pedigree unknown.

Beaconsfield Teneriffe by Beaconsfield Temporize out of Beaconsfield Theocracy.

Beaconsfield Theocracy (J. Thompson) by Bellerby Bishop out of Nellie (NT).

Beaconsfield Tourist 123A (J. Cook) 1894 by Tip (NT) (Armstrong) out of Lil (NT) (Adamson). Blue.

Beaconsfield Toxopholite 446P (J. Cook) 1907 by Beaconsfield Tavy out of Diana R5369. Bred by G. Brown. Blue.

Beaconsfield Treasure 1001B, bitch (J. Cook) 1896 by Elswick Lad (NT) (Thornton) out of Sally Day (NT) (Day). Blue. There was also a **dog** called Beaconsfield Treasurer by Sir Goldsmith out of Nettle (Brown), born in 1898.

Beaconsfield Triumph 1267B (J. Cook) 1894 by Tip (NT) (Armstrong) out of Nettle (NT) (Goodison). Blue. There seem to have been several Tips belonging to Armstrong and I am very sorry that I cannot sort them out or give their pedigree which would be very helpful. There seems to have been one by a well-known dog called Hanlon out of Bagatelle and another by a certain Tyrolean out of a Nettle and I think there were others but I have no means of distinguishing them. Can anyone help?

Beaconsfield Typhoon. See Clyde Boy.

Beadle Blue Nettle (W. Cole) by Leo out of Lady Aggalade. Bred by owner.

Beauburn Gyp (J. D. Davey) 1906 by Berwick Blue Boy out of Hillburn Lass (NT) (Lugton).

Beetle, The 355NN (Mrs Harman) 1928 by Rathangan Piper out of Knowlton Jill. Bred by Miss Sturt. Blue.

Beetly Vixen by Redstart out of Floss (NT).

Belah 146GG (T. R. Osborn) 1924 by Hop-a-long out of Tweedie (NT). Bred by W. A. Brown. Blue.

Bella Ross (C. A. Gilzean) 1920 by Jock's Lodge out of Daisy R5875. Bred by owner.

Bellerby Bishop 1487K, Champion (W. B. Baty) 1904 by Elswick Piper out of Afton Jessie. Bred by J. Blench.

Bellerby Surprise 484N (W. B. Baty) 1907 by Deansfield Piper out of Goxhill Frisk. Bred by Grayshon. Blue. Originally named Stonehouse Piper.

Ben Lady 1920 by Breakwater Chieftain out of Salamander Lass. Bred by A. Pow.

Benton Bridesmaid. See Nettle R354.

Benwell Joe (T. Lamb) 1912 by Bellerby Surprise out of Princess Diana. Bred by G. Brown.

Benwell Prince (G. Brown) 1907 by Beaconsfield Tavy out of Diana R5369. Bred by owner.

Berwick Blue Bell 1892 by Berwick Brick out of Merry Jyp 27810.

Berwick Blue Boy 649L, Champion (J. Blench) 1905 by Deansfield Piper out of Firefly R5277. Bred by R. Edminson. Blue.

Berwick Brick 32374 (J. Blench) 1890 by Rattler O out of Stonehouse Gipsy. Dark Blue.

Berwick Brigadier (J. Blench) 1906 by Berwick Blue Boy out of Afton Jessie. Bred by W. Onions.

Berwick Lass 18594 (J. Blench) 1884 by Clansman out of Fly. Bred by C. C. Spragget. Blue.

Berwick Surprise 1896 by Jethart Jet out of Berwick Jewel (NT).

Bess R49 (Smith) by Dante R46 out of Bitter (Gibbs) who is said to have been a sister of Ebchester Tip.

Bessema (T. R. Osborn) 1922 by Jock's Lodge out of Bluey R5704. Bred by owner.

Bet of Bransways 1988PP (Miss E. S. M. Branfoot) 1932 by Deckham Oprecious out of Binnacle Bella. Bred by Morton. Blue.

Betsy Prig (W. Scott) 1928 by Fly Bob out of Moving Cheek. Bred by A. Wilkinson.

Betty R47 (Dodd) by Rattler R34 out of

Jess (NT) (Gibbs). This is according to a pedigree in K.C.S.B. 1892 under Dark Flyer. The pedigree of Strathblane, however, says that Betty was sister to Clark's Daisy, i.e., was by Scamp out of Meg. Yet another pedigree I have seen makes her by Rattler out of Meg (Gibbs).

Betty R5663 (F. Ellis) by Eccleshill Blue Boy out of Floss R5664.

Betty of Wynfield (Mrs Teverson) 1923 by Mercury 1192CC out of Bessema. Bred by T. R. Osborn.

Betty's Fancy 1303FF (T. R. Osborn) 1924 by Ridge Hill Jock out of Betty of Wynfield. Bred by Mrs Teverson. Blue.

Betty's Girl (Dr J. Wilkinson) 1930 by Peg's Pal out of Betsy Prig. Bred by W. Scott.

Biddy R5711 (C. Webster) by Breakwater Major out of Moorhouse Lady.

Billangho 1559KK (S. Mercer) 1928 by Azure Cast out of Sandshade. Bred by owner. Blue.

Bill of Harnish 1614PP (Mrs Hallowell-Carew) 1932 by Cribden Chutney out of Peggy of Ember. Bred by Miss R. E. Holland. Blue. Originally registered as Pickles of Woodhay.

Billy R23 (William Clark of Bedlington) by Billy R29 out of Wasp R22. See History.

Billy R29 (W. Cowney) by J. Maugham's Bustle out of a bitch of William Weatherburn's. No particulars of this dog and bitch can be given but see remarks in History.

Billy R341 (Wheaton) by Choker 15651 out of Floss R342.

Bingle Nanette 958HH (J. Rumjahn) 1926 by Newsham Dragon out of Fairplay. Bred by owner. Blue.

Binnacle Bella (Dr J. F. Knight) 1929 by Worton Demon out of Honeysuckle. Bred by owner.

Bit of Fashion 1152HH (A. Maddison) 1926 by Silvery Tweed out of Longscar. Bred by owner. Blue.

Bitter (Gibbs) said in pedigree of Strathblane to be sister to Ebchester Tip, which see.

Blackmail 1917 by Piper R5199 out of Nellie R5682. Bred by Taylor.

Blacksmith R5522 by Coatsworth King out of Coatsworth Lil.

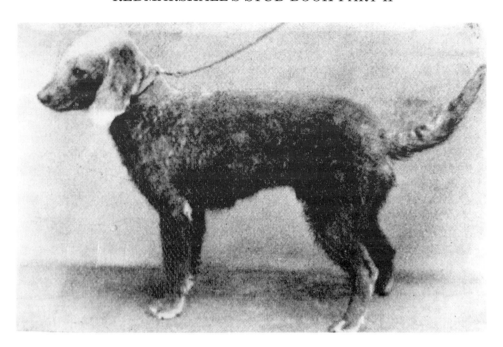

Jack Warkworth 188–.

Blyth Bob 1897.

Blue Adeline by Benwell Prince out of Gipsy Girl (NT).

Blue Bandeau (J. A. Carrington) 1922 by Charlie R5266 out of Queen (NT). Bred by W. J. Gingell.

Blue Beauty (Robson) 1924 by Chota Sahib out of Phoebe R5678. Bred by R. Allison.

Blue Bell R5419 (J. Spurgeon) by Goxhill Tatters out of Holloway Floss.

Blue Bell Maid 180FF (C.S. Bell) 1924 by Moving Knight out of Lady Betty. Bred by W. S. Wright. Blue.

Blue Bird (Mrs Martin) by Breakwater Chief out of Breakwater Zena.

Blue Blood 15148. See Vic R668.

Blue Boy 1919 by Buckenham Blue out of Barnaby Rudge. Bred by J. Flint.

Blue Bussell 1480KK (D. Pitt) 1928 by King's Pawn out of Merry Jyppy R6976. Bred by owner. Blue.

Blue China 279KK (Mrs T. Walker) 1927 by Sing-to-me out of Princess Peggy. Bred by owner. Blue.

Blue Day (Miss A. M. Worrell) 1928 by Moving Knight out of Rye Nellie. Bred by C. G. Worrell.

Blue Flame (C. Seddon) 1917 by Midmoor Jock out of Rose (NT). Bred by H. Ramsdon.

Blue Flash 530KK (H. Telfer) 1928 by Cadbury Sam out of Vera of Mottisfont. Bred by Mrs E. Lee. Blue.

Bluehouse Barnabas 624JJ (Mrs W. G. Magee) 1927 by Moving Knight out of Bluey's Pride. Bred by owner. Blue.

Bluehouse Larry (Mrs W. G. Magee) 1931 by Bluehouse Barnabas out of Deckham Opia. Bred by owner.

Bluehylda 220GG (T. R. Osborn) 1925 by Shothanger Rector out of Bluey's Pride. Bred by owner. Blue.

Blue Iris (J. A. Carrington) 1923 by Croxteth Blue Imp out of Blue Bandeau. Bred by owner.

Bluejacket (J. Spurgeon) 1905 by Cranley Blue Boy out of Twilight. Bred by owner.

Blue Kestrel 1921 by Croxteth Blue Boy out of Fairy Flax. Bred by Haynes.

Blue King (A. McEwen) 1927 by Moving Knight out of Lady Chemist. Bred by G. Widey.

Blue Label 1920 by Breakwater Chieftain out of Nellie (NT). Bred by H. P. Forshaw.

Blue Lad (M. Knight) 1920 by Blue Coat (NT) out of Rose (NT). Bred by J. Wood. As to the sire see under Nellie R5512.

Blue Lambkin (Dr Bevan) 1924 by Hell for Leather out of Redwings O'Phipson. Bred by T. Osborn.

Blue Lassie 896BB, Champion (Mrs Towers Minors) 1920 by Lo Ben out of Saucy Peggy. Bred by J. Mooney. Blue.

Blue Maid (W. M. Atchison) 1923 by Handyman out of Phoebe R5689. Bred by M. Robson.

Blue Mignon (Miss P. Ellis) 1926 by Shothanger Rector out of Chinchilla Jeanne. Bred by Miss Edwards.

Blue Moment 1058QQ (Miss V. Cross) 1933 by May the Devil Take You out of Bright Lass. Bred by Miss F. M. Sturt. Blue.

Blue Nanette (Miss W. M. Bickham) 1925 by Field House Jock out of Phoebe of Great Warford. Bred by Mrs R. Bennett.

Blue Pansy 1913 by Breakwater Treasure out of Raggles. Bred by Mrs Mead.

Blue Passion (W. Yates) 1926 by Siddow Sentry out of Bess (NT). Bred by S. England.

Blue Revival (E. Ashley) 1922 by Eccleshill Blue Boy out of Switch (NT). Bred by C. Howarth.

Blue Rival (C. Seddon) 1925 by Blue Revival out of Blue Flame. Bred by owner.

Blue Sahib (Gowland) 1924 by Chota Sahib out of Peggy (NT). Bred by R. Allison.

Blue Sam 1914 by Breakwater Pierrot out of Blue Pansy. Bred by W. Tait.

Blue Surprise. There is an uncertainty about the breeding of this bitch, the dam of Ch. Deckham Crest, which I have been unable to clear up. In Crest's stud card she is said to have been by Blue Sam out of Jock's Image and her owner to have been T. Fields. But Fields at the same time had a bitch named Blue Surprise which he registered at the K.C. as by Blue Sam out of Durham Lass. In Crest's registration Blue Surprise was shown as an unregistered bitch. As there is another mistake in the stud card pedigree I cannot accept it as reliable and therefore can here only give Blue Surprise as by Blue Sam out of?

Blue Tassie 1534NN Champion (Mrs Llewellyn Ward) 1931 by Night Express out of Elizabet. Bred by R. Boucher. Blue.

Blue Thunder 20588 QQ (Miss C. E. Dobbie) 1934 by Bluehouse Barnabas out of Knowlton Junora. Bred by owner. Blue.

Blue Tib (J. Winchester) 1921 by Patrick's Blue out of Cobledene Floss (NT). Bred by Mrs M. Rayner.

Blue Tinsell (Mrs N. Bullivant) 1931 by Cribden Chutney out of Battery Girl. Bred by H. Seddon.

Blue Vera (Mrs M. Webster) 1921 by Lucky Lad out of Floss (NT). Bred by J. King.

Blue Vixon (J. H. Taylor) 1921 by Blue Boy out of Proud Peggy. Bred by H. Taylor. In K.C.S.B. and in Blue Vixon's registration the sire is given as Boy Blue and he is shown as registered. The only registered dog of that name about that time was however born two years later than Blue Vixon. I have no doubt that the sire was Blue Boy by Buckenham Blue out of Barnaby Rudge to whom Proud Peggy seems to have been mated several times.

Bluey R5704 (T. R. Osborn) by Brompton Bobby out of Meg R5705.

Bluey's Pride (T. R. Osborn) 1922 by Jock's Lodge out of Bluey R5704. Bred by owner.

Blyth Barmaid 1914 (Oct.) by Coalcutter out of Isabella Newsham. Bred by L. Peacock.

Blyth Baronet 1914 (Feb.) by Budget out of Isabella Newsham. Bred by L. Peacock.

Blyth Bob 1173E (J. Douglas) 1897 by Seghill Sweep out of Golden Wreath (often called Golden Reef). Bred by G. Hall. Blue.

Blyth Briton by Blyth Bob out of Blyth Jennie (NT).

Bobby Dazzler 1499LL (S. Barker) 1928 by Cribden Chutney out of Breezehill Opal. Bred by owner. Liver.

Bobrikoff (R. C. Irving) 1904 by Els-

wick Type out of Orpington Lass. Bred by Williams.

Bobs R5377 by Craghead Surprise out of Craghead Kwamaxosa.

Bogus Prince 453KK (Misses M. M. and C. R. Carr) 1928 by Cribden Chutney out of Lucky Lass. Bred by J. Bennett. Blue.

Bomb Girl 1914 by Breakwater Ruler out of Curragh Belle. Bred by J. Latham. This bitch was not registered at the K.C. till June 1920 and in the meantime seems to have been sometimes known as Breakwater Nell under which name she occurs in pedigrees. There was however also another earlier Breakwater Nell R349.

Bongrace (H. Bottomley) 1926 by Robert out of Grace. Bred by W. A. Wright.

Boniface 1541L (R. C. Irving) 1906 by Bobrikoff out of Miretta. Bred by owner. Liver.

Bontesse of Simonside 1002NN (Mrs A. Burney-Cumming) 1930 by Deckham Oprecious out of Sotheron Blue. Bred by W. Herring. Blue.

Bonzette 531FF (Mrs Salmon) 1924 by Ridge Hill Jock out of Rita. Bred by owner. Blue.

Boota 862HH (W. G. Magee) 1926 by Hop-a-long out of Shothanger Sally. Bred by Mrs Magee. Blue.

Bouncing Girl 1302FF (J. Davey) 1924 by Hop-a-long out of Midmoor Avis. Bred by W. Savage.

Bowman Vixen 22FF (F. Ellis) 1923 by Ruddigore out of Tance (NT). Bred by G. Colburn. Liver.

Boxmoor Mary (Mrs T. N. Keith) 1921 by Alexander of Cromdale out of Miss Mischief R5193. Bred by T. W. Lawrence. Blue.

Boy of Anfield 562NN (C. G. Worrell) 1931 by Piper of Ryton out of Blue Day. Bred by Miss A. M. Worrell.

Break of Dawn (T. Griffiths) 1922 by Desperado out of Little Lady (NT). Bred by T. Dinsdale.

Breakwater Baron. See Sir Goldsmith.

Breakwater Chief 404R, Champion (Mrs P. R. Smith) 1910 by Goxhill Tatters out of Breakwater Fashion. Bred by owner. Blue. Not to be confused, as I have sometimes seen in pedigrees, with Ch. Breakwater Chieftain.

Breakwater Chieftain 820AA, Champion (P. R. Smith) 1916 by Deansfield Monarch out of Flora R5195. Bred by Mrs Burns. Was originally registered as Deansfield Chieftain under which name he still sometimes appears in pedigrees.

Breakwater Eclipse 381Q, Champion (Mrs P. R. Smith) 1908 by Dudley Blue Boy out of Ewood Floss. Bred by J. Ward. Blue. Originally registered as Ewood Marquis.

Breakwater Fashion 485N, Champion (J. Deane Willis) 1907 by Afton Wallace out of Nettle R5357. Bred by T. Maddison. Liver. Originally registered as Tweedside Queen.

Breakwater Fisher 556T, Champion (Mrs P. R. Smith) 1912 by Breakwater Chief out of Breakwater Zena. Bred by owner. Blue.

Breakwater Flash 1287G (Mrs P. R. Smith) 1899 by Blyth Bob out of Sweet Afton. Bred by Messrs Hunter and Bell. Blue. Formerly known as Mansfield Boy.

Breakwater Flora. See Minley Flora.

Breakwater Lorna 1912 by Bellerby Surprise out of Breakwater Fashion. Bred by H. Grayshon. First registered as Goxhill Beauty.

Breakwater Major 178FF (Mrs P. R. Smith) 1923 by Ruddigore out of Tance (NT). Bred by G. Colburn. Liver.

Breakwater Nell R349 by Beaconsfield Tyrolean (NT) out of Daisy (NT).

Breakwater Nell R5668. See Bomb Girl. See also above.

Breakwater Nipper 1896 by Beaconsfield Triumph out of Breakwater Nell R349.

Breakwater Peer 551M (Mrs P. R. Smith) 1906 by Bellerby Bishop out of Afton Actress. Bred by Bell. Blue.

Breakwater Pierrot 1913 by Gollyway out of Minley Flora. Bred by Mrs Currie.

Breakwater Princess (Mrs P. R. Smith) 1899 by Breakwater Squire out of Breakwater Nipper. Bred by owner.

Breakwater Ruler 432S (Mrs P. R. Smith) 1910 by Goxhill Tatters out of Breakwater Fashion. Bred by owner. Blue.

Breakwater Squire 1294C, Champion (Mrs P. R. Smith) 1896 by Premier out of Nell R347. Bred by J. Georgeson. Blue.

Breakwater Test by Jack R5423 out of Nellie R5424.

Breakwater Treasure by Goxhill Tatters out of Breakwater Fashion.

Breakwater Zena 433S (Mrs P. R. Smith) 1910 by Goxhill Tatters out of Sperkeforde Judy. Bred by E. B. Aylward. Blue.

Breezehill Opal (J. W. Bennett) 1925 by Odds On out of Fishwick Blue Bird. Bred by W. Cooke.

Bridget 21371 (G. Coulter) 1885 by Piper R309 out of Nell R308. Bred by Taylor. Blue.

Bright Eyes 1510HH (H. Lee) 1926 by Square Deal out of Whetstone Lady. Bred by J. T. Barnes. Blue.

Bright Lass (J. Rogers) 1926 by Rodio out of Blue Lambkin. Bred by Dr A. Bevan.

Brightstone Venture 131QQ, Champion (Miss G. Lawis) 1933 by Gardeners Supremacy out of Esperanza. Bred by Mrs E. H. Bartlett. Blue.

Brisco Kim by Bluejacket out of Blue Bell R5419.

Brisco Mart by Breakwater Test out of Nellie R5420.

Brompton Bobby 556M (F. Ward) 1907 by Jock of Oran out of Little Demon. Bred by owner. Blue.

Broomilea 277HH (D. Pitt) 1926 by Sudston Panther out of Merry Jyppy R6976. Bred by owner. Blue.

Broomilea Peggy (D. Pitt) 1927 by Sudston Panther out of Merry Jyppy R6976. Bred by owner.

Broughton Fireball 1216JJ (H. Hartley) 1927 by Cribden Chutney out of Alston Peggy. Bred by owner. Liver.

Broughton's Memory 1375HH (Mrs H. Hartley) 1927 by Cribden Chutney out of Alston Peggy. Bred by H. Hartley. Blue.

Brown Sugar or Harnish (Mrs E. Hallowell-Carew) 1929 by Cribden Chutney out of Breezehill Opal. Bred by S. Barker.

Bubble of Harnish 1899MM, Champion (Mrs M. E. O'Brien) 1931 by Cranley Jim out of Busy of Harnish. Bred by Mrs Hallowell-Carew. Blue.

Afton Wallace 1899.

Cranley Blue Boy 1903.

Buckenham Blue 1915 by Benwell Joe out of Findern Blue Bell.

Budget 382Q (R. Brown) 1909 by Dudley Blue Boy out of Dudley Blue Girl. Bred by M. Robson. Blue.

Busy of Harnish (Mrs Hallowell-Carew) 1929 by Bluehouse Barnabas out of Jill of Mottisfont. Bred by H. Cox.

C.

Cadbury Sam (C. T. D. Burchell) 1926 by The Deil out of Garw Hilda. Bred by W. J. Lewis.

Camperdown Jean 1917 by Jock's Lodge out of Whilensleaf. Bred by R. M. Roberts. Liver.

Camwood Gipsy or Colmswood Gipsy by Ewood Eclipse out of Midmoor Jean. I am uncertain as to the correct form of the name.

Cap of Gold 693LL (Mrs Hallowell-Carew) 1928 by Ishmel out of Golduma. Bred by Mrs B. Holgate. Blue and tan.

Capricious 1621HH (A. C. Tolhurst) 1926 by Pugnacity out of Valpre Jip. Bred by owner. Blue.

Captain Kettle 2057JJ (Dr and Mrs French) 1927 by Blue Rival out of Silvo (NT). Bred by R. Ball. Blue.

Castleton Puss by Castleton Twig out of Priscilla Punch.

Castleton Twig by Clyde Boy out of Mab (NT) (Croisdale's).

Charlie R5266 by Midmoor Jock out of Sudston Pearl.

Chelsea Blue Girl (L. Jafrate) 1909 by Boniface out of Tweedside Girl. Bred by R. C. Irving. I have seen another breeding given for this bitch in an otherwise apparently reliable pedigree, but the above are the facts as stated when she was registered by the K.C. and afterwards confirmed in K.C.S.B.

Chhota Peg (Mrs H. S. Brown) 1923 by Laird Joe out of Morning Light.

Chhota Sahib (H. S. Brown) 1922 by Stepdancer out of Rose R5680. Bred by Bower. Blue.

Chief 6665 (Jackson) 1870 by Redman (NT) (Mavin) out of Meg (NT) (Gibbs).

Child's Lad by Berwick Blue Boy out of Nettle (NT).

Chinchilla Jeanne (Misses Edwards) 1923 by Tatters R5632 out of Romping Rags. Bred by F. R. Day.

Chippinghouse Piper (W. H. Parker) 1923 by Park Blue Boy (NT) out of Sadie. Bred by J. W. Cooper.

Choker 15651 (H. B. Watson) 1880 by Tipper R666 out of Rosebud R305. Bred by J. Black.

Christmas Daisy 1197CC (Mrs Thompson) 1920 by Jock's Lodge out of Princess Floss.

Chum R5190 by Sudston Prince out of Nell or Floss (NT). This pedigree is somewhat doubtful.

Chutney Revival 27JJ, Champion (J. W. Bennett) 1927 by Cribden Chutney out of Tamar Implacable. Bred by A. T. Sutton. Blue.

Chutney's Double 438LL (A. S. Watson) 1929 by Cribden Chutney out of Tamar Implacable. Bred by J. Bennett. Blue.

Clansman 9581 (G. Ross) 1878 by Sam R158 out of Wasp R130. Blue. Weighed 24½lb. at 10 years old. Height 15½ins.

Clansman of Critonia 931HH (J. H. Woodward) 1926 by King's Own out of Bonzette. Bred by owner. Blue.

Cleg or Meg R244 (Henderson or Young) by Rattler R5697 out of Phoebe R160.

Cleopatra (Mrs Dawes) 1922 by Shothanger Robert out of Boxmoor Mary. Bred by Mrs T. N. Keith.

Clive Blue Maid (W. Williams) 1924 by Syringa out of Clive Fly (NT). Bred by owner.

Clyde Bob 1897 by Prymas (NT) out of Diamond Queen (NT).

Clyde Boy 41318, Champion (W. Wears) 1894 by Tip (NT) (A. Armstrong) out of Nell (NT) (R. Jordison). In some pedigrees the dam's name is given as Nettle but the K.C. registration and stud book give it as above. The stud book says 'further pedigree unknown'. For some time this dog was known as Beaconsfield Typhoon. For Tip, see note on Beaconsfield Triumph.

Clyde Boy's Ghost (H. Clay) 1924 by Deckham Crest out of Little Gem. Bred by J. Pearson.

Clyde Girl (J. Donnison) by Tip (NT)

(Armstrong) out of Nettle R352. For Tip, see note on Beaconsfield Triumph.

Clyde Peach 37239, dogs (Wears and Patterson) 1890 by Peach (Brewis) out of Nettle R354. Bred by H. White. Liver.

Clyde Pincher 152J (W. Wears) 1903 by Deansfield Piper out of Pride of Dudley. Bred by M. Robson. Blue.

Clyde Wallace 1270B (Wears formerly Jordison) 1896 by Tip (NT) (Armstrong) out of Beaconsfield Tourist. Liver. For Tip see note on Beaconsfield Triumph.

Coalcutter 1913 by Coalstriker out of Lady Newsham.

Coalstriker (L. Peacock) 1912 by Beaconsfield Toxophilite out of Isabella Newsham. Bred by owner.

Coatsworth King (J. Joicey) by Victor Wild out of Clyde Girl.

Coatsworth Lill 1362D (H. Graham) 1898 by Travers (NT) out of Pleasant Lass. Bred by Messrs Elliot and Devlin. Blue.

Cobledene Meg by Deansfield Monarch out of Junora.

Cobledene Pat 1914 by Piper (NT) (Mooney) out of Rose (NT). Bred by Burns.

Cobledene Squire 1912 by Piper (NT) (Gibson) out of Rosey (NT). Bred by Burns.

Collingham Keeper 1906 by Deansfield Piper out of Goxhill Frisk.

Colmswood Gipsy. See Camwood.

Colonel (Nixon) 1877 by Lion (Dunn) out of Jess (NT) or Wasp (NT). See note on Jamie who was Colonel's brother.

Comicator 1920 by Bagpipes out of Trixie (NT). Bred by M. Fish.

Commercial Lady (W. S. Wright) 1927 by Moving Didy out of Glendale Nellie. Bred by J. Heal.

Copsewood Blue Boy 27HH (Mrs Lang) 1925 by Willycrags out of Ellington Jenny. Bred by W. Waddell. Blue.

Copsterhill Blue Girl (B. W. Tweedale) 1924 by Moving Knight out of Lively Judy. Bred by Miss Evans.

Copsterhill Dinkie 132LL (B. W. Tweedale) 1929 by Square Deal out of Copsterhill Blue Girl. Bred by owner. Blue.

Corrella (J. Stephenson) 1930 by Scottie out of Hydesville Jean. Bred by R. Edminson.

Corrig Pincher (C. H. Redhead) 1915 by Rambler out of Seaham Hall. Bred by owner.

Corrig Sally (C. H. Redhead) 1915 by Rambler out of Seaham Hall. Bred by owner.

Corstorphine Lass (Mrs Laidlaw) 1923 by Croxteth Blue Imp out of Corrig Sally. Bred by C. H. Redhead.

Cottage Rose (J. Hedley) 1924 by Music out of Wannie (NT). Bred by J. J. Bower. The dam was the same bitch that appears as the dam of Leo but I have not been able to find how she was bred.

Country Girl R355 by Clyde Boy out of Nettle (NT). I have not found that this bitch was ever registered at K.C. but another of the same name by Beaconsfield Technical out of Goxhill Rags was born in 1909 and registered in 1911. Another was registered in 1923. See below.

Country Girl R6967 (G. Cairns) 1923 by Music Master out of Cranbrook Jean (NT). Bred by S. Gilholme.

Craghead Eclipse 1911 by Breakwater Eclipse out of Nellie (NT) (Pearson).

Craghead Kwamaxosa 407R (W. R. Scott) 1910 by Tim R5707 out of Myrtle R5708. Bred by H. E. Barber. Liver.

Craghead Piper (W. R. Scott) 1912 by Craghead Surprise out of Green Lane Vixen. Bred by owner.

Craghead Surprise 408R (W. R. Scott) 1910 by Bellerby Surprise out of Nettle (NT). Bred by J. Wilson. Blue.

Cramling Peggy (H. J. Skillings) 1926 by Active Lad out of Nell (NT). Bred by Mrs Steele.

Cranley Blue Belle 369H (H. Warnes) 1903 by Silversmith out of Miss Oliver. Bred by owner. Blue.

Cranley Blue Boy 368H (H. Warnes) 1903 by Silversmith out of Miss Oliver. Bred by owner. Blue.

Cranley Jim 21MM (H. Warnes) 1928 by King's Pawn out of Cranley Judy. Bred by owner. Blue.

Cranley Jix 1561KK (H. Warnes) 1928 by King's Pawn out of Cranley Judy. Bred by owner. Blue.

Cranley Judy 121HH (H. Warnes) 1926 by Cribden Chutney out of Highland Princess. Bred by W. S. Wright. Blue.

Cranley Peggy 434S (H. Warnes) 1911 by Breakwater Eclipse out of Northern Girl. Bred by owner. Blue.

Cranley Rosette 281F (H. Warnes) 1900 by Clyde Bob out of Miss Oliver. Bred by owner. Liver.

Cranley Sentinel 487N (H. Warnes) 1907 by Deansfield Piper out of Cross House Beauty. Bred by S. Gilholm. Blue.

Cranley Tatters by Elswick Piper out of Cranley Blue Belle.

Cribden Centaur 786NN (Misses Maunsell and Hamilton) 1930 by Cribden Conservative out of Cribden Clytie. Bred by A. S. Watson. Blue.

Cribden Choice (A. S. Watson) 1924 by Garw Jim out of Ellington Nell. Bred by owner.

Cribden Chutney 725FF, Champion (A. S. Watson) 1924 by Moving Knight out of Glendale Nellie. Bred by J. Heal. Blue. Formerly known as Mountain Rover.

Cribden Clytie (A. S. Watson) 1927 by Deckham Crest out of Winfield Lady. Bred by J. T. Barnes.

Cribden Connie 147GG (A. S. Watson) 1925 by Moving Knight out of Glendale Nellie. Bred by J. Heal. Blue.

Cribden Conservative (A. S. Watson) 1924 by Garw Jim out of Ellington Nell. Bred by owner.

Cribden Cracker 131LL (A. S. Watson) 1928 by Gingerino out of Mona (NT). Bred by E. Williams. Blue. Formerly registered as Glendale Jim.

Cross House Beauty 554M (W. Jobson) 1904 by Fountain Boy out of Lady Ord. Bred by owner. Liver.

Crossley Result 29951 (E. Taylor) 1889 by Warkworth Hotspur out of Miss Burton. Bred by owner. Blue.

Crowner R128 (Rutter) by Dante R46 out of Betty R47. There were other Crowners.

Croxteth Blue Boy 1920 by Breakwater Chieftain out of Salamander Lass. Bred by A. Pow.

Croxteth Blue Imp 1179CC (C. A. Haynes) 1920 by The Piper R5202 out of Curragh Belle. Bred by Davies.

Curragh Belle (A. J. Warburton) 1909 by Darnall Blue Boy out of Torfield Peggy. Bred by owner.

Cut-tailed Piper (T. Urron) by Ch. Piper 7698 out of Jess R165 also called Cuttail Piper.

D.

Dainty Girl (Mrs E. Bruce-Low) 1927 by Gingerino out of Clive Blue Maid. Bred by W. Williams.

Dainty Lady 1978HH, Champion (Miss Edwards and Mr Clifford) 1925 by Hop-a-long out of Chinchilla Jeanne. Bred by the Misses Edwards. Blue.

Daisy R25 (William Clark of Bedlington) by J. Curley's Scamp out of Meg R24. The parentage of Curley's Scamp is not known. He must be distinguished from his grandson, Clark's Scamp R27. See History. There is a good deal of difficulty in distinguishing between the various early Daisies.

Daisy R25A (also Clark's) by Billy R23 out of Meg R24A. See also Daisy R25. Clark had at least two Daisies and two Megs. See History.

Daisy R30 (Bagalee) by Viper 'the Moorhouse dog' out of an unnamed bitch. It seems probable that the Moorhouse dog was a descendant of Piper R15 and Phoebe R14 but see History.

Daisy R44 (Gibbs) by Rattler R34 out of Meg (NT) (Gibbs).

Daisy R48 or Young Daisy (Gibbs) by Dante R46 out of Daisy R25. I have seen it suggested also that the dam was Daisy R44.

Daisy R197 (J. Monkman also C. T. Maling) by Rustic late Victor R303 out of Hannah Dobbs. Bred by Monkman.

Daisy R5666 (J. Holt) by Tweedside Lad out of Portland Lass (NT).

Daisy R5875 (C. A. Gilzean) 1916 by Titch out of Queenie R5186. Bred by R. C. Irving.

Dancing Jimmy 617HH (W. J. Gingell) 1925 by Moving Knight out of Flashlight. Bred by owner. Blue.

Dancing Molly (W. Whitaker) 1924 by Eccleshill Blue Boy out of Laughing Tansie. Bred by J. Jennings.

Champion Seaham Hall 1908.

Tak-a-Bit 1908.

Dante R46 (J. Gibbs) by Rattler R34 out of Jess (NT), sister to Gibbs's Bitter. So given in pedigree of Strathblane. In pedigree of Sentinel the dam is given as Gibbs's Bess, which I am inclined to think is a slip of the pen, but am not confident about it. There were at least two other Dantes and, perhaps because it does not appear a particularly appropriate name for a Bedlington, it is frequently corrupted to Dainty. See History.

Dark Dinah by Coquet Lad (NT) out of Coquet Lass (NT).

Darnall Blue Boy (A. J. Warburton) by Clyde Pincher out of Nettle R5208.

Darville's Desire (F. J. Smith) 1923 by Eccleshill Blue Boy out of Gandy Bridge Jewel. Bred by W. Neil.

Dawn of Day 39LL (W. J. Onions) 1928 by Fly Bob out of Moving Cheek. Bred by A. Wilkinson. Blue.

Day Express 1482FF (A. Wilkinson) 1924 by Moving Knight out of Express Delight. Bred by owner. Blue.

Dazzler Demon 22MM (S. Barker) 1929 by Cribden Chutney out of Breezehill Opal. Bred by owner. Liver.

Dazzler Gem 1357MM, Champion (S. Barker) 1930 by Cribden Chutney out of Breezehill Opal. Bred by owner. Liver.

Dazzler Queen 526MM (S. Barker) 1930 by Cribden Chutney out of Breezehill Opal. Bred by owner. Blue.

Dazzler Queenie 789NN (S. Barker) 1930 by Cribden Chutney out of Breezehill Opal. Bred by owner. Blue.

Deansfield Chieftain. See Breakwater Chieftain.

Deansfield Jean (J. Donnison) 1926 by Moving Knight out of Rytonian Blue Girl. Bred by T. E. Brown.

Deansfield Monarch 203W 1913 by Bellerby Surprise out of Junora. Bred by C. Lindi.

Deansfield Piper 1621J, Champion (J. Donnison) 1901 by Coatsworth King out of Floss R5272. Bred by R. Donnison. Blue and tan. The great sire of the beginning of the present century. I believe his name appears somewhere in every pedigree that can be traced back so far. Seventeen of his sons and daughters appear in this list.

Deansfield Tip by Ord out of Clyde Girl.

Dear Goodness 863DD, Champion (Misses Maunsell and Hamilton) 1922 by Sperksforde Jackanapes out of Heart of Hell. Bred by owners. Blue.

Death or Glory (Messrs Rudge and Robson) 1907 by Deansfield Piper out of Cross House Beauty. Bred by S. Gilholm.

Deckham Aid (W. J. Onions) 1919 by Eccleshill Blue Boy out of Breakwater Lorna. Bred by J. King.

Deckham Crest 1023DD, Champion (W. J. Onions) 1922 by Stoneferry Jock's Double out of Blue Surprise. Bred by T. Fields. Blue.

Deckham Ocorey 1478GG (W. J. Onions) 1925 by Night Express out of Flare Light. Bred by Mrs Wilson. Blue.

Deckham Odream 578MM (W. J. Onions) 1928 by Deckham O'Great out of Deckham Oever Queen. Bred by J. J. Bower. Liver. Originally registered as Light Revere.

Deckham Oever Queen (W. J. Onions) 1927 by Moving Didy out of Glendale Nellie. Bred by J. Heal.

Deckham Ogim 274KK (W. J. Onions) 1928 by Night Express out of Old Hall Lass. Bred by R. Dagless. Blue.

Deckham O'Great 1340JJ, Champion (W. J. Onions) 1927 by Moving Knight out of Dinton Blue Gown. Bred by J. Nixon. Liver. Originally registered as Flambrough Hero.

Deckham Olad 1300FF (W. J. Onions) 1924 by Moving Knight out of Pride of Hetton. Bred by J. Hughes. Blue.

Deckham Omay 563GG (W. J. Onions) 1925 by Piper (NT) out of Minnie (NT). Bred by W. Elliott. Blue.

Deckham Onlaw 1355MM (W. J. Onions) 1930 by Gardeners Perfection out of Milbourne Flo. Bred by W. E. Miles. Liver.

Deckham Only 26HH (W. J. Onions) 1926 by Piper R5690 out of Patsy R5691. Bred by J. Watson. Blue.

Deckham Onnie 1344KK W. J. Onions) 1929 by Worton Demon out of Glendale Nellie. Bred by J. Heal. Blue.

Deckham Opia 524JJ (W. J. Onions) 1927 by Rough Night out of Glendale Lucy. Bred by Mrs M. Wilson. Liver.

Deckham Oprecious 1560KK, Champion (Misses M. M. and C. R. Carr) 1928 by Saval Boy out of Bit of Fashion. Bred by A. Maddison. Blue.

Deckham Oprince 528KK (W. J. Onions) 1928 by Scottie out of Nell (NT). Bred by owner. Blue.

Deckham Oprincess 1302GG (W. J. Onions) 1925 by Night Express out of Flare Light. Bred by Mrs Wilson. Blue.

Deckham Oreal 1270LL (W. J. Onions) 1929 by Scottie out of Nancy (NT). Bred by Mrs S. Collin. Liver.

Deckham Oreany 957HH (W. J. Onions) 1926 by Duplicate out of Minnie (NT). Bred by owner. Blue.

Deckham Shepherd 198CC, Champion W. J. Onions) March 1921 by Willycraggs out of Dolly Tint. Bred by M. Harrison. Blue.

Deckham Stamp 1181CC, Champion (W. J. Onions) October 1921 by Willycraggs out of Dolly Tint. Bred by owner. Liver.

Deckham Stormer 288DD (W. J. Onions) 1921 by Mickel out of Nell (NT). Bred by C. Newman.

Deil, The, 1600EE (W. J. Lewis) 1922 by Desperado out of Miss Dewley. Bred by R. Young. Liver.

Derryvolgie 1288G (Mrs W. B. Baty) 1901 by Piper (NT) (Harvey) out of Rosey (NT). Bred by J. McGlade. Blue.

Desperado 1920 by Coalstriker out of Lady Bomersund. Bred by Messrs Laws and Shiel.

Diana R5369 (G. Brown) by Silversmith out of Little Nell (NT). Meg is given as the dam in another pedigree I have seen.

Dimple 1916 by Sperkeforde Jackanapes out of Dinah's Double. Bred by W. P. Tate.

Dina R5368 by Bellerby Surprise out of Junora.

Dinah R149 (Crow) by Past I R241 out of Jess 6678.

Dinah Grey (C. Haworth) 1926 by Eccleshill Blue Boy out of Switch (NT). Bred by owner.

Dinah's Double 821AA 1915 by Benwell Joe out of Findern Blue Bell. Bred by E. E. Farrer. Blue.

Dinkie's Double (R. Boucher) 1931 by Night Express out of Welldon. Bred by Miss M. Pattison.

Dinton Blue Gown (J. Nixon) 1924 by Garw Jim out of Dinton Rightaway. Bred by W. Orkney.

Dinton Rightaway (W. Orkney) 1923 by Moving Knight out of Lady (NT). Bred by owner.

Dolly Tint 1919 by Patrick's Blue out of War Baby. Bred by J. McGlade.

Domino 13176 (Watson) 1881 by Petrarch out of Bagatelle.

Doneraile Boy 410R (W. Crabb) 1910 by Brompton Bobby out of Doneraile Girl. Bred by owner. Liver.

Doneraile Gem 1632S (W. Crabb) 1910 by Brompton Bobby out of Chelsea Blue Girl. Bred by W. Clanzy. Blue.

Doneraile Girl (W. Crabb) by Boniface out of Tweedside Girl.

Don Jeanette (H. Grain) 1926 by Sing-to-me out of Gipsy (NT). Bred by J. Grain.

Don't be Talkin' (Misses Maunsell and Hamilton) 1923 by Sperkeforde Jackanapes out of Heart of Hell. Bred by owners.

Dracula 525MM (Miss Herdman) 1929 by Chutney Revival out of Rytonian Galaxy. Bred by Miss Irwin. Liver.

Dragon Fly. See Arrah-go-on.

Driscoll Jerry (J. Smith) 1922 by Breakwater Chieftain out of Hopwood Girl. Bred by owner.

Dudley Blue Boy 653L (M. Robson) 1904 by Deansfield Piper out of Pride of Dudley. Bred by owner. Blue.

Dudley Blue Girl (M. Robson) 1904 by Deansfield Piper out of Pride of Dudley. Bred by owner.

Duns Blue Lady 1343JJ (F. Mawson) 1926 by Moving Knight out of Hidden Treasure. Bred by C. S. Bell. Blue.

Duplicate 679FF (W. Shiel) 1924 by Stepdancer out of Ellington Nell. Bred by Waddell.

Dusky Queen by Tyndale Roger (NT) out of Kit (NT). Bred by G. Morton.

E.

Ebchester Tip R42 1869 (Stoddart) by Dante R46 out of Bess (NT) (Dodd). Bred as above according to pedigree of Sentinel. In Strathblane's pedigree the dam is given as Clark's Daisy R25. I cannot say with absolute certainty which is correct, but incline to the version given above.

Eccleshill Blue Boy 822AA 1917 by Bellerby Surprise out of Floss R5183. Bred by G. W. Darking. Blue. There are twenty of his children named in this list.

Eccleshill Lucky Boy (J. King) 1923 by Piper's Surprise out of Bess (NT). Bred by G. Holmes.

Eccleshill Trumpeter 1920 by Eccleshill Blue Boy out of Nell (NT). Bred by A. Messenger.

Elizabet (R. Boucher) 1929 by Deckham O'Great out of La Reine. Bred by W. Shiel.

Ellington Jenny (W. Waddell) 1923 by Stepdancer out of Ellington Nell.

Ellington Nell 326FF (W. Waddell) 1921 by Desperado out of Ellington Swank. Bred by owner. Blue.

Ellington Swank (W. Waddell) by Take Me out of Gyp R5270.

Elswick Piper (J. Blench) 1902 by Silversmith out of Miss Wilson. Bred by W. Wilson.

Elswick Type 1278H (J. Blench) 1903 by Clyde Boy out of Regalia Regina. Bred by owner. Liver.

En Garde 130PP (D. Morgan) 1930 by Billongho out of Blue Passion. Bred by W. Yates. Blue.

England Rose 1917 by Coalstriker out of Jess R5681. Bred by L. Peacock.

Esmeralda (F. R. Day) 1926 by Pugnacity out of Perversity. Bred by W. E. Philpots.

Esperanza 563NN, Champion (Mrs E. M. Bartlett) 1931 by Cribden Chutney out of Tamar Implacable. Bred by J. Bennett. Blue.

Euxton Lad 956HH (R. Forshaw) 1924 by Driscoll Jerry out of Nett (NT). Bred by W. J. Jackman. Blue.

Evelyn (J. Heal) 1925 by Saval Boy out of Queenie R5710. Bred by M. Lewis.

Ewood Eclipse 204W 1913 by Falinge Blue Boy out of Ewood Floss. Bred by J. Ward.

Ewood Floss 489N (J. Ward) 1907 by Berwick Brigadier out of Tweedside Lady. Bred by Mrs Mather. Dark blue.

Ewood Nell by Ewood Eclipse out of Pitland Nell.

Express Delight (W. R. Peacock) 1921 by Willycraggs out of England Rose. Bred by owner.

F.

Fairplay 1183CC (W. L. Peacock) 1921 by Willycraggs out of England Rose. Bred by owner.

Fairy Flax 1918 by Ewood Eclipse out of Daisyfield Floss (NT). Bred by M. Lee.

Falinge Blue Boy (A. Kershaw) 1911 by Rory O'More out of Dinah (NT). Bred by J. Ward. Blue.

Fancy R45 (Gibson) by Piper (NT) (Revel) out of Phoebe (Coates). I presume that Phoebe is meant to be Phoebe R14, the dam of Ainsley's Piper R16 but I doubt whether it can be correct. The item is obtained from the pedigree of one of the late Mr Alcock's dogs in the K.C.S.B. for 1889. It would make Clansman, who was born in 1878, the great-great-grandson of Phoebe R14, who was born before 1820, and I think there must have been more generations between them.

Fern Bank Biddy by Barmoor Squire (NT) (J. Steele) out of Madame Camwal.

Fettler (W. Brewis) by Billy R341 out of Jess R344.

Field House Jock (Mrs Messenger) 1922 by Deckham Aid out of Lady (NT). Bred by owner.

Fife Lady by Blyth Briton out of Country Girl (NT). I have seen this bitch appear in a pedigree as 'Fifi,' but I hope that the other is the correct version. I do not know which Country Girl was the dam. See note under that name.

Findern Blue Bell (J. Warburton) 1911 by Breakwater Chief out of Findern Queen. Bred by E. E. Farrer.

Findern Queen 412R (Rev E. E. Farrer) 1910 by Goxhill Tatters out of Biddy (NT). Bred by owner. Liver.

Falinge Blue Boy 1911.

Champion Breakwater Chieftan 1911.

Firefly R5277 (Edminson) by Silver-smith out of Beaconsfield Teaser. There was, I think, also another Firefly.

Fishwick Blue Bird (Cooke) 1923 by Driscoll Jerry out of Golbourne Lass (NT). Bred by J. Woan.

Flare Light (W. J. Gingell) 1923 by Girardville Boy out of Ruby R5267. Bred by owner.

Flashlight (W. J. Gingell) 1923 by Rhondda Billy out of Lady Evelyn. Bred by J. Heal.

Flint, or Old Flint (Squire Trevelyan of Netherwitton). His parents are un-known but it is said that he was whelped in the year 1782 or 1792 which is the oldest date recorded in Bedlington annals – though we can hardly claim the name of Bedlington for him. See History.

Flora R5195 (Mrs E. Burns) by Break-water Fisher out of Wild Lassie.

Florrie R5670 by Hammond alias Jolly Barber out of Clyde Girl.

Floss R342 (T. Urron) by Pat I R241 out of Jess 6678.

Floss R5183 (G. W. Darking) by River-side Rufus out of Beetly Vixen.

Floss R5272 (R. Donnison) by Deansfield Tip out of Florrie R5670.

Floss R5664 by Piper R5665 out of Nancy R3980.

Floss R5696 (G. Bramley) by Break-water Chief out of Venus (NT).

Flowerseller (R. Edminson) 1927 by Moving Didy out of Glendale Nellie. Bred by J. Heal.

Fly (C. C. Spragget) by Young Devon out of Cleg or Meg R244.

Fly Bob (T. Topham) 1927 by Blue Sahib out of Mornington Minnie. Bred by owner.

Forgotten Fashion (J. Wright) 1926 by Moving Knight out of Lady Lintie. Bred by owner.

Founding Peg (G. H. Rowe) 1926 by Break of Dawn out of Tatters R5679. Bred by Davies.

Fountain Boy (W. Jobson) by Break-water Flash out of Nellie (NT).

Fraiflor (W. Williams) 1908 by Bromp-ton Bobby out of Jethart Clyde Girl. Bred by Dower.

Fury R248 (Gough) by Jack 3412 out of Tyne 3430.

G.

Gandy Bridge Jewel 1920 by Le Roy out of Recruiting Lady. Bred by T. Roper.

Gardeners Admiration 564NN (E. Metcalfe) 1931 by Cribden Chutney out of Lady Gay. Bred by Mrs Jolley. Liver.

Gardeners Alderman 500QQ (E. Met-calf) 1933 by Gardeners Supremacy out of Kirkhill Maid. Bred by J. Alder. Blue.

Gardeners Barmaid (E. Metcalf) 1929 by Gardeners Mark out of Night Barmaid. Bred by owner.

Gardeners Choice 1987PP (E. Metcalf) 1933 by Gardeners Supremacy out of Betty's Girl. Bred by Dr J. Wilkin-son. Blue.

Gardeners Eclipse 18PP (E. Metcalf) 1932 by Gardeners Supremacy out of Welldon. Bred by Miss M. Pattison. Blue.

Gardeners Elegance 1989PP, Cham-pion (E. Metcalf) 1933 by Gardeners Supremacy out of Welldon. Bred by Miss M. Pattison. Blue.

Gardeners Elite 861HH (E. Metcalf) 1926 by Night Express out of Blue Maid. Bred by owner. Blue.

Gardeners Essential 739PP, Cham-pion (Dr J. Wilkinson) 1932 by Gardeners Supremacy out of Well-don. Bred by Miss M. Pattison. Blue.

Gardeners Express (E. Metcalf) 1926 by Night Express out of Cottage Rose. Bred by J. Hedley.

Gardeners Exquisite 439LL (E. Met-calf) 1929 by Gardeners Mark out of Night Barmaid. Bred by owner. Blue.

Gardeners Ideal 1218JJ (E. Metcalf) 1927 by Gardeners Mark out of Tatters R5679. Bred by B. Davies. Blue.

Gardeners Jewel 1900MM (E. Metcalf) 1931 by Night Express out of Gar-deners Barmaid. Bred by owner. Blue.

Gardeners Mark 1850HH (E. Metcalf) 1926 by Night Express out of Blue Maid. Bred by owner. Blue.

Gardeners Perfection 275KK, Cham-pion (E. Metcalf) 1928 by Gardeners Mark out of Tatters R5679. Bred by B. Davies. Blue.

Gardeners Poacher 525JJ (Miss C. R. Carr) 1927 by Night Express out of Cottage Rose. Bred by J. Hedley. Blue.

Gardeners Renown 694LL (E. Metcalf) 1929 by Gardeners Mark out of Night Barmaid. Bred by owner. Blue.

Gardeners Sublime 1693MM (E. Metcalf) 1930 by Night Express out of Beadle Blue Nettle. Bred by W. Cole. Blue.

Gardeners Supremacy 21NN, Champion (E. Metcalf) 1930 by Gardeners Exquisite out of Gardeners Supreme. Bred by owner. Blue.

Gardeners Supreme 1219JJ, Champion (E. Metcalf) 1927 by Night Express out of Beadle Blue Nettle. Bred by W. Cole. Blue.

Garw Hilda 13DD (W. J. Lewis) 1922 by Willycraggs out of Bella Ross. Bred by owner.

Garw Jess (W. J. Lewis) 1923 by Garw Rags out of Joffreta. Bred by owner.

Garw Jim 862DD, Champion (W. J. Lewis) 1922 by Deckham Shepherd out of Moon Maiden. Bred by owner. Blue.

Garw Rags (W. J. Lewis) 1922 by Willycraggs out of Bella Ross. Bred by owner.

Gay Billy 284RR (D. Pitt) 1934 by Knowlton Peter Pan out of Blue Bussell. Bred by owner.

Gentle Mary 278KK (J. G. Burrell) 1927 by Jock's Surprise out of Bongrace. Bred by H. Bottomley. Blue.

Geordie's Fancy (G. Brown) 1929 by Peg's Pal out of Scotch Jean. Bred by Mrs N. Foggan.

Gibbs's liver-coloured dog by Billy R23 out of Wasp R22. This animal, whose name, if any, has not been preserved, has a place in history as sire of Gibbs's Rattler R34. He was brother to Clark's Meg R24. See History.

Gingerino (Williams) 1925 by Moving Knight out of Glendale Nellie. Bred by J. Heal.

Ginger Piper (W. Cavanagh) 1927 by Moving Knight out of Lady Changeful. Bred by J. A. Ure. Liver.

Gipsy R5692 by Piper R5693 out of Jessie R5694.

Girardville Boy (T. Lanyan) 1922 by Ewood Eclipse out of Nell (NT). Bred by A. W. Smith. This dog sometimes appears in pedigrees as Gerald Villa Boy but he was registered at the K.C. as I have given it.

Glendale Lucy (J. Heal) 1925 by Moving Knight out of Glendale Nellie. Bred by owner.

Glendale Nellie (J. Heal) 1921 by Charlie R5266 out of Ruby R5267. Bred by W. J. Gingell.

Glevum Knight (A. Gardner) 1924 by Moving Knight out of Glevum Meggy. Bred by owner.

Glevum Meggy (A. Gardner) 1922 by Sperkeforde Jackanapes out of Undine. Bred by R. P. Wilson.

Glooper 163NN (E. and P. Wears) 1929 by Night Express out of Deckham Oever Queen. Bred by J. J. Bower. Blue.

Go Bang (J. Kennedy) 1893 by The Goldsmith out of Berwick Blue Bell.

Gold Dust R5523 by Goldfinder out of Mollie (NT). Name also written Goldust.

Golden Wonder 1001NN (Mrs F. Palmer) 1931 by Night Cap out of Meditation. Bred by owner. Liver.

Golden Wreath by The Goldsmith out of ??????. This bitch's name generally appears in pedigrees as Golden Reef but is given as Wreath by K.C. in Blyth Bob's registration and in K.C.S.B. for 1901.

Goldfinder 1895 by Goldseeker out of Miss Chance.

Goldseeker 1321A, Champion (J. Kennedy) 1894 by Alnwick Cadger out of Go Bang. Bred by owner. Liver.

Goldsmith, The 32387 (J. Dryden) 1890 by Hammond alias Jolly Barber out of Needle. Bred by H. White. Liver. In the K.C.S.B. entry of The Goldsmith in 1892 it is stated that the pedigree of the dam Needle is unknown. This should be authoritative, but I have seen her parentage given as by Venture (Rogerson) out of Nettle (White) which is unlikely and impossible unless White had two Nettles.

Goldsmith's Daughter 1894 by The Goldsmith out of Polly Burton.

Golduma (Mrs B. Holgate) 1927 by Sing-to-me out of Guard. Bred by owner.

Gollyway 490N, Champion (W. Crabb) 1907 by Jock of Oran out of Ye Bonnie Lass. Bred by Sibley. Dark blue.

Goodness Gracious 221GG (W. Shiel) 1925 by Stepdancer out of The Imp. Bred by owner. Liver.

Goxhill Beauty. See Breakwater Lorna.

Goxhill Blue Boy (H. Grayshon) 1922 by Piper's Surprise out of Nellie R5374. Bred by G. Farrer.

Goxhill Frisk (H. P. Ward) 1904 by Silversmith out of Nellie R5355.

Goxhill Rags (S. Richards) 1906 by Deansfield Piper out of Goxhill Frisk. Bred by Messrs Grayshon and Crawford.

Goxhill Tatters 557M, Champion (Messrs Grayshon and Crawford) 1906 by Deansfield Piper out of Goxhill Frisk. Bred by owners. Blue.

Grace (W. A. Wright) 1922 by Stoneferry Jock's Double out of Rose (NT). Bred by Headland.

Green Lane Brum (F. Perry) 1906 by Deansfield Piper out of Glory Quayle (NT). Bred by T. R. Jones.

Green Lane Vixen (F. Perry) 1907 by Bellerby Bishop out of Green Lane Brum. Bred by owner.

Griselda 628JJ (Mrs N. Hallows) 1926 by Glevum Knight out of Sheila. Bred by owner. Blue.

Guard 1185CC (B. Holgate) 1921 by Breakwater Chieftain out of Jenny (or Jeany) R5662. Bred by B. Whipp. Light liver and tan.

Guardsman 1948QQ (H. Scott-Dun) 1933 by En Garde out of Azure Model. Bred by D. Morgan. Liver.

Gyp R5270 by Askme out of Wass (NT).

Gyp R5430 by Breakwater Chief. The dam is said to have been named Floss but I feel very doubtful of the pedigree from which I have gathered these particulars and would like to have it confirmed.

Gyp R5683 by Piper R5684 out of Nell R5685.

Gyp R5701 (John Ainsley) by Scamp R27 out of Wassy R5702. See History.

Gypeena (Mrs C. H. Martin) 1917 by Brompton Bobby out of Blue Bird. Bred by owner.

H.

Hadaway Piper (Mrs E. A. Carr) 1932 by Dinkie's Double out of Deckham Oever Queen. Bred by J. J. Bower.

Hairdresser 14417, Champion (A. N. Dodd) 1882 by Projectile out of Vic R668 alias Blue Blood. Bred by owner. Blue. Mr Dodd was a great authority on the breed but gave up showing as a protest against the over-trimming and what he considered the 'faking' which became prevalent. The name he gave this dog was probably therefore a mild sarcasm.

Half Holiday 1920 by Lo Ben out of Saucy Peggy. Bred by J. Mooney.

Hammond (Hoggins) by Barber (Barnes) out of Jess R5671. Was some time known as Jolly Barber.

Handyman 1186CC, Champion (M. C. Hamilton) 1921 by Lo Ben out of Camperdown Jean. Bred by owner. Liver.

Hannah Dobbs (Monkman) by Colonel (Nixon) out of Kate Webster.

Happy Go Lucky 726FF (Misses Maunsell and Hamilton) 1923 by Moving Knight out of Sperkeforde Witch. Bred by owners. Liver.

Harwood Meg by Breakwater Chieftain out of Ewood Nell.

Hawfinch 918EE (M. C. Hamilton) 1923 by Handyman out of Redwings O'Phipson. Bred by Mrs Mitchison. Liver.

Heart of Hell 777GG (Misses Maunsell and hamilton) 1921 by Corrig Pincher out of Dimple. Bred by W. P. Tate. Blue.

Heebie Jeebie 503QQ (S. Barker) 1933 by Dazzler Demon out of Dazzler Queen. Bred by owner. Blue.

Heir Apparent, The, 871FF (Mrs Hallowell-Carew) 1924 by King's Own out of Heart of Hell. Bred by Misses Maunsell and Hamilton. Liver.

Hell for Leather (Misses Maunsell and Hamilton) 1922 by Sperkeforde Jackanapes out of Heart of Hell. Bred by owners.

Hell of a Night 930HH (Misses Maunsell and Hamilton) 1925 by The Kybosh out of Merry Hell. Bred by R. M. Bassett. Blue.

Champion Doneraile Snowball 1910.

A study in type. Champion Sperkeford Jackanapes 1911.

Hell's Belle 837KK (Dr Nolan) 1927 by Moving Knight out of Arrah-go-on. Bred by Misses Maunsell and Hamilton). Blue.

Hell's Bells 1359MM (W. Shiel) 1930 by Glooper out of La Reine. Bred by owner. Blue.

Hell's Delight (Mrs M. Harper) 1929 by Rathangan Piper out of Hell's Belle. Bred by Dr J. N. Greene Nolan.

Henry Codrington 65DD (Mrs Beck) 1922 by Jock's Lodge out of Queen Bee. Bred by R. C. Irving.

Her Ladyship 934HH (A. J. Lord) 1926 by Square Deal out of Lady Wynforem. Bred by owner. Blue.

Hidden Treasure (C. S. Bell) 1925 by Principality out of Hawfinch. Bred by W. E. Philpots.

Highland Lassie 1562KK (W. S. Wright) 1928 by King's Pawn out of Cranley Judy. Bred by H. Warnes. Blue and tan.

Highland Princess 179FF, Champion (W. S. Wright) 1924 by Moving Knight out of Lady Betty. Bred by owner. Blue.

Highwayman 901BB 1920 by Deansfield Monarch out of Camperdown Jean. Bred by M. C. Hamilton.

Hold Your Whisht 1966LL (Misses Maunsell and Hamilton) 1930 by The Kybosh out of Precious Nonsense. Bred by owners. Blue and tan.

Holloway Floss by Beaconsfield Technical out of Holloway Venus (NT).

Honeysuckle (Dr J. F. Knight) 1925 by Hop-a-long out of Chinchilla Jeanne. Bred by the Misses Edwards.

Hop-a-long 184EE (T. N. Keith) 1921 by Stepdancer out of Half Holiday. Bred by M. C. Hamilton. Blue.

Hopwood Girl (J. Smith) by Bagpipes out of Peggy R5525. I suspect that Peggy, dam of Hopwood Girl, was really Cranley Peggy, as she was bred the same way. Hopwood Girl was not registered at the K.C. so I cannot verify it.

Horncliffe Lass by Royal Stag out of Nettle (NT).

Hot Pickles (C. G. Worrell) 1931 by Cribden Chutney out of Battery Girl. Bred by H. Seddon.

Hotspur. See Warkworth Hotspur.

Hydesville Jean (R. Edminson) 1928 by Saval Boy out of Gallacher (NT). Bred by O'Brien.

Hydesville Night Hawk (R. Edminson) 1928 by Worton Demon out of Evelyn. Bred by J. Heal.

I.

Imp, The (W. Shiel) 1923 by Moving Knight out of Queen (NT). Bred by W. Onions.

Imperial 529FF (R. C. Irving) 1924 by Jock's Lodge out of Winsome Wendy. Bred by Mrs Needham. Blue.

Indigo Lad 1920 by Eccleshill Blue Boy out of Daisy R5666. Bred by J. Holt.

Intombi 1916 by Blue Coat (NT) out of Ganny (NT). Bred by Swoerby.

Irish Elegance (Miss Hallowell-Carew) 1923 by croxteth Blue Imp out of Corrig Sally. Bred by C. H. Redhead.

Isabella Newsham 413R (L. Peacock) 1910 by Askme out of Seaham Hall. Bred by E. Thirlwell. Blue.

Ishmael 1341JJ (Mrs B. Holgate) 1927 by Pugnacity out of Rose Dew. Bred by owner. Blue.

J.

Jack R116 (Caris or Robson) by Tartar (NT) (Pickett) out of Gip (NT) (Smith). I think, but am not quite certain, that it was this Jack that was the sire of Jess 6678.

Jack R5423 by Goxhill Tatters out of Breakwater Daisy (NT).

Jack 3412 (Lee, afterwards H. E. James) pedigree unknown. Liver. Was imported into Plymouth in a collier. Was entered in K.C.S.B. for 1874. Exhibited at many shows all over the country, and at Paris; he had a great success. He was most affectionate to human beings but would attack anything else that moved in his sight and eventually had to be destroyed.

Jacksonette (J. Jennings) 1920 by Mackley Mac (NT) out of Floss (NT). Bred by Colburn.

Jake (J. Pearson) 1922 by Blue Lad out of School Girl. Bred by S. Broad.

Jamie R151 about 1877, brother to Nixon's Colonel, by Lion (Dunn) out of Jess (NT) or Wasp (NT) (Wall or Spoor). There is a considerable divergence of opinion about the dam;

Spoor's Wasp seems the favourite but Jess or Jessie (Wall), Nettle (Moul) and Nell (Dunn) have also been given.

Jan R5181 (R. C. Irving) by Brompton Bobby out of Goxhill Rags.

Jane of Harnish 509PP (Mrs Hallowell-Carew) 1932 by Glooper out of Flowerseller. Bred by R. Edminson. Blue.

Jean R17 or Jin by Piper R15 out of Phoebe R14, and therefore sister to Piper R16. See History.

Jean R5709 (B. Robinson) by Son of a Knight out of Miss Echo.

Jenny or Jeany R5662 (B. Whipp) by Brisco Kim out of Brisco Mart.

Jennie the Piper 1303GG (A. Burton) 1924 by Stepdancer out of Ellington Nell. Bred by W. Waddell. Blue.

Jess R165 (Hedley) by Pat I R241 out of Jess 6678.

Jess R344 (Cook) by Tip R345 out of Meg (NT) (Gibson).

Jess R5371 (D. Ritchie) by Beaconsfield Tavy out of Diana R5369.

Jess R5671 (Perry) by Elswick Lad (NT) out of Jess (NT) (Hedley). There was more than one Elswick Lad and Hedley had more than one Jess and I do not know which these were.

Jess R5672 (Rundle) pedigree unknown. Came from Hartman's Kennels, Saltram House.

Jess R5681 (L. Peacock) by Beaconsfield Toxophilite out of Beaconsfield Temianka.

Jes 6678 (W. Matthews) 1874 by Jack R116 out of Victoria alias Meg R240. Bred by R. Robson. Liver.

Jessie R5694 by Bellerby Bishop out of Nellie (NT).

Jethart Clyde Girl (J. C. Dower) 1905 by Bobs (owner) (NT) out of Jethart Jenny (NT). Bred by owner. The sire is not the same as Bobs R5377.

Jethart Jess (A. Crawfurd) 1892 by Berwick Brick out of Merry Jyp 27810. Bred by Chambers.

Jethart Jet 1895 by Orme out of Jethart Jess.

Jiggles 1798KK (J. W. Bennett) 1928 by Cribden Chutney out of Queenie (NT). Bred by J. Smith. Blue.

Jill of Mottisfont 828JJ, Champion (H. Cox) 1927 by Copsewood Blue Boy out of Susan of Mottisfont. Bred by Commander Holbrook, V.C. Blue.

Jimmy of Braganza 692LL (Langford) 1927 by the Kybosh out of Sea Fire. Bred by Mrs Shapcott. Blue.

Jock of Duart (C. A. Gilzean) 1907 by Jock of Oran out of Tweedside Girl. Bred by R. C. Irving. See note under Top Hole who was really identical with this dog.

Jock of Oran 1538L (R. C. Irving) 1906 by Bobrikoff out of Tweedside Girl. Bred by owner. Blue.

Jock's Lodge 269V, Champion (R. C. Irving) 1914 by Top Hole out of Jan R5181. Bred by owner. Blue. This dog was the leading sire of the war years and those immediately following, and appears in a very great number of modern pedigrees. He died in 1924. This list contains the names of twenty-five of his sons and daughters.

Jock's Surprise (J. G. Burrell) 1925 by Cinders (NT) out of Nell (NT). Bred by L. Marsh.

Joffreta (H. A. Tutt) 1922 by Eccleshill Blue Boy out of Tegwen. Bred by owner.

Jolly Barber. The same as Hammond, which see.

Jon 1482JJ (Mrs F. Hamilton) 1927 by Leader Duke out of Rose Marie. Bred by owner. Blue.

Jubilee Surprise (J. Bibby) 1926 by Square Deal out of Little Minnie. Bred by C. Smith.

Judy R5210 by Spark (NT) (? Shark) out of Gipsy (NT).

Judy Pop (F. Royles) 1921 by Eccleshill Blue Boy out of Nellie (NT). Bred by J. Pearson.

Juno 10911 (H. E. James) 1879 by Jamie R151 out of Phoebe R5674. Bred by J. Calderwood. Liver.

Junora 1912 by Bluejacket out of Blue Bell R5419. Bred by Spurgeon. This bitch's name is often given as Genora.

Jyppy's Tibby 154MM (W. J. Onions) 1930 by Gardeners Perfection out of Merry Jyppy. Bred by D. Pitt. Blue.

K.

Kate Webster (J. Monkman) by Colonel (Nixon) out of Meg R225.

Killingholme Stickler 1919 by Breakwater Chieftain out of Sudston Pearl. Bred by Mrs Mead.

King's Own 324FF (Mrs Hallowell-Carew) 1923 by Le Roy out of Express Delight. Bred by A. Wilkinson. Blue.

King's Pawn 119HH, Champion (Mrs Hallowell-Carew) 1924 by King's Own out of Irish Elegance. Bred by owner. Blue.

Kirkhill Maid (J. Alder) 1931 by Gardeners Sublime ouf of Sunmaid. Bred by G. Tait.

Kiss in the Ring (Misses Maunsell and Hamilton) 1927 by Moving Knight out of Dear Goodness. Bred by owners.

Kitty Flyn (W. H. Barnes) 1923 by Deckham Stamp out of School Girl. Bred by Mrs Broad.

Klondyke Girl (P. Lugton) 1897 by Berwick Surprise out of Irene (NT). Bred by owner.

Knowlton Jill 626JJ (Miss F. M. Sturt) 1927 by Swift Knight out of Esmeralda. Bred by owner. Blue.

Knowlton John 740PP (Miss F. M. Sturt) 1930 by Knowlton Piper out of Moving Flash. Bred by owner. Blue.

Knowlton Junora (Miss C. E. Dobbie) 1932 by Cribden Centaur out of Bright Lass. Bred by Miss F. F. Sturt.

Knowlton Peter Pan 23MM, Champion (Miss F. M. Sturt) 1929 by Knowlton Piper out of Perdita. Bred by Mrs Day and owner. Blue. Died 1934.

Knowlton Piper 27NN (Miss F. M. Sturt) 1928 by Rathangan Piper out of Knowlton Jill. Bred by owner. Blue.

Knowlton Starlight 1990PP (Miss F. M. Sturt) 1931 by Knowlton Peter Pan out of Moving Flash. Bred by owner. Blue.

Kybosh, The 13188EE (Misses Maunsell and Hamilton) 1923 by Moving Knight out of Sperkeforde Witch. Bred by owners. Blue.

L.

Lady Aggalade (W. Cole) 1923 by Willycraggs out of Miss Dewley. Bred by R. Young.

Lady Betty 903BB 1920 by Eccleshill Blue Boy out of Fairy Flax. Bred by A. Hanes.

Lady Bomersund 1917 by Blyth Baronet out of Blyth Barmaid. Bred by J. H. Douglas.

Lady Changeful (J. Watson) 1926 by Piper R5690 out of Patsy R5691. Bred by owner. Blue.

Lady Chemist (G. Sidey) 1926 by Pugnacity out of Perversity. Bred by W. E. Philpots.

Lady Dazzler 40LL (S. Barker) 1928 by Cribden Chutney out of Breezehill Opal. Bred by owner. Liver.

Lady Donner 615NN (D. Henrey) 1931 by Bobby Dazzler out of Deansfield Jean. Bred by J. Donnison.

Lady Emma 2297HH (E. Williams) 1925 by Moving Knight out of Flashlight. Bred by W. J. Gingell. Blue.

Lady Evelyn 1917 by Jock's Lodge out of Findern Blue Bell.

Lady Gay (Mrs Jolley) 1928 by Gardeners Mark out of Night Betty. Bred by D. Jolley.

Lady Go Lightly (S. Atkin) 1921 by Eccleshill Blue Boy out of Nellie (NT). Bred by J. Pearson.

Lady Hazeldene 1919 by Buckenham Blue out of Bomb Girl. Bred by M. Lee. Her registration gives her dam as Breakwater Nell but this was apparently a name by which Bomb Girl was known before being registered.

Ladyhead Piper (A. Cunningham) 1929 by Moving Knight out of Ringlady. Bred by T. Roper.

Lady Lintie (J. Wright) 1925 by Stepdancer out of Country Girl. Bred by G. Cairns.

Lady Maureen. See Skin the Goat.

Lady Newsham (Menier) by Beaconsfield Tavy out of Diana R5369.

Lady of the Rock 414R (R. Allan) 1911 by Snowdoun Piper out of Jess R5371. Bred by D. Ritchie. Blue.

Lady Ord by Clyde Wallace out of Nettle (NT).

Lady Trail 1920 by Deansfield Monarch out of Camperdown Jean. Bred by M. C. Hamilton.

Lady Wynforem 1490EE (Mrs M.

Champion Night Express 1924.

Champion Ulsterman.

Thompson) 1923 by Le Roy out of Xmas Daisy. Bred by owner. Blue.

Laird Joe (Mrs Weeks) 1922 by Desperado out of Miss Dewley. Bred by R. Young.

Langside Lass (D. Ross) 1884 by Strathblane out of Meg R190. Bred by owner. Blue.

Langside Olive (D. Ross) by Clansman 9581 out of Langside Lass.

Langside Squire 29955 (D. Ross) 1889 by Rocket R292 out of Maid of Langside. Bred by owner. Blue.

Lap End (G. Sanderson) 1928 by Step Up out of Wannie II (NT). Bred by T. H. Miller.

La Reine 618HH (W. Shiel) 1926 by Duplicate out of Blue Bell Maid. Bred by C. S. Bell. Blue.

Lauder Baronet 1400LL (J. Ballantyne) 1928 by Moving Knight out of Rye Nellie. Bred by C. G. Worrall. Liver.

Laughing Tansie (J. Jennings) 1923 by Patricks Blue out of Blue Marvel (NT). Bred by Tyzack.

Leader Duke (J. Ballantyne) 1925 by Moving Knight out of Perversity. Bred by W. E. Philpots.

Leader of Simonside 569MM (W. J. Onions) 1930 by Deckham Oprecious out of Sotheron Blue. Bred by P. C. Herring. Blue. Was exported to America.

Leo (J. J. Bower) 1923 by Le Roy out of Wannie (NT). Bred by owner. The dam was the same Wannie that appears as dam of Cottage Rose but I do not know how she was bred.

Le Roy 1915 by Atton Gem out of Afton Daisy. Bred by A. Green. As sire of Ch. Moving Knight as well as of other good Bedlingtons, his name occurs very frequently in modern pedigrees.

Linthouse Blue Girl (J. Ferguson) 1924 by Eccleshill Blue Boy out of Tarfield Teasem (NT). Bred by J. Pearson.

Lion (Dunn) by Tearem 3429 out of Phoebe (MT) (Wall).

Little Boy Blue 562T (J. W. Blench) 1911 by Breakwater Eclipse out of Berwick Bella (NT). Bred by owner. Blue.

Little Demon (F. Ward) 1904 by Derryvolgie out of Dusky Queen. Bred by J. Cornforth.

Little Gem (J. Pearson) 1923 by Jake out of Judy Pop. Bred by P. J. Webstr.

Little Joker 1915 by Shield's Bluie out of Queen Bess. Bred by J. McGlade.

Little Minnie (C. Smith) 1924 by Sporting Chance out of Needle (NT). Bred by owner.

Little Remnant 1913 by Benwell Joe out of Miss Rhona. Bred by T. Roper.

Lively Judy (Miss Evans) 1922 by Breakwater Chieftain out of Ryeside Maid. Bred by J. Patrick.

Lo Ben 826AA, Champion 1914 by Breakwater Pierrot out of Nell (NT). Liver.

Long Odds of Bransways 1061QQ (Miss E. S. M. Branfoot) 1933 by Bluehouse Larry out of Sheisin. Bred by Miss Wallis. Liver.

Longscar (A. Maddison) 1922 by Sporting Chance out of Harwood Meg. Bred by G. Nicholson.

Lord Roberts by Chum R5190 out of Rose or Nellie (NT). The pedigrees from which I have got this are very doubtful and as neither the dog nor his alleged parents were registered I have been unable to verify it.

Lucky Lady 1919 by Breakwater Chieftain out of Nell R5194. Bred by W. Bramwell. Blue.

Lucky Lass (J. Bennett) 1924 by Ridge Hill Jock out of Bessema. Bred by T. Osborn.

M.

Machen Pride (F. J. Webb) 1907 by Boniface out of Nell (NT). Bred by owner.

Madame Camwal (G. Coulter) 1901 by Silversmith out of Nellie (NT). Bred by Law.

Maggie Murphy 1892 by Rodsley Bill (NT) out of Bridget 21371.

Magill Mysa 1913 by Sperkeforde Jackanapes out of Cranley Peggy. Bred by W. W. Savage.

Maid of Langside (D. Ross) 1885 by Clansman 9581 out of Langside Lass. Bred by owner. Blue and tan.

Majestic of Simonside 1799KK (Misses M. M. and C. R. Carr) 1929 by Moving Knight out of Broomilea Peggy. Bred by D. Pitt. Blue.

Mansfield Boy. See Breakwater Flash.

Marion of Dovesland 1919 by Jack (NT) out of Pamela. Bred by Allison.

Maritza of Critonia (Misses M. M. and C. R. Carr) 1926 by King's Own out of Prudence of Critonia. Bred by J. H. Woodward.

Markfield Monarch 1734LL (J. Bennett) 1930 by Cribden Chutney out of Tamar Implacable. Bred by owner. Blue.

Marks Dream 24MM (A. L. Bartlett) 1929 by Gardeners Mark out of Tatters R5679. Bred by B. Davies. Blue.

Masquerade (G. W. Kent) 1925 by Principality out of Blue Label. Bred by owner.

Mat 5580 (L. Batty) 1872 by Piper R50 out of Topsy R51. Bred by owner. Dark liver with wiry coat and light linty crown. Weighed 21 lbs. at 7 years old. Height 14⅝ inches. See History.

Matchem R2 (Mills of Netherwitton) by Flint, generally known as Old Flint belonging to Mr Trevelyan of Netherwitton. Dam unknown. See history.

Matchem R9 (Sherwood of Longhorsley) by Pincher R7 out of a bitch of William Wardle of Framlington. See history.

Maurena of Eldale 164NN (E. P. and E. W. Wears) 1931 by Leader of Simonside out of Nell (NT). Bred by Mrs G. Blenkinsop.

May the Devil Take You 734MM (Misses Maunsell and Hamilton) 1930 by The Kybosh out of Kiss in the Ring. Bred by owners. Blue.

Meditation (Mrs F. Palmer) 1929 by Gardeners Perfection out of Phantom Queen. Bred by Parsons.

Meg R19 (James Anderson) by Tug (R. Bell) out of Jean R17. See history.

Meg R24 (William Clark of Bedlington) by Billy R23 out of Wasp R22. Wasp was also Billy's dam. See History.

Meg R24A (also Clark's) sire said to be 'Capt. Pott's dog'. See History.

Meg R190 (D. Ross) by Senator out of Domino.

Meg R225 (J. Monkman) by Gauntlet (NT) out of Jess (NT) (Lynn).

Meg R229 (J. Reed) by Senator out of Vic R230 who was also called Old Vic (Hedley).

Meg R240 (R. Robson) by Dante R46 out of Daisy R44. This bitch was apparently also called Victoria.

Meg R5220 (Snowdoun) by Beaconsfield Temporize out of Beaconsfield Treasure.

Meg R5675 (Pratt) by The Goldsmith out of Tweedmouth Lass.

Meg R5705 by Blyth Briton out of Northern Lass.

Mellbeck's Mildred by Bluejacket out of Phoebe (NT).

Mercury 1192CC (T. W. Lawrence) 1921 by Jock's Lodge out of Trixie (NT). Bred by owner. Blue.

Mercury R5706 by Ventor (NT) out of Nettle (NT).

Merry Hell (Misses Maunsell and Hamilton) 1924 by Sandpiper out of Gyp R5683. Bred by R. M. Bassett. Formerly registered as Nora.

Merry Jyp 27810 (Chambers) 1888 by Warkworth Hotspur out of Daisy R197. Bred by C. T. Maling. Blue.

Merry Jyppy R6976 (D. Pitt) 1924 by Moving Knight out of Lady Betty. Bred by W. S. Wright.

Michael of Rugely 34KK (Miss P. Wolseley) 1926 by Night Express out of Susan of Mottisfont. Bred by Miss N. Dixon. Blue.

Mickel 828AA 1917 by Jock's Lodge out of Whilensleaf. Bred by W. J. Onions. Blue.

Middleton Pride (H. Taylor) by Lord Roberts out of Gyp R5430.

Midmoor Avis 89AA, Champion (W. W. Savage) 1919 by Jock's Lodge out of Ursula. Bred by Miss M. Cross. Blue.

Midmoor Chassis 1301FF, Champion (Mrs Savage) 1924 by Hop-a-long out of Midmoor Avis. Bred by W. W. Savage. Blue.

Midmoor Fay 1713DD (W. W. Savage) 1923 by Jock's Lodge out of Midmoor Avis. Bred by owner.

Midmoor Jean 1915 by Jock's Lodge out of Cranley Peggy. Bred by W. W. Savage.

Midmoor Jock 207W (W. W. Savage) 1915 by Jock's Lodge out of Cranley Peggy. Bred by owner.

Midmoor Micawber 124FF (W. W. Savage) 1924 by Hop-a-long out of Midmoor Avis. Bred by owner. Blue.

Midmoor Miranda 933HH (W. W. Savage) 1924 by Hop-a-long out of Midmoor Avis. Bred by owner. Blue.

Mignonette 550QQ (Mrs F. L. Franks) 1933 by Cribden Chutney out of Powder Puff. Bred by Miss P. Ellis. Blue.

Milbourne Flo (W. Miles) 1928 by Jubilee Surprise out of Trixie (NT). Bred by C. Smith.

Milton Marvel 1477GG (J. Napier) 1925 by Williamfield Piper out of Milton Nell. Bred by owner. Blue.

Milton Nell 181FF (J. Napier) 1923 by Deckham Stormer out of Jennie (NT). Bred by J. Bowes. Liver and tan.

Minley Flora 430S (Mrs L. Currie) 1909 by Beaconsfield Tavy out of Beauburn Gyp. Bred by P. Lugton. Blue. Formerly known as Breakwater Flora.

Minnie R5214 by Beaconsfield Temporize out of Nettle (NT).

Minnie R5687 by Benwell Prince out of Nettle R5688.

Minnie Clyde 19087 (W. Morris) 1884 by Piper (NT) (McKay) out of Daisy (NT) (Weir).

Minstrel Boy 1194CC (J. J. Bower and J. Arkie) 1921 by Music Master out of Biddy (NT). Bred by E. Rutter.

Miretta (R. C. Irving) 1903 by Deansfield Piper out of Queen's Pride (NT). Bred by Donnison.

Miss Burton 27809 (E. Taylor) 1888 by Fettler out of Bridget 21371. Bred by G. Coulter. Blue.

Miss Chance (Kennedy). Registered at K.C. in 1895 as pedigree unknown.

Miss Dewley 1919 by Breakwater Chieftain out of Recruiting Lady. Bred by T. Roper.

Miss Echo (T. H. Maddison) 1927 by Saval Boy out of Garw Jess. Bred by R. Edminson.

Miss Gaysum 788NN, Champion (Miss M. Hallowell-Carew) 1931 by Hydesville night Hawk out of Jean R5709. Bred by B. F. Robinson. Liver.

Miss Jock 829AA 1919 by Deansfild Monarch out of Queenie R5186. Bred by R. C. Irving. Blue.

Miss Mischief R5193 (T. W. Lawrence) by Breakwater Chieftain out of Nell R5194.

Miss Oliver 1272B, Champion (J. Smith, formerly J. Blench) 1896 by Dick (NT) (Dowan) out of Meg R5675. Bred by Pratt. Liver. Died in 1911.

Miss Pink (Miss P. Ellis) 1927 by Midmoor Micawber out of Blue Mignon. Bred by owner.

Miss Rhona 439S (T. Roper) 1910 by Askme out of Princess Dolly. Bred by owner. Blue.

Miss South 37253 (A. Reekie) 1893 by Crossley Result out of Sweetheart II. Blue.

Miss Wilson by Sir Goldsmith out of Goldsmith's Daughter.

Mist of Harnish 36KK (Mrs Hallowell-Carew) 1928 by Square Deal out of Don Jeanette. Bred by H. Grain. Blue.

Misty Dawn (Miss W. Bickham) 1932 by Oh Boy out of Blue Nanette. Bred by owner.

Mollie R5201 by Budget out of Rose (NT).

Molly Boyle 1919 by Coalstriker out of Jess R5681. Bred by L. Peacock.

Moon Maiden 1919 by Breakwater Chieftain out of Nell R5194. Bred by J. Dennison.

Moorhouse Lady (Mrs M. Webster) 1921 by Killingholme Stickler out of Nell (NT). Bred by J. Burrell.

Morning Light 1920 by Willycraggs out of Molly Boyle. Bred by R. Boucher.

Mornington Minnie (Topham) 1923 by Laird Joe out of Morning Light. Bred by R. Boucher.

Moss House Beauty by Barney Boy out of Fife Lady.

Most Precious Treasure 527MM (Misses Maunsell and Hamilton) 1930 by The Kybosh out of Precious Nonsense. Bred by owners. Blue and tan.

Mottisfont Jeff 1597JJ (Commander Holbrook, V.C.) 1927 by Copsewood Blue Boy out of Susan of Mottisfont. Bred by owner. Blue.

Mountain Rover. See Cribden Chutney.

Moving Cheek 222GG (J. A. Ure) 1924 by Moving Knight out of Glendale Nellie. Bred by J. Heal. Blue.

Moving Cracker 177FF (J. A. Ure) 1924 by Moving Knight out of Glendale Nellie. Bred by J. Heal. Liver.

Mrs P. R. Smith (Breakwater) 1899.

*Champion Gardeners
Supremacy 1930.*

Moving Day (J. A. Ure) 1919 by Step-dancer out of Lady Bomersund. Bred by Messrs Law and Shiel. Blue.

Moving Didy (J. A. Ure) 1925 by Moving Knight out of Flashlight. Bred by W.J. Gingell.

Moving Flash 932HH (J. A. Ure) 1926 by Moving Knight out of Flashlight. Bred by W. J. Gingell. Liver.

Moving Knight 671DD, Champion (J. A. Ure) 1922 by Le Roy out of Moving Day. Bred by owner. Blue. This dog has had a wonderful success as the leading sire of his day and his name appears in a very great number of modern pedigrees. No less than fifty-eight Bedlingtons sired by him appear in this edition.

Moving Monarch (J. A. Ure) 1929 by Moving Knight out of Lady Change-ful. Bred by owner.

Musha (Misses Maunsell and Hamilton) 1922 by Sperkeforde Jackanapes out of Top o' the Morning. Bred by owners.

Music (J. J. Bower) 1922 by Minstrel Boy out of Wannie (NT). Bred by owner.

Music, alias Wassy R43 (W. Taylor) by Piper (NT) (Bowman) out of Meg (NT) (Taylor). Bred by owner. In an entry in the K.C.S.B. for 1889 Taylor's Meg was said to be descended from Donkin's Old Peachem.

Musician (J. J. Bower) 1924 by Music out of Wannie (NT). Bred by owner.

Music Lady (R. Jobling) 1925 by Musician out of Flare Light. Bred by J. J. Bower.

Music Master (J. Wright) 1919 by Ewood Eclipse out of Sally (NT). Bred by A. Pearson.

My Blue Delight 1345KK (E. Smith) 1928 by Gardeners Express out of Blue Iris. Bred by J. A. Carrington. Blue.

My Choice 133QQ (E. W. Wears) 1933 by Dinkie's Double out of Geordie's Fancy. Bred by Miss E. Hindmarsh. Blue.

Myrtle R5708 (H. E. Barber) by Mercury R5706 out of Cranley Tatters.

Mysterious Billy 38LL (J. Bennett) 1929 by Chutney Revival out of Rytonian Galaxy. Bred by Miss F. V. M. Irving. Blue.

N.

Nancy R3980 (S. Gee) 1898 by Clyde Boy out of Breakwater Nipper.

Nancy of Standlynch (Miss G. Lawis) 1929 by Bluehouse Barnabas out of Jill of Mottisfont. Bred by H. Cox.

Neat Kettle (W. Cole) 1927 by Willy-craggs out of Music Lady. Bred by R. Jobling.

Needle (H. White). See note under The Goldsmith.

Nell R308 (J. Taylor) by Ch. Piper 7698 out of Bess (NT) (Donkin).

Nell R347 (J. Georgeson) by The Gold-smith out of Nellie (NT).

Nell R5194 (J. Dennison or W. Bramwell) by Benwell Prince out of Dina R5368.

Nell R5685 by Blackmail out of Minnie R5687.

Nellie R5355 by Sweep R5363 out of Swap R5364.

Nellie R5374 (G. Farrer) by Breakwater Chieftain out of Camwood (or Colms-wood) Gipsy. There is a doubt about the spelling of the dam's name.

Nellie R5375 (G. Farrer) by Bobs R5377 out of Tatters R5416.

Nellie R5420 by Goxhill Tatters out of Fern Bank Biddy.

Nellie R5424 by Winn for Beer out of Nancy (NT).

Nellie R5512 by Bluecoat (Spurgeon) out of Gamey (NT). I can find no dog of Spurgeon's registered as Bluecoat and suspect that this is merely another name for Bluejacket (J. Spurgeon), which see. The name of Bluecoat (Spurgeon) does however appear several times as an unreg-istered sire in different registrations but such a mistake would easily occur.

Nellie R5521 (W. B. Baty) by Blyth Bob out of Superba.

Nellie R5682 by Beaconsfield Tavy out of Northern Girl. Was sister of Ch. Cranley Jess.

Nellie Burton 37254 (Coulter, formerly Brewis) 1890 by Peach R353 out of Nettle R354. Bred by H. White. Liver.

Nettle R352 by Clyde Wallace out of Clyde Pet (NT).

Nettle R354 (H. White) 1889 by Ham-mond alias Jolly Barber out of Needle

(White). This bitch was registered as Benton Bridesmaid but generally appears as Nettle.

Nettle R5208 by Goldseeker out of Lassy (NT).

Nettle R5357 (T. Maddison) by Berwick Blue Boy out of Tweedside Jessie.

Nettle R5431 (Mrs D. Foord) by Nip R5511 out of Nellie R5512.

Nettle R5688 by Dudley Blue Boy out of Minnie (NT).

Newsham Dragon (W. H. St. Aubyn) 1924 by Siddow Sentry out of Blue Kestrel. Bred by owner.´

Night Alarm 836KK (D. Jolley) 1928 by Gardeners Mark out of Night Betty. Bred by owner. Blue.

Night Barmaid 776GG (E. Metcalf) 1925 by Moving Knight out of Ellington Jenny. Bred by W. Waddell. Blue.

Night Betty 596HH, Champion (D. Jolley) 1926 by Night Express out of Jennie (NT). Bred by W. Taylor. Blue.

Night Cap 976MM (Mrs E. Bruce-Low) 1927 by Rough Night out of Glendale Lucy. Bred by Mrs M. Wilson. Blue.

Night Express 1481FF, Champion (E. Metcalf) 1924 by Moving Knight out of Express Delight. Bred by Mrs A. Wilkinson. Blue.

Nimble R20 (Bagalee) by Piper R16 out of Meg R19. See History.

Nimble R28 (Thomas Thompson) by Tip out of Nimble R20. The sire Tip was probably the same Old Tip who was the sire of Viper R21 and I believe him to have been a son of Piper R15 and Phoebe R14, but there is no definite evidence. See however History.

Nip R5511 (A. Cope) by Deansfield Monarch out of Flora R5195.

Northern Girl (A. Dawson) 1904 by Afton Topic out of Minnie R5214.

Northern Lass by Clyde Boy out of Nettle (NT).

Northern Leader 29957, Champion (J. Blench) 1886 by Hairdresser out of Berwick Lass. Bred by owner. Blue.

O.

Odds On (F. Snalam) 1924 by Ridge Hill Jock out of Bessema. Bred by T. R. Osborn.

Oh Boy (Miss P. Ellis) 1930 by What'll I Do out of Pierette. Bred by owner.

Old Hall Lass (R. Dagless) 1926 by Break of Dawn out of Tatters R5679. Bred by B. Davies.

Ord 1322A (J. Smith) 1895 by Tip the Tinker (NT) out of Jess (NT) (Grant). Blue.

Orme 34955 (J. Smith) 1891 by Langside Squire out of Langside Olive. Bred by D. Ross. Liver.

Orpheus 19PP (J. Hutton) 1931 by Ladyhead Piper out of Brucefield Echo (NT). Bred by owner. Blue.

Orpington Lass 1618J (W. A. Williams) 1903 by Moses (NT) (Williams) out of Breakwater Princess. Bred by owner. Blue.

P.

Pamela 1916 by Breakwater Fisher out of Magill Mysa. Bred by Miss Wallace.

Pat I R241 (J. Thompson) by Weardale R142 out of Wasp R242.

Patrick's Blue 1917 by Cobledene Pat out of Squire's Daughter. Bred by T. Robson.

Patsy R5691 (J. Watson) by Laird Joe out of Morning Light.

Payment (W. Taylor) 1931 by Roy (NT) out of Nell (NT). Bred by owner.

Peach R353, dog (W. Brewis) by Piper (NT) (Brewis) out of Nellie (NT) (Brewis).

Peachem R1, or Old Peachem. A kennel Terrier belonging to Mr Edward Donkin of Flotterton near Rothbury. The great forefather of the breed. Pedigree unknown but see History.

Peachem R13 (Cowen's, afterwards Joseph Ainsley's) by Burdett (Cowen's) out of a bitch of David Moffat's of Howick. Further pedigree unknown. See History.

Peachem R5699. In some notes left by the late Mr Alcock he was said to belong to Lucas and to be by Rothbury Piper (NT) out of an unnamed bitch, but in the pedigree of Sentinel he is given as by Ebchester Tip and out of Topsy and as belonging to John Parker.

Peachem 3422 (W. Carrick) by Rock R32 out of Music alias Wassy R43.

Peggy R5525 by Breakwater Eclipse out of Northern Girl. I suspect this Peggy is Cranley Peggy who was bred the same way.

Peggy of Ember (Miss R. E. Holland) by Mottisfont Jeff out of Midmoor Fay.

Peggy the Piper 1913 by Snowdoun Defender out of Lady of the Rock. Bred by R. Allan.

Peg o' Wycombe 1616PP (Miss M. E. Binns) 1931 by Knowlton Peter Pan out of Westell Beauty. Bred by Mrs W. Beattie. Blue.

Pegs Pal (Miss M. E. Simm) 1928 by Gardeners Mark out of Forgotten Fashion. Bred by J. Wright.

Pennycraig Lucy 37KK (Mrs M. K. M. Williamson) 1926 by Moving Knight out of Hidden Treasure. Bred by C. S. Bell. Liver.

Peridita (F. R. Day) 1926 by Shothanger Rector out of Saucy Sue. Bred by Major Fill.

Perdita Joy 977MM (W. J. Onions) 1928 by King's Pawn out of Capricious. Bred by A. C. Tolhurst. Blue and tan.

Perplexity 145GG (W. E. Philpots) 1925 by Moving Knight out of Perversity. Bred by owner. Blue.

Perversity 1562DD, Champion (W. E. Philpots) 1922 by Principality out of Express Delight. Bred by owner. Blue.

Petanna 1059QQ (Mrs I. Pettigrew) 1932 by Piper of Ryton out of Petena. Bred by owner. Blue.

Petena 131PP (Mrs I. Pettigrew) 1930 by Deckham Oprecious out of Princess Wee One of Simonside. Bred by Misses M. M. and C. R. Carr. Blue.

Pethommie 1016PP (Miss B. Statham) 1932 by Right Choice of Simonside out of Petita. Bred by Mrs I. Pettigrew. Blue.

Petita (Mrs I. Pettigrew) 1930 by Deckham Oprecious out of Princess Wee One of Simonside. Bred by Misses M. M. and C. R. Carr.

Petrarch (T. Urron) 1880 by Ch. Piper 7698 out of Phoebe R262. Bred by owner.

Phantom Boy (J. Pearson) 1927 by Clyde Boy's Ghost out of Linthouse Blue Girl. Bred by owner.

Phantom Queen (Miss B. Pearson) 1928 by Phantom Boy out of Queen of the Lake. Bred by H. J. Clements.

Philwood Proximity 486HH (W. E. Philpots) 1926 by Pugnacity out of Perversity. Bred by owner. Blue.

Philwood Tess (W. E. Philpots) 1926 by Square Deal out of Philwood Proximity. Bred by owner.

Phoebe R8 (John Dodd of Longhorsley) by Peachem R1 out of Vixen R6. See History.

Phoebe R12 (Christopher Dixon of Longhorsley) by Matchem R9 out of Phoebe R8. See History.

Phoebe R14, generally known as Coates's Phoebe, but really belonging first to Andrew Riddell of Framlington and afterwards to Joseph Ainsley of Bedlington. By the Rennington dog out of his sister Wasp R10. For description of her, see History.

Phoebe R31 (J. Dodd) by Tip (NT) (Hutchinson) out of Bess (NT) (Dodd).

Phoebe R126 (G. Ross) by Crowner R128 out of Violet R127.

Phoebe R160 (J. Pickard) 1879 by Weardale R142 out of Poll R245.

Phoebe R262 (T. Urron) by Ch. Piper 7698 out of Phoebe R606.

Phoebe R361 (J. Cook) by Berwick Brick out of Nettle (NT).

Phoebe R606, also called Atkinson's Phoebe (E. K. Little) by Crowner R128 out of Topsy R263.

Phoebe R5674 (J. Calderwood) by Peachem R5699 out of Wasp R5700.

Phoebe R5678 by Victor (NT) out of Rose (NT).

Phoebe R5689 (M. Robson) by Pip out of Rebecca.

Phoebe R5695 by Sandy (NT) out of ?— —?. I cannot decipher the dam's name in the pedigree I have seen.

Phoebe of Great Warford (Mrs R. Bennett) 1922 by Don (NT) out of Luce (NT). Bred by Messrs Furness and Kessler.

Phoebe of Harnish (Mrs Hallowell-Carew) 1930 by Gardeners Perfection out of Milbourne Flo. Bred by W. E. Miles.

Pick (T. H. Urron) by Peachem 3422 out of Meg (NT) (Bendle).

Mrs Mead and her Sudstons 1910–1940.

*Champion
Gardeners
Supreme
1927.*

Pickles of Woodhay. See Bill of Harnish.

Pierrette (Miss P. Ellis) 1929 by Midmoor Micawber out of Blue Mignon. Bred by owner.

Pincher R5 (William Turnbull of Holystone) by Peachem R1 out of Venom R4. See History.

Pincher R7 (Edward Donkin). Probably the son of Peachem R1 but see History.

Pip 1916 by Jock's Lodge out of Cranley Peggy. Bred by W. W. Savage.

Piper R15, or Old Piper (James Anderson of Rothbury Forest) by Peachem R13 out of Phoebe R12. For description of him see History.

Piper R16, generally known as Ainsley's Piper, and sometimes to distinguish him from his sire, as Young Piper, was whelped in 1825 and was the first dog to be known as a Bedlington Terrier, that name having been coined by Joseph Ainsley of Bedlington, his breeder and owner. He was by Piper R15 out of Phoebe R14. He died in 1840. See also History.

Piper R26, or Joicee's Piper, by Rock R32 out of Meg R24. See History.

Piper R50 (John Ainsley) by Scamp R27 out of Gyp R5701. The more famous Ainsley's Piper is R16. See History.

Piper R249 (Fender) by Piper R5703 out of Fancy R45.

Piper R309 (Tupps) by Piper 7699 out of ?——?

Piper R360 (J. Cook or Armstrong) by Lord Byron (NT) out of Jeanette (NT).

Piper R5199 by Askme out of Mollie R5201.

Piper R5665 by Berwick Bob (NT) out of Jean (NT).

Piper R5684 by Afton Gem out of Afton Ida.

Piper 7698, Champion (J. A. Baty) 1876 by Pick (Urron) out of Vic R33. Blue. This was one of the great pillars of the breed and appears in many pedigrees. He died in 1885.

Piper 7699 (G. Ross) 1876. Blue. No pedigree given in K.C.S.B. G. Ross had at least four Pipers.

Piper R5690 by Tango out of Gipsy R5692.

Piper R5693 by Deansfield Piper out of Goxhill Frisk.

Piper R5703 (G. Gibson) by Rock (NT) (Spoor) out of Phoebe (NT) (Gibson).

Piper, The, R5202 by Bellerby Surprise out of Queenie R5203.

Piper of Ryton 518LL (T. E. Brown) 1929 by Gardeners Mark out of Deansfield Jean. Bred by J. Donnison. Blue.

Pipers Success 1566 QQ, Champion (C. G. Worrell) 1933 by Piper of Ryton out of Blue Day. Bred by owner. Liver.

Piper's Surprise 1920 by Eccleshill Blue Boy out of Nellie R5375. Bred by G. Farrer.

Pitland Lass 1914 by Blue Coat (NT) out of Blue Bell R5419. Bred by J. Spurgeon. With regard to the sire see under Nellie R5512. He is probably the dog registered as Bluejacket.

Pitland Nell 1918 by Tweedside Lad out of Pitland Lass. Bred by J. Mills.

Pitsmoor Peg (W. Gillatt) 1918 by Jock's Lodge out of Cranley Peggy. Bred by W. W. Savage.

Pitswood General (L. Alderson) 1929 by Sing-to-me out of Water Lily. Bred by owner.

Pleasant Lass 1368D (Elliot and Devlin) 1896 by Lord Clyde (NT) out of Nettle (NT) (Geordison). Blue.

Plymouth Lad (H. E. James) by Jack 3412 out of Juno 10908. Sometimes appears as Plym Lad.

Polar Boy by My Boy (NT) out of Blue Girl (NT). I have an idea that this dog's name was really Poplar Boy.

Poll R245 (Shaw) by Mat 5580 out of ?——?

Polly Burton (W. Brewis) 1892 by Fettler out of Nellie Burton. Bred by owner.

Popcorn of Bransways 741PP (Miss E. S. M. Branfoot) 1932 by Knowlton Peter Pan out of Barley of Bransways. Bred by owner. Blue.

Powder Puff (Miss P. Ellis) 1931 by Deckham Oprecious out of Blue Mignon. Bred by owner.

Precious Jim of Simonside 1689QQ (Misses M. M. and C. R. Carr) 1933 by Deckham Oprecious out of Binnacle Bella. Bred by owners. Blue.

Precious Michael of Simonside 542PP (Misses M. M. and C. R. Carr) 1932 by Deckham Oprecious out of Maritza of Critonia. Bred by owners. Blue.

Precious Night 625JJ (A. C. Tolhurst) 1927 by Stormy Night out of Judy Pop. Bred by F. Royles. Blue.

Precious Nonsense 627JJ, Champion (Misses Maunsell and Hamilton) 1927 by Moving Knight out of Dear Goodness. Bred by owners. Blue.

Premier (Weatherspoon) by Pelton Fell (NT) out of Nettle (NT).

President Lincoln 1293H (W. J. Onions) 1899 by Sir Goldsmith out of Nellie (NT). Bred by Lumsden. Blue.

President Squire 1619J (R. C. Irving) 1902 by President Lincoln out of Nellie (pedigree unknown). Bred by R. Armstrong. Blue.

Pride of Dudley (M. Robson) 1901 by Blyth Bob out of Minnie (NT). Bred by Donnison.

Pride of Hetton (J. W. Hughes) 1922 by Blue Boy out of Middleton Pride. Bred by H. Taylor.

Prim Press 1356MM (J. Bennett) 1930 by Cribden Chutney out of Rytonian Galaxy. Bred by owner. Blue.

Princess Diana 386Q, Champion (G. Brown) 1909 by Beaconsfield Tavy out of Diana R5369. Bred by owner. Blue.

Princess Dolly (T. Roper) by Benwell Prince out of Gipsy Girl (NT).

Princess Floss by Deansfield Monarch out of Treaford (?) Topsy (NT). I am not sure of the dam's name.

Princess Peggy (Mrs T. Walker) 1924 by Ruddigore out of Floss (NT). Bred by C. E. Thresk.

Princess Wee One of Simonside (Misses M. M. and C. R. Carr) 1928 by Sing-to-me out of Gardeners Poacher. Bred by owners.

Principality 905BB (W. E. Philpots) 1920 by Eccleshill Blue Boy out of Somme Girl. Blue.

Priscilla Punch by Goldseeker out of Beaconsfield Tartaress.

Projectile 10902, Champion (Watson, formerly A. Armstrong) 1879 by Ch. Piper 7698 out of Jess 6678. Blue.

Proud Girl of Simonside 20PP (Misses M. M. and C. R. Carr) 1930 by Deckham Oprecious out of Princess Wee One of Simonside. Bred by owners. Blue.

Proud Peggy (H. Taylor) 1919 by Lord Roberts out of Gyp R5430. Bred by F. P. Shearman.

Prudence of Critonia (J. H. Woodward) 1925 by Le Roy out of Sperkeford Betsey. Bred by Major E. B. Aylward.

Pugnacity 530FF (W. E. Philpots) 1924 by Moving Knight out of Miss Jock. Bred by owner. Blue.

Q

Quayside Lad (D. Ross, also Armstrong) by Petrarch out of Bagatelle.

Queen Bee 831AA 1916 by Titch out of Queenie R5186. Bred by R. C. Irving. Blue.

Queen Bess (J. McGlade) 1909 by Benwell Prince out of Hexham Rose (NT). Bred by J. Dyke.

Queenie R5186 (R. C. Irving) by Top Hole out of Jan R5181.

Queenie R5203 by Child's Lad out of Dark Dinah.

Queenie R5710 (M. Lewis) by Cymro (NT) out of Apple Tree Blossom.

Queen of the Lake (E. Lucas) 1923 by Jake out of Lady Go-Lightly. Bred by S. Atkin.

Quick Change 2059QQ (Miss M. A. Roberts) 1931 by Moving Monarch out of Cramling Peggy. Bred by H. J. Skillings. Blue.

Quick Step (T. Griffiths) 1924 by Step-dancer out of Ellington Nell. Bred by W. Waddell.

Qui Vive 564GG (Mrs Salmon) 1925 by Hop-a-long out of Rita. Bred by owner. Blue.

Quorndon Katja 872FF (Mrs E. Farnham) 1924 by Jock's Lodge out of Half Holiday. Bred by R.C. Irving. Blue and tan.

R.

Radiance of Wrinstone 1615PP, Champion (Mrs L. Ward) 1933 by Gardeners Supremacy out of Phoebe of Harnish. Bred by owner. Blue.

Raggles (Mrs Mead) 1909 by Trusty out of Vic R5217. Bred by E. Hurtley.

Rambler 563T (C. H. Redhead) 1909 by Goxhill Tatters out of Retribution. Bred by owner. Blue and tan.

Rathangan Piper 622CC (Carlisle) 1920 by Corrig Pincher out of Dimple. Bred by W. P. Tate. Blue.

Rattler R34 (J. Gibbs) by Gibbs's liver-coloured dog. Dam unknown. The sire, whose name has not been recorded will be found in this list under Gibbs. See also History.

Rattler R5697 (Ramshaw or Young) by Tearem R5698 out of Phoebe (NT) (Charlton).

Rattler O (J. Weatherburn) by Northern Leader out of Phoebe (NT) (Rankin).

Rebecca (M. Robson) 1911 by Budget out of Rose (NT). Bred by G. Graham.

Recruiting Lady 1917 by Deansfield Monarch out of Little Remnant. Bred by G. Brown.

Red Gauntlet (Mrs F. Nisbet) 1922 by Square Measure out of Doris (NT). Bred by H. Baigent.

Red King (G. Tait) 1928 by Scottie out of Day Express. Bred by owner.

Redstart (J. Lowrie) 1911 by Young Piper (NT) (Walker) out of Wasp (NT). Bred by J. Walker.

Redwings O'Phipson (B. G. Greenup) 1922 by Deckham Shepherd out of Miss Jock. Bred by owner.

Regalia Regina (J. Blench) 1899 by Breakwater Squire out of Klondyke Girl. Bred by P. Lugton.

Regilded of Radynden 121RR (Miss B. Brett) 1933 by Bluehouse Larry out of Sheisin. Bred by Miss N. Wallis.

Rennington dog, The by Pincher R5 out of an unnamed bitch of William Wardle of Framlington, whose parents are not recorded. See History. Was brother to Wasp R10 to whom he was afterwards mated.

Retaliation (C. H. Redhead) 1905 by Deansfield Piper out of Miss Oliver. Bred by H. Warnes.

Retribution (C. H. Redhead) 1906 by Retaliation out of Afton Water. Bred by owner.

Rhondda Billy (W. J. Gingell) 1921 by Charlie R5266 out of Queen (NT). Bred by owner.

Riddle of Wrinstone 2060QQ (Mrs M. Duncan) 1933 by Gardeners Supremacy out of Phoebe of Harnish. Bred by Mrs Llewellyn Ward. Blue.

Ridge Hill Jock 1559DD, Champion (R. C. Irving) 1923 by Jock's Lodge out of Blue Lassie. Bred by Mrs Towers Minors.

Right Choice of Simonside 1692MM

(Misses M. M. and C. R. Carr) 1930 by Dracula out of Miss Pink. Bred by Miss E. V. Herdman. Liver.

Ringlady (T. Roper) 1927 by Square Deal out of Lady Wynforem. Bred by A. J. Lord.

Rita 291DD (T. Roper) 1922 by Mickel out of Marion of Dovesland. Bred by J. Fulton.

Riverside Rufus by Triumph out of Machen Pride.

Robert (Miss L. Johnson) 1924 by Goxhill Blue Boy out of Sea Swallow. Bred by Mrs Shapcott.

Rock R32 also known as Rocky III by Pincher (Dodd) (NT) out of an unrecorded bitch. There is reason to believe that Rock was descended from Piper R15 and Phoebe R14. See History.

Rocket R292 (D. Ross) by Clansman 9581 out of Langside Lass.

Rodio (R. C. Irving) 1924 by Jock's Lodge out of Half Holiday. Bred by owner.

Romping Rags (F. R. Day) 1921 by Jock's Lodge out of Recruiting Lady. Bred by Major Dixon.

Rory O'More 558M, Champion (R. C. Irving) 1907 by Jock of Oran out of Little Demon. Bred by F. Ward. Blue.

Rose R162 (W. Redhead) by Young Flint (NT) out of Wasp (NT).

Rose R5680 (Bower) by Patrick's Blue out of Nettle (NT).

Rosebud R305 (F. Armstrong and J. Black) by Weardale R142 out of Nellie (NT) (Davy).

Rose Bud 1358MM (W. McEwen) 1930 by Blue King out of Commercial Lady. Bred by owner. Blue.

Rose Dew (Mrs B. Holgate) 1926 by Ruddigore out of Guard. Bred by owner.

Rosemaid 1920 by Coalstriker out of Lady Bomersund. Bred by J. Laws.

Rose Marie 152JJ (Mrs F. Hamilton) 1925 by Red Gauntlett out of Corstorphine Lass. Bred by Mrs E. M. Laidlaw. Blue.

Rosette R5353 (A. W. Smith) by Blacksmith R5522 out of Gold Dust R5523.

Rosie Bell 1567QQ (W. McEwen) 1932 by Billangho out of Rose Bud. Bred by owner. Blue.

Roughdown Diana 1979HH (D. P. Horne) 1926 by Cribden Chutney out

Billy Onions (Deckham).

Champion Deckham Oprecious 1932. Owned by The Misses Carr. (Thomas Fall).

of Highland Princess. Bred by W. S. Wright. Blue.

Rough Night 118HH, Champion (E. Metcalf) 1925 by Moving Knight out of Ellington Jenny. Bred by W. Waddell. Blue.

Royal Stag (Watson) by Cut Tailed Piper out of Vic R668 alias Blue Blood, or out of Jess, or out of Gip (Hedley). It will be seen that three different bitches are given as dam by various authorities and I cannot choose between them.

Ruby R5267 (W. J. Gingell) 1917 by Coalstriker out of Vanity. Bred by E. Hurtley. Blue.

Ruby R5667 (W. H. Cowpe) by Eccleshill Blue Boy out of Lady Hazeldene.

Ruddigore 289DD (F. Ellis) 1921 by Lucky Lad out of Betty R5663. Bred by owner.

Rustic, late Victor R303 (Dodd) by Choker 15651 out of Meg R229.

Rye Nellie (C. G. Worrell) by Gasyard Bill (NT) out of Blue Tib.

Ryeside Maid 1920 by Corrig Pincher out of Dimple. Bred by W. P. Tate.

Rytonian Blue Girl (T. E. Brown) 1923 by Tatters R5632 out of Romping Rags. Bred by F. R. Day.

Rytonian Forager 1598JJ (T. E. Brown 1928 by Moving Knight out of Rytonian Blue Girl. Bred by owner. Blue.

Rytonian Frobisher 35KK (T. E. Brown) 1928 by Moving Knight out of Rytonian Blue Girl. Bred by owner. Blue.

Rytonian Galaxy 1342JJ, Champion (W. J. Onions) 1927 by Moving Knight out of Rytonian Blue Girl. Bred by T. E. Brown. Blue.

Rytonian Nettle 120HH, Champion (T. E. Brown) 1926 by Moving Knight out of Rytonian Blue Girl. Bred by owner. Blue.

Rytonian Nipper 485HH (T. E. Brown) 1926 by Moving Knight out of Rytonian Blue Girl. Bred by owner. Blue.

Rytonian Nugget 860HH (T. E. Brown) 1926 by Moving Knight out of Rytonian Blue Girl. Bred by owner. Liver.

S.

Sadie (J. W. Cooper) 1921 by Conn (NT) out of Pitsmoor Peg. Bred by W. Gillatt.

Salamander Lass 1915 by Blue Billy (NT) (Turnbull) out of Nell (NT). Bred by A. Pow.

Sam R158 (Harbottle) by Dante R46 out of Daisy R44. Sometimes called 'the Sandyford Lane dog'.

Sandpiper (Mrs Shapcott) 1922 by Sperkeforde Jackanapes out of Heart of Hell. Bred by Misses Maunsell and Hamilton.

Sandshade 278HH (S. Mercer) 1926 by Deckham Crest out of Kitty Flyn. Bred by W. A. Barnes. Liver.

Sarah of Nonington 950QQ (Mrs M. E. O'Brien) 1932 by Right Choice of Simonside out of Deckham Oreal. Bred by Miss G. Lawis. Liver.

Saucy Peggy 1916 by Little Joker out of Pip (NT). Bred by J. Mooney.

Saucy Sue (Major Fill) 1924 by Ridge Hill Jock out of Nettle R5431. Bred by Mrs D. Foord.

Saucey Sue of Portlight 696LL (Dr and Mrs French) 1929 by Ishmael out of Bright Eyes. Bred by owners. Blue, tan on legs and feet.

Saval Boy (J. Heal) 1924 by Moving Knight out of Glendale Nellie. Bred by owner.

Scamp R27 (William Clark of Bedlington) by Piper R26 out of Daisy R25, his parents being half-brother and half-sister. He is one of the great pillars of the breed and lived in the 1860's. See History.

School Girl (S. Broad) 1920 by Breakwater Chieftain out of Lady Evelyn. Bred by owner.

Scotch Jean (Mrs N. Foggan) 1925 by Break of Dawn out of Tatters R5679. Bred by B. Davies.

Scottie 955HH, Champion (C. S. Bell) 1926 by Duplicate out of Blue Bell Maid. Bred by owner. Liver.

Sea Fire (Mrs Shapcott) 1925 by Henry Codrington out of Sea Swallow. Bred by owner.

Seaham Hall 457P, Champion (E. Thirlwell) 1908 by Silksworth Prince out of Meg R5220. Bred by Snowdoun. Blue.

Sea Swallow (Mrs Shapcott) 1922 by Charlie R5266 out of Ruby R5267. Bred by W. J. Gingell.

Seghill Sweep by Hairdresser out of Seghill Jennie (NT).

Senator 13171, Champion (Watson) 1880 by Tip R161 out of ? Bred by W. Redhead. Blue. I cannot make out who was Ch. Senator's dam.

Sentry's Select 1480FF (R. Statham) 1923 by Siddow Sentry out of Wharfe Lady. Bred by owner. Blue.

Sheila 681FF (Mrs Hallows) 1923 by Le Roy out of Christmas Daisy. Bred by Mrs Thompson. Blue.

Sheisin (Miss N. M. S. Wallis) 1931 by Cranley Jim out of Nancy of Standlynch. Bred by Miss G. Lawis.

Sherley Poppy of Mincingait 1949QQ (Mrs R. A. Martin) 1934 by Welhead Whoopee out of Misty Dawn. Bred by owner. Blue.

Shield's Bluie (R. McVay) 1910 by Butcher Lad (NT) (Robson) out of Nellie (NT). Bred by D. Clark.

Shothanger Rector 983EE, Champion (T. N. Keith) 1923 by Hop-a-long out of Boxmoor Mary. Bred by Mrs T. N. Keith. Blue.

Shothanger Robert (Mrs T. N. Keith) 1915 by Sperkeforde Jackanapes out of Cranley Peggy. Bred by W. W. Savage.

Shothanger Sally (Mrs T. N. Keith) 1922 by Shothanger Robert out of Boxmoor Mary. Bred by owner.

Siddow Sentry 1921 by Indigo Lad out of Lady Trail. Bred by W. Hirst.

Silksworth Lass by Beaconsfield Triumph out of Meg (NT) (Patterson).

Silksworth Prince by Silversmith out of Silksworth Lass.

Silver Doctor 11RR (Mrs H. S. Harman) 1934 by Knowlton Peter Pan out of Esperanza. Bred by A. L. Bartlett.

Silver Sea (W. Scott) 1929 by Pegs Pal out of Betsy Prig. Bred by owner.

Silversmith (W. H. Scott) 1898 by Sir Goldsmith out of Polly Burton. Bred by J. Guildford.

Silver Spray (W. Scott) 1931 by Red King out of Silver Seal. Bred by owner.

Silvertop Gem 735MM (Mrs G. Rutherford and Miss F. M. Sturt) 1929 by Cribden Chutney out of Capricious. Bred by Mrs G. Day. Blue.

Silvertop Teenie 695LL (Mrs G. Day) 1929 by Cribden Chutney out of Capricious. Bred by owner. Blue.

Silvery Tweed (J. Blench) 1923 by Moving Knight out of Lively Judy. Bred by Miss Evans.

Sing-to-me 1372HH (J. Jennings) 1924 by Eccleshill Blue Boy out of Laughing Tansie. Bred by owner. Blue.

Sir Goldsmith 1297C (W. Brewis) 1897 by Terror out of Victoria R357. Bred by P. H. Freeman. Blue. Name afterwards changed to Breakwater Baron.

Skin the Goat 507PP (Mrs H. S. Harman) 1931 by Knowlton Peter Pan out of Moving Flash. Bred by Miss F. M. Sturt. Blue. Originally registered as Lady Maureen.

Smiling Thru 12RR (C. G. Worrell) 1934 by Hadaway Piper out of Tess of my Heart. Bred by owner. Blue.

Snowdoun Defender 417R (W. H. McShean) 1910 by Snowdoun Piper out of Mellbeck's Mildred. Bred by J. Harker. Blue.

Snowdoun Piper 458P (W. H. McShean) 1907 by Berwick Blue Boy out of Jess R5371. Bred by D. Ritchie. Blue.

Somme Girl 1917 by Brompton Bobby out of Blue Bird. Bred by Mrs Martin.

Son of a Knight (E. Metcalf) 1926 by Moving Knight out of Hidden Treasure. Bred by C. S. Bell.

Son Of Surprise 2296HH (B. Davey) 1927 by Sing-to-me out of Stanningley Surprise. Bred by owner. Blue.

Sotheron Blue (P. C. Herring) 1926 by Midmoor Micawber out of Darville's Desire. Bred by F. J. Smith.

Sperkeforde Betsey (E. B. Aylward) 1923 by Sperkeforde Jackanapes out of Heart of Hell. Bred by Misses Maunsell and Hamilton.

Sperkeforde Jackanapes 130S, Champion (E. B. Aylward) 1911 by Bellerby Surprise out of Sperkeforde Jill. Bred by owner. Blue.

Sperkeforde Jill (E. B. Aylward) 1907 by Berwick Blue Boy out of Rosette R5353. Bred by A. W. Smith.

Sperkeforde Judy 162R (E. B. Aylward) 1908 by Breakwater Peer out of Sperkeforde Jill. Bred by owner. Blue and tan.

Sperkeforde Juggins 723GG (E. B. Aylward) 1925 by Le Roy out of

Sperkeforde Betsy. Bred by owner. Blue.

Sperkeforde Witch (E. B. Aylward) 1922 by Principality out of Heart of Hell. Bred by Miss D. Hamilton.

Splendid Surprise 680FF (F. R. Day) 1922 by Piper's Surprise out of Jacksonette. Bred by J. Jennings. Blue.

Sporting Chance (Mrs G. Kershaw) 1921 by Mickel out of Marion of Dovesland. Bred by J. Fulton. Originally registered as Cartside Boy.

Sporting Prince 132QQ (E. W. Wears) 1933 by Dinkie's Double out of Silver Spray. Bred by W. Scott. Blue.

Springhill Polly 325FF (W. M. Greenshaw) 1923 by Girardville Boy out of Ruby R5267. Bred by W. J. Gingell. Blue.

Square Deal 144GG, Champion (C. F. Simpson) 1924 by Sentry's Select out of Ruby R5667. Bred by W. H. Cowpe. Blue.

Square Measure (W. S. Wright) 1921 by Highwayman out of Ben Lady. Bred by owner.

Squeak of Harnish 610NN (Mrs E. Binnie) 1931 by Cranley Jim out of Busy of Harnish. Bred by Mrs Hallowell-Carew. Blue.

Squire's Daughter 1915 by Cobledene Squire out of Queen Bess. Bred by J. McGlade.

Stanningley Surprise 1374HH (B. Davey) 1925 by Eccleshill Lucky Boy out of Tance (NT). Bred by A. Colburn. Blue.

Startler 1460PP (Mrs W. J. Onions) 1933 by Piper (NT) out of Corrella. Bred by R. Edminson. Blue.

Stepdancer 1917 by Coalstriker out of Peggy the Piper. Bred by W. Shiel.

Step Up (G. Tait) 1927 by Stepdancer out of Day Express. Bred by owner.

Stirabout 787NN (Misses Maunsell and Hamilton) 1931 by Cribden Centaur out of Hell's Delight. Bred by Mrs M. Harper. Liver.

Stocksbridge Bess (W. R. Turner) 1922 by Breakwater Chieftain out of Blue Vixon. Bred by J. H. Taylor.

Stoneferry Jock's Double 1196CC (J. G. Burrell) 1921 by Jock's Lodge out of Daisy R5875. Bred by R. C. Irving.

Stonehouse Gipsy 27813 (H. E. James) 1886 by Projectile out of Stonehouse Vixen. Bred by owner. Liver.

Stonehouse Vixen 15927 (H. E. James) 1883 by Young Victor out of Wasp R5676. Liver. Show weight 23 lbs. Height 16 inches.

Stormy Night 1668HH (T. Webster) 1925 by Moving Knight out of Blue Vera. Bred by owner. Blue.

Strathblane 13173 (W. Morris, afterwards D. Ross) 1881 by Tell out of Phoebe R126. Bred by Ross. Liver. The dam is given as Daisy originally in K.C.S.B. but afterwards corrected to Phoebe.

Stump Cross Tim (H. Wainwright) 1923 by Ruddigore out of Intombi. Bred by owner.

Sudston Pamela 125FF (Mrs Mead) 1924 by Sudston Panther out of Sudston Pandora. Bred by owner. Blue.

Sudston Pandora (Mrs Mead) 1919 by Breakwater Chieftain out of Sudston Pearl. Bred by owner.

Sudston Panther 179EE (Mrs Mead) 1922 by Jock's Lodge out of Dinah (NT). Bred by Ching. Blue.

Sudston Pearl 565T (Mrs Mead) 1912 by Tak-a-bit out of Raggles. Bred by owner. Blue.

Sudston Pedlar 29MM (Mrs Mead) 1930 by King's Pawn out of Sudston Princess. Bred by owner. Blue.

Sudston Periwinkle 165NN (Mrs Mead) 1930 by King's Pawn out of Sudston Princess. Bred by owner.

Sudston Posey 348JJ (Mrs Mead) 1927 by Sudston Panther out of Merry Jyppy R6976. Bred by D. Pitt. Blue.

Sudston Prince 1911 by Breakwater Chief out of Findern Queen. Bred by E. Farrer.

Sudston Princess 279HH (Mrs Mead) 1926 by Sudston Panther out of Merry Jyppy R6976. Bred by D. Pitt. Blue.

Sugar Baby 22NN (Miss E. V. Herdman) 1931 by Dracula out of Brown Sugar of Harnish. Bred by owner.

Sunflower of Rogate 506PP, Champion (Miss E. B. Herdman) 1932 by Dracula out of Brown Sugar of Harnish. Bred by owner. Liver.

Sunmaid (G. Tait) 1928 by Scottie out of Day Express. Bred by owner.

Sunshine Duchess 2061QQ (J. T. Flint) 1933 by Sunshine Shone out of Payment. Bred by owner. Blue.

Sunshine Girl 1269LL, Champion (J. T. Flint) 1929 by Moving Knight out of Broomilea Peggy. Bred by D. Pitt. Blue.

Sunshine Princess 1148QQ (J. T. Flint) 1933 by Sunshine Shone out of Payment. Bred by owner. Blue.

Sunshine Shone (J. B. Campbell) 1931 by Knowlton Peter Pan out of Sunshine Girl. Bred by J. T. Flint.

Sunshine Susie 549QQ (Miss V. Cross) 1931 by Knowlton Peter Pan out of Sunshine Girl. Bred by J. T. Flint. Blue.

Superba 1897 by Goldseeker out of Miss South.

Susan of Mottisfont (Commander Holbrook, V.C.) 1925 by Hop-a-long out of Cleopatra. Bred by T. N. Keith.

Sut R35 (W. Morris) by Dante R46 out of Bess (NT) (Heron).

Swap R5364 by Clyde Boy out of Breakwater Nell R349.

Sweep R5363 by Jack (NT) out of Sedgehill Jeanie (NT).

Sweet Afton 1181E (Messrs Hunter and Bell) 1897 by Tip (NT) (Armstrong) out of Nettle (NT) (Georgeson) Blue. For Tip see note under Beaconsfield Triumph.

Sweetheart II 29979 (A. Reekie) 1886 by Northern Leader out of Horncliffe Lass. Bred by owner. Liver.

Swift Knight (Miss F. M. Sturt) 1926 by Night Express out of Blue Beauty. Bred by T. Robson. Blue.

Sycamore Gem 1373HH (W. Holmes) 1926 by Moving Knight out of Rosemaid. Bred by J. Laws. Blue.

Syringa (W. Williams) 1921 by Ewood Eclipse out of Nell (NT). Bred by A. W. Smith.

T.

Tak-a-bit 418R (A. Rudham) 1908 by Beaconsfield Tavy out of Beaconsfield Tibbie (NT). Bred by J. Cook. Blue.

Take Me 1913 by Askme out of Rebecca. Bred by M. Robson.

Tamar Implacable 276KK, Champion (J. W. Bennett) 1926 by Deckham Crest out of Cribden Choice. Bred by A. S. Watson. Blue.

Tammany of Simonside 548QQ (Misses M. M. and C. R. Carr) 1933 by Precious Michael of Simonside out of Princess Wee One of Simonside. Bred by owners. Blue.

Tam's Wares 277KK (G. Nicholson) 1928 by Cribden Chutney out of Dinah Grey. Bred by C. Haworth. Blue.

Tango by Badger out of Phoebe R5695.

Tattered Jim 177GG (W. Neil) 1923 by Eccleshill Blue Boy out of Gandy Bridge Jewel. Bred by owner. Blue.

Tatters R5416, bitch by Craghead Eclipse out of Green Lane Vixen.

Tatters R5632, dog 1920 by Eccleshill Blue Boy out of Floss R5696. Bred by G. Bramley.

Tatters R5679, bitch (B. Davies) by Chhota Sahib out of Chhota Peg.

Tearem 3429, Champion (T. J. Pickett) 1869 by Scamp R27 out of Daisy R25. Scamp was the son of the Daisy to whom he was mated. Tearem was brother to Tyne 3430 and subsequently mated to her. A note dealing with the pedigree of a certain Rosebud appended to an article by Hugh Dalziel in the *Field* states that the dam of Tearem and Tyne was Gibbs's 'Daisy by Gibbs's dog out of J. Dodd's Bess', but this is a mistake. There is a terrible amount of confusion among these early Daisies. Tearem and Tyne were very famous Bedlingtons in their day. See also History.

Tearem R5698 (Anderson) by Dante R46 out of ?——?.

Tegwen (H. A. Tutt) 1921 by Lucky Lad out of Betty R5663. Bred by F. Ellis.

Tell by Tearem 3429 out of Daisy or Young Daisy R48 (Gibbs).

Terror (G. Hall) by Tip (NT) out of Nelly (NT).

Tess of my Heart (C. G. Worrell) 1932 by Boy of Anfield out of Hot Pickles. Bred by owner.

Thread of Gold (L. Alderson) by Moving Knight out of Foundling Peg.

Tim R5707 (H. E. Barber) by Blyth Briton out of Northern Lass.

The author's first dogs, the wire was two weeks older and shared his bottle. The Bedlington, Maid of Harnish, by Champion Shothanger Rector, whelped 1929, set his ideals on the Bedlington coat.

T. Alder.

Tip R36 (W. Liddel) by Ebchester Tip R42 out of Phoebe R31 (J. Dodd), or Daisy (NT) (J. Dodd). Different authorities give these different names for the dam. I cannot say which is correct. Possibly they both refer to the same bitch.

Tip R42 (Stoddart). See Ebchester Tip.

Tip R161 (Hedley) by Ch. Piper 7698 out of Rose R162.

Tip R345 (W. Todd) by Senator 13171 out of Vic R230.

Tip 4645 (J. Parker) 1874 by Ebchester Tip R42 out of Topsy. Bred by owner. I think the dam was Topsy R51 but am not sure.

Tipper R666, late Tip (J. A. Baty) 1879 by Ch. Piper 7698 out of Jess R165. Bred by W. Hedley. Colour described as silver. K.C.S.B. 14425.

Titch by Jock's Lodge out of Chelsea Blue Girl.

Tommy Foster (Pickett) by Nailer (NT) (Talbot) out of 'Snowdon's bitch'.

Tom Tom 1343KK (J. E. Turner) 1926 by Chippinghouse Piper out of Stocksbridge Bess. Bred by W. R. Turner. Liver.

Top Hole 1907 by Jock of Oran out of Tweedside Girl. Bred by R. C. Irving. This dog was registered in 1913 as Jock of Duart but by an oversight his name was given in its old unregistered form when his famous son Ch. Jock's Lodge was registered and he has gone down to posterity as Top Hole. As he appears under that name in hundreds of pedigrees, it is no use trying to alter it now.

Toppin (Major W. P. Groves) by Rex (NT) out of Belle (NT) Registered by K.C. in 1933 as 'breeder and date of birth unknown'.

Top o' the Morning (Misses Maunsell and Hamilton) 1917 by Brisco Kim out of Brisco Mart. Bred by E. Hocking.

Topsy R51, or Old Topsy (Batty) by Tearem 3429 out of Old Meg (NT) (Shields). See History.

Topsy R263 (N. Armstrong) about 1871 by Sep (NT) (Talbot) out of Meg (NT) (Snowden).

Torfield Peggy (J. Pearson also A. J. Warburton) by Polar Boy out of Judy R5210.

Treasure's Son 347JJ (F. Mawson) 1927 by Moving Swell (NT) out of Hidden Treasure. Bred by C. S. Bell. Liver.

Triumph 388Q (J. Wilson) 1907 by Collingham Keeper out of Castleton Puss. Bred by owner. Blue.

True Blue of Simonside 508PP (Misses M. M. and C. R. Carr) 1932 by Barny out of Bontesse of Simonside. Bred by owners. Blue.

Trump Card (J. Blench) 1907 by Jock of Oran out of Miss Nelson (NT). Bred by R.C. Irving.

Trusty (Mrs Mead) 1908 by Trump Card out of Tweedmouth Lady. Bred by H. Young.

Tug (Robert Bell of Wingate) by Dusty, belonging to Robert Dixon of Longhorsley, out of Music, a bitch of the Makepiece breed belonging to John Thompson. The parentage of Dusty and Music is not known, but see History.

Tweedmouth Lady (H. Young) by President Squire out of Hillburn Lass (NT).

Tweedmouth Lass (J. Blench) 1892 by Berwick Brick out of Venus alias Jess (NT) (Purvis).

Tweedside Girl 1616J (R. C. Irving) 1903 by Elswick Piper out of Tweedside Lady. Bred by W. M. Mather. Liver.

Tweedside Jessie by Elswick Piper out of Tweedside Lady.

Tweedside Lad 1913 by Little Boy Blue out of Tweed Lass (NT). Bred by A. Watson.

Tweedside Lady (W. M. Mather) by Blyth Bob out of Cranley Rosette.

Twig 10907 (Farquharson) 1878 by Chief 6665 out of Dinah R149. Bred by Crow. Light liver.

Twilight (J. Spurgeon) 1904 by Derryvolgie out of Dusky Queen. Bred by J. Cornforth.

Tyne 3430, Champion (T. J. Pickett) 1869 by Scamp R27 out of Daisy R25. See note on Tearem 3429 who was Tyne's brother and also see History.

Tyneside Lass R115 (T. J. Pickett) by Tearem 3429 out of Tyne 3430.

U.

Undine (R. P. Wilson) 1921 by Jock's Lodge out of Simba (NT). Bred by owner.

Ursula 1914 by Sperkeforde Jackanapes out of Cranley Peggy. Bred by W. W. Savage.

V.

Valpre Jip (A. C. Tolhurst) 1923 by Tatters R5632 out of Fluff (NT). Bred by C. Elwes.

Vanity by Trusty out of Vic R5217. Bred by E. Hurtley.

Vectis by Deansfield Piper out of Flash Point (NT).

Venom R4 (William Turnbull of Holystone) by Matchem R2 out of Fan. The dam Fan also belonged to Turnbull but her parents are not recorded. See History.

Venture R358 (Rogerson) by Young Clansman (NT) out of Minnie Clyde.

Vera of Mottisfont (Miss N. Dixon) 1926 by Night Express out of Susan of Mottisfont. Bred by owner.

Vic R33 (W. Liddell) by Tip R36 out of Sut R35.

Vic R230, also called Old Vic (Hedley) by Sam R158 out of Meg (NT) (Thompson).

Vic R668 (W. Hedley) 1879 by Ch. Piper 7698 out of Wasp R246. Bred by W. Morris. Blue. This bitch was afterwards registered as Blue Blood K.C.S.B. 15148 but generally appears as Vic. Hedley had at least one other, Vic, see above.

Vic R5217 (E. Hurtley) 1908 by Bellerby Bishop out of Nellie R5521. Bred by W. B. Baty. Blue. This bitch was registered at K.C. in 1914 as Abus Vic but was generally known without the prefix and so appears in many pedigrees.

Vicarage Supreme 219PP (Miss M. Pattison) 1932 by Gardeners Supremacy out of Welldon. Bred by owner. Blue.

Victor R303. See Rustic.

Victoria R357 (P. H. Freeman) by Happy Lad (NT) out of Maggie Murphy.

Victoria, alias Meg R240. See Meg R240.

Victor Wild by Hammond alias Jolly Barber out of Wild Rose (NT).

Violet R127 by Crowner R128 out of Bess R49.

Viper R21 (Bagalee) by Thomas Thompson's Old Tip out of Nimble R28. For Old Tip see remarks under Nimble R28 and also in History.

Vixen R6 (Andrew Evans of Holystone) by the Miller's dog at Felton out of a bitch belonging to Mr Carr of Felton Hall. The pedigree of these two Terriers is unknown. See History.

W.

Walker Girl 1750EE (J. Wilkins) 1920 by Ewood Eclipse out of Bomb Girl. Bred by M. Lee. Blue.

War Baby 1917 by Cobledene Pat out of Cobledene Meg. Bred by J. McGlade.

Warkworth Hotspur 23355 (C. T. Maling) 1884 by Quayside Lad out of Meg (NT). Bred by W. Heads. Liver with tan legs. The prefix was apparently added later and the dog sometimes appears as Hotspur.

Wasp R10 (Andrew Riddell of Framlington) by Pincher R5 out of an unnamed bitch of William Wardle of Framlington whose parents are not recorded. Was sister to the Rennington dog to whom she was afterwards mated. See History.

Wasp R22 (William Clark of Bedlington) by Viper R21 out of Daisy R30. See History.

Wasp R130 (Douglas) by Piper R249 out of Wasp (NT) (Fender).

Wasp R242 (J. Thompson) by Weardale R142 out of ?——?.

Wasp R246 (J. Morris) by Tip 4645 out of Meg (NT) (Morris).

Wasp R5676 (J. Mead) by Clansman 9581 out of Meg, described as a bitch of unknown pedigree.

Wasp R5677 (Spoor or Wall) by Tip (NT) (Foster) out of Jess (NT) (Spoor or Wall).

Wasp R5700 (Hunter) by Old Crowner (NT) out of Fan (NT). There were several Crowners and I do not know which this is.

Wassy R32. See Music.

Wassy R5702 (Joicee) by Piper R26 out of Daisy R25A. See History.

Water Lily (L. Alderson) 1927 by Stump Cross Tim out of Dancing Molly. Bred by W. Whitaker.

Weardale R142 (G. J. Soulsby) about 1872 by Tearem 3429 out of Tyne 3430.

Welhead Wallet 1280QQ, Champion (Mrs B. Holgate) 1933 by Ishmael out of Silvertop Gem. Bred by owner. Blue.

Welhead Warrior 547QQ (Mrs B. Holgate) 1933 by Ishmael out of Silvertop Gem. Bred by owner. Blue.

Welhead Whisper 285RR (Mrs B. Holgate) 1934 by Knowlton Peter Pan out of Silvertop Gem. Bred by owner.

Welhead Whoopee 1017PP, Champion (Mrs B. Holgate) 1932 by Knowlton Peter Pan out of Silvertop Gem. Bred by owner. Blue.

Welhead Wynot (Mrs B. Holgate) 1931 by Ishmael out of Golduma. Bred by owner.

Welhead Wynport 1060QQ, Champion (Mrs R. A. Martin) 1933 by Sudston Pedlar out of Welhead Wynot. Bred by A. Aspinall. Blue.

Welldon (Miss M. Pattison) 1929 by Lap End out of Neat Kettle. Bred by W. Cole.

Welldon Adorable 782QQ, Champion (Miss M. Pattison) 1933 by Gardeners Supremacy out of Welldon. Bred by owner. Blue.

Westagate Boy 1430NN, Champion (E. W. and P. Wears, and W. J. Onions) 1931 by Scottie out of Nellie (NT). Bred by L. Doyle. Blue.

Westell Beauty (Mrs W. V. Beattie) 1928 by Moving Knight out of Westella (NT). Bred by S. Caris.

Wharfe Lady 1920 by Eccleshill Blue Boy out of Somme Girl. Bred by H. Kershaw.

What'll I do (Mrs B. Holgate) 1927 by Pugnacity out of Rose Dew. Bred by owner.

Whetstone Lady (J. T. Barnes) 1924 by Deckham Crest out of Winfield Lady. Bred by owner.

Whilensleaf 1915 by Coalstriker out of Peggy the Piper. Bred by J. Wright.

Wild Lassie R5527 by Clive Boy (NT) out of Fraiflor.

Wild Woodbine 529KK (W. J. Onions) 1928 by Son of a Knight out of Daisy (NT). Bred by T. Maddison. Liver.

Williamfield Piper (R. Allan) 1922 by Willycraggs out of Williamfield Sensation. Bred by owner.

Williamfield Sensation (R. Allan) 1921 by Mickel out of Marion of Dovesland. Bred by J. Fulton.

Willycraggs 832AA 1917 by Blyth Baronet out of Blyth Barmaid. Blue.

Winfield Lady (J. T. Barnes) 1922 by Breakwater Chieftain out of Peggy (NT). Bred by M. Dyson.

Winn for Beer 1484K (W. J. Onions, 1904 by Afton Wallace out of Nell (NT). Bred by J. White. Liver.

Winning Princess 28HH (T. Griffiths) 1925 by Quick Step out of Lady Aggalade. Bred by W. Cole. Blue.

Winsome Wendy 46EE (Mrs Needham) 1923 by Jock's Lodge out of Blue Lassie. Bred by Mrs Towers Minors. Blue and tan.

Wolecurb Trix 440LL, Champion (Mrs Bruce-Low) 1929 by Worton Demon out of Glendale Nellie. Bred by J. Heal. Liver.

Wolecurb Woodnymph 1461PP Mrs Bruce-Low) 1932 by Knowlton Peter Pan out of Dainty Girl. Bred by owner. Blue.

Worton Demon (Mrs Williamson) 1923 by Goxhill Blue Boy out of Musha. Bred by owner. Blue.

X.

Xmas Daisy. See Christmas Daisy.

Y.

Ye Bonnie Lass (A. Sibley) 1905 by Deansfield Piper out of Miss Oliver. Bred by H. Warnes.

Young Devon (Henderson) by Young Nailer 7706 out of Fury R248.

Young Nailer 7706 (Turner) 1876 by Tommy Foster out of Tyneside Lass R115. Bred by T. J. Pickett. Linty blue.

Young Victor by Plymouth Lad out of Jess R5672.

ADDENDA TO STUD BOOK.

The following dogs have qualified for admission to the Stud Book since this volume went to press.

I have not had time in every case to trace their pedigrees further back.

Afton Girl (A. Fraser) 1932 by Rags (NT) out of Moving Cheek. Bred by R. Allison.

Gardeners Starturn 660RR (E. Metcalf) 1934 by Gardeners Supremacy out of Queen of All. Bred by Miss M. E. Simm.

Gardeners Supreme Lady 955RR (E. Metcalf) 1933 by Gardeners Supremacy out of Kirkhill Maid. Bred by J. Alder.

Gay Miss of Simonside 661RR (Misses M. M. and C. R. Carr) 1934 by Deckham Oprecious out of Miss Gaysum. Bred by Miss Hallowell-Carew. Blue.

Khaki (Miss E. Upton) 1931 by Cribden Chutney out of Belgrano Judy. Bred by R. Bleasdale.

Lapis Lazuli, Champion (Miss J. Nicholson) 1933 by Dazzler Demon out of Our Rhoda. Bred by F. Watson.

Minimum of Simonside 658RR, Champion (Misses M. M. and C. R. Carr) 1934 by Deckham Oprecious out of Miss Gaysum. Bred by Miss Hallowell-Carew. Blue.

Our Rhoda (F. Watson) 1930 by Fiddlers Boy out of Pride of the Lane. Bred by owner.

Pec's Fancy 666RR (P. Simm) 1933 by Gardeners Supremacy out of Afton Girl. Bred by A. Fraser.

Rival of Wrinstone (Mrs Llewellyn Ward) 1934 by Brightstone Venture out of Riddle of Wrinstone. Bred by owner.

Woodrow Waterboy 659RR (Miss V. Cross) 1934 by Gardeners Supremacy out of Sunshine Susie. Bred by owner.

Woodrow Wizard 701RR, Champion (Miss V. Cross) 1934 by Welhead Whoopee out of Khaki. Bred by Miss E. Upton.

— 10 —

Show record and breeding of
Challenge Certificate winners since Redmarshall's stud book

Redmarshall, in his addenda, takes us to the thirties and we now follow up the record from that date. Until 1948 the Kennel Club only published the names of Challenge Certificate winners but from 1949 the reserve winners were also shown.

The following lists give the show, judge and dog and bitch winners.

Unfortunately, it has not been possible to continue Redmarshall's Stud Book section but two generation pedigrees are given of all Challenge Certificate winners since and it is hoped that students of the breed will gain useful information therefrom. A dog's name appears in the first year in which it won a major award and no regard is given to age.

Every effort has been made to maintain accuracy but errors can and do occur in records and the reader is urged to correct any mistake.

Challenge Certificate Winners

1930

National Terrier   *Judge* S Graham
GARDENERS PERFECTION
TAMAR IMPLACABLE

Crufts   P R Smith
CH GARDENERS PERFECTION
SUDSTON PRINCESS

Bath   W P Charlton
CHUTNEYS DOUBLE
GARDENERS SUPREME

Great Joint Terrier   J Cook
DECKHAM O'PRECIOUS
CH GARDENERS SUPREME

Taunton   Miss Hamilton
CHUTNEY'S DOUBLE
GARDENERS RENOWN

Sheffield   G S Thomas
CH GARDENERS PERFECTION
SUNSHINE GIRL

Edinburgh   W J Onions
PIPER OF RYTON
CH RYTONION NETTLE

Kennel Club   H Grayshon
DECKHAM O'PRECIOUS
PENNYCRAIG LUCY

Metropolitain & Essex   T R Osborn
CH DECKHAM O'PRECIOUS
PENNYCRAIG LUCY

Birmingham   E Metcalf
HOLD YOUR WHISHT
CH TAMAR IMPLACABLE

1931

National Terrier   *Judge* Mrs Ben Holgate

SUDSTON PEDLAR
WOLECURB TRIX

Crufts   W S Wright
CH DECKHAM O'PRECIOUS
SUNSHINE GIRL

Bath   J Cook
DAZZLER DEMON
CH SUNSHINE GIRL

Great Joint Terrier   T E Brown
LEADER OF SIMONSIDE
WOLECURB TRIX

Taunton   T R Osborn
KNOWLTON PETER PAN
CH PENNYCRAIG LUCY

Cardiff   E Calvert Butler
LEADER OF SIMONSIDE
PERDITA JOY

Edinburgh   J J Holgate
DECKER ONLAW
DAZZLER GEM

Kennel Club   W J Onions
GINGER PIPER
CH WOLECURB TRIX

Metropolitan & Essex   T N Keith
RIGHT CHOICE OF SIMONSIDE
DAZZLER GEM

Birmingham   Miss V A C Maunsell
DAZZLER DEMON
GARDENERS JEWEL

1932

National Terrier   *Judge* Mr Hallowell-Carew
GARDENERS SUPREMACY
CH DAZZLER GEM

Crufts   P R Smith
KNOWLTON PETER PAN
DAZZLER QUEEN

CHALLENGE CERTIFICATE WINNERS

Bath   Maj E B Aylward
GARDENERS SUPREMACY
ESPERANZA

Great Joint Terrier   F Calvert Butler
RIGHT CHOICE OF SIMONSIDE
ESPERANZA

Taunton   J R Parsons
BOBBY DAZZLER
STIRABOUT

Richmond   Mrs Ben Holgate
CH KNOWLTON PETER PAN
CH ESPERANZA

Edinburgh   W S Wright
WESTGATE BOY
SUGAR BABY

Kennel Club   H K McCausland
WESTGATE BOY
BLUE TASSIE

Metropolitain & Essex Mrs E Bruce-Low
CH WESTAGATE BOY
SUGAR BABY

Birmingham   J A Ure
CH GARDENERS SUPREMACY
CH SUGAR BABY

1933

National Terrier   *Judge*
                Miss V Maunsell
CH CHUTNEY'S DOUBLE
MARKS DREAM

Crufts   J Cook
GARDENERS ECLIPSE
VICARAGE SUPREME

Bath   T R Osborn
CH RIGHT CHOICE OF SIMONSIDE
MISS GAYSUM

Great Joint Terrier   W J Onions
CH DAZZLER DEMON
JANE OF HARNISH

Taunton   Maj E J Aylward
GARDENERS ESSENTIAL
MISS GAYSUM

Richmond   Mrs Hallowell-Carew
PETHOMMIE
SUNFLOWER OF ROGATE

Edinburgh   G Wallwork
WELHEAD WHOOPEE
SUNFLOWER OF ROGATE

Kennel Club   P R Smith
WELHEAD WHOOPEE
RADIANCE OF WRINSTONE

Metropolitain & Essex   T N Keith
CH WELHEAD WHOOPEE
DAZZLER QUEEN

Birmingham   Miss D Hamilton
GARDENERS CHOICE
CH MISS GAYSUM

1934

National Terrier   *Judge*
             H K McCausland
BUBBLE OF HARNISH
RADIANCE OF WRINSTONE

Crufts   H Grayshon
BRIGHTSTONE VENTURE
CH RADIANCE OF WRINSTONE

Bath   Miss V A Maunsell
GARDENERS ESSENTIAL
CH RADIANCE OF WRINSTONE

Great Joint Terrier   T Wallace
WELHEAD WARRIOR
CH RADIANCE OF WRINSTONE

Taunton   F W Morris
GARDENERS ALDERMAN
GARDENERS ELEGANCE

Richmond   Mrs H E Magee
BRIGHTSTONE VENTURE
CH SUNFLOWER OF ROGATE

Leeds   P R Smith
CH GARDENERS ESSENTIAL
CH RADIANCE OF WRINSTONE

Harrogate   Mrs M Llewellyn Ward
CH BRIGHTSTONE VENTURE
CH SUNFLOWER OF ROGATE

Edinburgh　　　　　　J Garrow
BUBBLE OF HARNISH
GARDENERS ELEGANCE

Kennel Club　　　　Maj E B Aylward
CH BRIGHTSTONE VENTURE
CH RADIANCE OF WRINSTONE

Metropolitain & Essex　　T R Osborn
WELHEAD WALLET
CH RADIANCE OF WRINSTONE

Birmingham　　　　　Miss M Sturt
GARDENERS ALDERMAN
GARDENERS ELEGANCE

1935

National Terrier　　Judge T E Brown
WELHEAD WALLET
BLUE TASSIE

Crufts　　　　　　J R Parsons
GUARDSMAN
SUNSHINE DUCHESS

Glasgow　　　　　　W J Onions
CH BUBBLE OF HARNISH
SARAH OF NONINGTON

Bath　　　　　　　J T Flint
WOODROW WATERBOY
GAY MISS OF SIMONSIDE

Great Joint Terrier　　T N Keith
CH WELHEAD WALLET
HEEBIE JEEBIE

Taunton　　　Miss V A Maunsell
WELHEAD WYNPORT
CH BLUE TASSIE

Richmond　　　Mrs Llewellyn Ward
CH WELHEAD WALLET
GAY MISS OF SIMONSIDE

Leeds　　　　　　　C Houlker
CH BRIGHTSTONE VENTURE
CH RADIANCE OF WRINSTONE

Harrogate　　　　　P R Smith
PRECIOUS MICHAEL OF SIMONSIDE
WELLDON ADORABLE

Edinburgh　　　　　S Crabtree
LAPIZ LAZULI
CH DAZZLER QUEEN

Kennel Club　　　Mrs Ben Holgate
WELHEAD WYNPORT
AWAUNI

Metropolitain & Essex　　Mrs E
　　　　　　　　Hallowell-Carew
MINIMUM OF SIMONSIDE
AWAUNI

Birmingham　　　　W Bullivant
CH WELHEAD WYNPORT
CH RADIANCE OF WRINSTONE

1936

National Terrier　Judge H Grayshon
LAPIZ LAZULI
CH RADIANCE OF WRINSTONE

Crufts　　　　　　E Metcalf
FOGGYFURZE ACE HIGH
CH AWAUNI

Glasgow　　　　　G Wallwork
CH LAPIZ LAZULI
CH RADIANCE OF WRINSTONE

Bath　　　Count V C Hollender
WOODROW WIZARD
WELHEAD WIDEAWAKE

Great Joint Terrier　Miss E Herdman
MINIMUM OF SIMONSIDE
CH RADIANCE OF WRINSTONE

Richmond　　　　　T N Keith
CH MINIMUM OF SIMONSIDE
WOODROW WATERNYMPH

Leeds　　　　　Mrs M E Mead
FOGGYFURZE ACE HIGH
SUNSHINE DUCHESS

Harrogate　　　Miss V Maunsell
GARDENERS PARAGON
CH SUNSHINE DUCHESS

Edinburgh　　　　J W H Beynon
CH FOGGYFURZE ACE HIGH
WELLDON ADORABLE

Kennel Club　　　　T R Osborn
GARDENERS PARAGON
CH RADIANCE OF WRINSTONE

CHALLENGE CERTIFICATE WINNERS

Metropolitain & Essex T E Brown
CH GARDENERS PARAGON
CH WELLDON ADORABLE

Birmingham J Flint
CH GARDENERS PARAGON
WOODROW WITCH GIRL

1937

National Terrier *Judge* W Bullivant
CH BRIGHTSTONE VENTURE
BRIGHTSTONE HARMONY

Crufts Mrs Llewellyn Ward
CH BRIGHTSTONE VENTURE
BRIGHTSTONE HARMONY

Glasgow J Garrow
GARDENERS IMPERIAL
CHERRY OF NONINGTON

Bath J Ure
GARDENERS IMPERIAL
CHERRY OF NONINGTON

Great Joint Terrier Mrs S Harman
REQUEST OF WRINSTONE
LINDUM LAVENDER

Taunton Mrs F M Herdman
WOODROW WIZARD
LINDUM LAVENDER

Richmond Mrs Ben Holgate
CH WOODROW WIZARD
CH LINDUM LAVENDER

Harrogate Mrs Hallowell-Carew
ROBIN OF SIMONSIDE
PYNELLO JANE

Edinburgh T Scott
ROBIN OF SIMONSIDE
CH CHERRY OF NONINGTON

Kennel Club Mrs M E Magee
CH ROBIN OF SIMONSIDE
CH LINDUM LAVENDER

Birmingham C G Worrall
REQUEST OF WRINSTONE
TRUE JOY OF SIMONSIDE

Metropolitain & Essex T N Keith
CH REQUEST OF WRINSTONE
PYNELLO JANE

1938

National Terrier *Judge*
Mrs Ben Holgate
PIPER'S SUCCESS
CH PYNELLO JANE

Crufts G Wallwork
BRAMBLEDENE BUCCANEER
LEADING LADY OF SIMONSIDE

W.E.L.K.S. Mrs E Hallowell-Carew
LIVESPARK OF SIMONSIDE
REALITY OF WRINSTONE

Bath Miss V A Maunsell
CH GARDENERS IMPERIAL
CUCKOO OF HARNISH

Great Joint Terrier H K McCausland
PIPER'S SUCCESS
FOLLY

Taunton Miss D Hamilton
GARDENERS FIDELITY
CHARM OF NONINGTON

Richmond J W H Beynon
GARDENERS FIDELITY
REALITY OF WRINSTONE

Leeds P R Smith
BRAMBLEDENE BUCCANEER
CH REALITY OF WRINSTONE

Harrogate Mrs M E Mead
LAMPLIGHTER
CHARM OF NONINGTON

Edinburgh H R Brown
CH GARDENERS FIDELITY
HENRIETTA OF NONINGTON

Birmingham S L Franks
CH PIPER'S SUCCESS
FOLLY

Metropolitain & Essex Mrs H E Magee
LAVERS LANCER
CH FOLLY

Kennel Club Mrs S Harman
LAVERS LANCER
LEADING LADY OF SIMONSIDE

1939

National Terrier   *Judge*
Mrs Llewellyn Ward
HENRY OF NONINGTON
WOODROW WAIT

Crufts   J Garrow
CH BRAMBLEDENE BUCCANEER
CH REALITY OF WRINSTONE

Ladies Kennel Assn.   T N Keith
GOOD KNIGHT
BRIGHTSTONE FLAME

W.E.L.K.S.   W Bullivant
CH LAVERS LANCER
TRUE JOY OF SIMONSIDE

Bath   J Flint
CH GARDENERS FIDELITY
CH CHARM OF NONINGTON

Great Joint Terrier   Mrs M E O'Brien
TITUS OF ROGATE
CH LEADING LADY OF SIMONSIDE

Taunton   Count V C Hollender
HENRY OF NONINGTON
HENRIETTA OF NONINGTON

Richmond   Miss C R Carr
DUNMAIL OF PITT
IRON DUCHESS

Leeds   V Hirst
CH HENRY OF NONINGTON
CH HENRIETTA OF NONINGTON

Harrogate   Mrs Ben Holgate
DUNMAIL OF PITT
FOGGYFURZE STARLIGHT

1946

Bedlington Terrier Assn.   *Judge*
Mrs Llewellyn Ward
LINDUM LIGHTNING
FOGGYFURZE GLAMOROUS

1947

Muswell Hill   Mrs M E O'Brien
BRAMBLEDENE BARON
FOGGYFURZE GLAMOROUS

Blackpool   Mrs Ben Holgate
LINDUM LIGHTNING
CH FOGGYFURZE GLAMOROUS

National Terrier   C G Worrall
CH LINDUM LIGHTNING
FOGGYFURZE TAILOR MADE

Leicester   W Worfolk
CH LINDUM LIGHTNING
FOGGYFURZE TAILOR MADE

Bedlington Terrier Assn.   Mrs H
BRAMBLEDENE BARON   Marshall
CH FOGGYFURZE TAILOR MADE

Ladies Kennel Assn.   J W Beynon
CH BRAMBLEDENE BARON
SALLY OF FOXINGTON

1948

Scottish Kennel Club   *Judge* J Robb
HIGHLAND DUKE
ROSETOP VICTORIOUS

W.E.L.K.S   Leo. Wilson
BRAMBLEDENE BRENDAN
JOYVENTURE

Blackpool   Mrs N Bullivant
WELHEAD WARRANT
JOYVENTURE

Richmond   S L Franks
FRIAR OF HEATHFIELD
BLUE DAY OF MANATON

Metropolitan & Essex   Mrs LL. Ward
BRACKNELL ROWLAND OF PITT
BLUE DAY OF MANATON

Stockton-on-Tees   F Gent
BRIGHT LAD
CULLERCOATS CINDERELLA

Leicester   J Flint
BRACKNELL ROWLAND OF PITT
ROSETOP VICTORIOUS

City of Birmingham   T Scott
CH BRACKNELL ROWLAND OF PITT
CULLERCOATS CINDERELLA

Kensington   A A Simmonds
FRIAR OF HEATHFIELD
CULLERCOATS CINDERELLA

Crufts   W Worfolk
CH FRIAR OF HEATHFIELD
SALLY OF FOXINGTON

Ladies Kennel Assn.   P R Smith
BRAMBLEDENE BRENDAN
BRAMBLEDENE BELINDA

National Terrier   Llewellyn Ward
BLUE DUSK OF MANATON
CH FOGGYFURZE GLAMOROUS

Croydon   J Saunders
CH BRAMBLEDENE BRENDAN
CH CULLERCOATS CINDERELLA

1949

Birmingham   *Judge*
     Mrs M E O'Brien
GOLDSTRIKE OF FOXINGTON
Ruler of Pitt
CH FOGGYFURZE GLAMOROUS
Chriselda of Nare

Scottish Kennel Club   Mrs C J Barber
CURLY CUT
Ruler of Pitt
SPRITRESS
Joyventure

W.E.L.K.S.   C G Worrall
GOLDSTRIKE OF FOXINGTON
Bright Lad
TOL-PEDN MERRY MAID
Anne of Foxington

Croydon   Mrs R J Martin
BLUE DUSK OF MANATON
Goldstrike of Foxington
MOORSRAIKE MOONLIGHT
Anne of Foxington

Chester   Leo C Wilson
CH GOLDSTRIKE OF FOXINGTON
Curly Cut
MOORSRAIKE MOONLIGHT
Foggyfurze Gilda

Blackpool   J W H Beynon
RULER OF PITT
Moscar Red Ensign
CH MOORSRAIKE MOONLIGHT
Rosetop Victorious

Richmond   W Bullivant
CH BLUE DUSK OF MANATON
Welhead Warrant
CH JOYVENTURE
Naomi of Nablus

Leicester   Miss E Nichols
RULER OF PITT
Rosetop Javelin
CH ROSETOP VICTORIOUS
Lovely Lady of Nonington

City of Birmingham   W Worfolk
CH RULER OF PITT
Moscar Red Ensign
CHRISELDA OF NARE
Pearly of Marasan

Bedlington Terrier Assn.   Mrs Ben
     Holgate
PYNELLO JACQUES
Ch Goldstrike of Foxington
STUTEVILLE STARLETTE
Sally of Foxington

Scottish Kennel Club   F Gent
BRIGHTSTONE SUNFLOWER OF PITT
Moscar Red Ensign
STUTEVILLE STARLETTE
Highland Duchess

Ladies Kennel Assn.   T Scott
CH BRAMBLEDENE BARON
Gambol of Heathfield
BRAMBLEDENE BRENDA
Ch Rosetop Victorious

National Terrier   S L Franks
GAMBOL OF HEATHFIELD
Brightstone Sunflower of Pitt
CH SALLY OF FOXINGTON
Tol-pedn Merry Maid

Birmingham   Dr M E Binns
CH BRAMBLEDENE BARON
Ch Goldstrike of Foxington
CH STUTEVILLE STARLETTE
Tol-pedn Merry Maid

Kensington   A A Simmonds
BRIGHTSTONE SUNFLOWER OF PITT
Moscar Red Ensign
LORETTE OF NONINGTON
Lovely Lady of Nonington

1950

Crufts   *Judge* Mrs M Llewellyn Ward
CH GOLDSTRIKE OF FOXINGTON
Ch Brambledene Baron
CH FOGGYFURZE GLAMOROUS
Brambledene Blue Beauty

Scottish Kennel Club   Leo C Wilson
CH BRIGHTSTONE SUNFLOWER OF PITT
State Express
SHEILA OF BLUE SEA
Fleecy Sprite

W.E.L.K.S.   Llewellwyn Ward
Withheld
Withheld
SHEILA OF BLUE SEA
Jocaster of Pendrill

Croydon   W Worfolk
MOSCAR RED ENSIGN
Gambol of Heathfield
NAOMI OF NABLUS
Reputation of Pitt

Chester   S L Franks
CH GOLDSTRIKE OF FOXINGTON
Rag A Tail
TOL-PEDN MERRY MAID
Anne of Foxington

Blackpool   A W Fullwood
CH GOLDSTRIKE OF FOXINGTON
Moscar Red Ensign
AZURE ATTRACTION
Brambledene Blue Beauty

Richmond   Mrs M E O'Brien
CH BRAMBLEDENE BARON
Richard of Pitt
CH TOL-PEDN MERRY MAID
Jolande of Pendrill

Durham   Mrs R J Martin
DAUNTLESS DINGO
Bright Lad
SPRING DANCER
Brambledene Blue Beauty

Leicester   W Bullivant
CH GOLDSTRIKE OF FOXINGTON
Gay Boy of Foxington
JOCASTER OF PENDRILL
Blue Sky of Manaton

Bedlington Terrier Assn.   T Neville
CH GOLDSTRIKE OF FOXINGTON   Keith
Curly Cut
JOCASTER OF PENDRILL
Blue Sky of Manaton

Metropolitan & Essex   Leo C Wilson
RAG A TAIL
Curly Cut
SPRING DANCER
Lorette of Nonington

Scottish Kennel Club   J W H Beynon
MOSCAR RED ENSIGN
Kisimul of Oransay
BRAMBLEDENE BLUE BEAUTY
Newbottle New Look

Ladies Kennel Assn.   Mrs S L Franks
RAG A TAIL
Blue Flame
JOLANDE OF PENDRILL
Jocaster of Pendrill

Birmingham   C G Worrall
GAY BOY OF FOXINGTON
Curly Cut
CH SPRING DANCER
Brambledene Blue Beauty

Kensington   J Saunders
CH MOSCAR RED ENSIGN
Foggyfurze Bell Boy
CH JOCASTER OF PENDRILL
Jolande of Pendrill

1951

Croydon   *Judge* Mrs R J Martin
GAY BOY OF FOXINGTON
Gambol of Heathfield
BRAMBLEDENE BONNIE
Brambledene Blue Beauty

National Terrier   Mrs Llewellyn Ward
CH GAY BOY OF FOXINGTON
Curly Cut
NEWBOTTLE NEW LOOK
Jolande of Pendrill

Crufts   Llewellyn Ward
CH GAY BOY OF FOXINGTON
Curly Cut
JOLANDE OF FOXINGTON
Bluebell of Foxington

Scottish Kennel Club W Worfolk	*Scottish Kennel Club* J Garrow
CH GOLDSTRIKE OF FOXINGTON	BRIGHT LAD
Curly Cut	Burleydene Rodger
BLUEBELL OF FOXINGTON	CH SHEILA OF BLUE SEA
Newbottle New Look	Lorette of Nonington

Manchester Mrs A J Hopwood
CH GAY BOY OF FOXINGTON
Curly Cut
MOSCAR RED RASCAL
Bluebell of Foxington

Bedlington Terrier Assn. Mrs F
CH RAG A TAIL   Herdman
Petkim
GLORIA OF CLAYDALE
Lorette of Nonington

W.E.L.K.S. F Gent
CURLY CUT
Ch Gay Boy of Foxington
BRAMBLEDENE BLUE BEAUTY
Sheila of Blue Sea

Ladies Kennel Assn. Mrs Bullivant
CH RAG A TAIL
Ingram of Pitt
GLORIA OF CLAYDALE
Burleydene Mischief

Leeds J W H Beynon
CH CURLY CUT
Burleydene Blue Lad
CH JOLANDE OF PENDRILL
Newbottle New Look

Birmingham Mrs S L Franks
CH GAY BOY OF FOXINGTON
Ch Rag A Tail
BLUE SKY OF MANATON
Newbottle New Look

Chester T Scott
CH CURLY CUT
Blue Victor
LORETTE OF NONINGTON
Azure Attraction

Kensington Mrs A J Hopwood
CH GOLDSTRIKE OF FOXINGTON
Ingram of Pitt
NALLA OF NONINGTON
Burleydene Mischief

Blackpool Mrs Ben Holgate
CH CURLY CUT
Burleydene Blue Lad
PYNELLO PIXIE OF NARE
Karswell Cassadora

1952

Crufts *Judge* T Neville Keith
CH GAY BOY OF FOXINGTON
Rosetop Javelin
KARSWELL CASSADORA
Joanna of Pendrill

Richmond Dr M E Binns
CH GAY BOY OF FOXINGTON
Rag A Tail
CH JOLANDE OF PENDRILL
Blue Sky of Manaton

Scottish Kennel Club W S Wright
JONASH GENTLEMAN
Moscar Blue Ensign
RARE GOLD
Lorette of Nonington

Leicester S L Franks
CH GAY BOY OF FOXINGTON
Foggyfurze Sundowner
JOANNA OF PENDRILL
Moscar Red Rascal

Manchester W Worfolk
CH GAY BOY OF FOXINGTON
Ch Curly Cut
WOODSMANSEY WASPISH
Karswell Cassadora

Southern Counties Mrs R J Martin
INGRAM OF PITT
Barwal Blue Print
NEWBOTTLE NEW LOOK
Tol-pedn Crinoline

National Terrier Mrs M E O'Brien
CH CURLY CUT
Ingram of Pitt
CH NEWBOTTLE NEW LOOK
Burleydene Mischief

W.E.L.K.S.   Mrs Llewellyn Ward
CH CURLY CUT
Ch Rag A Tail
BLUE SKY OF MANATON
Woodsmansey Waspish

Leeds   Leo C Wilson
CH GAY BOY OF FOXINGTON
Westfen Panther
KARSWELL CASSADORA
Ch Sheila of Blue Sea

Chester   J Saunders
INGRAM OF PITT
Lorette of Nonington
BURLEYDENE MISCHIEF
Woodsmansey Waspish

Blackpool   V Hirst
CH GAY BOY OF FOXINGTON
Ch Curly Cut
BURLEYDENE MISCHIEF
Karswell Cassadora

Richmond   Mrs Llewellyn Ward
TOL-PEDN SMUGGLER
Inspector of Pitt
BLUE DAWN OF MANATON
Blue Sky of Manaton

Southern Counties   Mrs A J Hopwood
CH GAY BOY OF FOXINGTON
Ingram of Pitt
CH BURLEYDENE MISCHIEF
Blue Sky of Manaton

Scottish Kennel Club   W Worfolk
WESTFEN PANTHER
Tol-pedn Miner
CH NEWBOTTLE NEW LOOK
Pippa of Nonington

Bedlington Terrier Assn. Dr M E Binns
CH GOLDSTRIKE OF FOXINGTON
Cullercoats Bobby Bach
CH BLUE SKY OF MANATON
Ch Burleydene Mischief

Birmingham   T B Corbett
CH RAG A TAIL
Ingram of Pitt
CH BURLEYDENE MISCHIEF
Foggyfurze Dipsy Doodle

Ladies Kennel Assn.   Mrs R J Martin
PILGRIM OF YOMA
Nicholas of Cherrydale
BRAMBLEDENE BRINELLA
Ch Sheila of Blue Sea

1953

Crufts   *Judge* Mrs N Bullivant
CH GAY BOY OF FOXINGTON
Westfen Panther
CH BURLEYDENE MISCHIEF
Blue Dawn of Manaton

Glasgow   A W Fullwood
NORBERT OF NONINGTON
Westfen Panther
CH BURLEYDENE MISCHIEF
Woodmansey Waspish

W.E.L.K.S.   H Winder
GOLDEN SUN OF MANATON
Mirage of Wynbriar
PYNELLO PRIM
Tol-pedn Mermaid

Leeds   Mrs A J Hopwood
FOGGYFURZE CLASSIC CUT
Westfen Panther
WOODMANSEY WASPISH
Pynello Prim

Chester   Tom Scott
MIRAGE OF WYNBRIAR
Norbert of Nonington
PYNELLO PRIM
Pippa of Nonington

Blackpool   Percy Roberts, USA
FOGGYFURZE CLASSIC CUT
Westfen Panther
CH PYNELLO PRIM
Tol-pedn Mermaid

Richmond   Mrs M E O'Brien
CH FOGGYFURZE CLASSIC CUT
Westfen Panther
CH PYNELLO PRIM
Woodmansey Waspish

Brighton   Mrs Llewellyn Ward
PILGRIM OF YOMA
Norbert of Nonington
LUCY LOCKET OF PITT
Nona of Nablus

Edinburgh   A J Edwards
WESTFEN PANTHER
Norbert of Nonington
CH LORETTE OF NONINGTON
Jewel of Marasan

Bedlington Terrier Assn.   Mrs F Franks
MIRAGE OF WYNBRIAR
Westfen Panther
CH PYNELLO PRIM
Golden Days of Manaton

National Terrier   F Gent
CH WESTFEN PANTHER
Norbert of Nonington
TOL-PEDN MERMAID
Nona of Nablus

Birmingham   H H Wilson
CH FOGGYFURZE CLASSIC CUT
Norbert of Nonington
CH WOODMANSEY WASPISH
Roberta of Nonington

Ladies Kennel Assn.   Mrs F M Herdman
JUVERNA LORD LIVER OF PITT
Ingram of Pitt
NONA OF NABLUS
Tol-pedn Mermaid

1954

Glasgow   *Judge* J Garrow
CH CURLY CUT
Mirage of Wynbriar
CH SHIELA OF BLUE SEA
Tol-pedn Mermaid

Manchester   V Hirst
GOLDEN SUN OF MANATON
Juverna Lord Liver of Pitt
AMANDA MIRABEAU OF NONINGTON
Foggyfurze Cute Cut

W.E.L.K.S.   Mrs A J Hopwood
CH MIRAGE OF WYNBRIAR
Tol-pedn Smuggler
CH BLUE SKY OF MANATON
Daleview Delma

Leeds   Tom Scott
CH PILGRIM OF YOMA
Norbert of Nonington
AMANDA MIRABEAU OF NONINGTON
Karswell Cassadora

Chester   A Murray
NORBERT OF NONINGTON
Blueprint of Mahidap
CH KARSWELL CASSADORA
Westfen Vivandiere

Blackpool   Mrs M E O'Brien
CH GOLDEN SUN OF MANATON
Ch Pilgrim of Yoma
CH KARSWELL CASSADORA
Foggyfurze Cute Cut

Cardiff   T N Keith
CH NORBERT OF NONINGTON
Tol-pedn Smuggler
FOGGYFURZE CUTE CUT
Amanda Mirabeau of Nonington

Brighton   W Bullivant
CH GOLDEN SUN OF MANATON
Ch Norbert of Nonington
LINDUM LOVE IN THE MIST
Nona of Nablus

Bedlington Terrier Assn.   F Gent
CH GOLDEN SUN OF MANATON
Juverna Lord Liver of Pitt
NONA OF NABLUS
Ch Pynello Prim

Edinburgh   J Robb
BLUE RODNEY OF MANATON
Ch Norbert of Nonington
FOGGYFURZE CUTE CUT
Foggyfurze Clean Cut

National Terrier   Llewellyn Ward
CH GOLDEN SUN OF MANATON
Inspector of Pitt
NONA OF NABLUS
Foggyfurze Bubble Cut

Richmond   Dr J Aubrey Ireland
DANCER'S PRIDE
Ch Golden Sun of Manaton
CH NONA OF NABLUS
Lindum Love in the Mist

Birmingham National   G Trueman
                                         Hewitt
LEASOWES TRY AGAIN
Wynbriar Willie Winkle
CH FOGGYFURZE CUTE CUT
Westfen Vivandiere

Ladies Kennel Assn.   S L Franks
BLUE RODNEY OF MANATON
Leasowes Try Again
WESTFEN VIVANDIERE
Ch Nona of Nablus

1955

Crufts   Judge Dr M E Binns
CH GOLDEN SUN OF MANATON
Blueprint of Mahidap
CH TOL-PEDN MERMAID
Ch Foggyfurze Cute Cut

Glasgow   A Murray
FOGGYFURZE CLASSIC
Blueprint of Mahidap
WESTFEN VIVANDIERE
Foggyfurze Lindylou

Manchester   H H Wilson
FOGGYFURZE CLASSIC
Triple Cut
CH WESTFEN VIVANDIERE
Daleview Delma

W.E.L.K.S.   A W Fullwood
CH GOLDEN SUN OF MANATON
Dancer's Pride
CH WESTFEN VIVANDIERE
Daleview Delma

Leeds   W Bullivant
BLUEPRINT OF MAHIDAP
Leasowes Try Again
CH WESTFEN VIVANDIERE
Lindum Lunaria

Blackpool   Mrs A J Hopwood
LEASOWES TRY AGAIN
Foggyfurze Classic
DALEVIEW DELMA
Foggyfurze Lindylou

Brighton   Leo C Wilson
NOVELLO OF NABLUS
Leasowes Try Again
CH AMANDA MIRABEAU OF NONINGTON
Nocturn of Nablus

Bedlington Terrier Assn.   Mrs F L
                                          Franks
CH GOLDEN SUN OF MANATON
Blue Rodney of Manaton
CH WESTFEN VIVANDIERE
Pat's Peach of Manaton

Edinburgh   T M Corbett
TRIPLE CUT
Foggyfurze Avenger
withheld on lack of merit

Richmond   Mrs Llewellyn Ward
CH FOGGYFURZE CLASSIC
Foggyfurze Avenger
TOL-PEDN FAIRMAID
Pat's Peach of Manaton

Ladies Kennel Assn.   Mrs W Barber
CH FOGGYFURZE CLASSIC
Dancer's Pride
NITA OF NABLUS
Lindum Lunaria

Birmingham National   V Hirst
CH FOGGYFURZE CLASSIC
Leasowes Try Again
CH DALEVIEW DELMA
Tol-pedn Fairmaid

1956

Crufts   Judge Llewellyn Ward
CH FOGGYFURZE CLASSIC
Jones of Pitt
FOGGYFURZE LINDYLOU
Ruffle Cut

Glasgow   Fentan Fitzgerald
CH FOGGYFURZE CLASSIC
Blue Rodney of Manaton
LINDUM LUNARIA
Daleview Delma

Manchester   H Winder
CH FOGGYFURZE CLASSIC
Clever Cut
RUFFLE CUT
Foggyfurze Lindylou

W.E.L.K.S.   Ken Bounden
CH FOGGYFURZE CLASSIC
Clever Cut
PAT'S PEACH OF MANATON
Foggyfurze Lindylou

Leeds   F Gent
CH LEASOWES TRY AGAIN
Burleydene Golden Lad
DALEVIEW DAWN
Lassie of Simonside

Three Counties   W Bullivant
DANCER'S PRIDE
Wynbriar Willie Winkle
CH DALEVIEW DELMA
Lindum Lunaria

Blackpool   W Burrow
GENTS CUT
Blueprint of Mahidap
DALEVIEW DAWN
Ruffle Cut

City of Birmingham   L R Wardman
CH FOGGYFURZE CLASSIC
Juverna Sunlit Milord
LINDUM LUNARIA
Belliza of Oldpost

Brighton   F Cross
CH FOGGYFURZE CLASSIC
Dancer's Pride
CH LINDUM LUNARIA
Foggyfurze Lindylou

Bedlington Terrier Assn.   C G Worrall
BLUE PIP OF CLOVERWAY
Foggyfurze Classical
FOGGYFURZE BABY MINE
Foggyfurze Sugar Baby

Edinburgh   Leo C Wilson
FOGGYFURZE CLASSICAL
No other award
FOGGYFURZE SUGAR BABY
Woodmansey Waspy

Richmond   Mrs M E O'Brien
GENTS CUT
Ch Golden Sun of Manaton
BRIGHT DAY OF MANATON
Pat's Peach of Manaton

Ladies Kennel Assn.   G Trueman Hewitt
CH FOGGYFURZE CLASSIC
Lindum High Octane of Vistablu
FOGGYFURZE SUGAR BABY
Pat's Peach of Manaton

Birmingham National   Miss E Nichols
CH GENTS CUT
Juverna Lord Liver of Pitt
TOL-PEDN FAIRMAID
Foggyfurze Sugar Baby

1957

Crufts   *Judge* S L Franks
CH GENTS CUT
Blueprint of Mahidap
CH FOGGYFURZE SUGAR BABY
Tol-pedn Fairmaid

Glasgow   W S Wright
CH FOGGYFURZE CLASSIC
Foggyfurze Shootingstar
CH FOGGYFURZE SUGAR BABY
Woodmansey Waspy

Manchester   F Cross
CH GENTS CUT
Foggyfurze Shootingstar
CH TOL-PEDN FAIRMAID
Ch Foggyfurze Sugar Baby

W.E.L.K.S.   Mrs A J Hopwood
CH DANCER'S PRIDE
Juverna Golden Maestro
CH TOL-PEDN FAIRMAID
Daleview Dawn

National Terrier   Dr Muriel Binns
BLUE PIP OF CLOVERWAY
Blueprint of Mahidap
CH TOL-PEDN FAIRMAID
Woodmansey Waspy

Leeds   L R Wardman
CH GENTS CUT
Blueprint of Mahidap
CH TOL-PEDN FAIRMAID
Woodmansey Waspy

Blackpool   H Winder
BLUEPRINT OF MAHIDAP
Wederbi Vigilante
CH TOL-PEDN FAIRMAID
Lassie of Simonside

Bedlington Terrier Assn.   Mrs M E O'Brien
CH GENTS CUT
Blueprint of Mahidap
CH TOL-PEND FAIRMAID
Nadia of Nablus

Edinburgh   W Burrow
FOGGYFURZE SHOOTINGSTAR
Foggyfurze Jackpot
WOODMANSEY WASPY
Classia of Nonington

Richmond   S L Franks
CH BLUEPRINT OF MAHIDAP
Blue Pip of Cloverway
CH TOL-PEDN FAIRMAID
Pat's Peach of Manaton

Ladies Kennel Assn.   V Hirst
FOGGYFURZE SHOOTINGSTAR
Tol-pedn Hoodwink
CH TOL-PEDN FAIR MAID
Foggyfurze Cute

Birmingham National   Mrs F Franks
CH FOGGYFURZE SHOOTINGSTAR
Little Willie of Vistablu
PAT'S PEACH OF MANATON
Ch Tol-pedn Fairmaid

1958

Crufts   *Judge* F Gent
CH GENTS CUT
Ch Golden Sun of Manaton
CH TOL-PEDN FAIRMAID
Foggyfurze Cute

Glasgow   J Robb
CH FOGGYFURZE SHOOTINGSTAR
Wee Mac of Mahidap
FOGGYFURZE SUGAR PUSS
Knotts Bluebelle

Manchester   A Murray
CH GENTS CUT
Ch Foggyfurze Shootingstar
FOGGYFURZE SUGAR PUSS
Daleview Dame

W.E.L.K.S.   Mrs R J Martin
LINDUM HIGH OCTANE OF VISTABLU
Ch Foggyfurze Shootingstar
CH PAT'S PEACH OF MANATON
Wederbi Mist

National Terrier   S L Franks
LITTLE WILLIE OF VISTABLU
Tol-pedn Seadog
CH PAT'S PEACH OF MANATON
Wederbi Mist

Leeds   Leo C Wilson
TOL-PEDN SEADOG
Blue Pip of Cloverway
CH FOGGYFURZE SUGAR PUSS
Spring Cut

Blackpool   Miss E Nichols
TOL-PEDN HOODWINK
Blue Pip of Cloverway
CH FOGGYFURZE SUGAR PUSS
Debutante of Cloverway

Brighton   Mrs A J Hopwood
CH BLUE PIP OF CLOVERWAY
Lindum High Octane of Vistablu
DALEVIEW DAME
Esmeralda of Nonington

City of Birmingham   Mrs M E O'Brien
TOL-PEDN SEADOG
Ch Blue Pip of Cloverway
SPRING CUT
Daleview Dame

Bedlington Terrier Assn. Mrs W Barber
TOL-PEDN HOODWINK
Workman of Nonington
SPRING CUT
Ch Pat's Peach of Nonington

Edinburgh   Dr J Aubrey Ireland
LINDUM HIGH OCTANE OF VISTABLU
Foggyfurze Hallmarked
KNOTTS BLUEBELLE
Drewcote Candy Floss

Richmond   F Gent
CH TOL-PEDN HOODWINK
Lindum High Octane of Vistablu
KNOTTS BLUEBELLE
Foggyfurze Cute

Ladies Kennel Assn.   F Cross
CH LINDUM HIGH OCTANE OF VISTABLU
Sankirk Scoundrel
ANGELINA OF LEASOWES
Ch Pat's Peach of Manaton

Birmingham National   Ken Bounden
WORKMAN OF NONINGTON
Lucky of Cloverway
CH KNOTTS BLUEBELLE
Foggyfurze Supersonic

1959

Crufts   *Judge* Mrs F L Franks
LITTLE WILLIE OF VISTABLU
Amerdale Half Nelson
CH KNOTTS BLUEBELLE
Mandy of Daletarn

Glasgow F Dempster
AMERDALE HALF NELSON
Leasowes Forester
AMERDALE DELIGHT
Belliza of Oldpost

Manchester L R Wardman
CH LITTLE WILLIE OF VISTABLU
Ch Blueprint of Mahidap
CH WESTFEN VIVANDIERE
Ch Knotts Bluebelle

W.E.L.K.S. V Hirst
WORKMAN OF NONINGTON
Foggyfurze Texan
ANGELINA OF LEASOWES
Debutante of Cloverway

National Terrier D Fenby
CH LINDUM HIGH OCTANE OF VISTABLU
Foggyfurze Tonto
CH DALEVIEW DAWN
Cinderella

Leeds Miss G M M Cousens
CH WORKMAN OF NONINGTON
Foggyfurze Texan
TOL-PEDN BALLERINA
Ch Daleview Dawn

Blackpool Miss Eunice Clark, USA
REDBOY OF MAHIDAP
Foggyfurze Texan
BIBSY OF MAHIDAP
Foggyfurze Delaware Doll

Brighton Miss E V Herdman
FOGGYFURZE TEXAN
Gun Metal of Wetop
CH ANGELINA OF LEASOWES
Cinderella

City of Birmingham Madame
Lisa Salser, France
SHENSTONE MASTER MACK
Gun Metal of Wetop
CINDERELLA
Foggyfurze Delaware Doll

Bedlington Terrier Assn. Ken Bounden
FOGGYFURZE TEXAN
Gun Metal of Wetop
CINDERELLA
Shenstone Miss Tesha

Edinburgh Miss E Nichols
CH FOGGYFURZE TEXAN
Jasper of Nonington
TOL-PEDN BALLERINA
Cinderella

Richmond Mrs F L Franks
JASPER OF NONINGTON
Ch Little Willie of Vistablu
CH CINDERELLA
Marydew Miss Marie

Ladies Kennel Assn. Mrs A J Hopwood
JASPER OF NONINGTON
Shenstone Master Mack
FOGGYFURZE DELAWARE DOLL
Tol-pedn Ballerina

Birmingham National Mrs M E O'Brien
CH LINDUM HIGH OCTANE OF VISTABLU
Gun Metal of Wetop
CH CINDERELLA
Amerdale Delight

1960

Crufts *Judge* Mrs W Barber
SHENSTONE MASTER MACK
Jasper of Nonington
CH CINDERELLA
Stanolly Sapphire

Glasgow G Leatt
Withheld
Withheld
FOGGYFURZE DELAWARE DOLL
Amerdale Delight

Manchester W Burrow
CH SHENSTONE MASTER MACK
Wederbi Houghtop Invader
STANOLLY SAPPHIRE
Foggyfurze Delaware Doll

W.E.L.K.S. Leo C Wilson
CH SHENSTONE MASTER MACK
Tol-pedn Frigate
CH FOGGYFURZE DELAWARE DOLL
Ch Cinderella

National Terrier L R Wardman
CH SHENSTONE MASTER MACK
Wederbi Houghtop Invader
CH FOGGYFURZE DELAWARE DOLL
No award (disqualification)

Leeds Lt.Col. H F Whitehead DSO
FOGGYFURZE DRUMBEAT
Wederbi Houghtop Invader
STANOLLY SAPPHIRE
Bibsy of Mahidap

Blackpool F Dempster
WEDERBI HOUGHTOP INVADER
Geordie of Craglough
CH STANOLLY SAPPHIRE
Bibsy of Mahidap

City of Birmingham H Winder
GUN METAL OF WETOP
Ch Shenstone Master Mack
CH STANOLLY SAPPHIRE
Amerdale Delight

Brighton S L Franks
CH SHENSTONE MASTER MACK
Gun Metal of Wetop
AMERDALE DELIGHT
Shenstone Blue Bliss of Vistablu

Bedlington Terrier Assn. F Gent
WEDERBI HOUGHTOP INVADER
Ch Shenstone Master Mack
NORTHCOTE LUCKY STRIKE
Bibsy of Mahidap

Edinburgh Fentan Fitzgerald
FOGGYFURZE DRUMBEAT
Jasper of Nonington
NORTHCOTE LUCKY STRIKE
Amerdale Delight

Richmond Ken Bounden
GUN METAL OF WETOP
Carlingwark Meljoy McCullough
CH STANOLLY SAPPHIRE
Maydew Miss Maverick

Ladies Kennel Assn. Mrs F L Franks
CH GUN METAL OF WETOP
Ch Shenstone Master Mack
CH AMERDALE DELIGHT
Shenstone Blue Bliss of Vistablu

Birmingham National F Cross
CH SHENSTONE MASTER MACK
Jasper of Nonington
SHENSTONE BLUE BLISS OF VISTABLU
Northcote Lucky Strike

1961

Crufts Judge Mrs M E O'Brien
FOGGYFURZE DANDY
Ch Gun Metal of Wetop
CH NORTHCOTE LUCKY STRIKE
Ch Amerdale Delight

Manchester Mrs A J Hopwood
FOGGYFURZE DANDY
Kay of Nonington
CH NORTHCOTE LUCKY STRIKE
Foggyfurze Wederbi Sceptre

Glasgow F Dempster
CH FOGGYFURZE DANDY
Carlingwark Meljoy McCullough
CH NORTHCOTE LUCKY STRIKE
Ch Amerdale Delight

W.E.L.K.S. Dr Muriel Binns
CH SHENSTONE MASTER MACK
Ch Foggyfurze Dandy
CH NORTHCOTE LUCKY STRIKE
Ch Amerdale Delight

Leeds Ken Bounden
CH WEDERBI HOUGHTOP INVADER
Carlingwark Meljoy McCullough
MELJOY JULIET DEMESNE
Ch Northcote Lucky Strike

National Terrier Mrs F L Franks
PILOT OF GORSEA
Shenstone New Orbit
SHENSTONE BLUE BLISS OF VISTABLU
Ch Amerdale Delight

Blackpool T M Corbett
REDBOY OF MAHIDAP
Carlingwark Meljoy McCullough
CH NORTHCOTE LUCKY STRIKE
Shenstone Blue Bliss of Vistablu

City of Birmingham G Leatt
MAYDEW MOONRAKER
Shenstone New Orbit
CH NORTHCOTE LUCKY STRIKE
Meljoy Juliet Demesne

Brighton F Cross
SHENSTONE NEW ORBIT
Pilot of Gorsea
AMERDALE DELIGHT
Meljoy Juliet Demesne

Bedlington Terrier Assn.   H Winder
SHENSTONE NEW ORBIT
Buttons of Wetop
MELJOY JULIET DEMESNE
Lavender Blue

Edinburgh   Miss G M M Cousens
CH FOGGYFURZE DANDY
Maydew Moonraker
CH NORTHCOTE LUCKY STRIKE
Amerdale Delight

Ladies Kennel Assn.   C G Worrall
WEDERBI MINTING
Jasper of Nonington
CH MELJOY JULIET DEMESNE
Ch Northcote Lucky Strike

Birmingham National   Mrs A Care
MAYDEW MOONRAKER
Shenstone New Orbit
CH MELJOY JULIET DEMESNE
Tol-pedn Ballerina

Richmond   Madame
Lisa Sulser, France
CH MAYDEW MOONRAKER
County Cut
MISS MUFFET OF WETOP
Amerdale Delight

1962

Crufts   *Judge* V Hirst
BUTTONS OF WETOP
Flashy Cut
CH AMERDALE DELIGHT
Shenstone Blue Bliss of Vistablu

Manchester   A Murray
FLASHY CUT
Ch Foggyfurze Dandy
CH NORTHCOTE LUCKY STRIKE
Ch Amerdale Delight

W.E.L.K.S.   Mrs M E O'Brien
TOL-PEDN FRIGATE
Buttons of Wetop
MISS MUFFET OF WETOP
Ch Amerdale Delight

National Terrier   Mrs M Laverick
WEDERBI MINTING
Jasper of Nonington
ATOMIC CUT
Foggyfurze Honey Chile

Glasgow   G Leatt
CH WEDERBI MINTING
Foggyfurze Darius
BOUGHTON NORTHCOTE LUCKYSTONE
Ch Amerdale Delight

Leeds   L R Wardman
CH WEDERBI MINTING
Flashy Cut
BOUGHTON NORTHCOTE LUCKYSTONE
Shenstone Blue Bliss of Vistablu

Blackpool   Leo C Wilson
CH WEDERBI MINTING
Flashy Cut
CH BOUGHTON NORTHCOTE LUCKYSTONE
Miss Muffet of Wetop

Ladies Kennel Assn.   Mrs F L Franks
CHARTLANDS FAIR DINKUM
Jasper of Nonington
CH BOUGHTON NORTHCOTE LUCKYSTONE
Foggyfurze Honey Chile

City of Birmingham   Fentan Fitzgerald
CH WEDERBI MINTING
Kay of Nonington
CH AMERDALE DELIGHT
Maydew Miss Muriel

Brighton   C D Adamson
CH WEDERBI MINTING
Jasper of Nonington
CH SHENSTONE BLUE BLISS OF VISTABLU
Atomic Cut

Bedlington Terrier Assn.   Mrs R J
Martin
CH FOGGYFURZE DANDY
Foggyfurze Statacco
CH NORTHCOTE LUCKY STRIKE
Chartlands Fair Ninette

Edinburgh   S Young
CH FOGGYFURZE DANDY
Ch Wederbi Minting
CH NORTHCOTE LUCHY STRIKE
Foggyfurze Honey Chile

Birmingham National   Ken Bounden
CH WEDERBI MINTING
Ch Foggyfurze Dandy
FOGGYFURZE HONEY CHILE
Ch Stanolly Sapphire

Richmond   S L Franks
CHARTLANDS FAIR DINKUM
Shenstone New Orbit
CH SHENSTONE BLUE BLISS OF VISTABLU
Dina Mite of Oldpost

1963

Crufts   *Judge* F Cross
CH WEDERBI MINTING
Chartlands Fair Dinkum
FOGGYFURZE HONEY CHILE
Ch Amerdale Delight

Manchester   N Stead
FOGGYFURZE STATACCO
Gold Coin of Foxington
CH MISS MUFFET OF WESTOP
Amerdale Astralita

W.E.L.K.S.   Mrs F M Herdman
CH WEDERBI MINTING
Tweedledee of Wetop
WEDERBI DAWN CHORUS
Lindum Lavina

National Terrier   D Fenby
FOGGYFURZE STATACCO
Buttons of Wetop
CH SHENSTONE BLUE BLISS OF VISTABLU
Pentavy Firedance of Tol-pedn

Glasgow   L R Wardman
CH FOGGYFURZE STATACCO
Amerdale Aviator
WEDERBI DAWN CHORUS
Amerdale Astralita

Leeds   Mrs M E O'Brien
CH FOGGYFURZE STATACCO
Chartlands Fair Dinkum
CH NORTHCOTE LUCKY STRIKE
Pentavy Firedance of Tol-pedn

Blackpool   Mrs A J Hopwood
CH FOGGYFURZE STATACCO
Gold Coin of Foxington
CH NORTHCOTE LUCKY STRIKE
Foggyfurze Parka

Paignton   A W Fullwood
BUTTONS OF WETOP
Yoma Brig
CH TOL-PEDN BALLERINA
Nitram Blue Slipper

Leicester   W Burrow
CH BUTTONS OF WETOP
Foggyfurze High Hat
FOGGYFURZE FAN TAN
Wederbi Dawn Chorus

Brighton   Mrs R J Martin
CH JASPER OF NONINGTON
Chartlands Fair Dinkum
LINDUM LAVINA
Amerdale Astralita

City of Birmingham   F Gent
NADWORNA STATESMAN
Ch Wederbi Minting
PENTAVY FIREDANCE OF TOL-PEDN
Maydew Miss Muriel

Bedlington Terrier Assn.   Mrs F L
AMERDALE AVIATOR   Franks
Copper Rogue
DINA MITE OF OLDPOST
Foggyfurze Samantha

Edinburgh   Lt. Col. H F Whitehead DSO
CH FOGGYFURZE STATACCO
Amerdale Aviator
DALEVIEW SHENSTONE AMBER LASS
Amerdale Astralita

Ladies Kennel Assn.   Leo C Wilson
NADWORNA STATESMAN
Tweedledee of Wetop
PENTAVY FIREDANCE OF TOL-PEDN
Northcote Strike Again

Birmingham National   Mrs M M Taunt
COPPER ROGUE
Ch Foggyfurze Statacco
MAYDEW MISS MURIEL
Foggyfurze Parka

Richmond   Mrs J Creasy
TWEEDLEDEE OF WETOP
Nathaniel of Nonington
MAYDEW MISS MURIEL
Pentavy Firedance of Tol-pedn

1964

Crufts   *Judge* C G Worrall
CH NADWORNA STATESMAN
House of Rima
GOLDEN ARROW
Lindum Lavina

Manchester   F Gent
CH NADWORNA STATESMAN
Stanolly Sports Tosca
DALEVIEW SHENSTONE AMBER LASS
Maydew Miss Muriel

W.E.L.K.S.   S L Franks
GOLD COIN OF FOXINGTON
Amerdale Aviator
CH PENTAVY FIREDANCE OF TOL-PEND
Chartlands Fair Ninette

Glasgow   W Burrow
NORTHCOTE WILL STRIKE
Amerdale Aviator
NORTHCOTE STRIKE AGAIN
Daleview Shenstone Amber Lass

National Terrier   C D Adamson
STANOLLY SPORTS TOSCA
Northcote Will Strike
CH MAYDEW MISS MURIEL
Lindum Lavina

Leeds   A Murray
RATHSRIGG LITTLE CAESAR
Gold Coin of Foxington
NORTHCOTE STRIKE AGAIN
Berengreave Foggyfurze Sky High

Blackpool   Mrs F L Franks
RATHSRIGG LITTLE CAESAR
Gold Coin of Foxington
CH DALEVIEW SHENSTONE AMBER LASS
Amerdale Astralita

Paignton   Mrs A M Laverick
GOLD COIN OF FOXINGTON
Chartlands Fair Dinkum
GOLDEN ARROW
Ch Pentavy Firedance of Tol-pedn

Leicester   G Leatt
MAYDEW MOUNTAIN MUSIC
Gold Coin of Foxington
CH NORTHCOTE STRIKE AGAIN
Ch Daleview Shenstone Amber Lass

Hove   Miss G Lawis
CH CHARTLANDS FAIR DINKUM
Gold Coin of Foxington
LINDUM LAVINA
Caeruleus Jessica

City of Birmingham   Mrs A Care
CH GOLD COIN OF FOXINGTON
Maydew Mountain Music
CH PENTAVY FIREDANCE OF TOL-PEDN
Lindum Lavina

Bedlington Terrier Assn.   L R Wardman
CH GOLD COIN OF FOXINGTON
Ch Chartlands Fair Dinkum
CH LINDUM LAVINA
Amerdale Astralita

Edinburgh   S Young
CH GOLD COIN OF FOXINGTON
Foggyfurze Fargo
AMERDALE ASTRALITA
Berengreave Foggyfurze Sky High

Ladies Kennel Assn.   F Cross
MAYDEW MOUNTAIN MUSIC
Ch Gold Coin of Foxington
CH PENTAVY FIREDANCE OF TOL-PEDN
Amerdale Astralita

Birmingham National   W G Siggers
CH MAYDEW MOUNTAIN MUSIC
Ch Gold Coin of Foxington
CH PENTAVY FIREDANCE OF TOL-PEDN
Silver Solitaire

Richmond   Miss J de Beauchamp-Green
CH CHARTLANDS FAIR DINKUM
Tol-pedn Late Extra
AMERDALE ASTRALITA
Amerdale Amanda

1965

Crufts   *Judge* Mrs R J Martin
CH RATHSRIGG LITTLE CAESAR
Ch Chartlands Fair Dinkum
CH AMERDALE ASTRALITA
Ch Northcote Strike Again

Glasgow   Reg Gadsden
AMERDALE AVIATOR
Foggyfurze Hurricane
CH AMERDALE ASTRALITA
Ch Northcote Strike Again

Manchester   Fentan Fitzgerald
CH GOLD COIN OF FOXINGTON
Centurion of Craglough
STANOLLY SPORTS TIPPI
Vardene Golden Gem

THE BEDLINGTON TERRIER

W.E.L.K.S.   Ken Bounden
TWEEDLEDEE OF WETOP
Foggyfurze Cyclone
STANOLLY SPORTS TIPPI
Amerdale Amanda

National Terrier   Mrs J Creasy
ROB ROY OF WETOP
Centurion of Craglough
SILVER SOLITAIRE
Leasowes Moorland Melody

Leeds   D Fenby
FREDDIE THE GENT OF VISTABLU
Ch Rathsrigg Little Caesar
AMERDALE AMANDA
Wederbi Dawn Chorus

Blackpool   F Dempster
CH GOLD COIN OF FOXINGTON
Northcote Titan
AMERDALE AMANDA
Amerdale Astralita

Paignton   B Johnson
FREDDIE THE GENT OF VISTABLU
Tweedledee of Wetop
CH PENTAVY FIREDANCE OF TOL-PEDN
Tol-pedn Seasprite

Hove   S L Franks
CH FREDDIE THE GENT OF VISTABLU
Chartlands Peter Pan
CH AMERDALE AMANDA
Chartlands Fair Ninette

City of Birmingham   F Warner Hill
CH MAYDEW MOUNTAIN MUSIC
Tweedledee of Wetop
CH AMERDALE AMANDA
Ch Maydew Miss Muriel

Leicester   Leo C Wilson
STANOLLY SPORTS TOSCA
Ch Maydew Mountain Music
STANOLLY SUNSPRITE
Wederbi Dawn Chorus

Bedlington Terrier Assn.   Miss G Lawis
TOL-PEDN SATCHMO
Chartlands Peter Pan
CH LINDUM LAVINA
Vardenc Golden Gem

Ladies Kennel Assn.   C D Adamson
NORTHCOTE TERPO
Ch Freddie The Gent of Vistablu
CH AMERDALE AMANDA
Petherwyn Sweetbriar

Birmingham National   L R Wardman
CH FREDDIE THE GENT OF VISTABLU
Tol-pedn Satchmo
CH AMERDALE AMANDA
Daisymay of Oldpost

Richmond   Mrs C Barber
CH FREDDIE THE GENT OF VISTABLU
Chartlands Peter Pan
CH AMERDALE AMANDA
Highquest Harmony

1966

Crufts   Judge Ken Bounden
NORTHCOTE TERPO
Stanolly Starcracker
CH AMERDALE AMANDA
Bystock Sapphire

Manchester   Reg Gadsden
CH STANOLLY SPORTS TOSCA
Grinkle Cut
CH AMERDALE AMANDA
Stanolly Sunsprite

W.E.L.K.S.   Mrs A Care
TOL-PEDN SATCHMO
Rob Roy of Wetop
CH AMERDALE AMANDA
Stanolly Sunsprite

Glasgow   A W Fullwood
STANOLLY SUPERSTAR
Edgemoor Berengreave Bonaparte
CH AMERDALE AMANDA
Amerdale Au Pair

National Terrier   W Clark
STANOLLY SUPERSTAR
Ch Stanolly Sports Tosca
STANOLLY SUNSPRITE
Midnight of Francistown

Leeds   F Cross
CH STANOLLY SUPERSTAR
Ch Gold Coin of Foxington
CH AMERADLE AMANDA
Lisetta of Craglough

Paignton   F Warner Hill
CH TOL-PEDN SATCHMO
Avanti of Moorside
CH AMERDALE AMANDA
Amerdale Au Pair

Hove   S L Franks
CH FREDDIE THE GENT OF VISTABLU
Tweedledee of Wetop
ROULETTE OF WETOP
Ch Amerdale Amanda

City of Birmingham   Mrs M M Taunt
ROB ROY OF WETOP
Ch Freddie The Gent of Vistablu
DAISYMAY OF OLDPOST
Amerdale Delightful

Leicester   Mrs I Sills
CH STANOLLY SUPERSTAR
Rob Roy of Wetop
CH LINDUM LAVINA
Ch Amerdale Amanda

Bedlington Terrier Assn.   Mrs M E O'Brien
CH STANOLLY SUPERSTAR
Tweedledee of Wetop
CH AMERDALE AMANDA
Amerdale Delightful

Ladies Kennel Assn.   S W Dangerfield
CH STANOLLY SUPERSTAR
Rogerholme Riding High
STANOLLY SUNBLUSH
Daisymay of Oldpost

Birmingham National   G Leatt
CH STANOLLY SUPERSTAR
Rogerholme Riding High
CH AMERDALE AMANDA
Stanolly Sunblush

Richmond   Mrs F L Franks
FANCYPANTS OF VISTABLU
Ch Stanolly Superstar
CH AMERDALE AMANDA
Stanolly Sunblush

1967

Crufts   *Judge* L R Wardman
FANCYPANTS OF VISTABLU
Ch Stanolly Superstar
STANOLLY SUNBLUSH
Highquest Holly Girl

Manchester   F Gent
STANOLLY STARBLAZE
Northcote Terpo
CH STANOLLY SUNBLUSH
Ch Amerdale Amanda

Glasgow   F Cross
STANOLLY STARBLAZE
Amerdale Au Revoir
CH AMERDALE AMANDA
Ch Stanolly Sunblush

W.E.L.K.S.   Mrs A M Laverick
CH STANOLLY STARBLAZE
Northcote Terpo
CH AMERDALE AMANDA
Highquest Holly Girl

National Terrier   Mrs J Creasy
CH STANOLLY STARBLAZE
Fancypants of Vistablu
CH STANOLLY SUNBLUSH
Midnight of Francistown

Leeds   H Stead
CH STANOLLY STARBLAZE
Fancypants of Vistablu
VARDENE AMAREE OF CANZO
Ch Stanolly Sunblush

Hove   Ken Bounden
CH STANOLLY STARBLAZE
Fancypants of Vistablu
CH STANOLLY SUNBLUSH
Amerdale Delicious

City of Birmingham   W A Topham
CH STANOLLY STARBLAZE
Northcote Terpo
VARDENE AMAREE OF CANZO
Stanolly Crystal Belle

Leicester   L R Wardman
CH STANOLLY STARBLAZE
Fancypants of Vistablu
CH VARDENE AMAREE OF CANZO
Ch Stanolly Sunblush

Bedlington Terrier Assn.   Mrs I Sills
CH STANOLLY STARBLAZE
Northcote Terpo
CH VARDENE AMAREE OF CANZO
Northcote Blue Dawn

Ladies Kennel Assn. Mrs A J Hopwood
CH STANOLLY STARBLAZE
Fancypants of Vistablu
CH VARDENE AMAREE OF CANZO
Ch Amerdale Amanda

Birmingham National
M van de Weijer, Holland
CH STANOLLY STARBLAZE
Berengreave Token
NORTHCOTE BLUE DAWN
Ch Vardene Amaree of Canzo

1968

Crufts *Judge* A W Fullwood
CH STANOLLY STARBLAZE
Maydew Music Master
HIGHQUEST HOLLY GIRL
Ch Amerdale Delicious

Manchester Ken Bounden
HIGHQUEST HIGH MIST
Northcote Lucky Mark
NORTHCOTE AILEEN
Ch Amerdale Delicious

W.E.L.K.S. F Gent
NORTHCOTE LUCKY MARK
Fancypants of Vistablu
BYSTOCK MACK'S GOLDEN PEARL
Northcote Aileen

Glasgow S Young
NORTHCOTE LUCKY MARK
Grinkle Cut
AMERDALE DELICIOUS
Northcote Aileen

Leeds Mrs I Sills
CH NORTHCOTE LUCKY MARK
Stanolly Starbeat
VARDENE GOLDEN GIRL
Stanolly Crystal Belle

National Terrier S L Franks
CH FANCYPANTS OF VISTABLU
Rob Roy of Wetop
AMERDALE DELICIOUS
Vardene Golden Girl

Hove Miss G Lawis
AMERDALE DEFIANT
Gold Classic
DOLLYROCKER OF VISTABLU
Ch Amerdale Delicious

Leicester Mrs O Stones
CH ROB ROY OF WETOP
Vardene Blue Grenadier
BERENGREAVE PINK PERRY
Ch Vardene Amaree of Canzo

City of Birmingham Ken Bounden
CH ROB ROY OF WETOP
Nadina Sundew
HIGHQUEST HOLLY GIRL
Bystock Mack's Golden Pearl

Bedlington Terrier Assn. Mrs F L Franks
GOLD CLASSIC
Stanolly Sandpiper
DOLLYROCKER OF VISTABLU
Berengreave Pink Perry

Ladies Kennel Assn. S W Dangerfield
VARDENE BLUE GRENADIER
Stanolly Sandpiper
STANOLLY CRYSTAL BELLE
Ch Amerdale Delicious

Birmingham National F Dempster
VARDENE BLUE GRENADIER
Maydew Music Master
BERENGREAVE PINK PERRY
Ch Amerdale Delicious

Richmond Mrs A J Hopwood
CH VARDENE BLUE GRENADIER
Berengreave Token
CH AMERDALE DELICIOUS
Dollyrocker of Vistablu

1969

Crufts *Judge* Mrs A M Laverick
CH VARDENE BLUE GRENADIER
Maydew Music Master
CH STANOLLY SUNBLUSH
Highquest Holly Girl

Manchester N Stead
CH VARDENE BLUE GRENADIER
Moorside Dandy Dolphin
FOGGYFURZE FESTIVAL
Ch Amerdale Delicious

W.E.L.K.S. W A Topham
CH VARDENE BLUE GRENADIER
Tol-pedn Rophine Gethin
FOGGYFURZE FESTIVAL
Ch Berengreave Pink Perry

Scottish Kennel Club   A W Fullwood
FOGGYFURZE FLAMINGO
Nadina Sundew
CH AMERDALE DELICIOUS
Ch Berengreave Pink Perry

National Terrier   R M James
CH VARDENE BLUE GRENADIER
Blue Happening of Vistablu
CH FOGGYFURZE FESTIVAL
Ch Berengreave Pink Perry

Leeds   Mrs P R Willemson
STANOLLY SANDPIPER
Nadina Moon Glow
CH BERENGREAVE PINK PERRY
Ch Foggyfurze Festival

Hove   Mrs F L Franks
CII VARDENE BLUE GRENADIER
Stanolly Sandpiper
CH HIGHQUEST HOLLY GIRL
Ch Amerdale Delicious

Leicester   S L Franks
CH VARDENE BLUE GRENADIER
Blue Happening of Vistablu
CH FOGGYFURZE FESTIVAL
Ch Amerdale Delicious

City of Birmingham   M van de Weijer
FOGGYFURZE FAN FARE
Blue Happening of Vistablu
CH AMERDALE DELICIOUS
Ch Foggyfurze Festival

Bedlington Terrier Assn. C D Adamson
FOGGYFURZE FAN FARE
Ch Vardene Blue Grenadier
CH FOGGYFURZE FESTIVAL
Ch Highquest Holly Girl

Ladies Kennel Assn.   H Wright
CH FOGGYFURZE FAN FARE
Ch Vardene Blue Grenadier
CH AMERDALE AMANDA
Ch Foggyfurze Festival

Birmingham National Mrs M M Taunt
BLUE HAPPENING OF VISTABLU
Ch Vardene Blue Grenadier
CH AMERDALE AMANDA
Berengreave Personality

Richmond   Ken Bounden
STANOLLY SANDPIPER
Gold Classic
CH AMERDALE AMANDA
Amerdale Amelia

1970

Crufts   *Judge* Mrs A J Hopwood
CH VARDENE BLUE GRENADIER
Ch Foggyfurze Fan Fare
CH FOGGYFURZE FESTIVAL
Ch Amerdale Delicious

Manchester   W Clark
CH STANOLLY SANDPIPER
Craglough Sebastian
CH BERENGREAVE PERSONALITY
Moorside Dainty Denise

Scottish Kennel Club   S Young
MOORSIDE DANDY DOLPHIN
Amerdale Defiant
CH AMERDALE DELICIOUS
Moorside Dainty Denise

W.E.L.K.S.   L L De Groen
CH STANOLLY SANDPIPER
Blue Happening of Vistablu
MARILENA POLLYANNA
Caerulius Clovette

National Terrier   R Highfield
FOGGYFURZE FANGIO
Ch Stanolly Sandpiper
BERENGREAVE PERSONALITY
Leasowes Dancing Shadow

Leeds   Mrs B Clifton
CH BLUE HAPPENING OF VISTABLU
Stanolly Spectacular
BERENGREAVE PERSONALITY
Amerdale Attraction

Paignton   Mrs E Gray-Brewer
STANOLLY SPECTACULAR
Nadina Moonglow
PERRIANNE PETULA
Ch Amerdale Delicious

Southern Counties   Ken Bounden
CH BLUE HAPPENING OF VISTABLU
Nadina Sundew
PEWTER GREY OF WETOP
Perrianne Petula

Leicester   Mrs A Clark
MOORSIDE DANDY DOLPHIN
Stanolly Spectacular
MOORSIDE DAINTY DENISE
Marilena Pollyanna

City of Birmingham   Mrs O Stones
CH BLUE HAPPENING OF VISTABLU
Vardene Blue Guardsman
PERRIANNE PETULA
Leasowes Dancing Shadow

Bedlington Terrier Assn.   L R Wardman
CH BLUE HAPPENING OF VISTABLU
Vardene Blue Guardsman
CH BERENGREAVE PERSONALITY
Leasowes Dancing Shadow

Ladies Kennel Assn.   R Gadsden
FOGGYFURZE FANGIO
Vardene Blue Guardsman
CH PERRIANNE PETULA
Searake Royal Gem

Birmingham National   Mrs I Sills
CH FOGGYFURZE FANGIO
Vardene Blue Guardsman
CH PERRIANNE PETULA
Ch Berengreave Personality

Richmond   W Burrow
STANOLLY SPECTACULAR
Ch Foggyfurze Fangio
PEWTER GREY OF WETOP
Stanolly Starbow

1971

Crufts   *Judge* S L Franks
CH VARDENE BLUE GRENADIER
Vardene Blue Guardsman
LEASOWES DANCING SHADOW
Amerdale Attractive

Manchester   R M James
CH FOGGYFURZE FANGIO
Stanolly Scooby Doo
CH PERRIANNE PETULA
Stanolly Starbow

National Bedlington Terrier Club
     J Clifton
CH STANOLLY SPECTACULAR
Stanolly Scooby Doo
CH PEWTER GREY OF WETOP
Berengreave Tia Maria

W.E.L.K.S.   Mrs M Taunt
STANOLLY SCOOBY DOO
Ch Stanolly Spectacular
STANOLLY STARBOW
Stanolly Amber Blush

Birmingham   R Gadsden
WETOP AQUARIUS
Vardene Blue Gunner
CH PEWTER GREY OF WETOP
Leasowes Dancing Shadow

Scottish Kennel Club   W E Foster
CH FOGGYFURZE FANGIO
Moorside Freddie Fox
MOORSIDE DAINTY DENISE

Leeds   Mrs O M Stones
VARDENE BLUE GUARDSMAN
Wetop Aquarius
CH PEWTER GREY OF WETOP
Tuppence Off of Vistablu

National Terrier   C Sills
VARDENE BLUE GUARDSMAN
Stanolly Scooby Doo
STANOLLY STARBOW
Leasowes Dancing Shadow

Paignton   Miss A Heron
GOLD CLASSIC
Wetop Aquarius
CH STANOLLY STARBOW
Ch Pewter Grey of Wetop

Southern Counties   Mrs A Dallison
STANOLLY SCOOBY DOO
Vardene Blue Gunner
CH PEWTER GREY OF WETOP
Ch Stanolly Starbow

Leicester   W A Topham
CH STANOLLY SCOOBY DOO
Vardene Blue Guardsman
AMERDALE ATTRACTIVE
Stanolly Amber Blush

City of Birmingham   Mrs A M Laverick
CH GOLD CLASSIC
Ch Stanolly Spectacular
TUPPENCE OFF OF VISTABLU
Leasowes Dancing Shadow

Bedlington Terrier Assn.   Mrs A Care
CH STANOLLY SCOOBY DOO
Wetop Aquarius
CH PEWTER GREY OF WETOP
Ch Stanolly Starbow

Ladies Kennel Assn.   Mrs I Sills
CH STANOLLY SCOOBY DOO
Vardene Blue Guardsman
CH PEWTER GREY OF WETOP
Amerdale Attractive

Richmond   Miss M Boggia
CH STANOLLY SCOOBY DOO
Wetop Aquarius
CH PEWTER GREY OF WETOP
Ch Stanolly Starbow

1972

Crufts   *Judge* F Gent
WETOP AQUARIUS
Ch Stanolly Scooby Doo
CH PEWTER GREY OF WETOP
Ch Stanolly Starbow

Manchester   F Dempster
CH VARDENE BLUE GUARDSMAN
Birkonbrae Bronze Bacchus
BIRKONBRAE BLUE BUNNY
Amerdale Attractive

National Bedlington Terrier Club
    Mrs B Reddington
CH VARDENE BLUE GRENADIER
Ch Vardene Blue Guardsman
AMERDALE ATTRACTIVE
Ch Pewter Grey of Wetop

W.E.L.K.S.   S Franks
DISQUALIFIED *on technicality*
Ch Vardene Blue Guardsman
CH TUPPENCE OFF OF VISTABLU
Ch Pewter Grey of Wetop

Birmingham   A J Chandler
CH STANOLLY SCOOBY DOO
Ch Vardene Blue Grenadier
CH TUPPENCE OFF OF VISTABLU
Ch Berengreave Personal Property

Scottish Kennel Club   J H J Braddon
CH MOORSIDE DANDY DOLPHIN
Birkonbrae Bronze Bacchus
BERENGREAVE PERSONAL PROPERTY
Stanolly Secret Surprise

Leeds   W Clark
CH STANOLLY SCOOBY DOO
Ch Vardene Blue Guardsman
CH PEWTER GREY OF WETOP
Ch Berengreave Personal Property

Blackpool   A T A Curnow
CH STANOLLY SCOOBY DOO
Moorside Freddie Fox
STANOLLY SECRET SURPRISE
Ch Perrianne Petula

National Terrier   Ken Bounden
CH WETOP AQUARIUS
Craglough Denarius
CH TUPPENCE OFF OF VISTABLU
Ch Pewter Grey of Wetop

Paignton   R Highfield
CH STANOLLY SCOOBY DOO
Ch Wetop Aquarius
CH PEWTER GREY OF WETOP
Ch Berengreave Personal Property

Southern Counties   R M James
CH STANOLLY SCOOBY DOO
Birkonbrae Bronze Bacchus
CH PEWTER GREY OF WETOP
Ch Tuppence Off of Vistablu

Leicester   Mrs B Clifton
CH STANOLLY SCOOBY DOO
Birkonbrae Bronze Bacchus
BERENGREAVE PERSONAL PROPERTY
Amerdale Attraction

City of Birmingham   M van de Weijer
WETOP FREE LANCE
Moorside Freddie Fox
CH STANOLLY STARBOW
Craglough Clematis

Darlington   N Stead
MOORSIDE FREDDIE FOX
Foggyfurze Fireboy
DOOLEY OF CRAGLOUGH
Ch Tuppence Off of Vistablu

Bedlington Terrier Assn.   Mrs A M
    Laverick
CH GOLD CLASSIC
Caeruleus Corinthian
CH TUPPENCE OFF OF VISTABLU
Dooley of Craglough

215

Ladies Kennel Assn.   Mrs A Care
CH STANOLLY SCOOBY DOO
Birkonbrae Bronze Bacchus
CH PEWTER GREY OF WETOP
Ch Tuppence Off of Vistablu

Richmond   H Wright
CH STANOLLY SCOOBY DOO
Wetop Free Lance
CH PEWTER GREY OF WETOP
Dooley of Craglough

1973

Crufts   *Judge* Mrs F Franks
CH STANOLLY SCOOBY DOO
Caeruleus Corinthian
CH TUPPENCE OFF OF VISTABLU
Foggyfurze Firenza

Manchester   L Clifton
CH STANOLLY SCOOBY DOO
Birkonbrae Bronze Bacchus
WETOP BLUE VELVET
Ch Berengreave Personal Property

National Bedlington Terrier Club
      C Sorensen
CH STANOLLY SCOOBY DOO
Wetop Free Lance
STANOLLY SCOOBY'S SOLO
Wetop Blue Velvet

W.E.L.K.S.   W A Topham
CH STANOLLY SCOOBY DOO
Birkonbrae Bronze Bacchus
VARDENE BLUE MISCHIEF
Lieberlamb Lucinda

Birmingham   C Sills
CH STANOLLY SCOOBY DOO
Birkonbrae Bronze Bacchus
STANOLLY SCOOBY'S SOLO
Lieberlamb Lucinda

Scottish Kennel Club   A J Chandler
BIRKONBRAE BRONZE BACCHUS
Moorside Freddie Fox
CH BERENGREAVE PERSONAL PROPERTY
Lieberlamb Lucinda

Leeds   W Spilstead
CH STANOLLY SCOOBY DOO
Wetop Free Lance
WETOP BLUE VELVET
Ch Berengreave Personal Property

National Terrier   L R Wardman
CH STANOLLY SCOOBY DOO
Birkonbrae Bronze Bacchus
CH TUPPENCE OFF OF VISTABLU
Vardene Blue Mischief

Blackpool   F Gent
WETOP FREE LANCE
Ch Stanolly Spectacular
LIEBERLAMB LUCINDA
Stanolly Scooby's Solo

Paignton   G Leatt
CH STANOLLY SCOOBY DOO
Tol-pedn The Laird
CH BERENGREAVE PERSONAL PROPERTY
Bleu Bacchic of Birkonbrae

Southern Counties   Mrs M M Taunt
CH STANOLLY SCOOBY DOO
Stanolly Scoostar Boy
CH BERENGREAVE PERSONAL PROPERTY
Stanolly Sundance

Leicester   R Gadsden
CH STANOLLY SCOOBY DOO
Wetop Free Lance
CH BERENGREAVE PERSONAL PROPERTY
Wetop Blue Velvet

City of Birmingham   S L Franks
BRENTBROOK GAY BOY
Rathsrigg Kings Pawn
LIEBERLAMB LUCINDA
Stanolly Sundance

Darlington   A Tait

Rathsrigg King's Pawn
CH STANOLLY SCOOBY'S SOLO
Foggyfurze Fina

Bedlington Terrier Assn. Ken Bounden
CRAGLOUGH DENARIUS
Rathsrigg King's Pawn
BIRKONBRAE BRONZE BON BON
Wetop Blue Velvet

Ladies Kennel Club   J Cartledge
CH STANOLLY SCOOBY DOO
Wetop Free Lance
CH WETOP BLUE VELVET
Stanolly Scoostar Tipsy

Richmond Mrs I Sills
CH STANOLLY SCOOBY DOO
Bredonvale Smoky Joe
CH LIEBERLAMB LUCINDA
Stanolly Scoostar Tipsy

1974

Crufts *Judge* Mrs O M Stones
BIRKONBRAE BRONZE BACCHUS
Wetop Free Lance
CH BERENGREAVE PERSONAL PROPERTY
Ch Tuppence Off of Vistablu

Manchester Miss M Boggia
RATHSRIGG KING'S PAWN
Wetop Free Lance
STANOLLY SCOOSTAR TIPSY
Marilena Portia

National Bedlington Terrier Club
Miss A Heron
CRAGLOUGH DENARIUS
Rathsrigg Opening Gambit
FOGGYFURZE FENWICK
Craglough Kittiwake

National Terrier Mrs A Clark
CH BIRKONBRAE BRONZE BACCHUS
Rathsrigg King's Pawn
STANOLLY SUNSTAR
Stanolly Scoostar Tipsy

W.E.L.K.S. Mrs N Howard
LEASOWES TANGO
Stanolly Scoostar Boy
CH LIEBERLAMB LUCINDA
Ch Berengreave Personal Property

Birmingham Mrs A Dallison
CH BIRKONBRAE BRONZE BACCHUS
Ch Wetop Free Lance
STANOLLY SCOOSTAR TIPSY
Leasowes Chorus Girl

Scottish Kennel Club F Dempster
VARDENE BLUE MARKSMAN
Ch Birkonbrae Bronze Bacchus
FOGGYFURZE FENWICK
Ch Berengreave Personal Property

Leeds L R Wardman
RATHSRIGG KING'S PAWN
Ch Birkonbrae Bronze Bacchus
CH FOGGYFURZE FENWICK
Ch Berengreave Personal Property

Blackpool R M James
CH STANOLLY SCOOBY DOO
Ch Birkonbrae Bronze Bacchus
CH BERENGREAVE PERSONAL PROPERTY
Stanolly Scoostar Tipsy

Paignton Mrs B Reddington
CH STANOLLY SCOOBY DOO
Ch Birkonbrae Bronze Bacchus
CH STANOLLY SCOOSTAR TIPSY
Bystock Blue Pearl

Southern Counties J L Clifton
CH BIRKONBRAE BRONZE BACCHUS
Highquest Hallmark
WETOP BLUE OPAL
Ch Lieberlamb Lucinda

Leicester C Sills
CH WETOP FREE LANCE
Leasowes Tango
CH STANOLLY SCOOSTAR TIPSY
Ch Lieberlamb Lucinda

City of Birmingham Mrs A Care
CH BIRKONBRAE BRONZE BACCHUS
Sturnbay Stupendous
LIEBERLAMB LEANDER
Ch Stanolly Scoostar Tipsy

Darlington F Gent
CH RATHSRIGG KING'S PAWN
Vardene Blue Marksman
DOOLEY OF CRAGLOUGH
Ch Stanolly Scoostar Tipsy

Bedlington Terrier Assn. Mrs F L
CAERULEUS CORINTHIAN Franks
Foggyfurze Fellmist
CH TUPPENCE OFF OF VISTABLU
Stanolly Sun Pride

Ladies Kennel Assn. Mrs D Hamilton
FOGGYFURZE FANDANGO
Petacrest Sir Prancelot
CH STANOLLY SCOOSTAR TIPSY
Lieberlamb Leander

Richmond G Leatt
FOGGYFURZE FANDANGO
Ch Birkonbrae Bronze Bacchus
BIRKONBRAE BRONZE BRIGHTIZE
Highquest Honor

1975

Crufts   *Judge* Mrs M M Taunt
CH FOGGYFURZE FANDANGO
Sturnbay Stupendous
WETOP BLUE OPAL
Ch Berengreave Personal Property

Manchester   Mrs B Clifton
CH BIRKONBRAE BRONZE BACCHUS
Phindol Blue Dolphin
PERRIANNE POPPY
Ch Berengreave Personal Property

National Bedlington Terrier Club
     R Ratcliffe
VARDENE BLUE MARKSMAN
Ch Rathsrigg King's Pawn
PERRIANNE POPPY
Lieberlamb Leander

W.E.L.K.S.   R Gadsden
BREDONVALE SMOKY JOE
Phindol Blue Dolphin
CH WETOP BLUE OPAL
Lieberlamb Leander

National Terrier   Miss M Boggia
BREDONVALE SMOKY JOE
Stanolly Shang-a-Lang
LIEBERLAMB LEANDER
Leasowes Chorus Girl

Birmingham   W A Topham
CH BREDONVALE SMOKY JOE
Stanolly Shang-a-Lang
PETACREST PERFECT ANGEL
Lieberlamb Leander

Scottish Kennel Club   J H J Braddon
CH VARDENE BLUE MARKSMAN
Birkonbrae Bleu Braggadocio
CRAGLOUGH KITTIWAKE
Moorside Happy Huntress

Leeds   Mrs B Reddington
STURNBAY STUPENDOUS
Caeruleus Corinthian
BIRKONBRAE BRONZE BRIGHTIZE
Amerdale Delectable

Blackpool   J Cartledge
PHINDOL BLUE DOLPHIN
Amerdale Silent Lad
AVILAS ATHENE OF FOGGYFURZE
Stanolly Salamanda

Windsor   A J Chandler
PHINDOL BLUE DOLPHIN
Stanolly Shang-a-Lang
PETACREST BEWITCHING BLUE
Lieberlamb Leander

Paignton   H van der Loo
GRANITOR FLINT
Petacrest Sir Prancelot
DOOLEY OF CRAGLOUGH
Petacrest Perfect Angel

Southern Counties   Mrs N Howard
CH PHINDOL BLUE DOLPHIN
Moorside Freddie Fox
CH LIEBERLAMB LEANDER
Stanolly Something Special

Leicester   Mrs A M Laverick
PETACREST SIR PRANCELOT
Caeruleus Corinthian
CH LIEBERLAMB LEANDER
Stanolly Sukina

City of Birmingham   R M James
STANOLLY SHOOBY DO A
Ch Phindol Blue Dolphin
STANOLLY SUKINA
Cribden Annabell

Darlington   R Highfield
STANOLLY SHANG-A-LANG
Amerdale Silent Lad
BYSTOCK BLUE PEARL
Tabitha of Craglough

Ladies Kennel Assn.   H Wright
CH PHINDOL BLUE DOLPHIN
Sturnbay Stupendous
CH LIEBERLAMB LEANDER
Stanolly Sukina

Bedlington Terrier Assn.   F Gent
TURTONHEIGHTS BLUE GALLANT
Stanolly Shang-a-Lang
PETACREST PERFECT ANGEL
Tabitha of Craglough

Richmond   P Thompson
PETACREST SIR PRANCELOT
Petacrest Perfect Gent
STANOLLY SUKINA
Ch Lieberlamb Leander

CHALLENGE CERTIFICATE WINNERS

1976

Crufts   *Judge* Ken Bounden
CH RATHSRIGG KING'S PAWN
Granitor Flint
CRAGLOUGH KITTIWAKE
Tabitha of Craglough

Manchester   A Tait
AVILAS ARIES OF FOGGYFURZE
Granitor Flint
LIEBERLAMB LUCKY STAR
Moorside Joyful Julie

National Bedlington Terrier Club
     N Stead
AVILAS ARIES OF FOGGYFURZE
Turtonheights Blue Gallant
CH STANOLLY SUKINA
Lieberlamb Lucky Star

W.E.L.K.S.   A J Chandler
STANOLLY SHANG-A-LANG
Ch Phindol Blue Dolphin
TABITHA OF CRAGLOUGH
Ch Stanolly Sukina

National Terrier   Mrs O M Stones
CH AVILAS ARIES OF FOGGYFURZE
Wetop Gay Knight
TABITHA OF CRAGLOUGH
Cribden Annabell

Birmingham   R Gadsden
CH AVILAS ARIES OF FOGGYFURZE
Ch Phindol Blue Dolphin
CH STANOLLY SUKINA
Lieberlamb Lucky Star

Scottish Kennel Club   W E Foster
TURTONHEIGHTS BLUE GALLANT
Avilas At Last
WHICKHAM MERRY DUCHESS
Ch Stanolly Sukina

Leeds   Mrs I Sills
CH AVILAS ARIES OF FOGGYFURZE
Ch Rathsrigg King's Pawn
LIEBERLAMB LUCKY STAR
Tabitha of Craglough

Southern Counties   H Wright
AVILAS AT LAST
Sturnbay Stupendous
HILLDYKE ARKADINA
Lieberlamb Lucky Star

Blackpool   Mrs B Reddington
CH STANOLLY SHANG-A-LANG
Birkonbrae Bleu Braggadocio
DALIP PETRINELLO
Stanolly Something Special

Windsor   Mrs A Care
CH AVILAS ARIES OF FOGGYFURZE
Sturnbay Stupendous
CH LIEBERLAMB LUCKY STAR
Petacrest Perfect Angel

Paignton   Ben Johnson
TOL-PEDN RED CLOUD
Bystock Piperson
BYSTOCK BLUE OPAL
Gold Dust of Vardene

Leicester   Miss J de Beauchamp-Green
WETOP NUTMEG
Woodman of Cullercoats
STANOLLY SUMMER LUV
Gold Dust of Vardene

City of Birmingham   M van de Weijer
AVILAS LUCKY LAD OF FOGGYFURZE
Avilas At Last
CH LIEBERLAMB LUCKY STAR
Ch Stanolly Sukina

Darlington   Mrs B Clifton
CH TURTONHEIGHTS BLUE GALLANT
Stanolly Shalako
CH STANOLLY SUKINA
Stanolly Summer Delight

Bedlington Terrier Assn.   Mrs A Clark
AVILAS LUCKY LAD OF FOGGYFURZE
Birkonbrae Bleu Braggadocio
WHICKHAM MERRY DUCHESS
Stanolly Summer Luv

Ladies Kennel Assn.   S Stones
WETOP NUTMEG
Woodman of Cullercoats
CH LIEBERLAMB LUCKY STAR
Tabitha of Craglough

Midland Bedlington Terrier Club
     R Highfield
CH AVILAS LUCKY LAD OF FOGGYFURZE
Avilas At Last
STANOLLY SUMMER LUV
Tabitha of Craglough

Richmond J Cartledge
AVILAS AT LAST
Foggyfurze Fenman
CH LIEBERLAMB LUCKY STAR
Wetop Copper Charm

1977

Crufts *Judge* W A Topham
FOGGYFURZE FENMAN
Ch Avilas Lucky Lad of Foggyfurze
CH LIEBERLAMB LUCKY STAR
Rathsrigg Raffle

Manchester R Ratcliffe
FOGGYFURZE FENMAN
Granitor Flint
GOLD DUST OF VARDENE
Petacrest Perfect Angel

National Bedlington Terrier Club
L R Wardman
CH FOGGYFURZE FENMAN
Woodman of Cullercoats
RATHSRIGG RAFFLE
Whispering Song of Stanolly

National Terrier W Clark
BIRKONBRAE BLEU BRAGGADOCIO
Ch Foggyfurze Fenman
TYNECOURT TRINKET
Rathsrigg Raffle

W.E.L.K.S. F Gent
RATHSRIGG RUIN
Wetop Nutmeg
CH TABITHA OF CRAGLOUGH
Rathsrigg Raffle

Birmingham Mrs A Clark
BIRKONBRAE BLEU BRAGGADOCIO
Wetop Gay Knight
WHISPERING SONG OF STANOLLY
Gold Dust of Vardene

Scottish Kennel Club Mrs D Hamilton
CH FOGGYFURZE FENMAN
Ch Avilas Lucky Lad of Foggyfurze
FOGGYFURZE FONDANT
Stanolly Salamanda

Leeds Miss A Heron
WOODMAN OF CULLERCOATS
Ch Avilas Lucky Lad of Foggyfurze
CRAGLOUGH KITTIWAKE
Foggyfurze Fondant

Southern Counties R M James
LIEBERLAMB LIKELY LAD
Birkonbrae Bleu Braggadocio
WHISPERING SONG OF STANOLLY
Whickham Merry Duchess

Blackpool Miss M Boggia
WOODMAN OF CULLERCOATS
Lemmy Out of Phindol
CH STANOLLY SUMMER LUV
Rathsrigg Raffle

Windsor J H J Braddon
STANOLLY SHIROCO
Wetop Gay Knight
SINGLETON GINGERBREAD LADY
Rathsrigg Raffle

Paignton R J Clay
CH WOODMAN OF CULLERCOATS
Wetop Nutmeg
CH WHISPERING SONG OF STANOLLY
Seabird of Tol-pedn

Leicester Mrs I Sills
CH AVILAS LUCKY LAD OF FOGGYFURZE
Stanolly Shiroco
FOGGYFURZE FONDANT
Ch Stanolly Summer Luv

Birmingham Mrs A Dallison
STANOLLY SHIROCO
Ch Avilas Lucky Lad of Foggyfurze
CH FOGGYFURZE FONDANT
Whickham Merry Duchess

Darlington Mrs B Reddington
CH BIRKONBRAE BLEU BRAGGADOCIO
Ch Turtonheights Blue Gallant
CH WHICKHAM MERRY DUCHESS
Tonymarg Tartan Tearaway

Richmond A J Chandler
CH STANOLLY SHIROCO
Ch Avilas Lucky Lad of Foggyfurze
CH WHICKHAM MERRY DUCHESS
Lieberlamb Leading Lady

L.K.A Mrs A M Laverick
CH WOODMAN OF CULLERCOATS
Vistablu Don Perro
CH WHISPERING SONG OF STANOLLY
Singleton Gingerbread Lady

Bedlington Terrier Assn. Ken Bounden
GRANITOR FLINT
Rathsrigg Ruin
CH TABITHA OF CRAGLOUGH
Tynecourt Trinket

Midland Counties   Mrs A Care
MOORSIDE LUCKY LAD
Ch Foggyfurze Fenman
CH WHICKHAM MERRY DUCHESS
Lieberlamb Leading Lady

1978

Crufts   *Judge* R J Gadsden
CH FOGGYFURZE FENMAN
Ch Stanolly Shiroco
CH WHISPERING SONG OF STANOLLY
Tonymarg Tartan Tearaway

Manchester   F Gent
GRANITOR ROCKET MAN
Granitor Flint
VARDENE BLUE WITCHCRAFT
Avilas Barmaid

National Bedlington Terrier Club
                    S Stones
GRANITOR ROCKET MAN
Wetop Gay Knight
AVILAS BARMAID
Vardene Blue Witchcraft

W.E.L.K.S.   W A Topham
BOUGHTON BLUFF
Rathsrigg Ruin
REPRINT OF TIDDLYMOUNT
Lieberlamb Louise

Birmingham   W Clark
RATHSRIGG RUIN
Sturnbay Stupendous
CH WHICKHAM MERRY DUCHESS
Reprint of Tiddlymount

Scottish Kennel Club   G Leatt
CH GRANITOR ROCKET MAN
Moorside Lucky Lad
CH WICKHAM MERRY DUCHESS
Mistyhaze Crystal

Leeds   Miss M Boggia
WETOP GAY KNIGHT
Rathsrigg Ruin
FOGGYFURZE FLUTTER
Ch Whickham Merry Duchess

Midland Bedlington Terrier Club
                    H Jordan
CH RATHSRIGG RUIN
Wetop Gay Knight
FOGGYFURZE FLUTTER
Ch Whickham Merry Duchess

Windsor   Mrs O M Stones
WETOP GAY KNIGHT
Ch Rathsrigg Ruin
BIRKONBRAE BRONZE BACCHANTE
Avilas Barmaid

Paignton   F Curnow
CH GRANITOR FLINT
Petacrest Patron Saint
LIEBERLAMB LOUISE
Lieberlamb Lorna

Leicester   H Wright
PETACREST PATRON SAINT
Dalip Huggy Bear
CH FOGGYFURZE FLUTTER
Avilas Barmaid

Birmingham   A J Chandler
DALIP HUGGY BEAR
Boughton Bluff
VARDENE BLUE WITCHCRAFT
Avilas Barmaid

Darlington   Miss A Heron
CH RATHSRIGG RUIN
Foggyfurze Fine Fare
VARDENE BLUE WITCHCRAFT
Flixbridge Zita

Richmond   R M James
FOGGYFURZE FINE FARE
Ch Rathsrigg Ruin
CH FOGGYFURZE FLUTTER
Lieberlamb Louise

Bedlington Terrier Assn.
                    Mme A E Pfohl
FOGGYFURZE FOREVER
Willow of Cullercoats
LIEBERLAMB LOUISE
Singleton Gingerbread Lady

Midland Counties   Mrs B Clifton
CH WETOP GAY KNIGHT
Foggyfurze Forever
BIRKONBRAE BRONZE BACCHANTE
Reprint of Tiddlymount

1979

Crufts   *Judge* Mrs A Care
DALIP HUGGY BEAR
Ch Wetop Gay Knight
CH LIEBERLAMB LOUISE
Reprint of Tiddlymount

Manchester   R Gadsden
CH WETOP GAY KNIGHT
Dalip Huggy Bear
CH WHICKHAM MERRY DUCHESS
Ch Lieberlamb Louise

National Bedlington Terrier Club
    R Highfield
CH RATHSRIGG RUIN
Lemmy Out of Phindol
STANOLLY SUMMER DELIGHT
Dalip Personality Girl

National Terrier   Miss D Aitkenhead
CH RATHSRIGG RUIN
Ch Granitor Rocket Man
CH VARDENE WITCHCRAFT
Ch Lieberlamb Louise

W.E.L.K.S.   A O Grindey
CH DALIP HUGGY BEAR
Arg. Ch. Ben Franklin of Vistablu
REPRINT OF TIDDLYMOUNT
Ch Lieberlamb Louise

Birmingham   M van der Weijer
FOGGYFURZE FOREVER
Ch Dalip Huggy Bear
CH LIEBERLAMB LOUISE
Dalip Personality Girl

Leeds   R Ratcliffe
CH RATHSRIGG RUIN
Westland Blue Star
CH LIEBERLAMB LOUISE
Craglough Comfrey

Scottish Kennel Club   A J Chandler
CH DALIP HUGGY BEAR
Foggyfurze Fuji
CH BIRKONBRAE BRONZE BACCHKA
Birkonbrae Bronze Bonfleur

Windsor   Mrs A Dallison
CH FOGGYFURZE FOREVER
Lieberlamb Laddie Sim
CH BIRKONBRAE BRONZE BACCHKA
Birkonbrae Bronze Bachique

Paignton   Ken Bounden
CH RATHSRIGG RUIN
Willow of Cullercoats
CRAGLOUGH COMFREY
Hilary of Highquest

Leicester   L R Wardman
FOGGYFURZE FINE FARE
Ch Rathsrigg Ruin
CH BIRKONBRAE BRONZE BACCHKA
Ch Lieberlamb Louise

Birmingham   W Topham
STANOLLY SUNFLASH
Ch Rathsrigg Ruin
CH LIEBERLAMB LOUISE
Ukwong September Morn of Vardene

Darlington   H Wright
CH AVILAS LUCKY LAD OF FOGGYFURZE
Lieberlamb Laddie Sim
RATHSRIGG REGIUS
Foggyfurze Fifi

Richmond   H Jordan
CH DALIP HUGGY BEAR
Wetop Tight Rope
BRENTBROOK PRECIOUS GEM
Ch Lieberlamb Louise

Bedlington Terrier Assn.   Mrs I Sills
CH AVILAS LUCKY LAD OF FOGGYFURZE
Lieberlamb Laddie Sim
CH LIEBERLAMB LOUISE
Foggyfurze Fifi

Midland Counties   S Stones
WETOP TIGHT ROPE
Westland Blue Star
UNWONG SEPTEMBER MORN OF VARDENE
Craglough Celeste

1980

Crufts   *Judge* Mrs B Clifton
CH DALIP HUGGY BEAR
Wetop Tight Rope
BIRKONBRAE BRONZE BACHIQUE
Tuppence of Tynecourt

Manchester   Mrs O Stones
WETOP TIGHT ROPE
Arg. Ch Vistablu Ben Franklin of Blue
    Happening
AVILAS BARMAID
Rathsrigg Regius

National Bedlington Terrier Club
D Harker
STANOLLY SUPERFLASH
Ch Granitor Rocket Man
RATHSRIGG ROSE
Elcroft Lillie Lady

W.E.L.K.S.　　　　　　　　R Clay
STANOLLY SUPERFLASH
Tickerton Hodder Sherry of Cullercoats
CRAGLOUGH CELESTE
Moorside Quite Quaint

Birmingham　　　　　R W B Pinches
CH STANOLLY SUPERFLASH
Lieberlamb Laddie Sim
CH LIEBERLAMB LOUISE
Birkonbrae Bronze Bachique

Scottish Kennel Club　　　Ben Johnson
CH STANOLLY SUPERFLASH
Lieberlamb Light Fantastic
STAR AUDITION OF STANOLLY
Birkonbrae Bronze Bachique

Leeds　　　　　　　　I J Phillips
CH FOGGYFURZE FINE FARE
Ch Granitor Rocket Man
MOORSIDE QUITE QUAINT
Craglough Celeste

Midland Bedlington Terrier Club
R Highfield
CH STANOLLY SUPERFLASH
Ch Dalip Huggy Bear
TUPPENCE OF TYNECOURT
Star Audition of Stanolly

Windsor　　　　　　Miss M Boggia
LIEBERLAMB LADDIE SIM
Tickerton Hodder Sherry of Cullercoats
MOORSIDE QUITE QUAINT
Rathsrigg Rose

Paignton　　　　　　　　W Clark
CH DALIP HUGGY BEAR
Ch Stanolly Superflash
RATHSRIGG ROSE
Tynecourt Truffle

Leicester　　　　　　　J Cartledge
VISTABLU BEN FRANKLIN OF BLUE
　HAPPENING
Foggyfurze Fireman
FOGGYFURZE FIFI.
Wetop Meg

Birmingham　　　　　　R M James
CH RATHSRIGG RUIN
Willow of Cullercoats
CH AVILAS BARMAID
Tuppence of Tynecourt

Darlington　　　　　　　R Ratcliff
LIEBERLAMB LADDIE SIM
Ch Granitor Rocket Man
FOGGYFURZE FIFI
Rathsrigg Rose

Richmond　　　　　　　R Gadsden
CH LIEBERLAMB LADDIE SIM
Ch Dalip Huggy Bear
CH AVILAS BARMAID
Tuppence of Tynecourt

Bedlington Terrier Assn
Miss D Aitkenhead
TICKERTON HODDER SHERRY OF
　CULLERCOATS
Stanolly Seanachia
SINGLETON GINGERBREAD LADY
Rathsrigg Rose

Midland Counties　　　　　L Clifton
CH RATHSRIGG RUIN
Hilldyke Distinguished
BIRKONBRAE BLEU BUBBLICIOUS
Elcroft Lilly Lady

1981

Crufts　　　　　*Judge* A J Chandler
CH DALIP HUGGY BEAR
Arg. Ch Vistablu Ben Franklin of Blue
　Happening
TUPPENCE OF TYNECOURT
Wetop Meg

Manchester　　　　　　　H Wright
RATHSRIGG REUBEN
Aurableue Ashmow Alick
STAR AUDITION OF STANOLLY
Rathsrigg Rose

National Bedlington Terrier Club
N Stead
CH RATHSRIGG RUIN
Rathsrigg Reuben
CH STAR AUDITION OF STANOLLY
Tuppence of Tynecourt

National Terrier Club   W A Topham
STANOLLY SUPER SWANK
Willow of Cullercoats
CH RATHSRIGG ROSE
Elcroft Lilly Lady

W.E.L.K.S.   Mrs A Dallison
BRICKBATS BROUGHTON
Stanolly Super Swank
CH STAR AUDITION OF STANOLLY
Birkonbrae Bleu Bubblicious

Birmingham   J H J Braddon
BLA SKUGGANS MOVIE STAR
Stanolly Super Swank
BLA SKUGGAN NEXT STAR
Tuppence of Tynecourt

Scottish Kennel Club   Miss M Boggia
CH RATHSRIGG REUBEN
Willow of Cullercoats
CH FOGGYFURZE FIFI
Tuppence of Tynecourt

Leeds   Mrs O Stones
CH RATHSRIGG REUBEN
Brickbats Broughton
WETOP MEG
Ch Rathsrigg Rose

Windsor   Mrs A Care
RED EAGLE OF TOL-PEDN
Stanolly Super Swank
WETOP MEG
Bla Skuggan Next Star

Paignton   Mrs I Bach
WILLOW OF CULLERCOATS
Red Eagle of Tol-pedn
VISTABLU WONDER WOMAN
Tuppence of Tynecourt

Welsh Kennel Club   Mrs B Clifton
CH DALIP HUGGY BEAR
Bla Skuggans Movie Star
CH BIRKONBRAE BLEU BUBBLICIOUS
Elcroft Lilly Lady

Leicester   Mrs A Clark
WILLOW OF CULLERCOATS
Red Eagle of Tol-pedn
CH TUPPENCE OF TYNECOURT
Moorside Quite Quaint

Birmingham   M van de Weijer
CH DALIP HUGGY BEAR
Stanolly Super Swank
CH FOGGYFURZE FIFI
Lieberlamb Lucky Star

Richmond   Mrs P Lay
PETACREST PSALM
Tynecourt Trooper
CH MOORSIDE QUITE QUAINT
Lieberlamb Lucky Charm

Darlington   S Stones
BLA SKUGGANS MOVIE STAR
Tynecourt Trooper
CH WETOP MEG
Vistablu Wonder Woman

Bedlington Terrier Assn.   L Wardman
CH WILLOW OF CULLERCOATS
Ch Avilas Lucky Lad of Foggyfurze
CH BIRKONBRAE BLEU BUBBLICIOUS
Foggyfurze Faberge

Midland Counties   B Johnson
BRICKBATS BROUGHTON
Stanolly Super Swank
BLA SKUGGANS NEXT STAR
Vistablu Wonder Woman

1982

Crufts   *Judge* H R Highfield
CH AVILAS LUCKY LAD OF FOGGYFURZE
Stanolly Super Swank
CH STAR AUDITION OF STANOLLY
Ch Rathsrigg Rose

Manchester   W A Topham
RATHSRIGG RULE
Tynecourt Trooper
CH STAR AUDITION OF STANOLLY
Tinkerbloo Chic Angelique

National Bedlington Terrier Club
    R J Clay
RED EAGLE OF TOL-PEDN
Brickbats Broughton
CH STAR AUDITION OF STANOLLY
Vistablu Wonder Woman

W.E.L.K.S.   G Down
CH BRICKBATS BROUGHTON
Stanolly Super Swank
VISTABLU WONDER WOMAN
Moonstep Lace

CHALLENGE CERTIFICATE WINNERS

Birmingham   R W B Pinches
CH BRICKBATS BROUGHTON
Bla Skuggans Movie Star
CH STAR AUDITION OF STANOLLY
Moonstep Lace

Scottish Kennel Club   R M James
CH BLA SKUGGANS MOVIE STAR
Tynecourt Trooper
CH BLA SKUGGANS NEXT STAR
Tynecourt Truffle

Midland Bedlington Terrier Club
     D Harker
CH RATHSRIGG RUIN
Stanolly Super Swank
VERANNA MISS VALENTINE
Tynecourt Truffle

Windsor   J H J Braddon
WETOP PARSLEY
Wetop Silver Spur
AURABLEUE ADELA
Singleton Ginger Bread Lady

Paignton   I Phillips
CH RED EAGLE OF TOL-PEDN
Craglough Cerberus
CRAGLOUGH CALINKA
Tinkerbloo Chic Angelique

Leeds   H Wright
AURABLEUE ASHMOW ALICK
Winfell Rustler
CH VISTABLU WONDER WOMAN
Rathsrigg Raze

Welsh Kennel Club   Mrs M Sugden
TYNECOURT TROOPER
Wetop Silver Spur
CH STAR AUDITION OF STANOLLY
Craglough Calinka

Leicester   Mrs O Stones
WETOP SILVER SPUR
Ch Brickbats Broughton
CH VISTABLU WONDER WOMAN
Rathsrigg Raze

Birmingham   R J Gadsden
STANOLLY SUPER SWANK
Lieberlamb Lester
CH STAR AUDITION OF STANOLLY
Tynecourt Truffle

Richmond   K Bounden
WETOP PARSLEY
Aurableue Ashmow Alick
TINKERBLOO CHIC ANGELIQUE
Hilary of Highquest

Darlington   J L Clifton
TYNECOURT TROOPER
Stanolly Secret Agent
VERANNA MISS VALENTINE
Birkonbrae Bronze Barbraela

Bedlington Terrier Assn.   Miss A Heron
AURABLEUE ASHMOW ALICK
Lieberlamb Lester
RATHSRIGG RAZE
Tynecourt Tonic at Shenandoah

Midland Counties   S Stones
WINFELL RUSTLER
Wetop Silver Spur
CH VISTABLU WONDER WOMAN
Stanolly Celestial Dream

1983

Crufts   *Judge* Mrs I Sills
CH AVILAS LUCKY LAD OF FOGGYFURZE
Lieberlamb Lester
CH STAR AUDITION OF STANOLLY
Moorside Summer Song

Manchester   D Harker
CH STANOLLY SUPER SWANK
Moorside So Your Sammy
MOORSIDE SUMMER SONG
Bleu Berrypie of Birkonbrae

National Bedlington Terrier Club
     B Clifton
WETOP SILVER SPURR
Moorside So Your Sammy
ELCROFT LILLY LADY
Bleu Berrypie of Birkonbrae

National Terrier Club   G R Down
LIEBERLAMB LESTER
Stanolly Secret Agent
ELCROFT LILLY LADY
Tinkerbloo Chic Angelique

W.E.L.K.S.   A J Chandler
CH WETOP SILVER SPURR
Vistablu Union Jack
DELLBREN BLUE FANTASY
Vistablu Fly The Flag at Sevray

225

Birmingham   Ben Johnson
LIEBERLAMB LESTER
Barnsnap Brigadier
CH SINGLETON GINGER BREAD LADY
Stanolly Celestial Dream

Scottish Kennel Club   C Williams
CH BRICKBATS BROUGHTON
Winfell Rustler
CH ELCROFT LILLY LADY
Bleu Berrypie of Birkonbrae

Windsor   H Wright
WINFELL RUSTLER
Lieberlamb Lester
CH ELCROFT LILLY LADY
Moorside Summer Song

Paignton   Mrs Aquina Meyer (U.S.A.)
LIEBERLAMB LESTER
Craglough Cedilla
MOORSIDE SUMMER SONG
Tol-pedn Sea Holly

Leeds   Miss B Anderson
MOORSIDE SO YOUR SAMMY
Winfell Rustler
CRAGLOUGH CALINKA
Ch Elcroft Lilly Lady

Welsh Kennel Club   W R Irving
TICKERTON HODDER SHERRY
    OF CULLERCOATS
Ch Brickbats Broughton
CH STAR AUDITION OF STANOLLY
Moorside Summer Song

Leicester   H R Highfield
CH WINFELL RUSTLER
Lieberlamb Lester
VERANNA MISS VALENTINE
Moorside Summer Song

Birmingham   Dr W Ommen Kloeke
                        (Holland)
CH LIEBERLAMB LESTER
Wetop Parsley
CH MOORSIDE SUMMER SONG
Veranna Miss Valentine

Richmond   Miss F Hamilton
MOORSIDE SO YOUR SAMMY
Aurableue Ashmow Alick
CH MOORSIDE SUMMER SONG
Tynecourt Thingamy Jig

Darlington   Ken Bounden
AURABLEUE ASHMOW ALICK
Sutcott Serendipity
WETOP SOPHIE
Craglough Calinka

Bedlington Terrier Assn.
              Mrs G Brewin (U.S.A.)
AURABLEUE ASHMOW ALICK
Sevray Singing Sailor
CH CRAGLOUGH CALINKA
Petacrest Polly Wagtail

Midland Counties   Miss D Aitkenhead
CH AURABLEUE ASHMOW ALICK
Highquest Hoodwink
CH MOORSIDE SUMMER SONG
Pelton Lucky Strike

1984

Crufts   *Judge* R Ratcliffe
CH AVILAS LUCKY LAD OF FOGGYFURZE
Ch Brickbats Broughton
CH CRAGLOUGH CALINKA
Tinkerbloo Chic Angelique

Manchester   Miss M Boggia
CH MOORSIDE SO YOUR SAMMY
Stanolly Secret Agent
STANOLLY CELESTIAL DREAM
Moorside Tinker Tailor of Tynecourt

National Bedlington Terrier Club
                    Mrs J Langstaff
TYNECOURT TALLY-HO
Ch Aurableue Ashmow Alick
RATHSRIGG RAZE
Stanolly Treveda Tula

W.E.L.K.S.   Miss L Beak
LIEBERLAMB LESTER
Stanolly Starburst
PETACREST POLLY WAGTAIL
Ch Craglough Calinka

Birmingham   Geo R Down
STANOLLY STARBURST
Stanolly Secret Agent
PETACREST POLLY WAGTAIL
Stanolly Celestial Dream

Scottish Kennel Club   R Clay
BARNSNAP BRIGADIER
Ch Brickbats Broughton
VARDENE BLUE TREASURE
Tynecourt Tonic of Shenandoah

Midland Bedlington Terrier Club
E Hill
CH MOORSIDE SO YOUR SAMMY
Stanolly Starburst
BOJEN BIANCA
Bleu Berrypie of Birkonbrae

Windsor   W Topham
WINFELL RAIDER
Stanolly Starburst
CH PETACREST POLLY WAGTAIL
Moorside Tinker Tailor of Tynecourt

Paignton   Mrs F Craig
MARLISH BLUE STONE
Barnsnap Brigadier
CH PETACREST POLLY WAGTAIL
Jenash Moonbeam

Leeds   D Harker
STANOLLY STARBURST
Winfell Raider
MOORSIDE TINKER TAILOR OF
   TYNECOURT
Bleu Bacio of Birkonbrae

Welsh Kennel Club   Miss B Anderson
WINFELL RAIDER
Stanolly Starburst
STANOLLY CELESTIAL DREAM
Dalip Venus in Blue Genes

Leicester   Ken Bounden
BARNSNAP BRIGADIER
Ch Aurableue Ashmow Alick
CAERULEUS CELTIC
Wetop Sophie

Birmingham   H Wright
CH STANOLLY STARBURST
Winfell Raider
AURABLEUE ADELA
Moorside Tinker Tailor of Tynecourt

Richmond   Mrs M Sugden
CH RATHSRIGG RULE
Ch Stanolly Starburst
CH MOORSIDE SUMMER SONG
Vistablu Fly The Flag at Sevray

Darlington   N Stead
CH RATHSRIGG RULE
Winfell Raider
CH MOORSIDE SUMMER SONG
Bojen Bianca

Bedlington Terrier Assn.   F Gent
CH AURABLEUE ASHMOW ALICK
Sevray Singing Sailor
CH MOORSIDE SUMMER SONG
Bojen Bianca

Midland Counties   R J Gadsden
CH AURABLEUE ASHMOW ALICK
Tynecourt Tally-Ho
MOORSIDE TINKER TAILOR OF
   TYNECOURT
Stanolly Silver Trinket

1985

Crufts   *Judge* S Stones
CH WINFELL RAIDER
Ch Aurableue Ashmow Alick
VISTABLU FLY THE FLAG AT SEVRAY
Stanolly Rising Star

Manchester   R M James
TYNECOURT TALLY-HO
Ch Winfell Raider
STANOLLY SILVER TRINKET
Stanolly Super Flare

National Terrier Club   T J Horner
CH AURABLEUE ASHMOW ALICK
Hogarth of Ashness
CH AURABLEUE ADELA
Moorside Vivacious Vixen of
   Lieberlamb

National Bedlington Terrier Club
I J Phillips
CRAGLOUGH CHERUBINO
Ch Aurableue Ashmow Alick
MOORSIDE VIVACIOUS VIXEN OF
   LIEBERLAMB
Bojen Bianca

W.E.L.K.S.   C Williams
SEVRAY SINGING SAILOR
Ch Winfell Raider
STANOLLY CELESTIAL DREAM
Dellbren Blue Fantasy

Birmingham   W R Irving
CH WINFELL RAIDER
Ch Stanolly Starburst
CH MOORSIDE TINKER TAILOR OF
   TYNECOURT
Stanolly Super Flare

Scottish Kennel Club   Mrs A Clark
MOORSIDE VICTOR IS NO VAGRANT
Tynecourt Tally-Ho
CH MOORSIDE TINKER TAILOR OF
   TYNECOURT
Ch Moorside Summer Song

Southern Counties   C Metcalfe
CANNY LAD OF SPENNYMOOR
Ch Aurableue Ashmow Alick
STANOLLY SILVER TRINKET
Tinkerbloo Chic Angelique

Midland Bedlington Terrier Club
                    W Kitchin
CRAGLOUGH CHERUBINO
Ch Rathsrigg Rule
DALIP VENUS IN BLUE GENES
Stanolly Silver Trinket

Windsor   Mrs A Dallison
MOORSIDE VICTOR IS NO VAGRANT
Vistablu Nelson Touch
STANOLLY SUPER FLARE
Diamonds Delight

Paignton   J Holden
CH CRAGLOUGH CHERUBINO
Tynecourt Tally-Ho
CRAGLOUGH CONSTANTIA
Ch Moorside Summer Song

Leeds   Mrs B Reddington
CH MOORSIDE VICTOR IS NO VAGRANT
Ch Stanolly Starburst
DALIP VENUS IN BLUE GENES
Bleu Bacio of Birkonbrae

Welsh Kennel Club   Mrs O Stones
VISTABLU NELSON TOUCH
Ch Winfell Raider
DANCERS DESIRE
Brynsire Morning Melody

Leicester   Mrs I Sills
CH STANOLLY STARBURST
Ch Moorside Victor Is No Vagrant
MOORSIDE VIVACIOUS VIXEN OF
   LIEBERLAMB
Stanolly Super Flare

Birmingham   F Jones
CH STANOLLY STARBURST
Sevray Singing Sailor
MOORSIDE UPPER UTOPIA
Ch Moorside Summer Song

Richmond   J Braddon
VISTABLU NELSON TOUCH
Barnsnap Brigadier
CH DALIP VENUS IN BLUE GENES
Moorside Upper Utopia

Bedlington Terrier Assn.   C Sills
CH AURABLEUE ASHMOW ALICK
Stanolly Shotgun Will
STANOLLY SUPER FLARE
Moorside Ursula Ula at Hilldyke

Midland Counties   B F Emsley
CH MOORSIDE VICTOR IS NO VAGRANT
Ch Aurableue Ashmow Alick
MOORSIDE VIVACIOUS VIXEN OF
   LIEBERLAMB
Stanolly Super Flare

1986

Crufts   *Judge* H Wright
CH CRAGLOUGH CHERUBINO
Ch Moorside Victor Is No Vagrant
CH MOORSIDE TINKER TAILOR OF
   TYNECOURT
Moorside Ursula Ula At Hilldyke

Manchester   Miss D Aitkenhead
SEVRAY SINGING SAILOR
Ch Moorside Victor Is No Vagrant
DANCERS DESIRE
Stanolly Springtime Melody

National Terrier Club   S Stones
CH VISTABLU NELSON TOUGH
Ch Craglough Cherubino
BLUE DIAMOND OF WETOP
Stanolly Rising Star

National Bedlington Terrier Club
                    D Harker
CH MOORSIDE VICTOR IS NO VAGRANT
Sevray Singing Sailor
CH STANOLLY SUPER FLARE
Rathsrigg Rina

W.E.L.K.S.   Mrs M Sugden
CH VISTABLU NELSON TOUCH
Winfell Rambler
CINNAMON OF CULLERCOATS
Ch Stanolly Super Flare

Birmingham   Mrs V Yates
WINFELL RAMBLER
Ch Moorside Victor Is No Vagrant
STANOLLY RISING STAR
Moorside Vivacious Vixen of Lieberlamb

Scottish Kennel Club   Ken Bounden
CH SEVRAY SINGING SAILOR
Ch Craglough Cherubino
CINNAMON OF CULLERCOATS
Craglough Constantia

Southern Counties   G Down
CH VISTABLU NELSON TOUCH
Barnsnap Brigadier
CH STANOLLY SILVER TRINKET
Dancers Desire

Midland Bedlington Terrier Club
     Mrs O Stones
STANOLLY STUPENDOUS LAD
Ch Craglough Cherubino
BLUE DIAMOND OF WETOP
Stanolly Celestial Dream

Windsor   R Clay
CH MOORSIDE VICTOR IS NO VAGRANT
Ch Vistablu Nelson Touch
CH MOORSIDE VIVACIOUS VIXEN OF
   LIEBERLAMB
Hot Gosip

Paignton   Mrs M Phillips
CH CRAGLOUGH CHERUBINO
Ch Moorside Victor Is No Vagrant
MOORSIDE UPPER UTOPIA
Wildfire at Westfell

Leeds   T Horner
CH VISTABLU NELSON TOUCH
Winfell Rambler
STANOLLY SPRINGTIME MELODY
Craglough Constantia

Welsh Kennel Club   R M James
CH VISTABLU NELSON TOUCH
Ch Moorside Victor Is No Vagrant
BRYNSIRE MORNING MELODY
Veranna Blue Venus

Leicester   Mrs J Langstaff
CH VISTABLU NELSON TOUCH
Ivycott Ironmaster
STANOLLY SPRINGTIME MELODY
Wildfire at Westfell

Birmingham   C Williams
CH CRAGLOUGH CHERUBINO
Grey Wolf of Tol-pedn
STANOLLY RISING STAR
Stanolly Springtime Melody

Richmond   H A Jordan
CH VISTABLU NELSON TOUCH
Ch Moorside Victor Is No Vagrant
CH BLUE DIAMOND OF WETOP
Barnsnap Ballerina

Darlington   W Topham
WINFELL RAMBLER
Ch Moorside Victor Is No Vagrant
CH STANOLLY SPRINGTIME MELODY
Casamanda Princess Gipsy

Bedlington Terrier Assn.   Mrs P Lay
CH VISTABLU NELSON TOUCH
Rowney Blue Slick
CH CRAGLOUGH CONSTANTIA
Dancers Desire

Midland Counties   Miss F Hamilton
CH VISTABLU NELSON TOUCH
Ch Moorside Victor Is No Vagrant
WILDFIRE AT WESTFELL
Sutcott Sunday Stroller

1987

Crufts   *Judge* Miss A Heron
STANOLLY STUPENDOUS LAD
Ch Craglough Cherubino
CH CINNAMON OF CULLERCOATS
Veranna Blue Velvet

Manchester   J Holden
CH CRAGLOUGH CHERUBINO
Ch Moorside Victor Is No Vagrant
RATHSRIGG RINA
Moorside Ursula Ula at Hilldyke

National Terrier Club   E Hill
CH MOORSIDE VICTOR IS NO VAGRANT
Ch Vistablu Nelson Touch
MOORSIDE BONNY BLOSSOM
Rathsrigg Rina

National Bedlington Terrier Club
     Miss D Aitkenhead
CH MOORSIDE VICTOR IS NO VAGRANT
Dalip Boy George of Solstice
RATHSRIGG RINA
Moorside Ursula Ula at Hilldyke

W.E.L.K.S.   Ken Bounden
CH CRAGLOUGH CHERUBINO
Highquest Hot Coffee At Lowbrook
CH DANCERS DESIRE
Diamonds Delight

Birmingham   H H Atkinson
CH WINFELL RAMBLER
Ch Stanolly Starburst
DALIP UPTOWN GIRL
Ch Stanolly Springtime Melody

Scottish Kennel Club
     Dr W K J J Van Ommen Kloeke
CH VISTABLU NELSON TOUCH
Ch Moorside Victor Is No Vagrant
CH RATHSRIGG RINA
Veranna Blue Venus

Bath   W Kitchin
CH VISTABLU NELSON TOUCH
Stanolly Stupendous Lad
DALIP UPTOWN GIRL
Sutcott Sunday Stroller

Southern Counties   Mrs I Sills
CH BARNSNAP BRIGADIER
Yarbach Hurricane Higgins
MOORSIDE BONNY BLOSSOM
Stanolly Silver Chord

Midland Bedlington Terrier Club
     S Power
CH CRAGLOUGH CHERUBINO
Dalip Boy George of Solstice
CH RATHSRIGG RINA
Dalip Uptown Girl

Windsor   J A S Stones
CH STANOLLY STUPENDOUS LAD
Ch Moorside Victor Is No Vagrant
RATHSRIGG ROMANCE
Lieberlamb Laurel of Vistablu

Paignton   W Topham
THE COUNT OF CRISPINO
Grey Wolf of Tol-pedn
BARNSNAP BALLERINA
Blue Velvet Lady

Leeds   Mrs O Stones
CH VISTABLU NELSON TOUCH
Stanolly Student Prince
CRAGLOUGH CORYANTHUS
Sutcott Sunday Stroller

Welsh Kennel Club   Mrs M Sugden
CH SEVRAY SINGING SAILOR
Yarbach Hurricane Higgins
VERANNA BLUE VENUS
Stanolly Silver Bell

Leicester   C Williams
CH CRAGLOUGH CHERUBINO
Ch Vistablu Nelson Touch
CH MOORSIDE BONNY BLOSSOM
Stanolly Summer Melody

Birmingham   Mrs A Dallison
CH MOORSIDE VICTOR IS NO VAGRANT
Ch Stanolly Starburst
STANOLLY SILVER BELL
Veranna Blue Venus

Richmond   Miss M Boggia
THE COUNT OF CRISPINO
Jenash Just A Dreamer
CH MOORSIDE BONNY BLOSSOM
Sutcott Sunday Stroller

Darlington   T Horner
CH VISTABLU NELSON TOUCH
Stanolly Swanky Doo
CH DALIP UPTOWN GIRL
Ch Craglough Constantia

Bedlington Terrier Assn.   Mrs I Phillips
CH VISTABLU NELSON TOUCH
Ch Craglough Cherubino
CRAGLOUGH CORYANTHUS
Ch Dancers Desire

Midland Counties   C Sills
CH STANOLLY STARBURST
Yarbach Hurricane Higgins
VERANNA BLUE VENUS
Barnsnap Ballerina

1988

Crufts   *Judge* R M James
FANTASTIC LUCKY BLUE
Ch Stanolly Starburst
MOORSIDE URSULA ULA AT HILLDYKE
Veranna Blue Venus

Manchester   I J Phillips
CH VISTABLU NELSON TOUCH
Stanolly Student Prince
BOJEN BELLE AMIE
Moorside Ursula Ula At Hilldyke

230

CHALLENGE CERTIFICATE WINNERS

National Bedlington Terrier Club
Mrs A Emsley
CH VISTABLU NELSON TOUCH
Stanolly Sunny Romero
CH CRAGLOUGH CORYANTHUS
Rathsrigg Romance

National Terrier Club
Miss D Aikenhead
CH VISTABLU NELSON TOUCH
Ch Stanolly Starburst
CH DALIP UPTOWN GIRL
Moorside Ursula Ula At Hilldyke

W.E.L.K.S.
Mrs F Craig
FANTASTIC LUCKY BLUE
Highquest Hot Trail
CH CRAGLOUGH CORYANTHUS
Jenash Moon Beam

Birmingham
R J Clay
CH VISTABLU NELSON TOUCH
Ain't Misbehavin' At Furrolly
CH DALIP UPTOWN GIRL
Ch Craglough Coryanthus

Scottish Kennel Club
D Harker
CH VISTABLU NELSON TOUCH
Stanolly Sunny Romero
MOORSIDE URSULA ULA AT HILLDYKE
Rathsrigg Rani

Bath
Miss L Beak
CH VISTABLU NELSON TOUCH
Dalip Limited Edition
CH VERRANNA BLUE VENUS
Hot Gossip

Southern Counties
Mrs P Lay
CH VISTABLU NELSON TOUCH
Jenash Just A Dreamer
BARNSNAP BALLERINA
Moorside Altar Once Again

Midland Bedlington Terrier Club
L F Hemstock
CH VISTABLU NELSON TOUCH
Stanolly Sunny Romero
CH DALIP UPTOWN GIRL
Rathsrigg Romance

Windsor
Ken Bounden
CH VISTABLU NELSON TOUCH
Count of Crispino
MISTIBLEU SINDERELLA
Vistablu Nora Batty

Paignton
Miss B Anderson
CH VISTABLU NELSON TOUCH
Stanolly Sunny Romero
RATHSRIGG ROMANCE
Vistablu Nora Batty

Leeds
V Mitchell
CH VISTABLU NELSON TOUCH
Stanolly Sunny Romero
CH DALIP UPTOWN GIRL
Vistablu Flying Duchess

Welsh Kennel Club
W J Clifton
STANOLLY SUNNY ROMERO
Ch Vistablu Nelson Touch
CH DALIP UPTOWN GIRL
Moorside Ursula Ula At Hilldyke

Leicester
W A Topham
CH VISTABLU NELSON TOUCH
Stanolly Sunny Romero
CH MOORSIDE URSULA ULA AT HILLDYKE
Rathsrigg Romance

Birmingham
Miss M Boggia
CH VISTABLU NELSON TOUCH
Rathsrigg Rags
RATHSRIGG RANI
Stanolly Rising Star

Richmond
H Wright
CH VISTABLU NELSON TOUCH
Stanolly Sunny Romero
CH DALIP UPTOWN GIRL
Mistibleu Sinderella

Darlington
Mrs I Sills
RATHSRIGG RAGS
Stanolly Sunny Romero
CH MOORSIDE URSULA ULA AT HILLDYKE
Rathsrigg Rani

Bedlington Terrier Assn.
E Hill
CH VISTABLU NELSON TOUCH
Rathsrigg Rags
VISTABLU NORA BATTY
Ch Dalip Uptown Girl

Midland Counties
J Holden
RATHSRIGG RAGS
Ch Vistablu Nelson Touch
CH MOORSIDE URSULA ULA AT HILLDYKE
Ch Craglough Coryanthus

231

1989

Crufts   *Judge* C Sills
RATHSRIGG RAGS
Moorside Richard The Rebel At
    Cottontops
MOORSIDE EVER SO ELEGANT AT
    COTTONTOPS
Hilldyke Lady Madeline

National Terrier Club   H Atkinson
CH VISTABLU NELSON TOUCH
Dalip Silverton Blue
CH CRAGLOUGH CORYANTHUS
Moorside Ever So Elegant at Cottontops

Manchester   W Kitchin
CH THE COUNT OF CRISPINO
Dalip Boy George of Sollstice
CH CRAGLOUGH CORYANTHUS
Vardene Blue Will O'Warbler of
    Birkonbrae

National Bedlington Terrier Club
               Mrs M Phillips
CH VISTABLU NELSON TOUCH
Highdene Huntsman
HILLDYKE LADY MADELINE
Sugar Is Sweet

W.E.L.K.S.   S Stones
CH THE COUNT OF CRISPINO
Dalip Boy George of Sollstice
CH CRAGLOUGH CORYANTHUS
Brynsire Morning Melody

Birmingham   Mrs A Dallison
CH VISTABLU NELSON TOUCH
Moorside Richard The Rebel At
    Cottontops
MOORSIDE EVER SO ELEGANT AT
    COTTONTOPS
Vardene Blue Will O'Warbler of
    Birkonbrae

Scottish Kennel Club   Mrs A Emsley
CH VISTABLU NELSON TOUCH
Ch Rathsrigg Rags
RATHSRIGG RANI
Highdene Huntsman

Bath   I Phillips
CH VISTABLU NELSON TOUCH
Jagmar Rigton Blaize
HILLDYKE LADY MADELINE
Moorside Eye Spy Eleanor At
    Cottontops

Southern Counties   Mrs F Craig
CH VISTABLU NELSON TOUCH
Jenash Just A Dreamer
SUGAR IS SWEET
Blue Pollyanna of Annamine

Midland Bedlington Terrier Club
               L Clifton
CH VISTABLU NELSON TOUCH
Bojen Barnaby
CH MOORSIDE EVER SO ELEGANT AT
    COTTONTOPS
Rathsrigg Rani

Paignton   C Saevich
CH VISTABLU NELSON TOUCH
Ch Rathsrigg Rags
CH RATHSRIGG RANI
Vistablu Nora Batty

Windsor   Miss D Aitkenhead
BOJEN BARNABY
Ch Vistablu Nelson Touch
CH DALIP UPTOWN GIRL
Highdene Solitaire

Leeds   B Emsley
CH VISTABLU NELSON TOUCH
Birkonbrae Bleu Blaque
CH RATHSRIGG RANI
Ch Craglough Coryanthus

Welsh Kennel Club   S Power
CH VISTABLU NELSON TOUCH
The Joinery Boy
CH CRAGLOUGH CORYANTHUS
Ch Rathsrigg Rani

Leicester   Mrs P Lay
CH RATHSRIGG RAGS
Rowney Blue Slick
CH DALIP UPTOWN GIRL
Bonny Kurly Kews

Birmingham   T Horner
DALIP BOY GEORGE OF SOLLSTICE
Count of Rupertino
VISTABLU NORA BATTY
Ch Dalip Uptown Girl

Richmond   R Clay
JENASH JUST A DREAMER
Ch Vistablu Nelson Touch
MOORSIDE EYE SPY ELEANOR AT
    COTTONTOPS
Moorside Dawns Delight at Furrolly

Darlington F Jones

CH VISTABLU NELSON TOUCH
Highdene Crying Curlew
CH HILLDYKE LADY MADELINE
Ch Moorside Ever So Elegant At
  Cottontops

Bedlington Terrier Assn. Ken Bounden

CH RATHSRIGG RAGS
Highquest Hot Coffee at Lowbrook
CH CRAGLOUGH CORYANTHUS
Moorside Dawns Delight at Furrolly

Driffield D Harker

CH VISTABLU NELSON TOUCH
Highdene Crying Curlew
MOORSIDE DAWNS DELIGHT AT
  FURROLLY
Ch Verranna Blue Venus

Midland Counties C Metcalfe

JENASH JUST A DREAMER
Ch Vistablu Nelson Touch
HIGHDENE SOLITAIRE
Ch Dalip Uptown Girl

C. C. Winners' *Pedigrees*

DOGS

1936

CH FOGGYFRUZE ACE HIGH 129SS, F. Gent, br. Owner, 6.5.35, blue, s. Foggyfurze Blue Boy (Ch Gardeners Supremacy – Busy Sue) ex Conveyers Pride (Gold Seal Express – State Express).

CH GARDENERS PARAGON 1266SS, E. Metcalf, Br Mrs E. H. Sutherland, 9.12.35, blue, s. Ch Night Express (Ch Moving Knight – Express Delight) ex Kirkhill Exquisite (Ch Gardeners Supremacy – Kirkhill Maid).

1937

CH GARDENERS IMPERIAL 625SS, E. Metcalf, br Miss M. E. Simm, 1.1.35, blue, s. Ch Night Express (Ch Moving Knight – Express Delight) ex Queen of All (Peg's Pal – Betsy Prig).

CH REQUEST OF WRINSTONE 762TT, Mrs Llewellyn Ward, br. Owner, 8.6.36, liver, s. Reason of Wrinstone (Rustic of Wrinstone – Riddle of Wrinstone) ex Phoebe of Harnish (Ch Gardeners Perfection – Milbourne Flo).

CH ROBIN OF SIMONSIDE 1577RR, (late Robin of Harnish) Misses M. M. & C. R. Carr, brs. Owners, 16.9.34, blue, s. Ch Welhead Whoopee (Ch Knowlton Peter Pan – Silvertop Gem) ex Jane of Harnish (Glooper – Flowerseller).

1938

CH PIPER'S SUCCESS 1566QQ, C. G. Worrall, br Owner, 9.5.33, liver, s. Piper of Ryton (Gardeners Mark – Deansfield Jean) ex Blue day (Ch Moving Knight – Rye Nellie).

CH BRAMBLEDENE BUCCANEER 125UU, Miss E. E. Marsh, br. Owner, 11.2.37, blue, s. Ch Woodrow Wizard (Ch Welhead Whoopee – Khaki) ex Welhead Whisper (Ch Knowlton Peter Pan – Silvertop Gem).

LIVESPARK OF SIMONSIDE 596UU, Misses M. M. & C. R. Carr, br Mrs J. English, 27.3.37, sandy, s. Ch Minimum of Simonside (Ch Deckham O'Precious – Ch Miss Gaysum) ex Mary Tudor (Dracula – Wolecurb Juliet).

CH GARDENERS FIDELITY 837UU, E. Metcalf, br. Owner, 15.8.37, blue, s. Gardeners Emblem (Glooper – Silver Lining) ex Gardeners Rosette (Ch Gardeners Supremacy – Quorndon Cocoa).

LAMPLIGHTER 127UU, J. Taylor, br. Mrs Hallowell-Carew, 27.6.37, blue, s. Ch Minimum of Simonside (Ch Deckham O'Precious – Ch Miss Gaysum) ex Luckless Lass of Harnish (Ch Robin of Simonside – True Blue of Simonside).

CH LAVERS LANCER 1988UU, Mrs L. Phipps, br. Owner, 15.7.37, blue, Ch Welhead Wynport (Sudston Pedlar – Welhead Wynot) ex Brambledene Bluebell (Ch Welhead Wallet – Welhead Whisper).

1939

CH HENRY OF NONINGTON 1989UU, Mrs F. M. Pershouse, br. Mrs M. E. O'Brien, 16.11.37, liver, s. Ch Woodrow Wizard (Ch Welhead Whoopee – Khaki) ex Sarah of Nonington (Ch Right Choice of Simonside – Deckham O'Real).

GOOD KNIGHT 217VV, Mrs G. D'Oyley-Hughes, br. Miss R. Gull, 25.6.37, liver, s. Ch Woodrow Wizard (Ch Welhead

Whoopee – Khaki) ex Goodness Knows (Ruling Passion – Peach).

TITUS OF ROGATE 673VV, Miss E. V. Herdman, br. Owner, 30.5.38, sandy, s. Dunmail of Pitt (Ch Minimum of Simonside – Knowlton of Prudence) ex Marigold of Rogate (Dracula – Constant Nymph of Rogate).

DUNMAIL OF PITT 689UU, Miss. C. Brewer (later Mrs A. Best), br. Owner, 27.5.37, blue, s. Ch Minimum of Simonside (Ch Deckham O'Precious – Ch Miss Gaysum) ex Knowlton Prudence (Ruling Passion – Knowlton Starlight).

1946

CHAMPION LINDUM LIGHTNING 960AD, H. Winder, breeder Mrs F. L. Franks, 5.2.43, liver, s. Pynello Jacques (Lamplighter – Ch Pynello Jane) ex Lindum Lobelia (Ch Piper's Success – Ch Lindum Lavender).

1947

CH BRAMBLEDENE BARON 411AE, Miss E. E. Marsh, br. Owner, 10.7.44, blue, s. David of Harnish (Ch Bubble of Harnish – Saddlewood Topsy) ex Brambledene Brione (Amma Blue – Welhead Whisper).

1948

HIGHLAND DUKE 840AF, A. H. E. Burns, br. Mrs E. Ebden, 28.12.46, blue, s. Wansbeck Nobleman (Lukr Moon – Express Belle) ex Jeanfield Priscilla (Randal of Pitt – Fiona of Wynfield).

CH BRAMBLEDENE BRENDAN 531AF, L. Elwick, br. Miss E. E. Marsh, 29.10.45, blue, s. Wansbeck Nobleman (Lukr Moon – Express Belle) ex Brambledene Brione (Amma Blue – Welhead Whisper).

WELHEAD WARRANT 951AF, Mrs B. Holgate, br. Owner, 19.7.47, blue, s. Tivoli Crack (Welhead General – Bubbles of Heathfield) ex Welhead Moscar Topaz (Moscar Attraction – Moscar Blue Lady).

CH FRIAR OF HEATHFIELD 1153AF, Mrs C. Abbott, br. Owner, 6.6.47, dark liver, s. Ch Lindum Lightning (Pynello Jacques – Lindum Lobelia) ex Binnie of Heathfield (Pynello Jacques – Lancers Princess).

CH BRACKNELL ROWLAND OF PITT 1205AF, Mrs C. Best, br. Mrs M. Lowe, 8.7.47, blue, s. Dunmail of Pitt (Ch Minimum of Simonside – Knowlton Prudence) ex Bracknell Rona (Ch Brambledene Baron – Charlotte of Pitt).

BRIGHT LAD 1872AE, Miss N. Hall, br. G. R. Johnson, 22.5.44, blue, s. Rye of Pitt (Dunmail of Pitt – Dilis of Blue Anchor) ex Bright Day (Blue Bob – Merel's Girl).

1949

CH GOLDSTRIKE OF FOXINGTON 23AG, H. Winder, br. Owner, 11.6.48, liver, s. Livespark of Foxington (Ch Lindum Lightning – Wendy Blue) ex Ch Moorsraike Moonlight (Dunmail of Pitt – Sally Wee).

CH CURLY CUT 26AG, N. Stead, br. Owner, 23.2.48, blue, s. Ch Brambledene Brendan (Wansbeck Nobleman – Brambledene Brione) ex Bounty Blue (Welhead General – Ringstone Rip. – unregistered).

CH RULER OF PITT 25AG, Mrs C. Best, br. Mrs T. James, 19.4.48, blue, s. Rover of Pitt (Dunmail of Pitt – Bonny Lass) ex Rainbow of Pitt (Pynello Jacques – Jill's Double).

PYNELLO JACQUES 1237AE, Dr M. E. Binns, br. Owner, 2.3.39, blue, s. Lamplighter (Ch Minimum of Simonside – Luckless Lass of Harnish) ex Ch Pynello Jane (Ch Woodrow Wizard – Petanis).

CH BRIGHTSTONE SUNFLOWER OF PITT 1877AG, Mrs de Beauchamp-Green, br. Miss G. Lawis, 22.7.48, liver, s. Blue Thundercloud (Ch Lindum Lightning – Blue Bamby) ex Brightstone Daffodil (Dunmail of Pitt – Sally Wee).

GAMBOL OF HEATHFIELD 2167AG, Mrs C. Abbott, br. Owner, 6.8.48, liver, s. Ch Lindum Lightning (Pynello Jacques – Lindum Lobelia) ex Binnie of Heathfield (Pynello Jacques – Lancer's Princess).

1950

CH MOSCAR RED ENSIGN 1456AF, Mrs B. E. Wardman, br. F. Barnes, 13.6.47, liver, s. Moscar Blue Knight (Boy of Sunshine – Moscar Witch) ex Moscar Gold Flake (Moscar Attraction – Moscar Blue Lady).

DAUNTLESS DINGO 1054AG, G. Newcombe, br. Owner, 9.6.47, blue, Sudston Panda (Brambledene Barrie – Lighter Vein) ex Sheila of Grovedele (Springhead Jerry – Woodland Sally).

CH RAG A TAIL 538AH, Mrs M. M. Taunt, br. E. J. C. Furze, 23.1.48, dark blue, s. Ch Lindum Lightning (Pynello Jacques – Lindum Lobelia) ex Newlyn Fashion (Floradale Tony – Artist's Model of Newlyn).

CH GAY BOY OF FOXINGTON 1201AH, H. Winder, br. Owner, 27.9.49, blue, s. Countryman of Foxington (Fisherman of Foxington – Ch Sally of Foxington) ex Ch Moorsraike Moonlight (Dunmail of Pitt – Sally Wee).

1951

INGRAM OF PITT 1157AJ, A. D. Isherwood, br. Mrs C. Best, 19.4.50, blue, s. Ch Brightstone Sunflower of Pitt (Blue Thundercloud – Brightstone Daffodil) ex Newlyn Iris of Pitt (Rover of Pitt – Rainbow of Pitt).

1952

JONASH GENTLEMAN 239AK, Mrs G. Jay, br. Owner, 4.3.50, blue, s. Ch Ruler of Pitt (Rover of Pitt – Rainbow of Pitt) ex Cannock Beauty (Foggyfurze Marauder – Kirkhill Rowena).

TOL-PEDN SMUGGLER 1134AK, Ken Bounden, br. Owner, 8.10.51, blue, s. Ch Goldstrike of Foxington (Livespark of Foxington – Ch Moorsraike Moonlight) ex Ch Tol-pedn Merry Maid (Rover of Pitt – Blue Bliss).

CH WESTFEN PANTHER 331AK, Mrs J. Fenby, br. Mrs J. Dearlove, 25.9.50, dark blue, s. Ch Brambledene Baron (David of Harnish – Brambledene Brione) ex Ch Stuteville Starlette (Ch Lindum Lightning – Sudston Prattle).

CH PILGRIM OF YOMA 2226AK, Miss F. Ireson, br Mrs M. E. Britton, 7.7.51, blue, s. Piper of Yoma (Ch Bracknell Rowland of Pitt – Yoma Stella) ex Fair Girl of Foxington (Countryman of Foxington – Ch Moorsraike Moonlight).

1953

CH NORBERT OF NONINGTON 2046AH, Mrs M. Kersley, br. Mrs M. E. O'Brien, 16.12.49, blue, s. Ch Friar of Heathfield (Ch Lindum Lightning – Binnie of Heathfield) ex Brambledene Brenda (David of Harnish – Brambledene Brione).

CH GOLDEN SUN OF MANATON 512AL, Mr & Mrs C. G. Worrall, br. C. G. Worrall, 6.8.52, liver, s. Robin of Bracken (Blue Night of Manaton – Celia) ex Ch Blue Day of Manaton (Pynello Jacques – Jill's Double).

CH FOGGYFURZE CLASSIC CUT 201AL, F. Gent, br. N. Stead, 26.6.52, blue, s. Ch Westfen Panther (Ch Brambledene Baron – Ch Stuteville Starlette) ex Ch Spring Dancer (Ch Brambledene Brendan – Bounty Blue) Exported to L. Terpenning, U.S.A.

CH MIRAGE OF WYNBRIAR 1966AK, Mr & Mrs N. Brierley, br. N. Brierley, 28.7.51, blue & tan, s. Blue Victor (Ch Brambledene Brendan – Blue Vision) ex Huntress of Foxington (Livespark of Foxington – Dainty Miss of Foxington) exported to Mrs Seeley Brewer, U.S.A.

JUVERNA LORD LIVER OF PITT 339AL, Mrs M. de Beauchamp-Green, br. Mrs C. Best, 6.8.51, liver, s. Ch Brightstone Sunflower of Pitt (Blue Thundercloud – Brightstone Daffodil) ex Gaiety Girl of Pitt (Ch Ruler of Pitt – Request of Pitt).

1954

BLUE RODNEY OF MANATON 239AM, Lt Col & Mrs R. M. Douglas, br. Mr & Mrs C. G. Worrall, 3.2.53, blue, s. Ch Lindum Lightning (Pynello Jacques – Lindum Lobelia) ex Ch Blue Sky of Manaton (Ch Bracknell Rowland of Pitt – Blue Dawn of Manaton) owners returned to United States with dog.

CH DANCERS PRIDE 1550AM, J. D. Churcher, br. Owner, 21.1.52, liver, Moonlight Dancer (Destiny of Derrywood – Blue Valley Rose) ex Prunella's Pet (Forest Wuppet – Bartley Prunella).

CH LEASOWES TRY AGAIN 1741AL, Mrs M. M. Taunt, br. Owner, 30.6.52, liver, s. Ch Rag A Tail (Ch Lindum Lightning – Newlyn Fashion) ex Leasowes Lucky Charm (Ch Friar of Heathfield – Yoma Juliet).

1955

CH FOGGYFURZE CLASSIC 313AN, F. Gent, br. Owner, 3.8.54, blue, s. Ch Curly Cut (Ch Brambledene Brendan – Bounty Blue) ex Foggyfurze Acey Ducey (Ch Foggyfurze Classic Cut – Foggyfurze Madcap).

CH BLUEPRINT OF MAHIDAP 238AM, T. Barker, br. Owner, 20.11.52, blue, s. Ramda (Drakefield Monarch – Peggie Pinkie) ex Cardwell Cassandra (Flash Wizard – Salford Tess).

NOVELLO OF NABLUS 1589AN, Mr & Mrs D. C. Bartlett, br. Mr & Mrs A. J. Hill, 1.7.54, liver, s. Ch Friar of Heathfield (Ch Lindum Lightning – Binnie of Heathfield) ex Nita of Nablus (Foggyfurze Bell Boy – Naomi of Nablus).

TRIPLE CUT, 505AN, N. Stead, br. Owner, 23.2.54, blue, s. Ch Westfen Panther (Ch Brambledene Baron – Ch Stuteville Starlette) ex Ch Spring Dancer (Ch Brambledene Brendan – Bounty Blue).

1956

CH GENTS CUT 1041AP, N. Stead, br. Owner, 18.6.55, blue, s. Ch Foggyfurze Classic (Ch Curly Cut – Foggyfurze Acey Ducey) ex Ch Spring Dancer (Ch Brambledene Brendan – Bounty Blue).

CH BLUE PIP OF CLOVERWAY 1620AN, J. W. Dawson, br. Owner, 13.6.55, blue, s. Crew Cut of Vistablu (Ch Foggyfurze Classic Cut – Dilly Day Dream of Vistablu) ex Dina of Jonkin (Ch Friar of Heathfield – Rosetop Reticent).

FOGGYFURZE CLASSICAL 1483AP, F. Gent, br. Owner, 21.9.55, blue, s. Ch Foggyfurze Classic (Ch Curly Cut – Foggyfurze Acey Ducey) ex Foggyfurze Lindylou (Ch Curly Cut – Dunholme Delight).

1957

CH FOGGYFURZE SHOOTING STAR 191AQ, F. Gent, br. Owner, 26.3.56, blue. s. Foggyfurze Eclipse (Ch Golden Sun of Manaton – Ch Tol-pedn Mermaid) ex Foggyfurze Acey Ducey (Ch Foggyfurze Classic Cut – Foggyfurze Madcap).

1958

CH LINDUM HIGH OCTANE OF VISTABLU 2069AP, Mrs S. L. Franks, br. Mrs I. Sills, 23.6.55, blue, s. Ch Curly Cut (Ch Brambledene Brendan – Bounty Blue) ex Classic Maid of Vistablu (Ch Foggyfurze Classic Cut – Dilly Day Dream of Vistablu).

CH LITTLE WILLIE OF VISTABLU 2306AQ, Mrs I. Sills, br. Owner, 4.12.56, blue, Ch Blue Pip of Cloverway (Crew Cut of Vistablu – Dilly Day Dream of Vistablu) ex Jenny Wren of Pitt (Ch Goldstrike of Foxington – Newlyn Iris of Pitt).

TOL-PEDN SEADOG 82AR, Ken Bounden, br. O. Gowing, 16.6.56, blue, s. Ch Westfen Panther (Ch Brambledene Baron – Ch Stuteville Starlette) ex Ch Tol-pedn Mermaid (Ch Goldstrike of Foxington – Ch Tol-pedn Merry Maid).

CH TOL-PEDN HOODWINK 2131AQ, Ken Bounden, br. Ken Bounden & Mrs J. Martin, 5.56, liver, s. Tol-pedn Merry Monk (Ch Curly Cut – Tol-pedn Barmaid) ex Ch Tol-pedn Fairmaid (Ch Golden Sun of Manaton – Ch Tol-pedn Mermaid).

CH WORKMAN OF NONINGTON 2070AP, Mrs M. E. O'Brien, br. Owner, 19.3.55, liver, s. Ch Norbert of Nonington (Ch Friar of Heathfield – Brambledene Brenda) ex Ch Lorette of Nonington (Ch Brambledene Barob – Jane of Nonington).

1959

AMERDALE HALF NELSON 79AS, W. Clark, br. H. Hooper, 8.4.58, blue, s. Ch Gents Cut (Ch Foggyfurze Classic – Ch Spring Dancer) ex Lassie of Simonside (Yoma Rightroyal – Peggy Maureen) exported to E. Crowley, U.S.A.

REDBOY OF MAHIDAP 1221AR, T. Barker, br. Mrs E. A. Birtwell, 22.6.57, liver, s. Ch Blueprint of Mahidap (Ramda – Cardwell Cassandra) ex Mayqueen of Mahidap (Goldsmith of Mahidap – Cardwell Cassandra).

CH FOGGYFURZE TEXAN 759AS, F. Gent, br. Owner, 6.6.58, blue, s. Ch Foggyfurze Classic (Ch Curly Cut – Foggyfurze Acey Ducey) ex Foggyfurze Baby Mine (Ch Foggyfurze Classic – Drewcote Marie Belle) exported to Mr & Mrs Virden Wilson, U.S.A.

CH SHENSTONE MASTER MASK 1727AS, E. Smith, br. Owner, 5.8.57, liver, Ch Leasowes Try Again (Ch Rag A Tail – Leasowes Lucky Charm) ex Ginger Popinette of Oldpost (Leasowes Humpty Dumpty – Cherie of Oldpost).

CH JASPER OF NONINGTON 1883AS, Mrs M. E. O'Brien, br. Owner, 4.7.58, blue, s. Ch Norbert of Nonington (Ch Friar of Heathfield – Brambledene Brenda) ex Ch Amanda Mirabeau of Nonington (Ch Westfen Panther – Ch Spring Dancer).

1960

FOGGYFURZE DRUMBEAT 202AT, F. Gent, br. Miss D. Aitkenhead, 27.7.59, blue, s. Ch Foggyfurze Classic (Ch Curly Cut – Foggyfurze Acey Ducey) ex Bibsy of Mahidap (Foggyfurze Diecast – Gipsy Queen of Mahidap).

CH WEDERBI HOUGHTOP INVADER 1882AS,
O. Gowing, br. Owner, 9.9.54, blue, Ch Golden Sun of Manaton (Robin of Bracken – Ch Blue Day of Manaton) ex Ch Tol-pedn Mermaid (Ch Goldstrike of Foxington – Ch Tol-pedn Merry Maid).

CH GUN METAL OF WETOP 1633AS, W. Topham, br. Owner, 26.2.58, blue, s. Blue Blazes of Foxington (Blue Flash of Foxington – Lady Lana of Foxington) ex The Linnet (Ch Brambledene Baron – Roxanna of Cherrydale).

1961

CH FOGGYFURZE DANDY 62AV, F. Gent, br. Miss D. Aitkenhead, 27.7.59, blue, s. Ch Foggyfurze Classic (Ch Curly Cut – Foggyfurze Acey Ducey) ex Bibsy of Mahidap (Foggyfurze Die Cast – Gipsy Queen of Mahidap) exported to Australia.

PILOT OF GORSEA 1007AV, H. W. Newman, br. Owner, 8.12.59, blue, s. Ch Little Willie of Vistablu (Ch Blue Pip of Cloverway – Jenny Wren of Pitt) ex Lindum Lilli (Ch Lindum High Octane of Vistablu – Ch Lindum Lunaria).

CH MAYDEW MOONRAKER 1804AV, H. R. Highfield, br. Owner, 3.10.60, blue, s. Stanolly Startrite (Moyvallee Minstrel – Shenstone Miss Tesha) ex Maydew Miss Marie Wynbriar Willie Winkle – Maydew Miss Madeline).

SHENSTONE NEW ORBIT 934AV, E. Smith, br. Owner, 17.4.60, blue, s. Stanolly Startrite (Moyvallee Minstrel – Shenstone Miss Tesha) ex Shenstone Saucy Sue (Ch Leasowes Try Again – Ginger Popinette of Oldpost) exported to Dr Dionisi, Italy.

CH WEDERBI MINTING 1803AV, Mrs M. Wray, br. O. Gowing, 5.9.59, liver, s. Ch Wederbi Houghtop Invader (Ch Golden Sun of Manaton – Ch Tol-pedn Mermaid) ex Wederbi Diadem (Ch Foggyfurze Classic – Ch Tol-pedn Fairmaid).

1962

CH BUTTONS OF WETOP 2070AV, W. Topham, br. Owner, 25.1.61, blue, s. Ch

Gun Metal of Wetop (Blue Blazes of Foxington – The Linnet) ex Ch Cinderella (Ch Goldstrike of Foxington – Storm Cloud).

FLASHY CUT 62AV, N. Stead, br. S. Wall, 7.5.60, blue, s. Ch Gents Cut (Ch Foggyfurze Classic – Ch Spring Dancer) ex Vicky of Mahidap (Ch Blueprint of Mahidap – May Queen of Wetop).

TOL-PEDN FRIGATE 725AT, Ken Bounden, br. Owner, 29.9.58, blue, s. Tol-pedn Seadog (Ch Westfen Panther – Ch Tol-pedn Mermaid) ex Tol-pedn Carefree (Blue Blazes of Foxington – Juverna Happy Go Lucky).

CH CHARTLANDS FAIR DINKUM 2456AV, C. D. Adamson, br. Owner & Ken Bounden, 14.9.60, liver, Ch Shenstone Master Mack (Ch Leasowes Try Again – Ginger Popinette of Oldpost) ex Ch Tol-pedn Fairmaid (Ch Golden Sun of Manaton – Ch Tol-pedn Mermaid).

1963

CH FOGGYFURZE STATACCO 2223AV, F. Gent, br. Owner, 17.1.62, blue, s. Ch Foggyfurze Classic (Ch Curly Cut – Foggyfurze Acey Ducey) ex Ch Foggyfurze Delaware Doll (Ch Foggyfurze Classic – Foggyfurze Baby Mine).

CH NADWORNA STATESMAN 2582AW, J. N. Slee, br. Owner, 24.10.62, blue, s. Ch Foggyfurze Dandy (Ch Foggyfurze Classic – Bibsy of Mahidap) ex Meljoy All Quality (Ch Foggyfurze Texan – Smart Cut).

AMERDALE AVIATOR 739AW, W. Clark, br. Owner, 27.7.62, blue, s. Northcote Lucky Guy (Ch Foggyfurze Dandy – Northcote Blue Belle) ex Ch Amerdale Delight (Ch Foggyfurze Classic – Ch Knotts Bluebell).

COPPER ROGUE 2224AV, D. R. Rogers, br. Owner & J. Constance, 21.11.60, liver, s. Ch Shenstone Master Mack (Ch Leasowes Try Again – Ginger Popinette of Oldpost) ex Mynydd Morwyn (Ch Golden Sun of Manaton – Glaswen).

TWEEDLEDEE OF WETOP 589AW, W. Topham, br. Owner, 29.5.62, liver, s. Night Hawk of Wetop (Ch Gun Metal of Wetop – Betty of Foxington) ex Ch Cinderella (Ch Goldstrike of Foxington – Storm Cloud).

1964

CH GOLD COIN OF FOXINGTON 1336AW, Mr & Mrs J. L. Clifton, br. H. Winder, 27.11.61, liver, s. Blue Blazes of Foxington (Blue Flash of Foxington – Lady Lana of Foxington) ex Merry Lass of Foxington (Blue Blazes of Foxington – Tiller Girl of Foxington).

NORTHCOTE WILL STRIKE 1866AX, R. R. Seaton, br. Owner, 25.7.63, blue, s. Ch Foggyfurze Classic (Ch Curly Cut – Foggyfurze Acey Ducey) ex Ch Northcote Lucky Strike – (Northcote Micky – Foggyfurze Cute).

CH STANOLLY SPORTS TOSCA 1639AX, Mrs O. M. Stones, br. Owner, 12.6.63, liver, s. Shenstone Merry Mac (Ch Shenstone Master Mack – Shenstone Felicity) ex Stanolly Sports Hilight (Ch Maydew Moonraker – Stanolly Starturn).

CH RATHSRIGG LITTLE CEASAR 1990AX, I. J. Phillips, br. Owner, 1.9.63, blue, s. Glendessary Blue Boy (Ch Foggyfurze Classic – Foggyfurze Amanda) ex Blankers Ballerina (Ch Leasowes Try Again – Yoma Merry Light).

CH MAYDEW MOUNTAIN MUSIC 2388AX, H. R. Highfield, br. Owner, 30.6.63, liver, Foggyfurze High Hat (Ch Foggyfurze Classic – Foggyfurze Wederbi Sceptre) ex Maydew Miss Muriel (Ch Maydew Moonraker – Maydew Miss Maverick).

1965

CH ROB ROY OF WETOP 2490AX, W. Topham, br. Owner, 15.10.63, blue, s. Ch Buttons of Wetop (Ch Gun Metal of Wetop – Ch Cinderella) ex Ch Miss Muffet of Wetop (Ch Gun Metal of Wetop – Rose of Rushby).

CH FREDDIE THE GENT OF VISTABLU 1446AX, Mrs I. Sills, br. Owner, 8.11.63, blue, s. Foggyfurze High Hat (Ch Foggy-furze Classic – Foggyfurze Wederbi Sceptre) ex Ch Shenstone Blue Bliss of Vistablu (Ch Shenstone Master Mack – Shenstone Blue Lustre) exported to Sra Raigorodsky, Srs. Caram & Saevich, Argentina.

CH TOL-PEDN SACHMO 2592AY, Ken Bounden & Mrs R. Hodgson, br. Ken Bounden & Miss S. Bate, 5.2.65, liver, s. Ch Tol-pedn Hoodwink (Tol-pedn Merry Monk – Ch Tol-pedn Fairmaid) ex Tol-pedn Moonstone (Ch Maydew Moon-raker – Ch Stanolly Sapphire).

NORTHCOTE TERPO 2856AY, R. R. Seaton, br. Owner, 8.10.64, blue, s. Ch Wederbi Houghtop Invader (Ch Golden Sun of Manaton – Ch Tol-pedn Mermaid) ex Ch Northcote Lucky Strike (Northcote Micky – Foggyfurze Cute).

1966

CH STANOLLY SUPERSTAR 1959AS, Mrs O. M. Stones, br. L. Bramley, 22.4.65, blue, s. Ch Stanolly Sports Tosca (Shen-stone Merry Mac – Stanolly Sports Hilight) ex Pat's Choice (Starbright – Stanolly Wayward Damsel) exported to Mr & Mrs Virden Wilson, U.S.A.

CH FANCYPANTS OF VISTABLU 1406AZ, Mrs I. Sills, br. Owner, 26.1.66, blue, s. Foggyfurze Ranger (Ch Foggyfurze Clas-sic – Foggyfurze Stargirl) ex With It of Vistablu (Foggyfurze High Hat – Ch Shenstone Blue Bliss of Vistablu).

1967

CH STANOLLY STARBLAZE 1580BA, Mrs O. Stones, br. Owner, 17.5.66, blue, s. Ch Stanolly Superstar (Ch Stanolly Sports Tosca – Pat's Choice) ex Ch Stanolly Sapphire (Moyvallee Minstrel – Shen-stone Miss Tesha) exported to Mr Tsujihara, Japan.

1968

HIGHQUEST HIGH MIST 35BC, Mrs F. Morgan-Jones, br. Owner, 1.3.67, blue, s. Ch Stanolly Superstar (Ch Stanolly Sports Tosca – Pat's Choice) ex High-quest Donnor (Kay of Nonington – Arabella of Nonington).

CH NORTHCOTE LUCKY MARK 2240BA, R. R. Seaton, br. Owner, 13.8.66, blue, s. Northcote Terpo (Ch Wederbi Houghtop Invader – Ch Northcote Lucky Strike) ex Northcote Double Strike (Ch Foggyfurze Classic – Ch Northcote Lucky Strike) Exported to Mr & Mrs Virden Wilson, U.S.A.

AMERDALE DEFIANT 652BC, W. Clark, br. Owner, 5.1.68, blue, s. Amerdale Au Revoir (Ch Nadworna Statesman – Ch Knotts Bluebelle) ex Ch Amerdale Astralita (Northcote Lucky Guy – Ch Amerdale Delight).

CH GOLD CLASSIC 851BC, Mrs P. Lay, br. Mr & Mrs J. Brooks, 22.5.67, liver, s. Bobby Ensign of Brinroth (Merryman of Foxington – Sweet Sue) ex Mintings Merry Maid (Ch Wederbi Minting – Amerdale Shady Lady).

CH VARDENE BLUE GRENADIER 2502BC, Mrs B. Clifton, br. Owner, 22.12.67, blue, Ch Stanolly Starblaze (Ch Stanolly Superstar – Ch Stanolly Sapphire) ex Vardene Golden Gem (Ch Gold Coin of Foxington – Tol-pedn Shanty).

1969

FOGGYFURZE FLAMINGO 732BD, F. Gent, br. Owner, 3.5.68, blue, s. Ch Northcote Lucky Mark (Northcote Terpo – North-cote Double Strike) ex Foggyfurze Babe (Ch Foggyfurze Classic – Ch Foggyfurze Delaware Doll).

CH STANOLLY SANDPIPER 2683BC, Mrs O. Stones, br. Owner, 6.3.68, liver, Ch Stanolly Starblaze (Ch Stanolly Super-star – Ch Stanolly Sapphire) ex Stanolly Sports Delight (Ch Maydew Moonraker – Stanolly Starturn exported to Mr Lars Adenby, Sweden.

CH FOGGYFURZE FAN FARE 2313BD, F. Gent, br. Owner, 23.9.68, blue, Ch Northcote Lucky Mark (Northcote Terpo – Northcote Double Strike) ex Foggy-furze Nina (Foggyfurze Tino – Foggy-furze Lulu).

CH BLUE HAPPENING OF VISTABLU 431BD, Mrs I. Sills, br. Owner, 13.6.68, s. Ch Fancypants of Vistablu (Foggyfurze Ranger – With It of Vistablu) ex Foggyfurze Merrymaid (Ch Foggyfurze Classic – Foggyfurze Amanda).

1970

CH MOORSIDE DANDY DOLPHIN 198BD, D. Harker, br. R. Ratcliffe, 1.5.68, blue, s. Ch Stanolly Sports Tosca (Shenstone Merry Mac – Stanolly Sports Hilight) ex Babsy of Moorside (Grinkle Cut – Moorside Gypsy).

CH FOGGYFURZE FANGIO 85BE, F. Gent, br. Owner, 23.9.68, blue, s. Ch Northcote Lucky Mark (Northcote Terpo – Northcote Double Strike) ex Foggyfurze Nina (Foggyfurze Tino – Foggyfurze Lulu) exported to H van der Loo, Holland.

CH STANOLLY SPECTACULAR 1037BE, Mrs O. Stones, br. Owner, 20.5.69, liver, s. Ch Stanolly Sandpiper (Ch Stanolly Starblaze – Stanolly Sports Delight) ex Ch Stanolly Sunblush (Ch Stanolly Sports Tosca – Ch Stanolly Sapphire).

1971

CH STANOLLY SCOOBY DOO 1560BF, Mrs O. Stones, br. Owner, 1.8.70, blue, Ch Stanolly Sandpiper (Ch Stanolly Starblaze – Stanolly Sports Delight) ex Stanolly Crystal Belle) (Ch Stanolly Superstar – Ch Stanolly Sapphire).

CH WETOP AQUARIUS 1731BF, W. Topham, br. Owner, 6.4.70, liver, s. The Count of Wetop (Tweedle Dee of Wetop – Stanolly Sports Cherub) ex Duett of Wetop (Ch Rob Roy of Wetop – Little Bo Peep of Wetop).

CH VARDENE BLUE GUARDSMAN 84BE, Mrs B. Clifton, br. Owner, 16.3.69, blue, s. Ch Vardene Blue Grenadier (Ch Stanolly Starblaze – Vardene Golden Gem) ex Ch Vardene Amaree of Canzo (Ch Gold Coin of Foxington – Blue Willow of Canzo).

1972

CH WETOP FREE LANCE 2587BG, W. Topham, br. Owner, 25.8.71, liver, s. Bartholomew the Beneficient (Hesselview Cavalier – Lucinda of Greymuir) ex Christmas Cracker of Wetop (Ch Rob Roy of Wetop – Little Bo Peep of Wetop).

MOORSIDE FREDDIE FOX 577BF, R. Ratcliffe, br. Owner, 24.7.70, blue, Ch Moorside Dandy Dolphin (Ch Stanolly Sports Tosca – Babsy of Moorside) ex Moorside Little Candy (Dales Cut – Altar Mary Jane).

1973

CH BIRKONBRAE BRONZE BACCHUS 779BF, Mr & Mrs R. J. Anderson, br. Owners, 10.6.70, liver, s. Ch Vardene Blue Grenadier (Ch Stanolly Starblaze – Vardene Golden Gem) ex Birkonbrae Bronze Bunyip (Flashy Cut – Copper Coin).

BRENTBROOK GAY BOY 80BH, Mrs E. Vincent, br. I. Hoyle, 26.6.71, blue, Ch Vardene Blue Grenadier (Ch Stanolly Starblaze – Vardene Golden Gem) ex Gaytime of Gorsea (Ch Fancy Pants of Vistablu – Goya of Gorsea).

CRAGLOUGH DENARIUS 1414BF, Miss D. Aitkenhead, br. Owner, 14.5.70, blue, s. Scipio of Craglough (Ch Shenstone Master Mack – Prisca of Craglough) ex Craglough Charisma (Ch Northcote Lucky Mark – Lisetta of Craglough).

1974

CH RATHSRIGG KING'S PAWN 1047BH, Mr & Mrs I. J. Phillips, brs. Owners, 2.4.72, dark blue, Ch Rathsrigg Little Ceasar (Glendessay Blue Boy – Blankers Ballerina) ex Louella Lively Lady (Ch Stanolly Starblaze – Dawn of Francistown).

LEASOWES TANGO 3693BH, Mrs M. M. Taunt, br. Owner, 9.8.72, liver, s. Ch Stanolly Scooby Doo (Ch Stanolly Sandpiper – Stanolly Crystal Belle) ex Leasowe Dancing Shadow (Greenayre Tory – Leasowes Barley Sugar).

CH VARDENE BLUE MARKSMAN 2020BI, Mrs B. Clifton, br. Owner, 17.2.73, blue, Ch Vardene Blue Guardsman (Ch Vardene Blue Grenadier – Ch Vardene Amaree of Canzo) ex Stanfos Blue Ilex (Ch Vardene Blue Grenadier – Northcote Aileen).

CAERULEUS CORINTHIAN 339BG, Mrs P. Lay, br. Mrs I. Bach, 8.1.71, blue, s. Ch Rathsrigg Little Ceasar (Glendessary Blue Boy – Blankers Ballerina) ex Caeruleus Clovette (Jason of Nonington – Miranda of Nonington).

CH FOGGYFURZE FANDANGO 2626BI, F. Gent, br. Owner, 26.7.73, blue, s. Ch Foggyfurze Fan Fare (Ch Northcote Lucky Mark – Foggyfurze Nina) Foggyfurze Fastidious (Ch Foggyfurze Fan Fare – Moorside Elegant Empress).

1975

CH BREDONVALE SMOKEY JOE 1415BF, Mrs J. M. Hufton, br. Mr & Mrs Bradley-Reynolds, 2.4.70, blue, s. Ch Foggyfurze Fan Fare (Ch Northcote Lucky Mark – Foggyfurze Nina) ex Bredonvale Brenda (Ch Vardene Blue Grenadier – Ballerina of Louella).

STURNBAY STUPENDOUS 229BI, S. Power, br. Mrs B. Clifton, 30.12.72, blue, s. Ch Stanolly Scooby Doo (Ch Stanolly Sandpiper – Stanolly Crystal Belle) ex Vardene Blue Gown (Ch Vardene Blue Grenadier – Vardene Golden Gem).

CH PHINDOL BLUE DOLPHIN 300BJ, D. Harker, br. Owner, 10.6.74, blue, s. Ch Moorside Dandy Dolphin (Ch Stanolly Sports Tosca – Babsy of Moorside) ex Polly Flinders of Phindol (Ch Vardene Blue Grenadier – Treasure of Nonington).

CH GRANITOR FLINT 2614BJ, J. Holden, br. Owner, 19.4.74, blue, s. Craglough Denarius (Scipio of Craglough – Craglough Charisma) ex Ch Dooley of Craglough (Craglough Sebastion – Candula of Craglough).

PETACREST SIR PRANCELOT 1464BI, Mrs S. Belvoir, br. Mrs A. Norgate, 29.10.73,

liver, s. Ch Stanolly Scooby Doo (Ch Stanolly Sandpiper – Stanolly Crystal Belle) ex Lamott Echappee De Soleil (Lamott Original Fella – Vardene Blue Gondalier).

STANOLLY SHOOBY DOO A 2971BJ, Mrs O. Stones, br. Owner, 29.12.74, blue, s. Ch Stanolly Scooby Doo (Ch Stanolly Sandpiper – Stanolly Crystal Belle) ex Ch Stanolly Starbow (Ch Stanolly Sports Tosca – Ch Amerdale Delicious) exported to Mr Tsujihara, Japan.

CH STANOLLY SHANG-A-LANG 582BJ, Mrs O. Stones, br. Owner, 3.7.74, blue, s. Ch Stanolly Scooby Doo (Ch Stanolly Sandpiper – Stanolly Crystal Belle) ex Ch Stanolly Starbow (Ch Stanolly Sports Tosca – Ch Amerdale Delicious).

CH TURTONHEIGHTS BLUE GALLANT 301BJ, Mr & Mrs J. C. Walker, brs. Owners, 16.11.73, blue, s. Ch Vardene Blue Grenadier (Ch Stanolly Starblaze – Vardene Golden Gem) ex Sweet Maid In Blue (Ch Foggyfurze Fangio – Moorside Elegant Empress).

1976

CH AVILAS ARIES OF FOGGYFURZE 3944BJ, F. Gent, br. Mrs E. Johnson, 1.4.75, blue, s. Ch Stanolly Scooby Doo (Ch Stanolly Sandpiper – Stanolly Crystal Belle) ex Stanfos Blue Choice (Ch Foggyfurze Fangio – Northcote Aileen) exported to H van der Loo, Holland.

AVILAS AT LAST 1998BK, Mrs E. Johnson & Mrs O. Stones, br. Mrs E. Johnson, 1.4.75, blue, s. Ch Stanolly Scooby Doo (Ch Stanolly Sandpiper – Stanolly Crystal Belle) ex Stanfos Blue Choice (Ch Foggyfurze Fangio – Northcote Aileen) exported to R. Kohijoki, Finland.

TOL-PEDN RED CLOUD 2641BK, Ken Bounden, br. Owner, 1.5.75, liver, s. Gutch Common Jarus (Gutch Common Rusty – Gutch Common Jays) ex Tol-pedn Liebling (Bystock Master Mack Dougall – Tol-pedn Edelweis).

CH WETOP NUTMEG 2536BJ, W. Topham, br. Owner, 30.6.74, liver, s. Ch Wetop

Aquarius (The Count of Wetop – Duett of Wetop) ex Ch Pewter Grey of Wetop (The Count of Wetop – Duett of Wetop).

CH AVILAS LUCKY LAD OF FOGGYFURZE 3278BK, F. Gent, br. Mrs E. Johnson, 1.4.75, blue, s. Ch Stanolly Scooby Doo (Ch Stanolly Sandpiper – Stanolly Crystal Belle) ex Stanfos Blue Choice (Ch Foggyfurze Fangio – Northcote Aileen).

1977

CH FOGGYFURZE FENMAN 3906BK, F. Gent, br. Owner, 3.11.75, blue, s. Ch Foggyfurze Fan Fare (Ch Northcote Lucky Mark – Foggyfurze Nina) ex Foggyfurze Fidella (Foggyfurze Ferrari – Foggyfurze Francesca).

CH BIRKONBRAE BLEU BRAGGADOCIO 3943BJ, Mr & Mrs R. J. Anderson, br. Owners, 5.9.74, blue, s. Ch Stanolly Scooby Doo (Ch Stanolly Sandpiper – Stanolly Crystal Belle) ex Bleu Bacchic of Birkonbrae (Ch Birkonbrae Bronze Bacchus – Judy of Balmoral).

CH RATHSRIGG RUIN 1102BL, Mr & Mrs I. J. Phillips, br. Owners, 27.4.76, blue, s. Ch Granitor Flint (Craglough Denarius – Ch Dooley of Craglough) ex Rathsrigg Check Mate (Ch Rathsrigg Little Caesar – Louella Miss Max).

CH WOODMAN OF CULLERCOATS 3601BK, Mrs P. Lay. br. Mr Gilbert, 24.6.75, liver, s. Caeruleus Corinthian (Ch Rathsrigg Little Caesar – Caeruleus Clovette) ex Wild Rose of Parsons Green (Gallant Pride – Moorside I'm Iris).

LIEBERLAMB LIKELY LAD 669BL, Mrs M. Sugden, br. Owner, 5.6.76, blue, s. Simple Simon of Kenstaff (Foggyfurze Fantastic – Foggyfurze Fidella) ex Ch Lieberlamb Lucinda (Ch Vardene Blue Grenadier – Lieberlamb Lynette) exported to Gisela Klostermann, Germany.

CH STANOLLY SHIROCO 1980BL, Mrs O. M. Stones. br. Owner, 9.6.76, blue, s. Ch Stanolly Shang-a-Lang (Ch Stanolly Scooby Doo – Ch Stanolly Starbow) ex Stanolly Spring Fancy (Ch Stanolly Scooby Doo – Stanolly Amber Blush) exported to Frau M. Raithel, Germany.

MOORSIDE LUCKY LAD 4242BL, R. Ratcliff, br. Owner, 30.3.76, blue, s. Foggyfurze Fantastic (Foggyfurze Ferrari – Foggyfurze Fava) ex Moorside Happy Huntress (Moorside Freddie Fox – Moorside Dainty Denise).

1978

CH GRANITOR ROCKET MAN 492BM, J. Holden, br. Owner, 3.9.76, blue, Foggyfurze Fantastic (Foggyfurze Ferrari – Foggyfurze Fava) ex Ch Dooley of Craglough (Craglough Sebastian – Craglough Candula).

BOUGHTON BLUFF 4241BL, Mrs F. Craig & Miss M. Boggia, br. Miss M. Boggia, 20.8.76, blue, s. Highquest Hallmark (Ch Bredonvale Smokey Joe – Moorside Little Candy) ex Marilena Philomela (Marilena Marketeer – Marilena Pollyanna).

CH WETOP GAY KNIGHT 496BK, W. A. Topham, br. Owner, 5.10.74, blue, s. Swank of Wetop (Peter Pan of Wetop – Erica of Wetop) ex Duett of Wetop (Ch Rob Roy of Wetop – Little Bo Peep of Wetop).

PETACREST PATRON SAINT 2130BM, Mrs A. Norgate, br. Owner, 24.10.77, blue, s. Foggyfurze Fantastic (Foggyfurze Ferrari – Foggyfurze Fava) ex Petacrest Perfect Angel (Ch Stanolly Scooby Doo – Lammott Exchappe de Soleil).

CH DALIP HUGGY BEAR 2748BM, Mrs P. Hall, br. Owner, 12.11.76, blue, s. Ch Stanolly Shang-a-Lang (Ch Stanolly Scooby Doo – Ch Stanolly Starbow) ex Dalip Petranello (Ch Stanolly Scooby Doo – Franzel Huntersmoon).

CH FOGGYFURZE FINE FARE 2890BM, F. Gent, br. Owner, 8.1.78, blue, s. Ch Avilas Lucky Lad of Foggyfurze (Ch Stanolly Scooby Doo – Stanfos Blue Choice) ex Foggyfurze Fidella (Foggyfurze Ferrari – Foggyfurze Francesca).

CH FOGGYFURZE FOREVER 1636BM, F. Gent, br. Owner, 8.1.78, blue, s. Ch Avilas Lucky Lad of Foggyfurze (Ch Stanolly Scooby Doo – Stanfos Blue

Choice) ex Foggyfurze Fidella (Foggy-furze Ferrari – Foggyfurze Francesca).

1979

CH STANOLLY SUPERFLASH 2738BN, Mrs O. M. Stones, br. Owner, 22.11.78, liver, s. Stanolly Sandman (Avilas At Last – Ch Stanolly Starbow) ex Ch Stanolly Summer Luv (Ch Stanolly Shang-a-Lang – Stanolly Hi Impulse).

WETOP TIGHT ROPE 1292BN, W. A. Topham, br. Owner, 29.4.78, blue, s. Ch Wetop Gay Knight (Swank of Wetop – Duett of Wetop) ex Ch Wetop Blue Velvet (Ch Rob Roy of Wetop – Donna of Wetop).

1980

CH LIEBERLAMB LADDIE SIM 1291BN, Mrs M.E. Sugden, br. Owner, 7.9.78, blue, s. Foggyfurze Fantastic (Foggyfurze Ferrari – Foggyfurze Fava) ex Ch Lieberlamb Lucinda (Ch Vardene Blue Grenadier – Lieberlamb Lynette).

ARG. CH VISTABLUE BEN FRANKLIN OF BLUE HAPPENING 1381BN, Mrs I. Sills, brs. Mr N. & Mrs S. Raigorodsky, 24.12.75, blue, s. Stillwater Scotch on the Rocks (Arg Ch Wildwind Clown of Blue Happening – Arg Ch Women's Lib of Vistablu) ex Old Flints Dahlia (Extra-vert of Blue Happening – Arg Ch Sunshine of Blue Happening).

CH TICKERTON HODDER SHERRY OF CULLERCOATS 823BP, Mrs P. Lay, br. J. Whittaker, 18.4.78, liver, s. Caeruleus Corinthian (Ch Rathsrigg Little Ceasar – Caeruleus Clovette) ex Singleton Gingerbread Lady (Toffee of Merryavon – Sapphire of Merryavon).

1981

CH RATHSRIGG REUBEN 0432BQ, Mr & Mrs I. J. Phillips, brs. Owners, 24.4.80, blue, s. Ch Foggyfurze Fenman (Ch Foggy-furze Fan Fare – Foggyfurze Fidella) ex Rosa of Rathsrigg (Ch Foggyfurze Fan Fare – Foggyfurze Farah).

CH STANOLLY SUPER SWANK 0493BQ, Mrs O. M. Stones, br. Owner, 23.7.80, blue, s. Ch Stanolly Scooby Doo (Ch Stanolly Sandpiper – Stanolly Crystal Belle) ex Ch Stanolly Summer Luv (Ch Stanolly Shang-a-Lang – Stanolly Hi Impulse).

CH BRICKBATS BROUGHTON 2942BP, Mrs C. A. Smallwood, br. Mrs S. M. Edwards, 28.8.79, blue, Wilnesden Silver ex Blue Print of Tiddly Mount (Avilas At Last – Ch Stanolly Starbow).

CH BLA SKUGGANS MOVIE STAR 1448BQ, (Nordic Ch Import) Mrs R. Lyberg, br. Owner, 18.11.77, blue, Bla Skuggans Following Star (Marilena Marketeer – Stanolly Sunstar) ex Wetop Mermaid (Swank of Wetop – Wetop Sea Pearl).

CH RED EAGLE OF TOL-PEDN 1605BQ, Ken Bounden, br. Mrs A. Norgate, 10.6.80, liver, s. Ch Rathsrigg Ruin (Ch Granitor Flint – Rathsrigg Check Mate) ex Pere-grine of Pentavy (Gutch Common Sur-prise – Tol-pedn Herring Gull).

CH WILLOW OF CULLERCOATS 1637BM, Mrs P. Lay, br. Mrs A. Norgate, 1.5.77, blue, s. Caeruleus Corinthian (Ch Rath-srigg Little Ceasar – Caerulius Clovette) ex Highquest Honor (Ch Gold Classic – Highquest Hebe).

PETACREST PSALM 2605BQ, Mrs M. Mc-Erlean, br. Mrs A. Norgate, 11.9.79, blue, s. Foggyfurze Fantastic (Foggyfurze Ferrari – Foggyfurze Fava) ex Peta-crest Perfect Angel (Ch Stanolly Scooby Doo – Lamott Echappe de Soleil).

1982

CH RATHSRIGG RULE 0120BR, Mr & Mrs I. J. Phillips, brs. Owners, 14.4.81, blue, s. Ch Rathsrigg Ruin (Ch Granitor Flint – Rathsrigg Check Mate) ex Rosa of Rathsrigg (Ch Foggyfurze Fan Fare – Foggyfurze Farah).

WETOP PARSLEY 0006BR, Mrs P. M. Lind-borg, br. W. A. Topham, 18.2.79, blue, s. Ch Wetop Gay Knight (Swank of Wetop – Duett of Wetop) ex Wetop Artic Mist (Ch Wetop Gay Knight – Ch Wetop Blue Opal).

CH AURABLEUE ASHMOW ALICK 0431BQ, Mrs A. Pogson, br. Owner, 11.1.79, blue, s. Ch Avilas Lucky Lad of Foggyfurze (Ch Stanolly Scooby Doo – Stanfos Blue Choice) ex Aurableue Michele (Vistablu Don Perro – Megonhoney).

TYNECOURT TROOPER 2607BQ, E. L. Hill, br. Owner, 20.9.80, blue, s. Ch Foggyfurze Fine Fare (Ch Avilas Lucky Lad of Foggyfurze – Foggyfurze Fidella) ex Tynecourt Truffle (Ch Foggyfurze Fenman – Trinket of Tynecourt).

CH WETOP SILVER SPUR 2784BR, W. A. Topham, br. Owner, 4.7.81, blue, s. Ch Wetop Gay Knight (Swank of Wetop – Wetop Duett) ex Wetop Blue Lambkin (Ch Wetop Gay Knight – Wetop Artic Mist).

CH WINFELL RUSTLER 2557BR, Mrs Y. Greenland, br. Owner, 20.2.81, liver, s. Ch Wetop Gay Knight (Swank of Wetop – Wetop Duett) ex Wetop Lady Isobelle (Ch Wetop Gay Knight – Wetop Gold Gem).

1983

CH LIEBERLAMB LESTER 4597BR, Mrs M. Sugden, br. Owner, 9.10.81, blue, s. Swirleymist Sensation (Lieberlamb Sir Lancelot – Lieberlamb Leading Lady) ex Ch Lieberlamb Louise (Foggyfurze Fantastic – Ch Lieberlamb Lucinda).

CH MOORSIDE SO YOUR SAMMY 0594BS, R. Ratcliffe, br. Owner, 11.12.82, blue, s. Ch Avilas Lucky Lad of Foggyfurze (Ch Stanolly Scooby Doo – Stanfos Blue Choice) ex Ch Moorside Quite Quaint (Ch Foggyfurze Fenman – Moorside Joyful Julie).

1984

TYNECOURT TALLY-HO 3208BT, E. L. Hill, br. Owner, 12.12.82, blue, s. Ch Avilas Lucky Lad of Foggyfurze (Ch Stanolly Scooby Doo – Stanfos Blue Choice) ex Tynecourt Truffle (Ch Foggyfurze Fenman – Trinket of Tynecourt).

CH WINFELL RAIDER 3207BT, Mrs N. Y. Greenland, br. Owner, 24.4.83, blue, s.

Ch Winfell Rustler (Ch Wetop Gay Knight – Wetop Blue Lambkin) ex Winfell Blueberry (Ch Avilas Lucky Lad of Foggyfurze – Wetop Lady Isobelle).

MARLISH BLUE STONE 2640BT, Mrs E. M. Inglis, brs. Mmes S. A. Coates & M. Davies, 27.4.80, blue, s. Yutree Angelo (Foggyfurze Fantastic – Petacrest Peaches and Cream) ex Sutcott Sail Easy (Ch Wetop Gay Knight – Lambsdown Suzy Jane).

CH STANOLLY STARBURST 1138BT, Mrs O. Stones, br. Owner, 11.6.83, blue, s. Stanolly Secret Agent (Ch Stanolly Super Swank – Ch Whispering Song of Stanolly) ex Stanolly Shimmering Lite (Ch Stanolly Shang-a-Lang – Stanolly Spring Fancy).

CH BARNSNAP BRIGADIER 0887BT, T. McErlean, br. Owner, 12.8.83, blue, s. Petacrest Psalm (Foggyfurze Fantastic – Petacrest Perfect Angel) ex Petacrest Brown Eyes Blue (Petacrest Sir Prancelot – Peregrine of Pentavy).

1985

CH CRAGLOUGH CHERUBINO 0312BU, Miss D. Aitkenhead, br. Owner, 30.5.84, blue, s. Ch Rathsrigg Reuben (Ch Foggyfurze Fenman – Rosa of Rathsrigg) ex Ch Craglough Calinka (Ch Foggyfurze Fenman – Ch Tabitha of Craglough).

CH SEVRAY SINGING SAILOR 5122BS, Mr & Mrs E. Rainsbury, br. Owners, 17.9.82, blue s. Foggyfurze Flashy (Ch Foggyfurze Fenman – Foggyfurze Fettle) ex Moonstep Lace (Argentine Ch Vistablu Ben Franklin of Blue Happening – Perrianne Primrose).

CH MOORSIDE VICTOR IS NO VAGRANT 0314BU, R. Ratcliffe, br. Owner, 21.2.84, blue, s. Ch Foggyfurze Fenman (Ch Foggyfurze Fan Fare – Foggyfurze Fidella) ex Ch Moorside Summer Song (Ch Avilas Lucky Lad of Foggyfurze – Ch Moorside Quite Quaint).

CANNY LAD OF SPENNYMOOR 0266BU, Mr & Mrs I. & Miss J. Chapman, br. F. Gent, 8.11.81, blue, s. Ch Foggyfurze

Fenman (Ch Foggyfurze Fan Fare – Foggyfurze Fidella) ex Ch Foggyfurze Fifi (Ch Avilas Lucky Lad of Foggyfurze – Foggyfurze Fidella).

CH VISTABLU NELSON TOUCH 2569BU, Mrs I. Sills, br. Owner, 1.11.84, blue, s. Ch Aurableue Ashmow Alick (Ch Avilas Lucky Lad of Foggyfurze – Aurableue Michelle) ex Ch Vistablu Wonder Woman (Agentine Ch Vistablu Ben Franklin of Blue Happening – Lieberlamb Lucy Locket).

1986

CH WINFELL RAMBLER 0878BV, Mrs N. Y. Greenland, br. Owner, 2.1.85, liver, s. Ch Winfell Raider (Ch Wetop Gay Knight – Wetop Blue Lambkin) ex Wetop Lady Isobelle (Ch Wetop Gay Knight – Wetop Golden Gem).

CH STANOLLY STUPENDOUS LAD 1739BV, Mr & Mrs J. Crumpton, br. Mrs O. Stones, 27.9.84, liver, s. Ch Stanolly Starburst (Stanolly Secret Agent – Stanolly Shimmering Lite) ex Ch Star Audition of Stanolly (Ch Stanolly Scooby Doo – Stanolly Summer Delight).

1987

CH THE COUNT OF CRISPINO 2917BW, Mr P. Ellis & Miss L. Cowley, br. Ownes, 23.10.85, blue, s. Wetop Silver Ruler (Ch Wetop Gay Knight – Wetop Blue Lambkin) ex Wetop Bluebell (Ch Wetop Silver Spurr – Ch Wetop Meg).

1988

FANTASTIC LUCKY BLUE 4708BU, Mr & Mrs S. Lockett, br. F. Gent, 21.5.83, blue, s. Ch Foggyfurze Fenman (Ch Foggyfurze Fan Fare – Foggyfurze Fidella) ex Ch Foggyfurze Fifi (Ch Avilas Lucky Lad of Foggyfurze – Foggyfurze Fidella).

STANOLLY SUNNY ROMERO 0533BX, Mrs G. Anselmi (Italy) br. Mrs O. Stones, 12.6.87, liver, s. Ch Stanolly Starburst (Stanolly Secret Agent – Stanolly Shimmering Lite) ex Ch Stanolly Springtime Melody (Ch Brickbats Broughton – Stanolly Summer Wine).

CH RATHSRIGG RAGS 2107BX, Mr & Mrs I. J. Phillips, br. Owners, 28.3.87, blue, s. Ch Rathsrigg Rule (Ch Rathsrigg Ruin – Rathsrigg Rosa) ex Ch Craglough Constantia (Ch Rathsrigg Reuben – Ch Craglough Calinka).

1989

BOJEN BARNABY 2089BY, Miss L. Parker, br. Mrs C. J. C. Martindale, 23.4.88, blue, s. Bojen Bacchus (Ch Foggyfurze Fenman – Moorside Wee Wren) ex Bojen Bonnie (Bojen Bracken – Bojen Bianca).

DALIP BOY GEORGE OF SOLLSTICE 0676BW, Mrs M. George, br. Mrs P. Hall, 10.4.86, blue, s. Crackerjack Blue Solstice (Ch Foggyfurze Fenman – Stanolly Salamanda) ex Dalip Sheer Genius (Stanolly Sandman – Dalip Blue Angel).

CH JENASH JUST A DREAMER 4565BW, Mmes C. Taylor & P. Tall, br. Mrs C. Taylor, 2.10.86, blue, s. Fantastic Lucky Blue (Ch Foggyfurze Fenman – Ch Foggyfurze Fifi) ex Janash Precious Pearl (Argentine Ch Vistablu Ben Franklin of Blue Happening – Janash Melting Moments).

BITCHES

1936

WELHEAD WIDEAWAKE 2084RR, Mrs Ben Holgate, br. Owner, 9.3.35, blue, s. Ch Welhead Wallet (Ishmael – Silvertop Gem) ex Welhead Windsorlass (Ch Welhead Whoopee – Maid of the Mist).

WOODROW WATERNYMPH 1058SS, Mrs N. Bullivant, br. Miss V. Cross, 20.3.35, blue, s. Ch Night Express (Ch Moving Night – Express Delight) ex Blue Moment (May the Devil Take You – Bright Lass).

WOODROW WITCH GIRL 1107SS, Miss V. Cross, br. Miss E. Upton, 7.7.34, blue, s. Ch Welhead Whoopee (Ch Knowlton Peter Pan – Silvertop Gem) ex Khaki (Ch Cribden Chutney – Belgrano Judy).

1937

BRIGHTSTONE HARMONY 20TT, Miss G. Lawis, br. V. Smith, 5.7.35, blue, s. Ch Brightstone Venture (Ch Gardeners Supremacy – Esperanza) ex Alice of Nonington (Ch Bubble Of Harnish – Jenny of Nonington).

CH CHERRY OF NONINGTON 1541SS, Mrs M. E. O'Brien, br. Owner, 4.1.35, blue, s. Ch Bubble of Harnish (Cranley Jim – Busy of Harnish) ex Ch Miss Gaysum (Hydesville Nighthawk – Jean R5709).

CH LINDUM LAVENDER 730SS, Mrs F. L. Franks, br. Owner, 11.3.35, blue, s. Ch Welhead Wynport (Ch Welhead Whoopee – Welhead Wynot) ex Mignoette (Ch Cribden Chutney – Powder Puff).

CH PYNELLO JANE 763TT, Miss M. E. Binns, br. R. G. Couley, 23.2.36, liver, s. Ch Woodrow Wizard (Ch Welhead Whoopee – Khaki) ex Petanis (Ch Right Choice of Simonside – Princee Wee One of Simonside).

TRUE JOY OF SIMONSIDE 1975TT, Misses M. M. & C. R. Carr, brs. Owners, 15.4.37, blue, Ch Robin of Simonside (Ch Welhead Whoopee – Jane of Harnish) ex True Blue of Simonside (Barny – Bontesse of Simonside).

1938

CH LEADING LADY OF SIMONSIDE 1595TT, Misses M. M. & C. R. Carr, br. L. Alderson, b. 14.6.36, liver, s. Ch Lapiz Lazuli (Ch Dazzler Demon – Our Rhoda) ex Golden Julien (Pip (unr.) Gay Lady).

CH REALITY OF WRINSTONE 1343TT, Mrs Llewellyn Ward, br. Owner, 8.6.36, liver, Reason of Wrinstone (Rustic of Wrinstone – Riddle of Wrinstone) ex Phoebe of Harnish (Ch Gardeners Perfection – Milbourne Flo).

CUCKOO OF HARNISH 1689RR, Messrs B. A. Hobson & W. E. Stubbs, br. Miss Hallowell-Carew, b. 13.1.34, blue, Ch Deckham O'Precious (Saval Boy – Bit of Fashion) ex Ch Miss Gaysum (Hydesville Nighthawk – Jean R5709).

CH FOLLY 128UU, Mrs R. J. Martin, br. Owner, 7.7.36, blue, s. Ch Welhead Wynport (Sudston Pedlar – Welhead Wynot) ex Welhead Blinkbonnie (Ch Knowlton Peter Pan – Silvertop Gem).

CH CHARM OF NONINGTON 295SS, Mrs M. E. O'Brien, br. Owner, 4.4.35, blue, Ch Bubble of Harnish (Cranley Jim – Busy of Harnish) ex Ch Miss Gaysum (Hydesville Nighthawk – Jean R5709).

CH HENRIETTA OF NONINGTON 1578UU, Mrs M. E. O'Brien, br. Owner, 16.11.37, liver, s. Ch Woodrow Wizard (Ch Welhead Whoopee – Khaki) Sarah of Nonington (Ch Right Choice of Simonside (Deckham O'Real).

1939

WOODROW WAIT 1696TT, Miss V. Cross, br. Owner, 21.12.36, blue, s. Ch Woodrow Wizard (Ch Welhead Whoopee – Khaki) ex Woodrow Blue Bird (Nap of Bransways – Billinge Typyst).

BRIGHTSTONE FLAME 352VV, Miss G. Lawis, br. Owner, 19.10.37, liver, s. Remnant of Wrinstone (Reason of Wrinstone – Phoebe of Harnish) Brightstone

Mystic (Ch Gardeners Supremacy – Deckham O'Real).

IRON DUCHESS 1862UU, Mrs Llewellyn Ward, br. Miss G. Lawis, 19.10.37, blue, s. Remnant of Wrinstone (Reason of Wrinstone – Phoebe of Harnish) ex Brightstone Mystic (Ch Gardeners Supremacy – Deckham O'Real).

FOGGYFURZE STARLIGHT 1255VV, F. Gent, br. J. Graham, 5.8.38, blue, s. Foggyfurze Blue Boy (Ch Gardeners Supremacy – Busy Sue) ex Recretion Lass (Glooper – Mary Hagan (unr.).

1946

CH FOGGYFURZE GLAMOROUS 962AD, F. Gent, br. A. Belgian, 19.10.44, dark blue, s. Rye of Pitt (Dunmail of Pitt – Dilys of Blue Anchor) ex Faithfull Lass (Blue Bob – Merel's Girl).

1947

CH FOGGYFURZE TAILOR MADE 412AE, F. Gent, br. Mrs S. L. Barras, 19.10.45, blue, s. Lamplighter (Ch Minimum of Simonside – Luckless Lass of Harnish) ex Silla Lass (Rye of Pitt – Bright Day).

CH SALLY OF FOXINGTON 2032AE, H. Winder, br. Mr Lewis, 11.4.45, liver, Ch Lindum Lightning (Pynello Jacques – Lindum Lobelia) ex The Blue Princess (Townsman of Simonside – Rona's Double).

1948

CH ROSETOP VICTORIOUS 80AF, Mrs C. Fisher, br. Mrs F. C. Neale, 20.6.45, liver, s. Foggyfurze Topper (Foggyfurze Blueboy – Recreation Lass) ex Tremola's Rose (Beaconsfield Tremando – Marigold).

CH JOYVENTURE 532AF, T. Almond, br. J. J. Wilson, 8.7.47, dark blue, s. Wansbeck Gentleman (Lukr Moon – Express Belle) ex Kirkhill Kelvina (Bright Delight – Lindylou).

CH BLUE DAY OF MANATON 963AD, C. G. Worrall, br. Owner, 9.2.45, blue, s. Pynello Jacques (Lamplighter – Ch Pynello Jane) ex Jill's Double (Dunmail of Pitt – Golden Jill).

CH CULLERCOATS CINDERELLA 1154AF, Mrs R. J. Martin, br. Owner, 2.12.46, blue, s. Brambledene Bandit (Lamplighter – Welhead Whisper) ex Fantasy (Titus of Rogate – Ch Folly).

BRAMBLEDENE BELINDA 983AE, Miss E. E. Marsh, br. Owner, 14.5.46, blue, s. Brambledene Bandit (Lamplighter – Welhead Whisper) ex Brambledene Bubbles (David of Harnish – Brambledene Brione).

1949

SPRITRESS 211AG, W. McEwan, br. C. S. Bell, 13.10.46, blue, s. Wansbeck Nobleman (Lukr Moon – Express Belle) ex Blue Duchess (Glooper – Quest).

CH TOL-PEDN MERRY MAID 605AG, Ken Bounden, br. Owner, 20.3.48, dark blue, s. Rover of Pitt (Dunmail of Pitt – Bonny Lass) ex Blue Bliss (David of Harnish – Juno of Pitt).

CH MOORSRAIKE MOONLIGHT 28AG, H. Winder, br. H. Poole, 13.1.46, blue, Dunmail of Pitt (Ch Minimum of Simonside – Knowlton Prudence) ex Sally Wee (Barnacle Ben (unr) – Woodrow Sandra).

CHRISELDA OF NARE 27AG, Mrs C. B. Gibson & Miss M. C. Porter, br. Owners, blue, s. Ch Brambledene Baron (David of Harnish – Brambledene Brione) ex Fuzzypeg of Nare (Randal of Pitt – Rosealia of Pitt).

CH STUTEVILLE STARLETTE 2323AF, Mrs J. Dearlove, br. Owner, 5.6.47, dark blue, s. Ch Lindum Lightning (Pynello Jacques – Lindum Lobelia) ex Sudston Prattle (Brambledene Barrie – Lighter Vein).

BRAMBLEDENE BRENDA 81AF, Mrs M. E. O'Brien, br. Miss E. E. Marsh, 10.7.44, blue, s. David of Harnish (Ch Bubble of Harnish – Saddlewood Topsy) ex Brambledene Brione (Amma Blue – Welhead Whisper).

CH LORETTE OF NONINGTON 2507AG, Mrs M. E. O'Brien, br. Owner, 7.6.47, blue, s. Ch Brambledene Baron (David of Harnish – Brambledene Brione) ex Jane of Nonington (Ch Henry of Nonington – Flirt of Nonington).

1950

CH SHEILA OF BLUE SEA 44AH, A. Smith, br. W. S. Wright, 17.1.48, blue, s. Wansbeck Gentleman (Wansbeck Nobleman – Betty Blue) ex Highland Duchess (Mystical Moonlight – Lupin Lady).

NAOMI OF NABLUS 1220AG, Mr & Mrs A. J. Hill, br. A. G. Day, 4.12.47, liver, s. Ch Lindum Lightning (Pynello Jacques – Lindum Lobelia) ex September Waif – pedigree unknown).

AZURE ATTRACTION 987AH, F. Hodgson, br. N. Brierley, 9.7.49, blue, s. Ch Brambledene Brendan (Wansbeck Nobleman – Brambledene Brione) ex Blue Vision (Springhead Jerry – Keldholme Floss).

CH SPRING DANCER 2027AG, N. Stead, br. Owner, 23.2.48, blue, s. Ch Brambledene Brendan (Wansbeck Nobleman – Brambledene Brione) ex Bounty Blue (Welhead General – Ringstone Rip).

CH JOCASTER OF PENDRILL 539AH, Mrs I. Asplen, br. G. Foster, 1.6.49, liver, Ch Friar of Heathfield (Ch Lindum Lightning – Binnie of Heathfield) ex Woodash Thursday (Bermont of Heathfield – Woodash Thisbe).

BRAMBLEDENE BLUE BEAUTY 42AH, L. Elwick, br. Miss E. E. Marsh, 13.2.48, blue, s. Bright Lad (Rye of Pitt – Bright) ex Brambledene Begonia (Brambledene Bandit – Brambledene Bubbles).

CH JOLANDE OF PENDRILL 1202AH, Mrs R. J. Martin, br. G. Foster, 1.6.49, liver, s. Ch Friar of Heathfield (Ch Lindum Lightning – Binnie of Heathfield) ex Woodash Thursday (Bermont of Heathfield – Woodash Thisbe).

1951

BRAMBLEDENE BONNIE 1206AF, Miss E. Marsh, br. Owner, 29.10.45, blue, s. Wansbeck Nobleman (Lukr Moon – Express Belle) ex Brambledene Brione (Amma Blue – Welhead Whisper).

CH NEWBOTTLE NEW LOOK 1939AH, Mrs C. Fisher, br. W. Luker, 28.2.49, blue, s. Wansbeck Gentleman (Wansbeck Nobleman – Betty Blue) ex Wansbeck Queen (Wansbeck Nobleman – Blue Duchess).

BLUEBELL OF FOXINGTON 131AJ, H. Winder, br. Owner, 12.4.50, blue, s. Ch Goldstrike of Foxington (Livespark of Foxington – Ch Moorsraike Moonlight) ex Starlight of Foxington (Ch Lindum Lightning – Angela of Foxington).

MOSCAR RED RASCAL 2240AH, F. Barnes, br. W. Owner, 10.6.49, liver, Moscar Blue Knight (Boy of Sunshine – Moscar Witch) ex Moscar Goldflake (Moscar Attraction Moscar Blue Lady).

CH PYNELLO PIXIE OF NARE 1158AJ, Dr M. E. Binns, br. Mrs C. B. Gibson & Miss C. M. Porter, 13.6.40, dark liver, s. Pynello Jacques (Lamplighter – Ch Pynello Jane) ex Rosealia of Pitt (Dunmail of Pitt – Lancers Rhapsody).

CH GLORIA OF CLAYDALE 1784AJ, Mrs D. A. Goodridge, br. Owner, 1.5.50, liver, Ch Friar of Heathfield (Ch Lindum Lightning – Binnie of Heathfield) ex Arabella of Pendrill (Not So Dusty – Woodash Thursday).

JOANNA OF PENDRILL 92AJ, Mr & Mrs G. Foster, br. G. Foster, 1.6.49, liver, Ch Friar of Heathfield (Ch Lindum Lightning – Binnie of Heathfield) ex Woodash Thursday (Bermont of Heathfield – Woodash Thisbe).

CH BLUE SKY OF MANATON 41AH, Mr & Mrs C. G. Worrall, br. Owners, 22.3.49, blue, Ch Bracknell Rowland of Pitt (Dunmail of Pitt – Bracknell Rona) ex Blue Dawn of Manaton (Blue Timothy of Abney – Edith of Pitt).

NALLA OF NONINGTON 2107AJ, Mrs M. E. O'Brien, br. Owner, 16.12.49, blue, s. Ch Friar of Heathfield (Ch Lindum Lightning – Binnie of Heathfield)

Brambledene Brenda (David of Harnish – Brambledene Brione).

1952

CH KARSWELL CASSADORA 1159AJ, T. Barker, br. Mrs D.A. Goodridge, 1.6.50, dark liver, s. Ch Friar of Heathfield (Ch Lindum Lightning – Binnie of Heathfield) ex Arabella of Pendrill (Not So Dusty – Woodash Thursday).

RARE GOLD 327AJ, J. O. Thorne, br. W. S. Wright, 23.1.50, liver, s. Highland Duke (Wansbeck Nobleman – Jeanfield Priscilla) ex Highland Duchess (Mystical Moonlight – Lupin Lady).

CH WOODSMANSY WASPISH 241AK, H. Wright, br. Mrs J. Dearlove, 25.9.50, blue, Ch Brambledene Baron (David of Harnish – Brambledene Brione) ex Ch Stuteville Starlette (Ch Lindum Lightning – Sudston Prattle).

CH BURLEYDENE MISCHIEF 891AJ, Mrs B. Wardman, br. L. Elwick, 26.1.50, blue, Ch Brambledene Brendan (Wansbeck Nobleman – Brambledene Brione) ex Brambledene Begonia (Brambledene Bandit – Brambledene Bubbles).

BLUE DAWN OF MANATON 1876AG, Mr & Mrs C. G. Worrall, br. Mrs M. Raffell, 20.5.46, blue, s. Blue Timothy of Abney (Pynello Jacques – Jill's Double) ex Edith of Pitt (Randal of Pitt – Rachel of Pitt).

BRAMBLEDENE BRINELLA 2227AK, Miss E. E. Marsh, br. Owner, 9.7.50, blue, Brambledene Beckles (Ch Brambledene Brendan – Brambledene Belinda) ex Brambledene Bonnie (Wansbeck Nobleman – Brambledene Brione).

1953

CH PYNELLO PRIM 511AL, Dr M. E. Binns, br. Owner, 19.4.52, blue, s. Ch Gay Boy of Foxington (Countryman of Foxington – Ch Moorsraike Moonlight) ex Pynello Pixie of Nare (Pynello Jacques – Rosealia of Pitt).

LUCY LOCKET OF PITT 1443AL, Mrs A. Best, br. Owner, 6.10.51, blue, s. Ch

Brightstone Sunflower of Pitt (Blue Thundercloud – Brightstone Daffodil) ex Gaiety Girl of Pitt (Ruler of Pitt – Request of Pitt).

CH TOL-PEDN MERMAID 337AL, O. G. Gowing, br. Ken Bounden, 8.10.51, blue, s. Ch Goldstrike of Foxington (Livespark of Foxington – Ch Moorsraike Moonlight) ex Ch Tol-pedn Merry Maid (Rover of Pitt – Blue Bliss).

CH NONA OF NABLUS 514AL, Mr & Mrs A. J. Hill, br. G. Heslop, 2.2.52, liver, s. Ch Goldstrike of Foxington (Livespark of Foxington – Ch Moorsraike Moonlight) ex Wansbeck Autocrat (Wansbeck Gentleman – Wansbeck Democrat).

1954

CH AMANDA MIRABEAU OF NONINGTON 236AM, Mrs M. E. O'Brien, br. N. Stead, 24.6.52, blue, s. Ch Westfen Panther (Ch Brambledene Baron – Ch Stuteville Starlette) ex Ch Spring Dancer (Ch Brambledene Brendan – Bounty Blue).

CH FOGGYFURZE CUTE CUT 237AM, F. Gent, br. Owner, 4.8.53, blue, s. Ch Foggyfurze Classic (Ch Curly Cut – Foggyfurze Acey Ducey) ex Ch Foggyfurze Glamorous (Rye of Pitt – Faithful Lass).

CH WESTERN VIVANDIERE 635AM, Mrs J. Fenby, br. Owner, 4.4.52, blue, Ch Westfen Panther (Ch Brambledene Baron – Ch Stuteville Starlette) ex Debonair Stephanie (Sudston Premier – Westfen Periwinkle).

LINDUM LOVE IN THE MIST 1236AK, Mrs F. L. Franks, br. Miss S. M. Wroath, 10.2.50, blue, s. Ch Lindum Lightning (Pynello Jacques – Lindum Lobelia) ex Polvarth Queen (Floradale Tony – Koldoran Lass).

1955

CH DALEVIEW DELMA 632AM, Mrs B. E. Wardman, br. Owner, 29.5.53, blue, s. Ch Brambledene Baron (David of Harnish – Brambledene Brione) ex Ch Burleydene Mischief (Ch Brambledene Brendan – Brambledene Begonia).

CH TOL-PEDN FAIRMAID 1995AN, Ken Bounden & C. D. Adamson, br. O. Gowing, 9.9.54, liver, s. Ch Golden Sun of Manaton (Robin of Bracken – Ch Blue Day of Manaton) ex Ch Tol-pedn Mermaid (Ch Goldstrike of Foxington – Ch Tol-pedn Merry Maid).

NITA OF NABLUS 1965AK, Mr & Mrs A. J. Hill, brs. Owners, 24.4.51, liver, Foggyfurze Bell Boy (Rustic Rydle – Foggyfurze Gracious) ex Naomi of Nablus (Ch Lindum Lightning – September Waif).

1956

FOGGYFURZE LINDY LOU 314AN, F. Gent, br. A. Tait, 1.6.54, dark blue, s. Ch Curly Cut (Ch Brambledene Brendan – Bounty Blue) ex Dunholme Delight (Wansbeck Gentleman – Wansbeck Democrat).

CH LINDUM LUNARIA 1817AM, Mrs S. L. Franks, br. Miss S. M. Wroath, 26.6.53, blue, s. Ch Lindum Lightning (Pynello Jacques – Lindum Lobelia) ex Polvarth Queen (Floradale Tony – Koldoran Lass).

RUFFLE CUT 65AP, N. Stead, br. Owner, 18.6.55, blue, s. Ch Foggyfurze Classic (Ch Curly Cut – Foggyfurze Acey Ducey) ex Ch Spring Dancer (Ch Brambledene Brendan – Bounty Blue).

CH PAT'S PEACH OF MANATON 1627AN, Mrs A. M. Laverick, br. Owner, 30.4.54, liver, Blue Rodney of Manaton (Ch Lindum Lightning – Ch Blue Sky of Manaton) ex Golden Day of Manaton (William of Westminster – Ch Blue Day of Manaton).

CH DALEVIEW DAWN 2338AN, Mrs B. E. Wardman, br. O. Gowing, 9.9.54, liver, Ch Golden Sun of Manaton (Robin of Bracken – Ch Blue Day of Manaton) ex Ch Tol-pedn Mermaid (Ch Goldstrike of Foxington – Ch Tol-pedn Merry Maid).

FOGGYFURZE BABY MINE 1618AP, F. Gent, br. A. Tait, 3.12.55, dark blue, s. Ch Foggyfurze Classic (Ch Curly Cut – Foggyfurze Acey Ducey) ex Drewcote Marie Belle (Blue Vision of Parsonby – Dunholme Delight).

CH FOGGYFURZE SUGAR BABY 1619AN, F. Gent, br. A. Tait, 3.12.55, dark blue, s. Ch Foggyfurze Classic (Ch Curly Cut – Foggyfurze Acey Ducey) ex Drewcote Marie Belle (Blue Vision of Parsonby – Dunholme Delight) exported to Mr & Mrs Virden Wilson, U.S.A.

BRIGHT DAY OF MANATON 1628AN, Mr & Mrs C. G. Worrall, br. Owners, 3.2.53, blue, s. Ch Lindum Lightning (Pynello Jacques – Lindum Lobelia) ex Ch Blue Sky of Manaton (Ch Bracknell Rowland of Pitt – Blue Dawn of Manaton).

1957

WOODSMANSEY WASPY 1789AP, H. Wright, br. Owner, 24.12.54, blue, s. Westfen Dragoon (Ch Westfen Panther – Debonair Stephanie) ex Ch Woodsmansey Waspish (Ch Brambledene Baron – Ch Stuteville Starlette).

1958

CH FOGGYFURZE SUGAR PUSS 213AR, F. Gent, br. Owner, 9.7.57, dark blue, s. Foggyfurze Jackpot (Clever Cut – Foggyfurze Acey Ducey) ex Foggyfurze Baby Mine (Ch Foggyfurze Classic – Drewcote Marie Belle) exported to Mr & Mrs Virden Wilson, U.S.A.

DALAVIEW DAME 214AR, Mrs B. E. Wardman, br. Owner, 14.4.57, blue, s. Ch Foggyfurze Classic (Ch Curly Cut – Foggyfurze Acey Ducey) ex Daleview Duskie (Ch Brambledene Baron – Ch Burleydene Mischief).

SPRING CUT 949AR, N. Stead, br. Owner, 18.1.57, blue, s. Ch Foggyfurze Classic (Ch Curly Cut – Foggyfurze Acey Ducey) ex Ch Spring Dancer (Ch Brambledene Brendan – Bounty Blue).

CH KNOTS BLUEBELLE 1848AQ, W. Clark, br. Owner, 15.6.56, dark blue, s. Ch Gents Cut (Ch Foggyfurze Classic – Ch Spring Dancer) ex Amberdale Lass (Showfield Jim – Tynefield Teaser).

CH ANGELINA OF LEASOWES 1549AN, Mrs M. M. Taunt, br. T. Rigg, 18.5.53, blue, s. Ch Leasowes Try Again (Ch Rag A

Tail – Leasowes Lucky Charm) ex Yoma Merrylight (Ch Bracknell Rowland of Pitt – Yoma Stella).

1959

CH AMERDALE DELIGHT 207AS, W. Clark, br. Owner, 30.4.58, blue, s. Ch Foggyfurze Classic (Ch Curley Cut – Foggyfurze Acey Ducey) ex Ch Knotts Bluebelle (Ch Gents Cut – Amerdale Lass).

CH TOL-PEDN BALLERINA 760AS, Ken Bounden & Mrs K. G. Holmes, brs. Ken Bounden & C. D. Adamson, 16.6.58, blue, s. Ch Foggyfurze Classic (Ch Curley Cut – Foggyfurze Acey Ducey ex Ch Tolpedn Fairmaid (Ch Golden Sun of Manaton – Ch Tol-pedn Mermaid).

BIBSY OF MAHIDAP 1199AS, Miss D. Aitkenhead, br. T. Barker, 14.3.58, blue, s. Foggyfurze Die Cast (Foggyfurze Eclipse – Foggyfurze Cornflower) ex Gipsy Queen of Mahidap (Goldsmith of Mahidap – Cardwell Cassandra).

CH CINDERELLA 858AS, W. Topham, br. E. Kirkham, 17.12.57, liver, s. Ch Goldstrike of Foxington (Livespark of Foxington – Ch Moorsraike Moonlight) ex Storm Cloud (Ch Brambledene Baron – Roxana of Cherrydale).

CH FOGGYFURZE DELAWARE DOLL 1198AS, F. Gent, br. Owner, 6.6.58, blue, s. Ch Foggyfurze Classic (Ch Curly Cut – Foggyfurze Acey Ducey) ex Foggyfurze Baby Mine (Ch Foggyfurze Classic – Drewcote Marie Belle).

1960

CH STANOLLY SAPPHIRE 80AT, Mrs O. M. Stones, br. Owner, 4.1.59, blue, s. Moyvallee Minstrel (Welhead Wistful – Knowlhead Flash) ex Shenstone Miss Tesha (Ch Leasowes Try Again – Ginger Popinette of Oldpost).

CH NORTHCOTE LUCKY STRIKE 189AT, R. R. Seaton, br. Owner, 13.8.59, blue, s. Northcote Micky (Foggyfurze Jackpot – Foggyfurze Dancer) ex Foggyfurze Cute (Ch Foggyfurze Classic – Ch Foggyfurze Cute).

CH SHENSTONE BLUE BLISS OF VISTABLU 1735AT, Mrs I. Sills, br. E. Smith, 5.6.59, blue, s. Ch Shenstone Master Mack (Ch Leasowes Try Again – Ginger Popinette of Oldpost) ex Shenstone Blue Lustre (Leasowes Simple Simon – Ginger Popinette of Oldpost).

1961

CH MELJOY JULIET DEMESNE 933AV, B. Howarth, br. Owner, 11.8.59, blue, s. Ch Foggyfurze Texan (Ch Foggyfurze Classic – Foggyfurze Baby Mine) ex Smart Cut (Ch Foggyfurze Classic – Ch Spring Dancer).

CH MISS MUFFET OF WETOP 64AV, W. Topham, br. Owner, 25.2.60, blue, s. Ch Gun Metal of Wetop (Blue Blazes of Foxington – The Linnet) ex Rose of Rushby (Ch Goldstrike of Foxington – Betty of Foxington).

1962

ATOMIC CUT 326AV, J. N. Slee, br. N. Stead, 26.1.61, blue, s. Foggyfurze Drumbeat (Ch Foggyfurze Classic – Bibsy of Mahidap) ex Meljoy All Quality (Ch Foggyfurze Texan – Smart Girl).

CH BOUGHTON NORTHCOTE LUCKY STONE 752AV, Miss M. Boggia, br. R. R. Seaton, 18.6.61, blue, s. Ch Foggyfurze Dandy (Ch Foggyfurze Classic – Bibsy of Mahidap) ex Northcote Bluebelle (Foggyfurze Jackpot – Foggyfurze Dancer).

FOGGYFURZE HONEY CHILE 751AV, F. Gent, br. Owner, 10.8.61, blue, s. Ch Foggyfurze Classic (Ch Curly Cut – Foggyfurze Acey Ducey) ex Foggyfurze Baby Mine (Ch Foggyfurze Classic – Drewcote Marie Belle).

1963

WEDERBI DAWN CHORUS 62AW, O. G. Gowing, br. Owner, 2.8.61, blue, s. Ch Wederbi Houghtop Invader (Ch Golden Sun of Manaton – Ch Tol-pedn Mermaid) ex Wederbi Diadem (Ch Foggyfurze Classic – Ch Tol-pedn Fairmaid).

FOGGYFURZE FAN TAN 1491AW, F. Gent, br. Owner, 24.5.62, blue, s. Ch Foggyfurze Classic (Ch Curly Cut – Foggy-furze Acey Ducey) ex Foggyfurze Wederbi Sceptre (Ch Wederbi Houghtop Invader – Wederbi Diadem).

CH LINDUM LAVINIA 587AW, Mrs F. L. Franks, br. Owner, 9.11.61, blue, s. Ch Chartlands Fair Dinkum (Ch Shenstone Master Mack – Ch Tol-pedn Fairmaid) ex Lindum Lucille (Ch Lindum High Octane of Vistablu – Ch Lindum Lunaria).

CH PENTAVY FIREDANCE OF TOL-PEDN 740AW, Ken Bounden & Mrs K. G. Holmes, brs. Owners, 19.8.62, liver, s. Ch Tol-pedn Hoodwink (Tol-pedn Merry Monk – Ch Tol-pedn Fairmaid) ex Ch Tol-pedn Ballerina (Ch Foggyfurze Classic – Ch Tol-pedn Fairmaid).

DINA MITE OF OLDPOST 2936AV, Mrs N. J. Howard, br. R. R. Seaton, 18.6.61, blue, s. Ch Foggyfurze Dandy (Ch Foggyfurze Classic – Bibsy of Mahidap) ex North-cote Bluebelle (Foggyfurze Jackpot – Foggyfurze Dancer).

CH DALEVIEW SHENSTONE AMBER LASS 2611AW, Mrs B. E. Wardman, br. E. Smith, 9.11.61, liver, Shenstone New Orbit (Stanolly Startrite – Shenstone Saucey Sue) ex Shenstone Felicity (Leasowes Simple Simon – Ginger Popinette of Oldpost).

CH MAYDEW MISS MURIEL 827AV, H. R. Highfield, br. Owner, 15.11.61, blue, s. Ch Maydew Moonraker (Stanolly Startrite – Maydew Miss Marie) ex Maydew Miss Maverick (Ch Shenstone Master Mack -- Bourneville Blue Mantle).

1964

GOLDEN ARROW 1553AX, Miss S. Marriott, br. Owner, 24.4.62, liver, s. Copper Rogue (Ch Shenstone Master Mack – Mynydd Morwyn) ex Petherwyn Nicola (Ch Tol-pedn Hoodwink – Lucille's Shadow).

CH NORTHCOTE STRIKE AGAIN 2740AW, R. R. Seaton, br. Owner, 13.12.62, blue, s. Ch Foggyfurze Classic (Ch Curly Cut

– Foggyfurze Acey Ducey) ex Ch North-cote Lucky Strike (Northcote Micky – Foggyfurze Cute).

CH AMERDALE ASTRALITA 312AW, W. Clark, br. Owner, 22.7.62, blue, s. North-cote Lucky Guy (Ch Foggyfurze Dandy – Northcote Bluebelle) ex Ch Amerdale Delight (Ch Foggyfurze Classic – Ch Knotts Bluebelle).

1965

STANOLLY SPORTS TIPPI 1031AX, Mrs O. M. Stones, br. Owner, 12.6.63, blue, Shenstone Merry Mac (Ch Shenstone Master Mack – Shenstone Felicity) ex Stanolly Sports Hilight (Ch Maydew Moonraker – Stanolly Starturn) exported to Mr Lars Adenby, Sweden.

SILVER SOLITAIRE 1638AX, Mrs J. E. Jackson, br. W. McCann, 3.8.62, blue, s. Ch Foggyfurze Dandy (Ch Foggyfurze Classic – Bibsy of Mahidap) ex Silver Sapphire (County Cut – Pynello Zoe).

CH AMERDALE AMANDA 1445AX, Mrs A. Clark, br. Owner, 19.11.63, blue, s. Amerdale Aviator (Northcote Lucky Guy – Ch Amerdale Delight) ex Amer-dale Blue Belle (Ch Gents Cut – Amer-dale Lass).

CH STANOLLY SUNSPRITE 2454AY, Mrs O. Stones, br. Owner, 19.7.64, liver, s. Ch Stanolly Sports Tosca (Shenstone Merry Mac – Stanolly Sports Hilight) ex Ch Stanolly Sapphire (Moyvallee Minstrel – Shenstone Miss Tesha) exported to Mr Lars Adenby, Sweden.

1966

ROULETTE OF WETOP 805AZ, W. Topham, br. Owner, 9.4.65, blue, s. Ch Rob Roy of Wetop (Ch Buttons of Wetop – Ch Miss Muffet of Wetop) ex Little Bo Peep of Wetop (Night Hawk of Wetop – Ch Cinderella).

DAISYMAY OF OLDPOST 1883AY, Mrs N. J. Howard, br. Mrs M. M. Taunt, 29.4.64, blue, s. Foggyfurze High Hat (Ch Foggy-furze Classic – Foggyfurze Wederbi Sceptre) ex Leasowes Lovely Lady (Ch

Shenstone Master Mack – Lolita Latour).

CH STANOLLY SUNBLUSH 843AS, Mrs O. Stones, br. Owner, 5.11.65, liver, s. Ch Stanolly Sports Tosca (Shenstone Merry Mac – Stanolly Sports Hilight) ex Ch Stanolly Sapphire (Moyvallee Minstrel – Shenstone Miss Tesha) exported to Mr M. Cash, U.S.A.

1967

CH VARDENE AMAREE OF CANZO 1581BA, Mr & Mrs S. J. L. Clifton, br. Mrs C. Taylor, 19.10.65, blue, s. Ch Gold Coin of Foxington (Blue Blazes of Foxington – Merrylass of Foxington) ex Blue Willow of Canzo (Blue Blazes of Foxington – Willow Marsh).

NORTHCOTE BLUE DAWN 2205BA, Mrs A. M. Norgate, br. R. R. Seaton, 25.11.65, blue, s. Northcote Terpo (Ch Wederbi Houghtop Invader – Ch Northcote Lucky Strike) ex Northcote Double Strike (Ch Foggyfurze Classic – Ch Northcote Lucky Strike).

1968

CH HIGHQUEST HOLLY GIRL 1263AY, Miss A. Heron, br. Mrs F. M. Jones, 7.12.64, liver, s. Ch Stanolly Sports Tosca (Shenstone Merry Mac – Stanolly Sports Hilight) ex Highquest Donnor (Kay of Nonington – Arabella of Nonington).

NORTHCOTE AILEEN 138BC, C. Stanley, br. R. R. Seaton, 23.2.67, blue, s. Northcote Terpo (Ch Wederbi Houghtop Invader – Ch Northcote Lucky Strike) ex Northcote Double Strike (Ch Foggyfurze Classic – Ch Northcote Lucky Strike).

BYSTOCK MACK'S GOLDEN PEARL 328BC, Miss V. Duckworth-Bradshaw, br. Owner, 17.3.65, liver, s. Ch Shenstone Master Mack (Ch Leasowes Try Again – Ginger Popinette of Oldpost) ex Bystock Sapphire (Ch Foggyfurze Dandy – Silver Sapphire).

CH AMERDALE DELICIOUS 2204BA, W. Clark, Br. Owner, 22.4.65, blue, s. Ch

Chartlands Fair Dinkum (Ch Shenstone Master Mack – Ch Tol-pedn Fairmaid) ex Ch Amerdale Astralita (Northcote Lucky Guy – Ch Amerdale Delight).

VARDENE GOLDEN GIRL 1937BC, Mrs B. Clifton, brs. Mr & Mrs J. L. Clifton, 13.4.67, liver, s. Ch Stanolly Sports Tosca (Shenstone Merry Mac – Stanolly Sports Hilight) ex Vardene Golden Gem (Ch Gold Coin of Foxington – Tol-pedn Shanty).

DOLLYROCKER OF VISTABLU 849BC, Mrs I. Sills, br. Owner, 8.11.67, s. Ch Fancypants of Vistablu (Foggyfurze Ranger – With It of Vistablu) ex Foggyfurze Merrymaid (Ch Foggyfurze Classic – Foggyfurze Amanda) exported to Saevich, Caram & Raigorodsky, Argentina.

CH BERENGREAVE PINK PERRY 2501BC, B. Reddington, br. Owner, 11.4.67, liver, s. Ch Stanolly Sports Tosca (Shenstone Merry Mac – Stanolly Sports Hilight) ex Berengreave Foggyfurze Sky High (Foggyfurze Drumbeat – Foggyfurze Stargirl).

STANOLLY CRYSTAL BELLE 586BA, Mrs O. Stones, br. Owner, 17.5.66, blue, s. Ch Stanolly Superstar (Ch Stanolly Sports Tosca – Pat's Choice) ex Ch Stanolly Sapphire (Moyvallee Minstrel – Shenstone Miss Tesha).

1969

CH FOGGYFURZE FESTIVAL 1537BD, F. Gent, br. Owner, 27.2.68, blue, s. Foggyfurze Dandini (Foggyfurze Fargo – Northcote Shadow) ex Foggyfurze Lulu (Foggyfurze Freelance – Foggyfurze Fiona) exported to Ms H. Cloppenburg, Holland.

1970

MARILENA POLLYANNA 2303BD, Mrs M. Metcalfe, br. Owner, 7.7.68, liver, s. Tweedle Dee of Wetop (Nighthawk of Wetop – Ch Cinderella) ex Symphony in Blue (Dick of Gutch Common – Jemima of Gutch Common).

CH BERENGREAVE PERSONALITY 2986BD, B. Reddington, br. Owner, 9.8.68, liver, s. Ch Stanolly Sports Tosca (Shenstone Merry Mac – Stanolly Sports Hilight) ex Berengreave Foggyfurze Sky High (Foggyfurze Drumbeat – Foggyfurze Stargirl).

CH PERRIANNE PETULA 1429BE, Miss A. Stoppard, br. Owner, 10.10.68, blue, s. Blueflower Clear Crystal (Ch Buttons of Wetop – Lavender Blue) ex Stanolly Blue Bubbles (Ch Stanolly Super Star – Ch Stanolly Sapphire).

CH PEWTER GREY OF WETOP 2062BE, W. Topham, br. Owner, 15.6.69, blue, s. The Count of Wetop (Tweedle Dee of Wetop – Stanolly Sports Cherub) ex Duett of Wetop (Ch Rob Roy of Wetop – Little Bo Peep of Wetop).

MOORSIDE DAINTY DENISE 23158BD, R. Ratcliffe, br. Owner, 1.5.68, blue, Ch Stanolly Sports Tosca (Shenstone Merry Mac – Stanolly Sports Hilight) ex Babsy of Moorside (Grinkle Cut – Moorside Gypsy).

1971

LEASOWES DANCING SHADOW 2314BD, Mrs M. M. Taunt, br. Mrs M. Braid, 14.7.68, blue, s. Greenayre Tory (Ch Foggyfurze Classic – Silver Slipper) ex Leasowes Barley Sugar (Foggyfurze High Hat – Leasowes Lovely Lady).

CH STANOLLY STARBOW 3147BE, Mrs O. Stones, br. W. Clark, 6.11.69, blue, s. Ch Stanolly Sports Tosca (Shenstone Merry Mac – Stanolly Sports Hilight) ex Ch Amerdale Delicious (Ch Chartlands Fair Dinkum – Ch Amerdale Astralita).

AMERDALE ATTRACTIVE 1038BE, W. Clark, br. Owner, 8.11.69, blue, s. Ch Stanolly Sports Tosca (Shenstone Merry Mac – Stanolly Sports Hilight) ex Ch Amerdale Delicious (Ch Chartlands Fair Dinkum – Ch Amerdale Astralita).

CH TUPPENCE OFF OF VISTABLU 1562BF, Mrs I. Sills, br. Owner, 1.1.70, blue, s. Ch Foggyfurze Fan Fare (Ch Northcote Lucky Mark – Foggyfurze Nina) ex Foggyfurze Merrymaid (Ch Foggyfurze Classic – Foggyfurze Amanda).

1972

BIRKONBRAE BLEU BUNNY 167BG, Mrs J. Walker, brs. Mr & Mrs R. J. Anderson, 10.6.70, blue, s. Ch Vardene Blue Grenadier (Ch Stanolly Starblaze – Vardene Golden Gem) ex Birkonbrae Bronze Bunyip (Flashy Cut – Copper Coin).

CH BERENGREAVE PERSONAL PROPERTY 854BG, Mr & Mrs B. Reddington, brs. Owners, 20.5.71, blue, s. Ch Vardene Blue Grenadier (Ch Stanolly Starblaze – Vardene Golden Gem) ex Ch Berengreave Pink Perry (Ch Stanolly Sports Tosca – Berengreave Foggyfurze Sky High).

STANOLLY SECRET SURPRISE 1416BF, Mrs B. Cowdall, br. Mrs O. Stones, 20.5.69, liver, s. Ch Stanolly Sandpiper (Ch Stanolly Starblaze – Stanolly Sports Delight) ex Ch Stanolly Sunblush (Ch Stanolly Sports Tosca – Ch Stanolly Sapphire).

CH DOOLEY OF CRAGLOUGH 168BG, J. Holden, br. Miss D. Aitkenhead, 30.7.70, blue, s. Craglough Sebastian (Ch Northcote Lucky Mark – Lisetta of Craglough) ex Candula of Craglough (Ch Nadworna Statesman – Bibsy of Mahidap).

1973

CH WETOP BLUE VELVET 3724BG, W. Topham, br. Owner, 23.8.71, blue, Ch Rob Roy of Wetop (Ch Buttons of Wetop – Ch Miss Muffet of Wetop) ex Donna of Wetop (Tweedle Dee of Wetop – Stanolly Sports Cherub).

CH STANOLLY SCOOBY'S SOLO 3725BG, Mrs O. Stones, br. Owner, 3.1.72, liver, s. Ch Stanolly Scooby Doo (Ch Stanolly Sandpiper – Stanolly Crystal Belle) ex Stanolly Sunblaze (Ch Stanolly Sports Tosca – Ch Stanolly Sapphire).

CH LIEBERLAMB LUCINDA 532BH, Mrs M. Sugden, br. Owner, 16.7.72, blue, Ch Vardene Blue Grenadier (Ch Stanolly Starblaze – Vardene Golden Gem) ex

Lieberlamb Lynette (The Count of Wetop – Stanolly Amber Blush).

BIRKONBRAE BRONZE BON BON 3202BH, Mr & Mrs A. Blaxter, brs. Mr & Mrs Anderson, 15.10.71, liver, s. Berengreave Action Man (Ch Stanolly Sandpiper – Ch Berengreave Pink Perry) ex Birkonbrae Bronze Bunyip (Flashy Cut – Copper Coin).

1974

CH STANOLLY SCOOSTAR TIPSY 3560BH, Mrs O. Stones, br. Owner, 11.1.73, blue, s. Ch Stanolly Scooby Doo (Ch Stanolly Sandpiper – Stanolly Crystal Belle) ex Ch Stanolly Starbow (Ch Stanolly Sports Tosca – Ch Amerdale Delicious).

CH FOGGYFURZE FENWICK 479BI, F. Gent, br. Owner, 7.2.73, blue, s. Foggyfurze Fantastic (Ch Foggyfurze Ferrari – Foggyfurze Fava) ex Foggyfurze Farah (Foggyfurze Tino – Foggyfurze Mura).

STANOLLY SUNSTAR 2683BH, Mrs A. M. Norgate, br. Mrs O. Stones, 20.9.72, liver, Ch Stanolly Scooby Doo (Ch Stanolly Sandpiper – Stanolly Crystal Belle) ex Stanolly Sunblaze (Ch Stanolly Sports Tosca – Ch Stanolly Sapphire).

CH WETOP BLUE OPAL 1533BI, W. Topham, br. Owner, 28.9.72, blue, s. The Count of Wetop (Tweedle Dee of Wetop – Stanolly Sports Cherub) ex Duett of Wetop (Ch Rob Roy of Wetop – Little Bo Peep of Wetop).

CH LIEBERLAMB LEANDER 480BI, Mrs. M. Sugden, br. Owner, 7.7.73, blue, s. Ch Vardene Blue Guardsman (Ch Vardene Blue Grenadier – Ch Vardene Amaree of Canzo) ex Lieberlamb Lorraine (The Count of Wetop – Stanolly Amber Blush).

BIRKONBRAE BRONZE BRIGHTIZE 2141BI, Mr & Mrs R. J. Anderson, brs. Owners, 27.8.73, liver, s. Ch Vardene Blue Grenadier (Ch Stanolly Starblaze – Vardene Golden Gem) ex Birkonbrae Bronze Bunyip (Flashy Cut – Copper Coin).

1975

PERRIANNE POPPY 1266BI, Miss A. Stoppard, br. Owner, 4.8.72, blue, Ch Stanolly Scooby Doo (Ch Stanolly Sandpiper – Stanolly Crystal Belle) ex Ch Perrianne Petula (Blueflower Clear Crystal – Stanolly Blue Bubbles).

PETACREST PERFECT ANGEL 848BJ, Mrs A. M. Norgate, br. Owner, 8.6.74, blue, s. Ch Stanolly Scooby Doo (Ch Stanolly Sandpiper – Stanolly Crystal Belle) ex Lamott Echappe de Soleil (Lamott Original Fella – Vardene Blue Gondalier).

CH CRAGLOUGH KITTIWAKE 478BI, Miss D. Aitkenhead, br. Owner, 15.3.73, blue, s. Craglough Denarius (Scipio of Craglough – Craglough Charisma) ex Craglough Cassiope (Craglough Sebastian – Candula of Craglough).

AVILAS ATHENE OF FOGGYFURZE 1320BJ, F. Gent, br. Mrs E. Johnson, 2.3.74, blue, s. Ch Stanolly Scooby Doo (Ch Stanolly Sandpiper – Stanolly Crystal Belle) ex Stanfos Blue Choice (Ch Foggyfurze Fangio – Northcote Aileen).

PETACREST BEWITCHING BLUE 2537BJ, Mrs J. Hawes, br. Mrs A. Norgate, 29.10.73, blue, Ch Stanolly Scooby Doo (Ch Stanolly Sandpiper – Stanolly Crystal Belle) ex Lamott Echappe de Soleil (Lamott Original Fella – Vardene Blue Gondalier).

CH STANOLLY SUKINA 2952BJ, Mrs O. Stones, br. Owner, 29.12.74, blue, Ch Stanolly Scooby Doo (Ch Stanolly Sandpiper – Stanolly Crystal Belle) ex Stanolly Hi Impulse) (Ch Stanolly Spectacular – Stanolly Sports Adoration) exported to Mrs Verschueen-Devriendt, Belgium.

BYSTOCK BLUE PEARL 1466BI, Miss V. Duckworth-Bradshaw, br. Owner, 20.2.73, blue, s. Ch Vardene Blue Grenadier (Ch Stanolly Starblaze – Vardene Golden Gem) ex Bystock Miss Sapphire (Bystock Master Mack Douglass – Bystock Sapphire).

1976

CH TABITHA OF CRAGLOUGH 3357BJ, Miss D. Aitkenhead, br. J. Holden, blue, 19.4.74, Craglough Denarious (Scipio of Craglough – Craglough Charisma) ex Ch Dooley of Craglough (Craglough Sebastian – Candula of Craglough).

CH WHICKHAM MERRY DUCHESS 3946BJ, E. L. Hill, br. Owner, 13.7.74, blue, s. Ch Foggyfurze Fandango (Ch Foggyfurze Fan Fare – Foggyfurze Fastidious) ex Whickham Invader (Barcas Marra – Pelton Pin-up Girl).

CH LIEBERLAMB LUCKY STAR 262BK, Mrs M. Sugden, br. Owner, 11.5.75, blue, s. Foggyfurze Fantastic (Foggyfurze Ferrari – Foggyfurze Fava) ex Ch Lieberlamb Lucinda (Ch Vardene Blue Grenadier – Lieberlamb Lynette) exported to Constance Friestedt, Sweden.

HILLDYKE ARKADINA 831BK, B. F. Emsley, br. Owner, 3.11.74, blue, s. Foggyfurze Fantastic (Foggyfurze Ferrari – Foggyfurze Fava) ex Hilldyke Elida May (Ch Stanolly Spectacular – Stanolly Blue Crystal).

DALIP PETRANELLO 2530BK, Mrs P. Hall, br. Owner, 12.5.74, blue, s. Ch Stanolly Scooby Doo (Ch Stanolly Sandpiper – Stanolly Crystal Belle) ex Franzel Huntersmoon (Ch Vardene blue Grenadier – Berengreave Sunset Gleam).

CH STANOLLY SUMMER LUV 3182BK, Mrs O. Stones, br. Owner, 17.7.75, liver, s. Ch Stanolly Shang-a-lang (Ch Stanolly Scooby Doo – Ch Stanolly Starbow) ex Stanolly Hi Impulse (Ch Stanolly Spectacular – Stanolly Sports Adoration).

1977

GOLD DUST OF VARDENE 4029BI, Mr & Mrs C. J. Rogers, br. Mrs J. Walker, 15.5.73, liver, s. Ch Vardene Blue Grenadier (Ch Stanolly Starblaze – Vardene Golden Gem) ex Birkonbrae Bleu Bunny (Ch Vardene Blue Grenadier – Birkonbrae Bronze Bunyip).

RATHSRIGG RAFFLE 2325BK, Mr & Mrs I. J. Phillips, br. Owners, 2.7.75, blue, s.

Ch Foggyfurze Fan Fare (Ch Northcote Lucky Mark – Foggyfurze Nina) ex Rathsrigg Check Mate (Ch Rathsrigg Little Caesar – Louella Miss Max).

CH WHISPERING SONG OF STANOLLY 1103B1, Mrs O. M. Stones, br. F. B. Oates, 28.5.76, Blue, s. Ch Stanolly Scooby Doo (Ch Stanolly Sandpiper – Stanolly Crystal Belle) ex Highquest Holiday Girl (Highquest High Mist – Highquest High Faith).

CH FOGGYFURZE FONDANT 1631B1, F. Gent, br. Owner. 19.5.76, blue, s. Ch Avilas Aries of Foggyfurze (Ch Stanolly Scooby Doo – Stanfos Blue Choice Foggyfurze Fidella (Ch Foggyfurze Ferrari – Foggyfurze Francesca).

CH SINGLETON GINGERBREAD LADY 2596BK, J. S. Whittaker, br. Mrs G. Jump, 28.11.74, liver, s. Toffee of Merryavon (Greenayre Hussar – Greenayre Nutmeg) ex Sapphire of Merryavon (Blue Knight of Sealham – Blue Melanie).

1978

CH VARDENE BLUE WITCHCRAFT 494BM, Mrs B. Clifton & Miss D. Middlehurst, br. Mrs B. Clifton, 30.10.76, blue, s. Ch Vardene Blue Grenadier (Ch Stanolly Starblaze – Vardene Golden Gem) ex Stanfos Blue Ilex (Ch Foggyfurze Fangio – Northcote Aileen).

CH AVILAS BARMAID 495BM, J. Mitchell, br. Mrs E. Johnson, 23.10.76, blue, s. Ch Stanolly Scooby Doo (Ch Stanolly Sandpiper – Stanolly Crystal Belle) ex Stanfos Blue Choice (Ch Foggyfurze Fangio – Stanfos Blue Choice).

REPRINT OF TIDDLYMOUNT 666BM, P. Gratton, br. Mrs O. M. Stones, 20.3.77, liver, s. Ch Stanolly Scooby Doo (Ch Stanolly Sandpiper – Stanolly Crystal Belle) ex Ch Stanolly Summer Luv (Ch Stanolly Shang a Lang – Stanolly Hi Impulse).

CH FOGGYFURZE FLUTTER 4240BL, F. Gent, br. Owner, 19.8.76, blue, s. Ch Avilas Aries of Foggyfurze (Ch Stanolly

Scooby Doo – Stanfos Blue Choice) ex Foggyfurze Fidella (Foggyfurze Ferrari – Foggyfurze Francesca).

BIRKONBRAE BRONZE BACCHANTE 1700BM, R. J. Anderson, br. Owner, 7.7.77, liver, s. Ch Stanolly Scooby Doo (Ch Stanolly Sandpiper – Stanolly Crystal Belle) ex Blue Bacchic of Birkonbrae (Ch Birkonbrae Bronze Bacchus – Judy of Balmoral).

CH LIEBERLAMB LOUISE 667BM, Mrs M. Sugden, br. Owner, 16.7.77, blue, s. Foggyfurze Fantastic (Foggyfurze Ferrari – Foggyfurze Fava) ex Ch Lieberlamb Lucinda (Ch Vardene Blue Grenadier – Lieberlamb Lynette).

1979

STANOLLY SUMMER DELIGHT 4153BK, W. Kitchin, br. Mrs O. Stones, 17.7.75, liver, s. Ch Stanolly Shang-a-Lang (Ch Stanolly Scooby Doo – Ch Stanolly Starbow) ex Stanolly Hi Impulse (Ch Stanolly Spectacular – Stanolly Sports Adoration).

CRAGLOUGH COMFREY 589BM, Miss D. Aitkenhead, br. Owner, 27.11.76, blue, s. Ch Granitor Flint (Craglough Denarius – Ch Dooley of Craglough) ex Craglough Quetzal (Scipio of Craglough – Craglouch Charisma).

RATHSRIGG REGIUS 963BN, Mr & Mrs I. J. Phillips, brs. Owners, 1.6.77, blue, s. Ch Foggyfurze Fenman (Ch Foggyfurze Fan Fare – Foggyfurze Fidella) ex Rathsrigg Check Mate (Ch Rathsrigg Little Ceasar – Louella Miss Max).

BRENTBROOK PRECIOUS GEM 1536BN, Mrs M. Burgess, br. I. Hoyle, 8.5.77, blue, s. Foggyfurze Fantastic (Foggyfurze Ferrari – Foggyfurze Fava) ex Brentbrook Gay Lib (Petacrest Sir Prancelot – Gaytime of Grosea).

UKWONG SEPTEMBER DAWN OF VARDENE 2352BN, Mrs B. Clifton, br. Miss M. J. Egerton, 1.9.78, blue, s. Ch Vardene Blue Grenadier (Ch Stanolly Starblaze – Vardene Golden Gem) ex Vardene Blue Madjic (Ch Vardene Blue Guardsman – Stanfos Blue Ilex).

1980

CH BIRKONBRAE BRONZE BACCHIQUE 293BN, Mr & Mrs R. J. & Miss B. Anderson, brs. Mr & Mrs R. J. Anderson, 7.7.77, liver, s. Ch Stanolly Scooby Doo (Ch Stanolly Sandpiper – Stanolly Crystal Belle) ex Bleu Bacchic of Birkonbrae (Ch Birkonbrae Bronze Bacchus – Judy of Balmoral).

CH RATHSRIGG ROSE 762BP, Mr & Mrs I. J. Phillips, brs. Owners, 1.12.78, blue, s. Ch Rathsrigg Ruin (Ch Granitor Flint – Rathsrigg Check Mate) ex Rosa of Rathsrigg (Ch Foggyfurze Fan Fare – Foggyfurze Farah).

CRAGLOUGH CELESTE 2394BN, Miss D. Aitkenhead, br. Owner, 3.4.78, blue, s. Ch Granitor Rocket Man (Foggyfurze Fantastic – Ch Dooley of Craglough) ex Ch Tabitha of Craglough (Craglough Denarius – Ch Dooley of Craglough).

CH STAR AUDITION OF STANOLLY 2092BP, Mrs O. M. Stones, br. W. Kitchin, 16.6.79, blue, s. Ch Stanolly Scooby Doo (Ch Stanolly Sandpiper – Stanolly Crystal Belle) ex Stanolly Summer Delight (Ch Stanolly Shang-a-Lang – Stanolly Hi Impulse).

CH MOORSIDE QUITE QUAINT 765BP, R. Ratcliff, br. Owner, 12.10.78, blue, s. Ch Foggyfurze Fenman (Ch Foggyfurze Fan Fare – Foggyfurze Fidella) ex Moorside Joyful Julie (Moorside Freddie Fox – Moorside Dainty Denise).

CH TUPPENCE OF TYNECOURT 489BP, E. L. Hill, br. F. Gent, 10.9.78, blue, s. Ch Avilas Lucky Lad of Foggyfurze (Ch Stanolly Scooby Doo – Stanfos Blue Choice) ex Foggyfurze Fidella (Foggyfurze Ferrari – Foggyfurze Francesca).

CH FOGGYFURZE FIFI 2393BN, F. Gent, br. Owner, 8.1.78, blue, s. Ch Avilas Lucky Lad of Foggyfurze (Ch Stanolly Scooby Doo – Stanfos Blue Choice) ex Foggyfurze Fidella (Foggyfurze Ferrari – Foggyfurze Francesca).

CH BIRKONBRAE BLEU BUBBLICIOUS 3452BP, Mr & Mrs R. J. & Miss B.

Anderson, brs. Owners, 7.1.80, blue, Ch Birkonbrae Bleu Braggadocio (Ch Stanolly Scooby Doo – Bleu Bacchic of Birkonbrae) ex Birkonbrae Bleu Brilliance (Ch Birkonbrae Bleu Braggadocio – Birkonbrae Bronze Brightize).

1981

CH BLA SKUGGANS NEXT STAR (NORDIC CH IMPORT) 0656BQ, Mrs R. Lyberg, br. Owner, 25.11.77, liver, s. Bla Skuggans Following Star (Marilena Marketeer – Stanolly Sunstar) ex Wetop Mermaid (Swank of Wetop – Wetop Sea Pearl).

CH WETOP MEG 2909BP, W. A. Topham, br. Owner, 29.4.79, liver, s. Ch Wetop Gay Knight (Swank of Wetop – Duett of Wetop) ex Wetop Copper Charm (Wetop Blue Boy – Donna of Wetop).

CH VISTABLU WONDER WOMAN 1641BQ, Mrs I. Sills, br. Owner, 24.4.80, blue, s. Arg. Ch Vistablu Ben Franklin of Blue Happening (Stillwater Scotch on the Rocks – Old Flints Dahlia) ex Lieberlamb Lucy Locket (Foggyfurze Fantastic – Ch Lieberlamb Lucinda).

1982

CH VERANNA MISS VALENTINE 2767BR, Mrs P. F. Pick, br. Owner, 14.2.80, blue, s. Ch Dalip Huggy Bear (Ch Stanolly Shang-a-Lang – Dalip Petranello) ex Bystock Blue Poppy (Foggyfurze Fantastic – Bystock Horatia).

CH AURABLEUE ADELA 3550BR, Mrs A. F. M. Pogson, br. Owner, 16.12.80, blue, s. Ch Rathsrigg Ruin (Ch Granitor Flint – Rathsrigg Check Mate) ex Aurableue Annabella (Ch Avilas Lucky Lad of Foggyfurze – Aurableue Michele).

CH CRAGLOUGH CALINKA 0208BR, Miss D. Aitkenhead, br. Owner, 24.8.80, blue, s. Ch Foggyfurze Fenman (Ch Foggyfurze Fan Fare – Foggyfurze Fidella) ex Ch Tabitha of Craglough (Craglough Denarius – Ch Dooley of Craglough).

TINKERBLOO CHICK ANGELIQUE 0124BR, Mrs P. M. Lindborg, br. Owner, 24.12.80, blue, s. Wetop Parsley (Ch Wetop Gay Knight – Wetop Artic Mist) ex Heathrose Caprice of Tinkerbloo (Arg Ch Vistablu Ben Franklin of Blue Happening – Perrianne Primrose).

RATHSRIGG RAZE 0127BR, Mr & Mrs I. J. Phillips, brs. Owners, 24.8.80, blue, s. Ch Foggyfurze Fenman (Ch Foggyfurze Fan Fare – Foggyfurze Fidella) ex Rosa of Rathsrigg (Ch Foggyfurze Fan Fare – Foggyfurze Farah).

1983

CH MOORSIDE SUMMER SONG 0504BS, R. Ratcliffe, br. Owner, 11.12.81, blue, s. Ch Avilas Lucky Lad of Foggyfurze (Ch Stanolly Scooby Doo – Stanfos Blue Choice) ex Ch Moorside Quite Quaint (Ch Foggyfurze Fenman – Moorside Joyful Julie).

CH ELCROFT LILLY LADY 764BP, W. Kitchin, Br. Owner, 16.6.79, liver, s. Ch Stanolly Scooby Doo (Ch Stanolly Sandpiper – Stanolly Crystal Belle) ex Stanolly Summer Delight (Ch Stanolly Shang-a-Lang – Stanolly Hi Impulse).

DELBREN BLUE FANTASY 0916BS, Mr & Mrs D. J. Rogers, brs. Owners, 2.3.81, blue, s. Ch Stanolly Shang-a-Lang (Ch Stanolly Scooby Doo – Ch Stanolly Starbow) ex Stanolly Bubbles Bon Bon of Delbren (Ch Stanolly Scooby Doo – Ch Stanolly Summer Luv).

WETOP SOPHIE 5108BS, Mrs A. Palmigiano, br. W. Topham, 2.5.82, liver, s. Ch Wetop Gay Knight (Swank of Wetop – Duett of Wetop) ex Ch Wetop Meg (Ch Wetop Gay Knight – Wetop Copper Charm).

1984

CH STANOLLY CELESTIAL DREAM 0125BR, Mrs C. A. Smallwood, br. Mrs O. Stones, 12.12.80, blue, s. Ch Stanolly Shang-a-Lang (Ch Stanolly Scooby Doo – Ch Stanolly Starbow) ex Ch Whispering Song of Stanolly (Ch Stanolly Scooby Doo – Highquest Holiday Girl).

CH PETACREST POLLY WAGTAIL 0206, K. Bounden & Mmes F. Littlejohn & A.

Norgate, br. Mrs A. Norgate, 10.6.80, blue, s. Ch Rathsrigg Ruin (Ch Granitor Flint – Rathsrigg Check Mate) ex Peregrine of Pentavy (Gutch Common Surprise – Tol-pedn Herring Gull).

VARDENE BLUE TREASURE, Mr & Mrs W. W. McCoy, brs. Misses Clifton & Middlehurst, 14.11.78, blue, s. Ch Turtonheights Blue Gallant (Ch Vardene Blue Grenadier – Sweet Maid in Blue) ex Ch Vardene Blue Witchcraft (Ch Vardene Blue Grenadier – Stanfos Blue Ilex).

BOJEN BIANCA 1970BT, Miss J. C. J. Pearce, br. Owner, 24.3.81, blue, s. Ch Rathsrigg Ruin (Ch Granitor Flint – Rathsrigg Check Mate) ex Foggyfurze Flair (Ch Foggyfurze Fenman – Foggyfurze Fettle).

CH MOORSIDE TINKER TAILOR OF TYNECOURT 0331BT, E. J. Hill, br. R. Ratcliffe, 1.9.82, blue, s. Ch Avilas Lucky Lad of Foggyfurze (Ch Stanolly Scooby Doo – Stanfos Blue Choice) ex Ch Moorside Quite Quaint (Ch Foggyfurze Fenman – Moorside Joyful Julie).

CAERULEUS CELTIC, Mrs I. Bach, br. Owner, 7.12.78, blue, s. Foggyfurze Fantastic (Foggyfurze Ferrari – Foggyfurze Favia) ex Caeruleus Lorette (Stanolly Shooby Do A – Highqest Herne Charity).

1985

VISTABLU FLY THE FLAG AT SEVRAY 0919BS, Mmes I. Sills & V. Rainsbury, br. Owner, 7.4.82, blue, s. Argentine Ch Vistablu Ben Franklin of Blue Happening (Stillwater Scotch on the Rocks – Old Flints Dhalia) ex Lieberlamb Lucy Locket (Foggyfurze Fantastic – Ch Lieberlamb Lucinda).

CH STANOLLY SILVER TRINKET 4204BT, Mrs C. Jacob, br. Mrs O. Stones, 12.4.83, blue, s. Ch Stanolly Super Swank (Ch Stanolly Scooby Doo – Ch Stanolly Summer Luv) ex Ch Whispering Song of Stanolly (Ch Stanolly Scooby Doo – Highquest Holiday Girl).

CH MOORSIDE VIVACIOUS VIXEN OF LIEBERLAMB 0267BU, Mr & Mrs M. & Mrs M. E. Sugden, br. R. Ratcliffe, 21.2.84, blue, s. Ch Foggyfurze Fenman (Ch Foggyfurze Fan Fare – Foggyfurze Fidella) ex Ch Moorside Summer Song (Ch Avilas Lucky Lad of Foggyfurze – Ch Moorside Quite Quaint).

CH DALIP VENUS IN BLUE GENES 4020BT, Mrs P. Hall, br. Owner, 9.3.83, blue and tan, s. Stanolly Sandman (Avilas At Last – Ch Stanolly Starbow) ex Dalip Blue Angel (Dalip Punchanello – Dalip Dream Girl).

CH CRAGLOUGH CONSTANTIA 2575BU, Mr & Mrs I. J. Phillips, br. Miss D. Aitkenhead, 30.5.84, blue, s. Ch Rathsrigg Reuben (Ch Foggyfurze Fenman – Rosa of Rathsrigg) ex Ch Craglough Calinka (Ch Foggyfurze Fenman – Ch Tabitha of Craglough).

CH DANCERS DESIRE 2571BU, Mr & Mrs C. Richardson, brs. Messrs R. & P. Garbutt, 22.12.83, blue, s. Ch Avilas Lucky Lad of Foggyfurze (Ch Stanolly Scooby Doo – Stanfos Blue Choice) ex Princess Jewel (Ch Foggyfurze Fenman – Foggyfurze Firedance).

MOORSIDE UPPER UTOPIA 4738BU, Mrs L. Butler, br. R. Ratcliffe, 11.1.84, blue, s. Ch Aurableue Ashmow Alick (Ch Avilas Lucky Lad of Foggyfurze – Aurableue Michelle) ex Ch Moorside Quite Quaint (Ch Foggyfurze Fenman – Moorside Joyful Julie).

CH STANOLLY SUPER FLARE 0103BU, Mr & Mrs Wee Teng Woon, br. Mrs O. Stones, 2.4.84, liver, s. Stanolly Secret Agent (Ch Stanolly Super Swank – Ch Whispering Song of Stanolly) ex Stanolly Shimmering Lite (Ch Stanolly Shang-a-Lang – Stanolly Spring Fancy).

1986

CH BLUE DIAMOND OF WETOP 4865BU, W. Topham, br. Mrs A. Palmigiano, 8.11.84, blue, s. Ch Wetop Silver Spur (Ch Wetop Gay Knight – Wetop Blue Lambkin) ex Wetop Sophie (Ch Wetop Gay Knight – Ch Wetop Meg).

CH CINNAMON OF CULLERCOATS 0879, Mrs P. Lay, br. Miss S. F. Seager, 23.1.84, sandy, s. Ch Willow of Cullercoats (Caeruleus Corinthian – Highquest Honor) ex Tao Suka (Caeruleus Corinthian – Wetop Suka).

STANOLLY RISING STAR 0253BU, Mrs C. Smallwood, br. Mrs O. Stones, 4.10.82, blue, s. Stanolly Super Fame (Ch Stanolly Scooby Doo – Stanolly Shimmering Lite) ex Ch Whispering Song of Stanolly (Ch Stanolly Scooby Doo – Highquest Holiday Girl).

CH STANOLLY SPRINGTIME MELODY 3197BV, Mrs O. Stones, br. Owner, 19.4.85, liver, s. Ch Brickbats Broughton (Wilnesden Silver – Blue Print of Tiddly Mount) ex Stanolly Summer Wine (Stanolly Secret Agent – Stanolly Shimmering Lite).

BRYNSIRE MORNING MELODY 2675BU, Mrs C. Smallwood, br. Owner, 19.9.84, blue, s. Ch Brickbats Broughton (Wilnesden Silver – Blue Print of Tiddly Mount) ex Ch Stanolly Celestial Dream (Ch Stanolly Shang-a-Lang – Ch Whispering Song of Stanolly).

1987

CH RATHSRIGG RINA 0710BV, Mr & Mrs I. J. Phillips, br. Owners, 27.2.85, blue, s. Petacrest Psalm (Foggyfurze Fantastic – Petacrest Perfect Angel) ex Rathsrigg Reeve (Ch Rathsrigg Rule – Rathsrigg Raze).

CH MOORSIDE BONNY BLOSSOM 0636BW, Mrs M. & Mr M. Sugden, br. R. Ratcliffe, 1.1.86, blue, s. Ch Aurableue Ashmow Alick (Ch Avilas Lucky Lad of Foggyfurze – Aurableue Michelle) ex Ch Moorside Summer Song (Ch Avilas Lucky Lad of Foggyfurze – Ch Moorside Quite Quaint).

CH DALIP UTOWN GIRL 1257BW, Mrs P. Hall, br. Owner, 11.4.86, blue, s. Crackerjack Blue Solstice (Ch Foggyfurze Fenman – Stanolly Salamanda) ex Dalip Sheer Genius (Stanolly Sandman – Dalip Blue Angel).

RATHSRIGG ROMANCE 0922BW, Mrs B. Sebire, br. Mr & Mrs I. J. Phillips, 17.11.85, blue, s. Craglough Cerberus (Ch Foggyfurze Fenman – Ch Tabitha of Craglough) ex Rathsrigg Raze (Ch Foggyfurze Fenman – Rosa of Rathsrigg).

BARNSNAP BALLERINA 1578BV, Mr & Mrs T. McErlean, br. Owners, 5.4.85, blue, s. Ch Rathsrigg Reuben (Ch Foggyfurze Fenman – Rosa of Rathsrigg) ex Petacrest Brown Eyes Blue (Petacrest Sir Prancelot – Peregrine of Pentavy at Cristaby).

CH CRAGLOUGH CORYANTHUS 2065BW, Miss D. Aitkenhead, br. Owner, 12.11.85, blue, s. Ch Craglough Cherubino (Ch Rathsrigg Reuben – Ch Craglough Calinka) ex Craglough Cachet (Ch Granitor Rocket Man – Ch Tabitha of Craglough).

CH VERANNA BLUE VENUS 3359BV, Mrs P. Pick, br. Owner, 17.6.85, blue, s. Ch Aurableue Ashmow Alick (Ch Avilas Lucky Lad of Foggyfurze – Aurableue Michelle) ex Perrianne Purdy (Perrianne Paladin – Perrianne Pennyfarthing).

STANOLLY SILVER BELL 3736BW, Mr & Mrs J. Hart, br. Mrs O. Stones, 17.7.86, blue, s. Stanolly Shotgun Will (Ch Stanolly Starburst – Ch Stanolly Summer Luv) ex Stanolly Summer Wine (Stanolly Secret Agent – Stanolly Shimmering Lite).

1988

CH MOORSIDE URSULA ULA AT HILLDYKE 4834BU, Mr B. F. Emsley, br. R. Ratcliffe, 11.1.84, blue, s. Ch Aurableue Ashmow Alick (Ch Avilas Lucky Lad of Foggyfurze – Aurableue Michelle) ex Ch Moorside Quite Quaint (Ch Foggyfurze Fenman – Moorside Joyful Julie).

BOJEN BELLE AMIE 0309BX, Mrs J. C. J. Martindale, br. Owner, 6.7.86, blue, s. Ch Foggyfurze Fenman (Ch Foggyfurze Fan Fare – Foggyfurze Fidella) ex Bojen Bianca (Ch Rathsrigg Ruin – Foggyfurze Flair).

MISTIBLEU SINDERELLA 5332BW, Mrs M. D. & Ms S. E. Baldwin, br. Mr & Mrs T. J. Read, 2.11.86, blue, s. Abnomali Blue Rain (Tawny Flintstone – Blue Sauce of Bamber) ex Ivycott Irresistable (Ch Wetop Silver Spur – Ivycott Innocent).

CH RATHSRIGG RANI 1546BX, Mr & Mrs I. J. Phillips, br. Owners, 28.3.87, blue, s. Ch Rathsrigg Rule (Ch Rathsrigg Ruin – Rathsrigg Rosa) ex Ch Craglough Constantia (Ch Rathsrigg Reuben – Ch Craglough Calinka).

CH VISTABLU NORA BATTY 3367BW, Mr & Mrs S. E. & Mr M. D. Baldwin, br. Mrs I. Sills, 25.11.85, blue, s. Ch Aurableue Ashmow Alick (Ch Avilas Lucky Lad of Foggyfurze – Aurableue Michelle) ex Ch Vistablu Wonder Woman (Argentine Ch Vistablu Ben Franklin of Blue Happening – Lieberlamb Lucy Locket).

1989

CH MOORSIDE EVER SO ELEGANT FROM COTTONTOPS 0078BY, Mrs L. S. Aspden, br. R. Ratcliffe, 3.10.87, blue, s. Ch Vistablu Nelson Touch (Ch Aurableue Ashmow Alick – Ch Vistablu Wonder Woman) ex Ch Moorside Summer Song (Ch Avilas Lucky Lad of Foggyfurze – Ch Moorside Quite Quaint).

CH HILLDYKE LADY MADELYN 0079BY, B. F. Emsley, br. Owner, 3.7.87, blue, s. Ch Rathsrigg Reuben (Ch Foggyfurze Fenman – Rathsrigg Rosa) ex Ch Moorside Ursula Ula At Hilldyke (Ch Aurableue Ashmow Alick – Ch Moorside Quite Quaint).

SUGAR IS SWEET 0638BY, Mr & Mrs S. J. Lockett, br. Owners, 20.4.87, blue, s. Fantastic Lucky Blue (Ch Foggyfurze Fenman – Ch Foggyfurze Fifi) ex Barnsnap Belinda (Ch Rathsrigg Reuben – Barnsnap Bronze Statuette).

MOORSIDE I SPY ELEANOR FROM COTTONTOPS 1323BY, Mr & Mrs E. S. Inglis, br. R. Ratcliffe, 3.10.87, blue, s. Ch Vistablu Nelson Touch (Ch Aurableue Ashmow Alick – Ch Vistablu Wonder Woman) ex Ch Moorside Summer Song (Ch Avilas Lucky Lad of Foggyfurze – Ch Moorside Quite Quaint).

MOORSIDE DAWNS DELIGHT AT FURROLLY 0663BY, Mrs C. A. Reaston, br. R. Ratcliffe, 13.2.87, blue, s. Ch Moorside Victor Is No Vagrant (Ch Foggyfurze Fenman – Ch Moorside Summer Song) ex Ch Moorside Quite Quaint (Ch Foggyfurze Fenman – Moorside Joyful Julie).

HIGHDENE SOLITAIRE 1631BY, Mr & Mrs C. Richardson, br. Owners, 3.7.87, blue, s. Ch Rathsrigg Rule (Ch Rathsrigg Ruin – Rathsrigg Rosa) ex Diamonds Delight (Ch Avilas Lucky Lad of Foggyfurze – Princess Jewel).

INDEX OF CHALLENGE CERTIFICATE WINNERS SINCE 1930

DOGS

Year of first win

AMERDALE HALF NELSON	1959
AMERDALE AVIATOR	1963
AMERDALE DEFIANT	1968
AVILAS AT LAST	1976
AVILAS ARIES OF FOGGYFURZE	1976
AVILAS LUCKY LAD OF FOGGYFURZE	1976
AURABLEUE ASHMOW ALICK	1982
BARNSNAP BRIGADIER	1984
BIRKONBRAE BRONZE BACCIIUS	1973
BIRKONBRAE BLEU BRAGGADOCIO	1977
BLA SKUGGANS MOVIE STAR	1981
BOJEN BARNABY	1989
BOUGHTON BLUFF	1978
BRAMBLEDENE BUCCANEER	1938
BRAMBLEDENE BARON	1947
BRAMBLEDENE BRENDAN	1948
BREDONVALE SMOKY JOE	1975
BRENTBROOK GAY BOY	1973
BRIGHT LAD	1948
BRICKBATS BROUGHTON	1981
CAERULEUS CORINTHIAN	1974
CHARTLANDS FAIR DINKUM	1962
CLOVERWAY, BLUE PIP OF	1956
COPPER ROGUE	1963
CRAGLOUGH DENARIUS	1973
CRAGLOUGH CHERUBINO	1985
CRISPINO, THE COUNT OF	1986
CULLERCOATS, WOODMAN OF	1977
CULLERCOATS, WILLOW OF	1981
CULLERCOATS, TICKERTON HODDER SHERRY OF	1980
CUT, CURLY	1949
CUT, TRIPLE	1955
CUT, GENTS	1956
CUT, FLASHY	1962
DALIP HUGGY BEAR	1978
DALIP BOY GEORGE OF SOLLSTICE	1989
DANCERS PRIDE	1954
DAUNTLESS DINGO	1950
FANTASTIC LUCKY BLUE	1988
FOGGYFURZE ACE HIGH	1936

FOGGYFURZE CLASSIC CUT	1953
FOGGYFURZE CLASSIC	1955
FOGGYFURZE CLASSICAL	1956
FOGGYFURZE SHOOTING STAR	1957
FOGGYFURZE TEXAN	1959
FOGGYFURZE DRUMBEAT	1960
FOGGYFURZE DANDY	1961
FOGGYFURZE STATACCO	1963
FOGGYFURZE FLAMINGO	1968
FOGGYFURZE FAN FARE	1969
FOGGYFURZE FANGIO	1970
FOGGYFURZE FANDANGO	1974
FOGGYFURZE, AVILAS ARIES OF	1976
FOGGYFURZE, AVILAS LUCKY LAD OF	1976
FOGGYFURZE FENMAN	1977
FOGGYFURZE FINE FARE	1978
FOGGYFURZE FOREVER	1978
FOXINGTON, GOLDSTRIKE OF	1949
FOXINGTON, GAY BOY OF	1950
FOXINGTON, GOLD COIN OF	1964
GARDENERS PARAGON	1936
GARDENERS IMPERIAL	1937
GARDENERS FIDELITY	1938
GOLD CLASSIC	1968
GOOD KNIGHT	1939
GORSEA, PILOT OF	1961
GRANITOR FLINT	1975
GRANITOR ROCKET MAN	1978
HEATHFIELD, FRIAR OF	1948
HEATHFIELD, GAMBOL OF	1950
HIGHLAND DUKE	1948
HIGHQUEST HIGH MIST	1968
JENASH JUST A DREAMER	1989
JONASH GENTLEMAN	1952
JUVERNA LORD LIVER OF PITT	1953
LAMPLIGHTER	1938
LAVERS LANCER	1938
LEASOWES TRY AGAIN	1954
LEASOWES TANGO	1974
LINDUM LIGHTNING	1948
LINDUM HIGH OCTANE OF VISTABLU	1958
LIEBERLAMB LIKELY LAD	1977
LIEBERLAMB LADDIE SIM	1980
LIEBERLAMB LESTER	1983

MAHIDAP, BLUEPRINT OF	1954	STANOLLY SCOOBY DOO	1971
MAHIDAP, REDBOY OF	1959	STANOLLY SHOOBY DO A	1975
MANATON, GOLDEN SUN OF	1953	STANOLLY SHANG-A-LANG	1975
MANATON, BLUE RODNEY OF	1954	STANOLLY SHIROCO	1977
MARLISH BLUE STONE	1984	STANOLLY SUPERFLASH	1979
MAYDEW MOONRAKER	1961	STANOLLY SUPER SWANK	1981
MAYDEW MOUNTAIN MUSIC	1964	STANOLLY STARBURST	1984
MOSCAR RED ENSIGN	1950	STANOLLY STUPENDOUS LAD	1986
MOORSIDE DANDY DOLPHIN	1970	SATNOLLY SUNNY ROMERO	1988
MOORSIDE FREDDIE FOX	1972	STURNBAY STUPENDOUS	1975
MOORSIDE LUCKY LAD	1977		
MOORSIDE SO YOUR SAMMY	1983	TOL-PEDN SMUGGLER	1952
MOORSIDE VICTOR IS NO VAGRANT	1985	TOL-PEDN HOODWINK	1958
		TOL-PEDN SEADOG	1958
NABLUS, NOVELLO OF	1955	TOL-PEDN FRIGATE	1962
NADWORNA STATESMAN	1963	TOL-PEDN SACHMO	1965
NONINGTON, HENRY OF	1939	TOL-PEDN RED CLOUD	1976
NONINGTON, NORBERT OF	1952	TOL-PEDN, RED EAGLE OF	1981
NONINGTON, WORKMAN OF	1958	TICKERTON HODDER SHERRY	
NONINGTON, JASPER OF	1959	OF CULLERCOATS	1980
NORTHCOTE WILL STRIKE	1964	TURTONHEIGHTS BLUE GALLANT	1975
NORTHCOTE TERPO	1965	TYNECOURT TROOPER	1982
NORTHCOTE LUCKY MARK	1968	TYNECOURT TALLY HO	1984
PETACREST PATRON SAINT	1978	VARDENE BLUE GRENADIER	1968
PETACREST PSALM	1981	VARDENE BLUE GUARDSMAN	1971
PITT, DUNMAIL OF	1939	VARDENE BLUE MARKSMAN	1974
PITT, BRACKNEL ROWLAND OF	1948	VISTABLU, LITTLE WILLIE OF	1958
PITT, RULER OF	1949	VISTABLU, FREDDIE THE GENT OF	1965
PITT, BRIGHTSTONE		VISTABLU, FANCYPANTS OF	1966
SUNFLOWER OF	1949	VISTABLU, BLUE HAPPENING OF	1969
PITT, INGRAM OF	1951	VISTABLU BEN FRANKLIN OF	
PHINDOL BLUE DOLPHIN	1975	BLUE HAPPENING	1980
PIPER'S SUCCESS	1938	VISTABLU NELSON TOUCH	1985
PYNELLO JACQUES	1939		
		WELHEAD WARRANT	1949
RAG A TAIL	1950	WESTFEN PANTHER	1952
RATHSRIGG LITTLE CEASAR	1964	WEDERBI HOUGHTOP INVADER	1960
RATHSRIGG KINGS PAWN	1974	WEDERBI MINTING	1961
RATHSRIGG RUIN	1977	WINFELL RUSTLER	1982
RATHSRIGG REUBEN	1981	WINFELL RAIDER	1984
RATHSRIGG RULE	1982	WINFELL RAMBLER	1986
RATHSRIGG RAGS	1988	WETOP, GUNMETAL OF	1960
ROGATE, TITUS OF	1939	WETOP, BUTTONS OF	1962
		WETOP, TWEEDLEDEE OF	1963
SEVRAY SINGING SAILOR	1985	WETOP, ROB ROY OF	1965
SHENSTONE MASTER MACK	1959	WETOP AQUARIUS	1971
SHENSTONE NEW ORBIT	1961	WETOP FREE LANCE	1972
SIMONSIDE, ROBIN OF	1937	WETOP NUTMEG	1976
SIMONSIDE, LIVESPARK OF	1938	WETOP GAY KNIGHT	1978
SPENNYMOOR, CANNY LAD OF	1985	WETOP TIGHT ROPE	1979
STANOLLY SPORTS TOSCA	1964	WETOP PARSLEY	1982
STANOLLY SUPERSTAR	1966	WETOP SILVER SPUR	1982
STANOLLY STARBLAZE	1967	WRINSTONE, REQUEST OF	1937
STANOLLY SANDPIPER	1969		
STANOLLY SPECTACULAR	1970	YOMA, PILGRIM OF	1952

CHALLENGE CERTIFICATE WINNERS

BITCHES

AMERDALE DELIGHT	1959
AMERDALE ASTRALITA	1964
AMERDALE AMANDA	1965
AMERDALE DELICIOUS	1968
AMERDALE ATTRACTIVE	1971
AURABLEUE ADELA	1982
AVILAS BARMAID	1978
AZURE ATTRACTION	1950
BARNSNAP BALLERINA	1987
BERENGREAVE PINK PERRY ,	1968
BERENGREAVE PERSONALITY	1970
BERENGREAVE PERSONAL	
PROPERTY	1972
BIRKONBRAE BLEU BUNNY	1972
BIRKONBRAE BRONZE BON BON	1973
BIRKONBRAE BRONZE BRIGHTISE	1974
BIRKONBRAE BRONZE	
BACCHANTE	1978
BIRKONBRAE BRONZE	
BACCHIQUE	1980
BIRKONBRAE BLEU BUBBLICIOUS	1980
BLUE SEA, SHEILA OF	1950
BLA SKUGGANS NEXT STAR	1981
BOJEN BIANCA	1984
BOJEN BELLE AMIE	1988
BOUGHTON NORTHCOTE	
LUCKY STONE	1962
BRAMBLEDENE BELINDA	1948
BRAMBLEDENE BRENDA	1949
BRAMBLEDENE BLUE BEAUTY	1950
BRAMBLEDENE BONNIE	1951
BRAMBLEDENE BRINELLA	1952
BRENTBROOK PRECIOUS GEM	1979
BRIGHTSTONE HARMONY	1937
BRIGHTSTONE FLAME	1939
BRYNSIRE MORNING MELODY	1986
BURLEYDENE MISCHIEF	1952
BYSTOCK MACK'S GOLDEN PEARL	1968
BYSTOCK BLUE PEARL	1975
CAERULEUS CELTIC	1984
CINDERELLA	1959
CLAYDALE, GLORIA OF	1951
CRAGLOUGH, DOOLEY OF	1972
CRAGLOUGH KITTIWAKE	1975
CRAGLOUGH, TABITHA OF	1976
CRAGLOUGH COMFREY	1979
CRAGLOUGH CELESTE	1980
CRAGLOUGH CALINKA	1982
CRAGLOUGH CONSTANTIA	1985
CRAGLOUGH CORYANTHUS	1987
CULLERCOATS CINDERELLA	1948
CULLERCOATS, CINNAMON OF	1986

CUT, RUFFLE	1956
CUT, SPRING	1958
CUT, ATOMIC	1962
DALEVIEW DELMA	1952
DALEVIEW DAWN	1956
DALEVIEW DAME	1958
DALEVIEW SHENSTONE	
AMBER LASS	1963
DALIP PETRANELLO	1976
DALIP VENUS IN BLUE GENES	1985
DALIP UPTOWN GIRL	1987
DANCERS DESIRE	1985
ELCROFT LILLY LADY	1983
FOGGYFURZE STARLIGHT	1939
FOGGYFURZE GLAMOROUS	1946
FOGGYFURZE TAILOR MAID	1947
FOGGYFURZE CUTE CUT	1954
FOGGYFURZE LINDY LOU	1956
FOGGYFURZE BABY MINE	1956
FOGGYFURZE SUGAR BABY	1956
FOGGYFURZE SUGAR PUSS	1958
FOGGYFURZE DELAWARE DOLL	1959
FOGGYFURZE HONEY CHILE	1962
FOGGYFURZE FAN TAN	1963
FOGGYFURZE FESTIVAL	1969
FOGGYFURZE FENWICK	1974
FOGGYFURZE, AVILAS ATHENE OF	1975
FOGGYFURZE FONDANT	1977
FOGGYFURZE FLUTTER	1978
FOGGYFURZE FIFI	1980
FOLLY	1938
FOXINGTON, SALLY OF	1947
FOXINGTON, BLUEBELL OF	1951
GOLDEN ARROW	1964
HARNISH, CUCKOO OF	1938
HIGHDENE SOLITAIRE	1989
HIGHQUEST HOLLY GIRL	1968
HILLDYKE ARKADINA	1976
HILLDYKE LADY MADELINE	1989
IRON DUCHESS	1939
JOYVENTURE	1948
KARSWELL CASSADORA	1952
KNOTTS BLUEBELL	1958
LEASOWES, ANGELINA OF	1952
LEASOWES DANCING SHADOW	1971
LIEBERLAMB LUCINDA	1973
LIEBERLAMB LEANDER	1974

LIEBERLAMB LUCKY STAR	1976	PENDRILL, JOCASTER OF	1950
LIEBERLAMB LOUISE	1978	PENDRILL, JOLANDE OF	1950
LIEBERLAMB, MOORSIDE		PENDRILL, JOANNA OF	1951
VIVACIOUS VIXEN OF	1985	PERRIANNE PETULA	1970
LINDUM LAVENDER	1937	PERRIANNE POPPY	1975
LINDUM LOVE IN THE MIST	1954	PETACREST PERFECT ANGEL	1975
LINDUM LUNARIA	1956	PETACREST BEWITCHING BLUE	1975
LINDUM LAVINIA	1963	PETACREST POLLY WAGTAIL	1984
		PITT, LUCY LOCKET OF	1953
MAHIDAP, BIBSY OF	1959	PYNELLO JANE	1937
MANATON, BLUE DAY OF	1948	PYNELLO PIXIE OF NARE	1951
MANATON, BLUE SKY OF	1951	PYNELLO PRIM	1953
MANATON, BLUE DAWN OF	1952		
MANATON, PAT'S PEACH OF	1956	ROSETOP VICTORIOUS	1948
MANATON, BRIGHT DAY OF	1956	RARE GOLD	1952
MARILENA POLLYANNA	1970	RATHSRIGG RAFFLE	1977
MAYDEW MISS MURIEL	1963	RATHSRIGG REGIUS	1979
MELJOY JULIET DEMESNE	1961	RATHSRIGG ROSE	1980
MISTIBLEU SINDERELLA	1988	RATHSRIGG RAZE	1982
MOORSRAIKE MOONLIGHT	1949	RATHSRIGG RINA	1987
MOORSIDE DAINTY DENISE	1970	RATHSRIGG ROMANCE	1987
MOORSIDE QUITE QUAINT	1980	RATHSRIGG RANI	1988
MOORSIDE SUMMER SONG	1983		
MOORSIDE UPPER UTOPIA	1985	SILVER SOLITAIRE	1965
MOORSIDE VIVACIOUS VIXEN		SIMONSIDE, TRUE JOY OF	1937
OF LIEBERLAMB	1985	SIMONSIDE, LEADING LADY OF	1938
MOORSIDE BONNY BLOSSOM	1987	SINGLETON GINGER BREAD LADY	1977
MOORSIDE URSULA ULA AT		SPRING DANCER	1950
HILLDYKE	1988	SPRITRESS	1949
MOORSIDE EVER SO ELEGANT		STUTEVILLE STARLETTE	1949
AT COTTONTOPS	1989	STANOLLY SAPPHIRE	1960
MOORSIDE I SPY ELEANOR		STANOLLY SPORTS TIPPI	1965
AT COTTONTOPS	1989	STANOLLY SUNSPRITE	1965
MOORSIDE DAWNS DELIGHT		STANOLLY SUNBLUSH	1966
AT FURROLLY	1989	STANOLLY CRYSTAL BELLE	1968
MOSCAR RED RASCAL	1951	STANOLLY STARBOW	1971
		STANOLLY SECRET SURPRISE	1972
NABLUS, NAOMI OF	1950	STANOLLY SCOOBY'S SOLO	1973
NABLUS, NONA OF	1953	STANOLLY SCOOSTAR TIPSY	1974
NABLUS, NITA OF	1955	STANOLLY SUNSTAR	1974
NARE, CHRISELDA OF	1949	STANOLLY SUKINA	1975
NEWBOTTLE NEW LOOK	1951	STANOLLY SUMMER LUV	1976
NONINGTON, CHERRY OF	1937	STANOLLY, WHISPERING SONG OF	1977
NONINGTON, CHARM OF	1938	STANOLLY SUMMER DELIGHT	1979
NONINGTON, HENRIETTA OF	1938	STANOLLY, STAR AUDITION OF	1979
NONINGTON, LORETTE OF	1949	STANOLLY CELESTIAL DREAM	1984
NONINGTON, NALLA OF	1951	STANOLLY SILVER TRINKET	1985
NONINGTON, AMANDA		STANOLLY SUPER FLARE	1985
MIRABEAU OF	1954	STANOLLY RISING STAR	1986
NORTHCOTE LUCKY STRIKE	1960	STANOLLY SPRINGTIME MELODY	1986
NORTHCOTE STRIKE AGAIN	1964	STANOLLY SILVER BELL	1987
NORTHCOTE BLUE DAWN	1966	SUGAR IS SWEET	1989
NORTHCOTE AILEEN	1968		
		TIDDLYMOUNT, REPRINT OF	1978
OLDPOST, DINA MITE OF	1973	TINKERBLOO CHIC ANGELIQUE	1982
OLDPOST, DAISY MAY OF	1966	TOL-PEDN MERRY MAID	1949

TOL-PEDN MERMAID	1953	VISTABLU FLY THE FLAG AT	
TOL-PEDN FAIRMAID	1955	SEVRAY	1985
TOL-PEDN BALLERINA	1959	VISTABLU NORA BATTY	1988
TOL-PEDN, PENTAVY FIREDANCE OF	1963		
TYNECOURT, TUPPENCE OF	1980	WEDERBI DAWN CHORUS	1963
TYNECOURT, MOORSIDE		WELHEAD WIDEAWAKE	1936
TINKER TAILOR OF	1984	WESTFEN VIVANDIERE	1954
		WETOP, MISS MUFFET OF	1961
VARDENE AMAREE OF CANZO	1967	WETOP, ROULETTE OF	1965
VARDENE GOLDEN GIRL	1968	WETOP, PEWTER GREY OF	1970
VARDENE, GOLD DUST OF	1977	WETOP BLUE VELVET	1973
VARDENE BLUE WITCHCRAFT	1978	WETOP BLUE OPAL	1974
VARDENE, UKWONG		WETOP MEG	1981
SEPTEMBER DAWN OF	1979	WETOP SOPHIE	1983
VARDENE BLUE TREASURE	1984	WETOP, BLUE DIAMOND OF	1986
VERANNA MISS VALENTINE	1982	WHICKHAM MERRY DUCHESS	1976
VERANNA BLUE VENUS	1987	WOODMANSEY WASPISH	1952
VISTABLU, SHENSTONE BLUE		WOODMANSEY WASPY	1957
BLISS OF	1960	WOODROW WATER NYMPH	1936
VISTABLU, DOLLY ROCKER OF	1968	WOODROW WITCH GIRL	1936
VISTABLU, TUPPENCE OFF OF	1971	WOODROW WAIT	1939
VISTABLU WONDER WOMAN	1981	WRINSTONE, REALITY OF	1938

NOTABLE DOGS SINCE 1937

It is difficult to choose a short list of animals for special mention. Some famous dogs may not have merited their exalted position and, conversely, some beautiful specimens were not shown sufficiently to gain prominence. Also, Bedlington people have not always appreciated the photographer's art and many important animals were never photographed. Too many of our illustrations fail to give a true impression of the subject. However, the following pages seek to do justice to dogs who have contributed something to the breed.

Comments are made that may throw some light on why certain virtues and faults are with the breed today. It is not the intention to belittle any dog and it is as well to remember the words of Rosslyn Bruce that there is not a dog alive without, at least, three faults. Degree of fault is our measure.

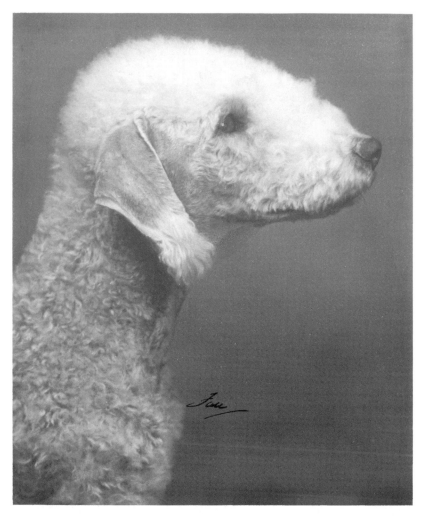

Champion Pynello Jane (Ch Woodrow Wizard – Petanis) 1936. Owned by Doctor Muriel Binns and bred by R. G. Couley. The ideal head and expression. (Thomas Fall).

Champion Brambledene Buccaneer (Ch Woodrow Wizard – Welhead Whisper) 1937. Owned and bred by Miss E. E. Marsh. The perfect coat. An excellent dog but his owner responsibly withdrew him from public when it was discovered he transmitted the corny feet of his granddam, Khaki. Was in the last six for Best in Show at the 1939 Crufts. (Thomas Fall).

Dunmail of Pitt (Ch Minimum of Simonside – Knowlton Prudence) 1937. Owned and bred by Mrs A. Best. A winner of two Challenge Certificates before the war put an end to his chances of becoming a Champion which he deserved to be. A great stud force.

Pynello Jacques 1 C.C. (Lamplighter – Ch Pynello Jane) 1939. Owned and bred by Dr Muriel Binns. A second important stud force born at a time when the war prevented a dog becoming a Champion. However, Jacques returned to the ring at the age of 11 years and won the C.C. at the Bedlington Terrier Association championship show under Mrs Ben Holgate. (Thomas Fall).

Champion Foggyfurze Glamorous (Rye of Pitt – Faithful Lass) 1944. Owned by Fred Gent and bred by A. Belgian. The first postwar Champion.

Champion Lindum Lightning. (Pynello Jacques – Lindum Lobelia) 1943. Owned by H. Winder and bred by Mrs F. Franks. The first postwar Champion male. (Thomas Fall).

Champion Foggyfurze Tailor Maid (Lamplighter – Silla Lass) 1945. Owned by Fred Gent and bred by Mrs S. L. Barras. The photograph shows her with Bill Taylor, the man that Fred Gent declared taught him all he knew about Bedlingtons.

Champion Golden Sun of Manaton. (Robin of Bracken – Ch Blue Day of Manaton) 1952. Owned by Mr and Mrs C. G. Worrall and bred by Mr Worrall. One of the best ever with the perfect head. (C. M. Cooke).

Champion Rag-a-tail (Ch Lindum Lighning – Newlyn Fashion) 1948. Owned by Mrs M. M. Taunt and bred by E. J. C. Furze.

Champion Spring Dancer (Ch Brambledene Brendan – Bounty Blue) 1948. Owned and bred by Norman Stead. A superb show specimen and winner-producer. An ideal size. Worked successfully with fox.

Ch Foggyfurze Classic (Ch Curly Cut – Foggyfurze Acey Ducey) 1954. Owned and bred by Fred Gent. Very successful show career but must be remembered as one of the most successful and influential sires of all time.

Champion Goldstrike of Foxington (Livespark of Foxington – Ch Moorsraike Moonlight) 1948. Owned and bred by H. Winder. A true terrier not as short in back as the photograph would indicate.

273

Champion Tol-pedn Fairmaid (Ch Golden Sun of Manaton – Ch Tol-pedn Mermaid) 1954. Owned by Ken Bounden and C. D. Adamson and bred by O. Gowing. The first Bedlington to win Best in Show at an English Championship show – the L.K.A. 1957. Bred from a litter containing three Champions, her brothers Ch Wederbi Houghtop Invader and Foggyfurze Eclipse both sired Champions and Fairmaid produced Champions in each of three litters. (C. M. Cooke).

Champion Wederbi Houghtop Invader (Ch Golden Sun of Manaton – Ch Tol-pedn Mermaid) 1954. Owned and bred by O. Gowing. Used to improve heads in the Foggyfurze time. (Anne Roslin-Williams).

English and American Champion Foggyfurze Sugar Baby 1955. Owned in England by Fred Gent and in America by Virden and Jessie Wilson. Was the first Bedlington to win Best in Show at a British all breed show (the Scottish Kennel Club). (C. M. Cooke).

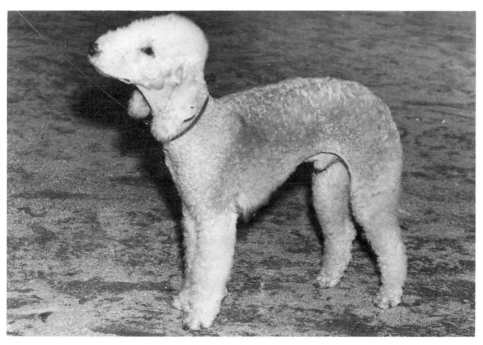

Champion Sheenstone Master Mack (Ch Leasowes Try Again – Ginger Popinette of Oldpost) 1957. Owned and bred by E. Smith. Spent latter part of his life in the ownership of Miss V. Duckworth-Bradshaw. (Sport and General Press Agency).

Champion Cinderella (Ch Goldstrike of Foxington – Storm Cloud) 1957. Owned and bred by W. Topham (Eric Curtis).

English and Argentine Champion Freddie the Gent of Vistablu (Foggyfurze High Hat – Ch Shenstone Blue Bliss of Vistablu) 1963. Owned and bred in England by Mrs I. Sills and exported to Susanna Saevich and brother Carlos Saevich, of Argentina. Established the breed in South America as foundation sire mated to American bred bitches and later English imports. (B. R. Hobbs).

Champion Amerdale Amanda (Amerdale Aviator – Amerdale Blue Belle) 1963. Owned and bred by Mrs A. Clark. Held record as top winning Bedlington for some years by winning 23 C.C.s.

Champion Vardene Blue Grenadier (Ch Stanolly Starblaze – Vardene Golden Gem) 1967. Owned and bred by Mrs B. Clifton. Best in Show and Group winner.

Champion Stanolly Scooby Doo (Ch Stanolly Sandman – Stanolly Crystal Belle) 1970. Owned and bred by Mrs O. Stones. The top winning dog of his day beating all previous records of C.C.s and Best in Show and Group awards. (Campbells).

Caeruleus Corinthian (Ch Rathsrigg Little Caesar – Caeruleus Clovette) 1971. Owned by Mrs P. Lay and bred by Mrs I. Bach. Winner of two C.C.s and, but for injury, could have been a champion.

*Foggyfurze Fidella (Cont. Ch Foggyfurze Ferrari – Foggyfurze Francesca) c. 1974.
Owned and bred by Fred Gent. A great winner producer.*

*Champion Wetop Gay Knight (Swank of Wetop – Duett of Wetop) 1974. Owned and
bred by W. Topham.*
  *A good winner but more successful as a sire, producing quality stock with
regularity. Must influence the future of the breed.*

Champion Birkonbrae Blue Braggadocio (Ch Stanolly Scooby Doo – Blue Bacchic of Birkonbrae) 1974. Owned and bred by Mr and Mrs R. J. Anderson.

Champion Avilas Lucky Lad of Foggyfurze (Ch Stanolly Scooby Doo – Stanfos Blue Choice) 1975. Owned by Fred Gent and bred by Mrs E. Johnson. Three times Best of Breed at Crufts and sire of many winners to a variety of bitch lines.

Champion Foggyfurze Fenman (Ch Foggyfurze Fan Fare – Foggyfurze Fidella) 1975. Owned and bred by Fred Gent. A prepotent sire that served the breed well.

Champion Rathsrigg Ruin (Ch Granitor Flint – Rathsrigg Check Mate) 1976. Owned and bred by Mr and Mrs I. Phillips. Successful in the ring and a great sire. (Dog World).

Champion Dalip Huggy Bear (Ch Stanolly Shang a Lang – Dalip Petranello) 1976. Owned and bred by Mrs P. Hall. Three times winner of Best of Breed at Crufts. (Barry Greenwood).

Champion Willow of Cullercoats (Caeruleus Corinthian – Highquest Honor) 1977. Owned by Mrs P. Lay and bred by Mrs A. Norgate (Frank Goswood).

Champion Moorside Summer Song (Ch Avilas Lucky Lad of Foggyfurze – Ch Moorside Quite Quaint) 1981. Owned and bred by R. Ratcliffe. (Datton).

Champion Lieberlamb Lester (Swirley-mist Sensation – Ch Lieberlamb Louise) 1981. Owned and bred by Mrs M. Sugden. (Frank Goswood).

Champion Winfell Raider (Ch Winfell Rustler – Winfell Blueberry) 1983. Owned and bred by Mrs N. Y. Greenland.

Champion Craglough Cherubino (Ch Rathsrigg Reuben – Ch Craglough Calinka) 1984. Owned and bred by Miss Dorothy Aitkenhead.

Champion Vistablu Nelson Touch (Ch Aurableue Ashmow Alick – Ch Vistablu Wonder Woman) 1984. Owned and bred by Mrs Ida Sills. Top winning Bedlington of all time. (E. T. Gascoigne).

APPENDICES

APPENDIX 1
COPPER TOXICOSIS

Advances in knowledge mean that these days we are aware of problems in animals and humans that no one dreamed of in the past. What were once sad mysteries are now so often diagnosed as specific disorders. Very many breeds are afflicted with hereditary faults and the Bedlington is no exception. Some are affected with Copper Toxicosis, a condition when the animal fails to get rid of excess copper which builds up in the liver. It is one of those strange conditions when an animal can be affected yet live a perfectly normal life, finally dying of old age. However, sometimes something stressful will trigger off a fatal illness in an affected subject. The dog becomes listless, jaundiced, vomits, dehydrates and dies within four days. Because the Bedlington was the first breed in which research was extensively done it was stupidly known as the 'Bedlington Disease'. At the time of writing, it is claimed in the United States that at least 24 breeds have the problem, ranging from West Highland Whites to Dobermans.

The condition is hereditary and it is obvious that breeds would be in danger of extinction if the problem were ignored and (unknowingly) only affected dogs were used for breeding. Sensible people who love the breed, and have a sense of responsibility, have their stock biopsied to discover whether they are affected. If it is, then a low copper diet and medication can be given. If the dog is not affected, it could still carry the undesirable gene and test-mating to an affected animal will prove whether or not it is a carrier. If five or more whelps result and all biopsy normal at six months of age, then the unaffected dog can be statistically classified as a non-carrier or clear. Of course the puppies will be carriers. If one does not test-mate but biopsy only, then the policy should be to mate a biopsied healthy animal to a similar one or, better still, to a proven non-carrier. The tables show the pattern of inheritance and the statistical reliability values of test-mating. Stud dogs and brood bitches of unknown status that have not been biopsied should be autopsied at death. Although too late for planned breeding, the information for geneticists to study could be of great value – especially in the case of much used animals. An arrangement made during a routine visit to the vet will eliminate the additional trauma of mentioning an autopsy when an old friend reaches the end of his days. No valid excuse can be made by an owner who has been ready to accept stud fees yet unwilling to seek the truth for the benefit of the breed.

The biopsy method normally used on the Bedlington is different to that for the human being, where a special hollow needle is inserted under local anaesthetic and a small section of the liver removed for examination. This is too dangerous for a flat sided, deep chested animal such as the Bedlington as the organ is not so readily located and an inexpert hand can pierce the gall bladder. In the biopsy of the Bedlington the animal should be given an anaesthetic and approximately a two inch incision made through which the surgeon reaches the liver and removes a piece the size of a match head. The operation is no more traumatic than spaying a bitch. The dog is dopey from the affects of the anaesthetic for a period of about 24 hours and is then back to its normal, lively state, dashing about the garden like a wild thing.

There are those who, for varying reasons (and not always honourable) have refused to co-operate in ridding the breed of the problem. Some, for motives best known to themselves, have opposed biopsy, spread stupid scare stories and even denigrated those working for the benefit of the breed. A 100 percent co-operation would have made the task easier but the dedicated are making progress and winning, healthy animals are being produced.

One of the silly claims made was that by breeding for healthy animals we would lose quality in the breed. That fallacy has been shown again and again for what it really is – nonsense.

It is hoped that true lovers of the breed will work together for the Bedlington and its future. Neither complacency nor panic are wanted but commonsense and responsibility should be the order of the day.

PATTERN OF INHERITANCE

Parents	Offspring
● + ● =	● ● ● ●
● + ◑ =	● ● ◑ ◑ ★
◑ + ◑ =	● ◑ ◑ ○
◑ + ○ =	◑ ◑ ○ ○
● + ○ =	◑ ◑ ◑ ◑ ★
○ + ○ =	○ ○ ○ ○

● = AFFECTED

◑ = CARRIER

○ = CLEAR

★ Possible test mating result when it is impossible to identify a carrier by other means.

- By following the above rules and breeding only from tested stock it is possible to produce clear from affected in two generations.

- Unfortunately , if the rules are ignored , the reverse is also true.

- Test mating is presently the only way to differentiate between carrier and clear animals.

STATISTICAL PERCENT RELIABILITY IN TESTMATING AN UNKNOWN DOG BY MATING WITH A KNOWN AFFECTED, CARRIER OR CLEAR DOG. (ANY RECESSIVE GENE)
97% to 100% is considered acceptable determining a test prospect.

Number of Biopsied Normal Puppies	Mated to Affected	Mated to Carrier	Mated to Clear
	%	%	
1	50	25	0
2	75	43.75	0
3	87.5	57.8	0
4	93.75	68.35	0
5	96.9	76.25	0
6	98.5	82.2	0
7	99.25	86.65	0
8	99.62	90	0
9	99.71	92.5	0
10	99.9	94.4	0
11		95.8	0
12		96.85	0
13		97.64	0
14		98.23	0
15		98.58	0
16		98.9	0
17		99.2	0
18		99.4	0
19		99.55	0
20		99.66	0

Using an affected to test an unknown, a resulting litter of 5 (with normal liver) is an acceptable result. Using a carrier, a total of 12 puppies would be required. This would mean two or more litters.

APPENDIX 2
GLOSSARY OF TERMS

The following are taken from the general doggy jargon as being applicable to the Bedlington terrier. It has to be realised that, in the world of dogs, expressions and terms are used that are incorrect, indeed meaningless, in normal use outside the fancy.

ACTION	Movement or gait.
AFFIX	Kennel name registered at the Kennel Club.
ALL-ROUNDER	A judge capable of judging a wide variety of breeds.
ANGULATION	Normally refers to the angle at the stifle but can refer to the angle formed at shoulder, elbow or hock.
ANORCHIDISM	The condition where one, or both, testicles are not placed in the scrotum. It is not necessary to go into the technicalities of monorchidism (one testis descended) or cryptorchidism (neither descended) but suffice to say that these conditions are highly undesirable. The fault is sometimes hereditary and one cannot condemn too strongly the use of afflicted stock for breeding purposes. The ultimate possibility of producing sterile dogs should prove the foolhardiness of ignoring the defect.
BAD FEET	See CORNY FEET.
BALANCE	See QUALITY.
BEEFY	Thick, heavy, sturdy.
BITCH	Female.
BITCHY	Feminine looking male.·
BITE	Meeting of the teeth.
BLOOM	Healthy condition with particular reference to coat.
BLOWN COAT or COAT ON THE BLOW	When the coat is dying.
BODIED	Mature in body.
BOSSY	Overloaded in shoulder muscle.
BRISKET	Lower region of ribcage between the forelegs.
CAMEL BACK	Incorrect formation of the backline with a high point just behind the withers from which

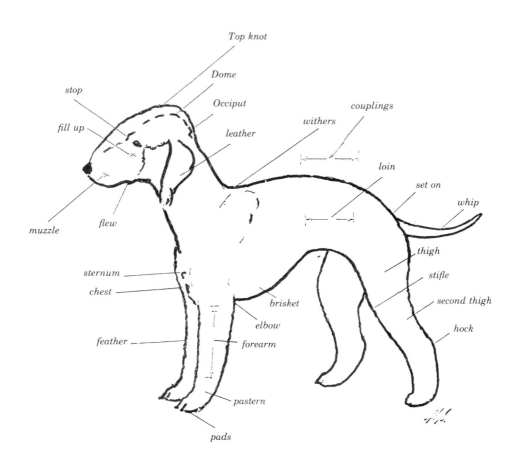

Top knot

Dome

stop

Occiput

couplings

fill up

withers

leather

loin

set on

whip

muzzle

flew

thigh

stifle

sternum

second thigh

chest

brisket

hock

feather

elbow

forearm

pastern

pads

POINTS OF THE DOG

the spine falls away in a straight line to the tail root. A bad fault.

CAT FOOT   Short, round foot. A fault in this breed.

CHALLENGE CERTIFICATE   Awarded to the best of each sex in a breed at certain Championship shows. It states, 'I am clearly of the opinion that No. . . . is of such outstanding merit as to be worthy of the title of Champion' and is signed by the judge on the day. The judge has the duty and the right to withold the award if he considers the best animals present are not of sufficiently high standard. Each breed has a limited number of certificates allotted to it annually, the number being reviewed by the Kennel Club and adjusted according to the number of entries in the breed at the previous year's shows. Often referrcd to as the C.C. or Ticket.

CHAMPION   Dog that has won three Challenge Certificates under three different judges, one after the age of 12 months. Overseas, other systems are used to qualify a dog for the title. The quality of Champions will, naturally, vary in different parts of the world and the Kennel Club, rightly, does not recognise the title International Champion. It is unfortunate, indeed regrettable, that, whilst a foreign title is always published in catalogues, etc. in this country the practice is not always reciprocated abroad. Why the Kennel Club has not insisted on common courtesy is an irritant to many British breeders.

CHAMPIONSHIP SHOW   Show where the Kennel Club has allocated sets of Challenge Certificates for competition. Not all breeds classified at a general Championship show have Certificates on offer.

CHANCE BRED   Good quality animal bred from indifferent stock and, therefore, unlikely to transmit its own good points.

CHEST   Part enclosed by ribcage.

CHISELLING   Refined shaping of contours, usually in reference to head.

CLODDY   Thick set, heavy build. A fault.

COBBY   Short in back and very compact in build. A fault in the breed.

COARSE   Lacking quality.

CORNY FEET,   Condition found in Bedlingtons, Dandie

CRACKED FEET	Dinmonts and Irish Terriers when the pads are hard, split and have excessive growth at the edges. Causes great discomfort to the dog and renders it useless as a worker. It is a symptom of a deficiency in the animal's system and 'cures' have been claimed with daily doses of vitamin H throughout the dog's natural life. The condition is hereditary and on no account should afflicted stock be used for breeding. To see a beautiful, faithful creature hobbling painfully on three legs is heartrending.
COUPLINGS	That part between the last rib and the hip.
CLOSE COUPLED	Short in couplings. A fault in the breed.
COVERING GROUND	Amount of ground covered by a dog in stance or on the move.
COW HOCKED	Hocks turned inwards as in the stance of a cow, a fault showing weakness of the hindquarters or lack of courage.
CRYPTORCHID	See Anorchidism.
DAM	Female parent.
DEW CLAWS	Fifth claw (thumb) an inch or so up the inside of the leg. Generally considered useless, opinion varies as to whether or not they should be removed; sometimes grow to a length that is a hindrance to the dog, catching on objects. Some assert it is of value to the dog when working. Removal best left to the experienced person in the first few days of a puppy's life.
DEWLAP	Loose skin hanging from the throat. A fault in any terrier. Sometimes called 'throatiness'. Whilst this state is undesirable it must be said that lack of easy mobility of a dog's skin is equally unwanted.
DISH-FACED	Foreface shallow, scooped out under the eye and the nose very slightly upturned. A fault in the Bedlington.
DOME	Skull rounded at the top. A feature of the breed although not as pronounced as in the Cocker Spaniel.
DOWN-FACE	The opposite to dish-faced, fairly common and usually seen with the sleepy eye so desirable in the breed.
DOWN AT PASTERN	Weak pasterns.
ELBOW	Back of upper joint of foreleg.

EX	Out of. Used when referring to the mother of an animal.
FALSE HEAT	In appearance a normal heat but the bitch comes into season again some weeks later. If mated, it should be repeated as she will not conceive on the first heat.
FALSE PREGNANCY	See Phantom pregnancy.
FEATHER, FEATHERING	Longer hair on legs and ears.
FELTED	Matted coat.
FILL-UP	Upper jaw below eye. Should not fall away but be strong and well developed.
FLAT-BONED	Bones of the leg in section. A Bedlington should not have round boned legs.
FLAT-CATCHER	An eye-catching, glamorous animal of inferior quality.
FLAT-SIDED	Ribs sprung but deep and not rounded when nearing sternum.
FLEWS	Pendulous corner of the lower lip. In the Bedlington the lip should be tight with no hint of a flew.
FLYING EARS	Ears not carried close to the cheek, falling further away when the dog points the nose high or when in a wind.
FOREARM	Front leg between elbow and pastern.
FOREHAND	Front part of the dog, including head, neck, chest, shoulders and front legs.
FOREQUARTERS	Front legs and shoulders.
FRINGES	Hair at the tip of the ear. Should never resemble a pom-pom.
FRONT	See forehand. Sometimes referring only to forelegs and chest when viewed from in front of the dog.
GAIT	Movement of legs and feet according to breed and speed.
GASKINS	Muscles between stifle and hock. Should be well developed in working and sporting breeds.
GAY, GAY CARRIAGE, GAY TAIL	Tail carried over the back. Not to be confused with carriage above the line of the back.
GOOSE RUMP	Ugly, round rump usually combining steep croup, lack of thigh muscle and limited stride.
GUARD HAIRS	Stiff hairs.
GUN BARREL	See Terrier Front.
HACKNEYING	High, short stepping action. A bad fault.

HARE FOOT	Long foot with well arched, strong toes. Pads thick. As in Greyhounds, Whippets and Bedlingtons.
HARE LIP	Lip split beneath the nose.
HAW	Red inner eyelid.
HEAT	Period of menstruation, occurring for the first time between seven and 11 months of age and then at six month intervals. It is becoming more commonplace for bitches to go beyond the normal six months and some have but one heat in the 12 months.
HEIGHT	Measured at the withers.
HERRING GUTTED	See Slab sided.
HINDQUARTERS	Rear part of the dog.
INBREEDING	Breeding to close relative. Brother to sister, half brother to half sister, parent to offspring etc.
LINE BREEDING	Breeding within the family. Animal to grandparent or repeatedly between descendents of a common ancestor.
LOADED SHOULDER	Too much muscle on the shoulder.
LOIN	That part of the side between the last rib and the sacrum.
LONG CAST	Too long in loin.
LUMBER	Too heavy bone.
MONORCHID	See Anorchidism.
MUZZLE	That part of the head forward of the eyes.
OCCIPUT	Peak at the back of the skull.
OPEN FEET	Condition where there is space between the toes, which are spread, not sufficiently arched and generally weak.
OUT OF COAT	Coat in poor condition.
OUT AT ELBOW	Elbows turned away from the rib. A bad fault.
OUTCROSSING	Mating of unrelated stock.
OVERSHOT	The upper incisors ranged in front of the lower with a definite gap between the two.
PACING	Moving of front and back legs of same side at one time.
PADS	Soles of the feet.
PASTERN	That part between foot and wrist.
PEAKED	When occiput is accentuated.
PHANTOM PREGNANCY	Sometimes a bitch will appear to be in whelp, increasing in size, even producing milk, although she has not been mated. After

making a bed and preparing for a family she gradually assumes natural proportions. This wishful thinking does no harm and such bitches usually make good mothers.

A similar performance can take place when a mated bitch does not have puppies. This is known as a false pregnancy.

PIG JAW
Very pronounced overshot condition caused by a short underjaw.

PIG TAIL
Tail with ring at the end.

PINCER JAW, PINCER BITE
When incisors meet in direct alignment, one set above the other.

PLAITING
Crossing of front legs when moving. Must not be confused with the slight rolling action seen at certain speeds in the breed.

POUNDING
Shorter stride of front legs with hesitant, hard step. A bad fault.

QUALITY
Observation on the usage of this word reveals different and, sometimes, confused thinking. When the larger masses of an animal are in correct proportion and relationship, one with another, we can say the subject is balanced. If the small details are in correct proportion, relationship, shape and colour then we can say the animal has quality. An animal can be balanced without having quality and have quality in parts without overall balance.

QUARTERS
See Forequarters and Hindquarters. 'Quarters' without qualifying fore or hind usually refers to the hindquarters.

RACY
Built on lines to suggest ability to gallop at great speed. This is a relative term and on no account should one consider as desirable the extremely 'racy' build of the Whippet. The Bedlington is a terrier, not a racing machine.

REACHY
With long neck.

REGISTRATION
Recorded particulars of a dog's breeding and ownership at the Kennel Club. Registration does not, as is sometimes mistakenly thought, make the owner a member of the Kennel Club.

ROACH
Curve of the back produced by arched loins. Must not be rigid but strong and supple.

SCIMITAR TAIL
Tail gently curved without small radial bends or sudden kinks.

SCISSORS BITE	When the edges of upper incisors are slightly in front of, but still touching the lower.
SEASON	See Heat.
SECOND THIGH	See Gaskins.
SET ON	Position of root of tail at root and ears.
SHALLOW	Applied to the head when it lacks depth, or to body when lacking in depth through the brisket.
SHELLY	Body small and light in proportion and, particularly, lacking substance.
SHORT COUPLED	Short in loin. A fault in this breed.
SICKLE HOCKS	There are now two uses of this term: (1) When the hocks are turned outward (viewed from behind) (2) When there is lack of angulation at the stifle but well bent hocks (viewed from the side).
SICKLE TAIL	See Scimitar Tail.
SINGLE TRACKING	When footprints are in line.
SIRE	Male parent.
SKULLY	Broad or coarse at cheeks.
SLAB-SIDED	Flat sides with insufficient spring of ribs.
SLIPPED PATELLA	Condition where patella is dislocated.
SNIPY	Weak, narrow, pointed foreface. Often found in breeds where there is a craze for exaggerated length of head and narrowness of skull.
SOFT FEET	Toes weak, lacking arch and spring.
SPLAYED FEET	See Open feet.
STEEP SHOULDERS	See Upright shoulders.
STERN	The tail.
STERNUM	Breast bone.
STIFLE	Upper joint of the hind leg.
STILTED	Stiff action from non flexing of the joints.
STRAIGHT IN PASTERN	Vertical pastern. Not correct for a Bedlington.
STRAIGHT IN STIFLE	Actually, it would be correct to say 'straight at stifle'. This is a fault with stilted action and lack of power resulting. Viewed from the side, a Bedlington's hind leg should be bent at the stifle – but not too much and certainly not to the excess of the present day German Shepherd.
STRINGING	Holding the dog's head high, standing or moving, by means of a tight, short, lead. A bad habit not to be indulged.

STOCKY	Solidly built animal. Although not necessarily lacking height, belonging to the shorter group.
STOCKY	A bitch that looks, and is capable of passing on her virtues to her offspring.
STOP	The drop, or step, at the eye, between the skull and the upper end of the foreface.
STUD DOG	Male for breeding purposes.
TERRIER FRONT	Having vertical front legs with narrower chest than is desirable in a Bedlington.
THIGH	Hind leg between hip and stifle.
THROATY	See Dewlap.
THROWBACK	When a dog bears one, or more, features which are not present in its immediate ancestors but found in a distant forebearer, then that dog is referred to as a throwback to that particular ancestor.
THROWOUT	A very poor specimen bred from good stock.
THROWING ELBOWS	Sometimes, a dog that stands correctly will turn out one, or both elbows when on the move.
TIED WITHERS	Wider space between the feet than at the chest.
TIGHT-LIPPED	Having no flews, or looseness, of the lips.
TIMBER	See Lumber.
TOP-KNOT	The silky hair on the top of the skull.
TRANSFER	Record of transfer of ownership at the Kennel Club.
TUCK UP	Belly line in breeds where ribs extend well below that line.
TUCKED UP	Excessive tuck up. Result of exaggerated arching of loin, or insufficient girth at loin.
UNDERSHOT	When the lower incisors are front of the upper. Very serious fault.
UPRIGHT SHOULDERS	Blades narrow and inclined to the vertical when viewed from the side.
VARMINTY	Expression produced by very small, deep set, round eye. Not correct in this breed.
WEAVING	See Plaiting.
WEEDY	Lacking in size and substance.
WHEELBACK	In profile, a symmetrically curved topline from withers to root of tail with little or no suppleness. Unhealthy and undesirable.
WHELP	See Puppy.

WHELPING	Birth of puppies.
WHIP	Tail.
WHIPPETY	Ultra racy build losing terrier characteristics.
WITHERS	Meeting of shoulder blade and back.

APPENDIX 3
MISCELLANY

Many are the tips, ideas, thoughts, warnings, legends, etc. that one picks up in a lifetime in dogs. No group of them could form a chapter with a beginning and an end, having any sense of continuity but, altogether, they make a pot pourri of varying interest and import.

Perfection There never was such a thing as a perfect dog and anyone that boasts that a perfect puppy is at home just waiting the day that it can compete, either has much to learn or is trying to brainwash everyone else in advance.

Crabbing It can be disheartening to the beginner exhibitor to learn that, although his dog wins, it has about every fault in the book. This comes from the sum total of the opinions of rival competitors, each contributing two or three points of criticism. The experienced person welcomes this as he suspects that the dog has the opposition really worried.

Health Hazard at Shows At the busier large shows thousands of people pass along the benches admiring or just looking at the exhibits. Hands reach out, stroke, tickle, grab or pinch the poor dog. The risk of spreading disease is obvious and it is not fair on the dog to subject him to such treatment. A cheap and simple way to protect the dog is to drape a rabbit netting across the front of the bench. Rolled up, the net takes little room in the dog bag and half a dozen clothes pegs or bulldog clips complete the equipment. A secure dog can doze happily until called upon to do his job in the ring. An added health precaution would be the wiping of the bench with disinfectant.

Orphan Dogs Some dog owners feel it necessary to leave instructions that, in the event of their deaths, the dogs owned by them are to be destroyed. No doubt the motive is for the benefit of the animal but this is a narrow and, possibly selfish, attitude. We must not delude ourselves into believing that no other person can give our dogs as good a life as ourselves. There are others just as capable and some even more so. Neither should we fall into the trap of thinking that the dogs will miss us so much as to grieve, for our pals do adjust and adapt themselves to change. If one wishes to safeguard dogs then the wise thing is to appoint someone reliable to find good homes for them. Any that do grieve can be put to sleep but we should give them the chance to enjoy a full life span.

Natural Culling A bitch knows better than us as to what should live and what should die in her brood. Natural culling of the inferior should be permitted and if a mother persistently pushes a whelp aside and refuses to suckle it there is something wrong and it should be allowed to perish. Some breeders in the past always had a bucket of water near a whelping bitch and if there were any obvious runts they were immediately drowned but out of sight of the mother. Some may find this callous but, however it is done, with or without a vet, culling of the weak or diseased is a commonsense respect for the laws of nature. Hand rearing out of pure sentiment or economics can mean the perpetration of unsound stock which will ultimately demand recognition. Of course, this only applies to the runt in an obviously bonny litter and a healthy mother. Should accident or illness handicap the mother then human assistance is fully justified.

History or Coincidence? Quote – 'There is a written record in existence, outside this country, that may throw some light on the Bedlington's origin. It is by a Hungarian of good family, Z. Molar, who visited England in 1702 and he appears to have stayed with the landed gentry in London and the North of England and did some hunting. He wrote of a fox hunt: Today we hunted well, Lord Charles mounted me on one of his best bays, a fine fellow. The fox we found gave us much sport, hard riding and one or two stout fellows lost their mounts. . . . after two good gallops we returned home just before dusk . . . On the way we passed a gypsy encampment, they are not as colourful as our gypsies in Hungary. These people have small Agar (Greyhound)-like dogs with hair like that on a lamb. Lord Charles told me they were great dogs on hare and rabbit and some of his grooms kept them for this sport. These woolly dogs were the red of brick.' Elsewhere a comment has been made in connection with the above that the traditional brick colour in Hungary was more yellow than red which leaves the question wide open whether the colour in the dogs was liver or sandy. At the same time we have to recall that 'red' was mentioned as a colour in the breed in an early description.

Who were the Authorities? It is tempting to read quotes from breeders or judges of old and select only what appeals personally as proof as to what was. The fact that strong arguments were hammered in the past would seem to infer that differences of opinion existed even then as to what was the true Bedlington and what the ideal should look like. The current controversy over the recognition by the Kennel Club of the Jack Russell Terrier should illustrate how wide the differences can be between contemporaries. Here, in the county of that breed's origin anything with a Chippendale front, slipped patella and a temperament bordering on the lunatic can be claimed as a real Jack Russell whereas in Dorset one sees paraded as true representatives of the breed animals longer and straighter in the leg and much more like the picture published by the Kennel Club of the boozy parson's tykes. The arguments between the different Jack Russell clubs have raged on the subject of what the breed should look like so perhaps the same thing could have happened in the early days of the Bedlington. The literate man could express himself in the sporting journals but were there other voices we have never heard?

Exaggeration Most adjectives applied to description of the dog are relative and one needs restraint in their understanding. A 'racey' Bedlington of 50 years ago was not the almost Whippet construction we encounter too often today. The Bedlington should look capable of galloping at great speed according to the Standard but it is a **terrier** and should never resemble a racing machine. Temporary exaggeration is found in the trimming of the coat of the Bedlington. Ideally, the trimmed coat should look as if it grew that way naturally so it follows that excess coat anywhere produces a caricature of an animal. Other breeds have suffered more than the Bedlington in exaggeration and it is sad that a standard that calls for a long head has resulted in a race for the longest head or the requirement of a short back has seen handlers string a poor mutt up with one hand holding the lead and the other trying hard to shove the tail between the ears. Not only are distortions ugly to the aesthetic eye but Nature will not tolerate our stupidity if we breed without respect and humility.

The Stinging Nettle (Overseas readers, sorry, you may not have this one)

The humble stinging nettle is available free to all who are willing to pick it. Known to herbalists, it has proved its value to dog people. Used by the 'old fashioned' as a blood tonic in the spring, more recently reports have been made of its efficacy in cases of arthritis. Boil the top leaves (making sure that the plant has not been sprayed by stupid man) and pour a tablespoon of the tea over the dog's food. A fresh supply has to be made every three days. The 'Spring Clean' covers a two week period of daily dosage.

APPENDIX 4
USEFUL ADDRESSES

At the time of writing there are three clubs devoted to the breed. The reader may not be interested in showing or breeding but these organisations can only serve to maintain the survival of the Bedlington if they have funds to work and the knowledge of the breed population that come from a substantial membership. Also, a club can help individual owners whether show or pet orientated. The National Bedlington Club is the oldest in the breed and will celebrate its centenary in 1998.

Bedlington Terrier Association
Hon. Sec. T. McErlean,
75, Nutley Crescent,
Worthing,
Sussex

National Bedlington Terrier Club
Hon. Sec. Mrs A. Emsley,
40, Leafield Crescent,
Eccleshill, Bradford,
Yorkshire BD2 3SO
01274 788773

Midland Bedlington Terrier Club
Hon. Sec. Mrs O. Stones,
3, Doulton Close,
Cheadle,
Staffordshire

The Kennel Club
1 Clarges Street,
London W1Y 8AB

Index

INDEX

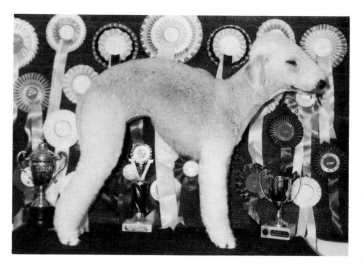

Fralex
Bedlington
Terriers

Alexander Lee Hurley has owned and bred Bedlington Terriers for 6 years.

Fralex Cosette Eponine by 2 years had won B.O.B. and 2 B.O.S. at Championship Shows and Best in Terrier Group K.C.J.O. Crufts 1988.

Both at the beginning of their Bedlington Terrier Career
would like to thank all members of the
Bedlington Terrier associations
for their advice and support.

*Enquiries: Alexander Lee Hurley,
Hillcrest, Princes Tower Road,
St. Saviour, Jersey, C.I.*

SIWASH KENNELS (reg.)

Home of Canada's Top Winning Bedlingtons

- No. 2 Terrier in Canada (1983)

- No. 3 Terrier in Canada (1984)

- Multiple Best in Show Winner

- BTCA – Chicago speciality Best of Breed, June, 1984

- Best of Opposite Sex – Montgomery County BTCA Speciality Oct – 1990

Ch. (Can & Am) Siwash Blue Keeley.

Ch. (Can & Am) Siwash Lady Luck (Keeley's daughter).

- Winners Bitch – Montgomery County BTCA Speciality Oct – 1987

- Best of Winners – Montgomery County BTCA Speciality Oct – 1988

- Best of Opposite Sex – Chicago BTCA Speciality June – 1989

Donald & Shirley Martin
3452 Sawmill Valley Drive
Mississauga, Ontario, L5L 3A4
416-820 8096

315

"Tyneside Bedlingtons"

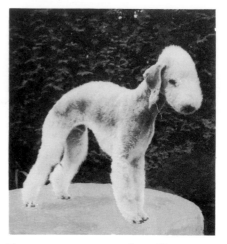

Ch. Tynecourt Tartan D.O.B. 5.1.78 by Ch. Foggyfurze Fenman ex Trinket of Tynecourt.

During his show career "Tartan" gained 11 Champion and Winner titles. Having sired 12 Champions or Winners, he is one of the breed's best stud dogs in Europe. But above all, this outstanding dog is a wonderful companion and a loved member of his owner's family.

Bred by: Ernie Hill GB, owned by: Dieter and Martha Heine.

Tartans promising grandson "Tootsie Tyneside" D.O.B. 16.3.88 by Ch. Wladimir v. Wetterstein German, Intern. Ch. NL. Luxemburger, VDH-Champ. Junior Ch., Dt., Ch. Nl-Klub Junior Ch. Bundes Jgd. Sieger, Ch-Klubsieger (one of Tartans Top winning son's) ex Ch. Karina Blue Diamonds.

Owned by: Kerstin Peper and Martha Heine.

"Tootsie" started his show career winning several European Junior Titles (German Junior Champion, Junior Ch. of Luxemburg, Bundesjugendsieger) and 3 C.C's, & B.O.B., 1 B.I.S., 1 Res.B.O.G.

His litter brother "Touch of Love" (2 C.C's) is living in Finland with well-known breeder Ritva Kohijoki ("Kisapirtin").

Both dogs are bred by Martha Heine.

"TYNESIDE-BEDLINGTONS"

Dieter and Martha Heine
Landwehrstrasse 23
D 6057 Dietzenbach
Phone 06074/23202